# Lecture Notes in Computer Science 733

Edited by G. Goos and J. Hartmanis

Advisory Board: W. Brauer  D. Gries  J. Stoer

Thomas Grechenig  Manfred Tscheligi  (Eds.)

# Human Computer Interaction

Vienna Conference, VCHCI '93, Fin de Siècle
Vienna, Austria, September 20-22, 1993
Proceedings

Springer-Verlag
Berlin Heidelberg NewYork
London Paris Tokyo
Hong Kong Barcelona
Budapest

Series Editors

Gerhard Goos
Universität Karlsruhe
Postfach 69 80
Vincenz-Priessnitz-Straße 1
D-76131 Karlsruhe, Germany

Juris Hartmanis
Cornell University
Department of Computer Science
4130 Upson Hall
Ithaca, NY 14853, USA


Volume Editors

Thomas Grechenig
Department of Computer Science, Vienna University of Technology
Resselgasse 3/188, A-1040 Vienna, Austria

Manfred Tscheligi
Department of Applied Computer Science, University of Vienna
Lenaugasse 2/8, A-1080 Vienna, Austria

CR Subject Classification (1991): D.2.2, H.1.2, H.5, I.2.7, I.7, K.3, K.4


ISBN 3-540-57312-7 Springer-Verlag Berlin Heidelberg New York
ISBN 0-387-57312-7 Springer-Verlag New York Berlin Heidelberg

© Springer-Verlag Berlin Heidelberg 1993
Printed in Germany

Typesetting: Camera-ready by author
Printing and binding: Druckhaus Beltz, Hemsbach/Bergstr.
45/3140-543210 - Printed on acid-free paper

# PREFACE

The scientific orientation of the VCHCI '93 corresponds to the mainstream HCI research spectrum which is represented by this year's prime events: INTERCHI '93 in Amsterdam and HCI '93 in Orlando.

The motto of the Viennese conference FIN DE SIÈCLE affiliates Vienna's intellectual tradition to the field's progressive development at the end of this century: Vienna in the FIN DE SIÈCLE was a place of intensity, disputes and rapid development in culture, politics and science. MODERNISM provoked both the moral-scientific tradition as well as the aesthetic-aristo-cratic ideal. By absorbing the fashionable poetic and plastic culture of all Europe in his language glowing darkly with purple and gold, the adolescent narcissus Hugo von Hofmannsthal became the idol of Vienna's culture-ravenous intelligentsia. Karl Kraus, the city's most acidulous moralist, poured contempt upon "THAT GEM-COLLECTOR" Hofmannsthal, who "FLEES LIFE AND LOVES THE THINGS WHICH BEAUTIFY IT" At that extra-ordinary time and location much of modern culture and thought was born out of a crisis of political and social disintegration. FREUD, MAHLER, SCHNITZLER, KLIMT were all working within a few steps from one another. ADLER, LOOS, SCHOENBERG at the same time discovered and developed their talents. KOKOSCHKA, SCHIELE and WITTGENSTEIN spent an inspiring youth then.

A century later, in today's fin de siècle, the VCHCI emphasizes on showing that HCI

- is more than AN AREA TO BEAUTIFY interaction with computers
- PROVOKES DISPUTES among its different contributing fields
- does not FLEE THE VITAL QUESTIONS for people using computers
- provides RADICALLY NEW opportunities for users

It is a pleasure to thank the invited speakers

| | |
|---|---|
| William Buxton | Xerox PARC & University of Toronto |
| Tom Hewett | Drexel University |

for accepting our invitation to give a keynote talk.

We are most grateful to the following cooperating organizations and their representatives:

| | |
|---|---|
| ACM-SIGCHI | Robert Jacob, Tom Hewett |
| BCS | Victoria Bellotti |
| GI | Horst Oberquelle |
| IFIP TC 13 | Brian Shackel |
| OCG | Günter Haring |

Scientists and engineers from industry, academia, and major research institutes from 19 countries have contributed to the Vienna Conference on Human Computer Interaction 1993 (VCHCI '93). All full papers have been judged by at least three members of the Programme Committee on technical soundness, originality and innovativeness of work, importance and relevance to HCI research, clarity of presentation and methods as well as credibility of results. Only submittals of high scientific quality were accepted as papers. Posters have been selected on the basis of potential interest of VCHCI attendees. All contributions address the latest research and application in the human aspects of design and use of computing systems. The accepted contributions cover a large field of human computer interaction including design, evaluation, interactive architectures, cognitive models, workplace environment, as well as HCI application areas.

We wish to thank the authors and the members of the Programme Committee who so diligently contributed to the success of the conference and the direction of these proceedings.

| | |
|---|---|
| Thomas Grechenig | Manfred Tscheligi |
| University of Technology Vienna | University of Vienna |

August 1993

# PROGRAMME COMMITTEE

| | |
|---|---|
| Beth Adelson | Rutgers University, Camden, USA |
| Bengt Ahlstrom | Royal Institute of Technology, Stockholm, SWE |
| Sandrine Balbo | LGI, Grenoble, FRA |
| Sebastiano Bagnara | University of Siena, ITA |
| David Benyon | Open University, Milton Keynes, UK |
| Meera M. Blattner | Lawrence Livermore National Laboratory, USA |
| Ahmet Cakir | Ergonomics Institute, Berlin, GER |
| Gilbert Cockton | University of Glasgow, UK |
| Prasun Dewan | Purdue University, West Lafayette, USA |
| Gitta Domik | University of Paderborn, GER |
| Sarah Douglas | University of Oregon, Eugene, USA |
| Wolfgang Dzida | GMD, Sankt Augustin, GER |
| Scott Elrod | Xerox PARC, Palo Alto, USA |
| Tom Erickson | Apple Computer, Cupertino, USA |
| Giorgio P. Faconti | CNR, Pisa, ITA |
| James Foley | Georgia Institute of Technology, Atlanta, USA |
| Andrew U. Frank | University of Technology Vienna, AUT |
| William W. Gaver | Xerox EuroPARC, Cambridge, UK |
| Peter Gorny | University of Oldenburg, GER |
| Richard A. Guedj | Institut National des Telecomm. Evry, FRA |
| Nuno M. Guimaraes | INESC, Lisbon, POR |
| Judy Hammond | University of Technology Sydney, AUS |
| Tom Hewett | Drexel University, Philadelphia, USA |
| James D. Hollan | Bellcore, Morristown, USA |
| Bradley Hartfield | University of Hamburg, GER |
| Ulrich Hoppe | GMD-IPSI, Darmstadt, GER |
| Robert J.K. Jacob | Naval Research Laboratory, Washington DC, USA |
| Peter Johnson | University of London, UK |
| Clare-Marie Karat | IBM United States, Greenwich, USA |
| John Karat | IBM Watson Res. Center, Yorktown Heights, USA |
| Wendy A. Kellogg | IBM Watson Res. Center, Yorktown Heights, USA |
| Werner Kuhn | Vienna University of Technology, AUT |
| David Kurlander | Microsoft Research, Redmond, USA |
| Clayton Lewis | University of Colorado, Boulder, USA |
| Jonas Lowgren | Linkoping University, SWE |
| Allan MacLean | Xerox EuroPARC, Cambridge, UK |
| David Maulsby | University of Calgary, CAN |
| James R. Miller | James R. Miller, Apple Computer, Cupertino, USA |
| Michael J. Muller | US WEST Advanced Techn., Boulder, USA |
| Dianne Murray | University of Surrey, UK |
| Robert Neches | University of South. Calif., Marina del Rey, USA |
| Gary M. Olson | University of Michigan, USA |
| Paolo Paolini | Politecnico di Milano, ITA |
| Franz Penz | Rutherford Appleton Laboratory, Chilton, UK |
| Christian Rathke | University of Stuttgart, GER |
| Matthias Rauterberg | ETH Zurich, CH |
| Harald Reiterer | GMD, St. Augustin, GER |

| | |
|---|---|
| Mary Beth Rosson | IBM Watson Res. Center, Yorktown Heights, USA |
| Gavriel Salvendy | Purdue University, West Lafayette, USA |
| Dominique L. Scapin | INRIA, Le Chesnay, FRA |
| Helmut Schauer | University of Zurich, CH |
| Franz Schiele | GMD-IPSI, Darmstadt, GER |
| Chris Schmandt | MIT Media Laboratory, Cambridge, USA |
| Chris Shaw | University of Alberta, CAN |
| John Stasko | Georgia Institute of Technology, Atlanta, USA |
| Tom Stewart | System Concepts, London, UK |
| Martha R. Szczur | NASA/Goddard Space Flight Center, Greenbelt, USA |
| Pedro Szekely | University of Southern California, Marina del Rey, USA |
| Michael Tauber | University of Paderborn, GER |
| Jo Tombaugh | Carleton University, Ottawa, CAN |
| Thomas S. Tullis | Canon Information Systems, Costa Mesa, USA |
| Andrew Turk | University of Melbourne, AUS |
| Gerrit van der Veer | Free University, Amsterdam, NLD |
| Ina Wagner | Vienna University of Technology, AUT |
| Yvonne Waern | Linkoping University, SWE |
| Pierre Wellner | Xerox EuroPARC, Cambridge, UK |
| Alan Wexelblat | MIT Media Laboratory, Cambridge, USA |
| Juergen Ziegler | Fraunhofer-Institut IAO, Stuttgart, GER |

## CONFERENCE CHAIRS

| | |
|---|---|
| Thomas Grechenig | Vienna University of Technology, AUT |
| Manfred Tscheligi | University of Vienna, AUT |

## ORGANIZING CHAIR

| | |
|---|---|
| Monika Fahrnberger | Vienna University of Technology, AUT |

**The VCHCI '93 is an in co-operation conference with ACM-SIGCHI. It is supported by BCS, GI, OCG and IFIP TC 13**

# TABLE OF CONTENTS

SUPPORTING THE DEVELOPERS

# Integrating Interactive 3D-Graphics into an Object-Oriented Application Framework

Dominik Eichelberg and Philipp Ackermann
University of Zurich, Department of Computer Science, Multi-Media-Lab
Winterthurerstrasse 190, CH-8057 Zürich, Switzerland
e-mail: eichel@ifi.unizh.ch, ackerman@ifi.unizh.ch

**Abstract.** This paper describes the integration of 3D graphics into the visual 2D part of an application framework. Most object-oriented application frameworks are built to ease the development of interactive graphical applications that use direct manipulation techniques. This study is based on the object-oriented application framework ET++ that provides predefined visual classes for text, 2D graphics display, and standard user interface components. We extended ET++ to support 3D graphics in a general way. It is now possible to integrate 3D graphics objects which may be placed wherever other visual objects can go, i.e. in scrollable views, as building blocks in dialogs or graphics editors, as characters in text editors, as items in lists or pop-up menus, etc. As a consequence 2D and 3D graphics are dealt in a uniform way. Interaction techniques on 3D graphics objects and 3D user interface components are supported.

**Keywords:** interactive 3D graphics, user interface, C++, object-oriented application framework, ET++

## 1. Introduction

Graphical user interfaces with direct manipulative interaction techniques based on 2D graphics are widely used in today's computer applications and have replaced command language and menu driven programs. Integrating new media such as 3D graphics, audio, and video into human computer interaction can enrich the user's abbilities to process complex context. The implementation of such interfaces often requires great efforts. The realization of modern user interfaces tend to consume a great part of a project time. The development of object-oriented application frameworks was very successful in reducing the complexity of 2D user interface programming. Examples are MacApp™ [Schmucker89], Interviews [Linton89], ET++ [Weinand89], and NeXTStep™ [NeXT92]. The purpose of our study is to investigate whether these object-oriented techniques are also suitable for multimedia extensions of the user interface. These extensions increase the accessibility and usability of computer applications that process complex data. In order to do these explorations the object-oriented application framework ET++ [Gamma88, Gamma92, Weinand89, Weinand92] is used. ET++ was chosen because it is highly portable, it integrates many features in a seamless fashion, and its source code is available in the public domain. As a first step of the multimedia extension the 2D graphics model of ET++ was extended to 3D graphics. In this paper we explain our motivation to integrate 2D and 3D graphics, introduce the object-oriented framework ET++, and present our approach to extend it with interactive 3D graphics.

## 2. Integrating 2D and 3D Graphics into the User Interface

The interactive direct manipulation paradigm of today's user interfaces is strongly coupled with the presentation and visualization of data objects. The information which is modeled and manipulated in applications becomes more and more complex as the processing power of workstations increases. New media such as interactive 3D graphics, animations, audio, and video are introduced in multimedia systems to allow richer presentation of complex data. It is extremely costly to implement user interfaces based on direct manipulation techniques for these new media. It takes a good deal of thought and care to create user interface components that combine visualization and manipulation of these media into useful and reusable software.

Not long ago 3D graphics was a field for specialists. They often were programmers and users of their programs in one person. They were not interested in software ergonomics, instead they concentrated their work on optimizing graphics performance. On the other hand there is little help in 3D graphics libraries for 2D interaction elements like pop-up and pull-down menus, buttons, sliders, scroll-bars, and so on. As a consequence, ad hoc solutions with no or separated 2D user interface components were developed. Today, 3D graphics is available on low cost workstations and users are not computer specialists that are satisfied with an ad hoc user interface. This means that 2D user interface components must be merged seamlessly with 3D graphics. In doing so it is even possible to add new 3D interaction components into the user interface. Realizing the interaction elements as a set of cooperative classes in an object-oriented framework will increase the software reusabilty.

## 3. The Object-Oriented Application Framework ET++

ET++ is an object-oriented class library integrating user interface building blocks, basic data structures, support for object input/output, printing, and high level application framework components. It eases the development of interactive textual and graphical applications with direct manipulation and high semantic feedback. ET++ is implemented with the programming language C++ and uses abstract classes as a portability layer and interface protocol to concrete window and operating systems (Figure 1). It is available for UNIX and VMS and runs either with SunView or with X11 window system.

In the domain of user interaction ET++ supports direct manipulation, efficient flicker-free screen update, multi-undoable commands, and a flexible mechanism to compose visual objects with declarative layout specification and automatic object positioning. Standard interaction components like pop-up and pull-down menus, buttons, scroll-bars, etc. are included as predefined classes that can be extended through inheritance. The application framework part of ET++ consists of abstract classes for the following concepts: application, manager, document, view, and command. These abstract classes define a generic application with predefined functionality that will be inherited by the respective subclasses of a concrete application. According to [Schmucker89] an application framework is a set of interconnected objects that provides the basic functionality of a working application, but which can be easily specialized (through subclassing and inheritance) into individual applications. An application framework not only allows the reuse of code as a class library, but also the reuse of design structures, because the dependencies between objects are preimplemented through predefined object composition possibilities, event dispatching mechanism and message flow control. The following functionality will automatically be part of any ET++ application:

- creating, saving, and opening of documents with a file dialog
- handling of several documents in different windows by one application
- scrolling of views through scroll-bars with auto-scrolling feature
- automatic layout management of visual components
- mouse and keyboard event handling
- multi-undoable commands
- clipboard cut/copy/paste, drag and drop
- flicker-free drawing with double-buffering
- device-independent printing
- change propagation
- program inspection by a programming environment based on run-time class information

Any extension of ET++ must be aware of this functionality and avoid conflicts with the sophisticated generic behavior of the application framework. In order to develop 3D graphics applications with ET++ to use its interface components and event handling mechanism, it is necessary to integrate 3D concepts into the application framework. The closer they fit into the philosophy of the framework, the better they will be usable by the programmer.

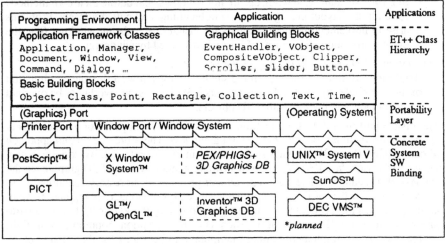

**Fig. 1.** The system architecture of ET++.

## 4. Concepts of Integrating 2D and 3D Graphics

Support for new media, such as 3D graphics, audio, and video, is added to workstation hardware so quickly that monolithic software is obsolete within a short time. The experience with ET++ has shown that good object-oriented design can obtain extensibility even for large and complex software systems. The extensibility and adaptability of ET++ is guaranteed by a portability layer (Figure 1) which consists of abstract classes defining method protocols. Beside code reuse, inheritance is used to propagate common method protocols in order to ensure flexible object composition. Concrete behaviour is realized in subclasses of the abstract classes. There exist concrete classes for specialized operating systems, window systems, and printers.

The ET++ class hierarchy only operates with the abstract classes of the portability layer and is therefore completely independent of a specific system environment. Dynamic binding is used to couple an abstract interface to a concrete realization. This architecture makes it easy to create adaptor classes for other system resources such as 3D graphics. The two following possibilities to integrate 3D graphics in the object-oriented application framework ET++ were investigated:

*a) Creating a New Window for Each 3D View*

Window systems such as the X11 Window System [Scheifler90] allow the allocation of windows not only for standard windows with their own borders, but also for many separate graphical objects in the main window. In the Xt toolkit these subwindows are called *widgets* and form a window hierarchy. By defining a widget for each 3D view it is possible to render 3D graphics in a separate window without disturbing the 2D part of the framework. There are some disadvantages inherent to such 3D interface objects:

- 3D object views are restricted to be rectangular on the 2D display since most window systems do not provide arbitrarily shaped windows.
- A 3D object cannot be covered by a visual object which is not a window.
- A 3D object cannot intersect 3D objects in a different widget or window.
- In ET++, standard visual objects are not windows, and define their own methods for clipping, layout management, event handling, and cut/copy/paste. Problems arise in implementing these methods for visual objects being windows (e.g. the event distribution mechanism of ET++ is disturbed by windows).

*b) Combining 2D and 3D Rendering in the Same Window*

Rendering 2D and 3D graphics in the same window allows a flexible combination of the two rendering modes. In this approach 3D objects can overlay or be overlaid by 2D objects and intersect other 3D objects.

The visible part of an ET++ application is hierarchically composed of visible objects called *VObjects*. In ET++, a *VObject* is not a window. Therefore, the second approach of combining 2D and 3D graphics in the same window is preferred. By deriving a new visible 3D object class *V3DObject* from *VObject*, the integration of 3D graphics in the framework is seamless. The class *V3DObject* provides all necessary functionality to work with the 2D part of ET++, e.g. it has methods for drawing, clipping and manipulating (resizing) the 2D content rectangle. In addition to the *VObject*, it defines parameters required for 3D visualization, such as camera position, zooming, twist, light source, etc. It also implements direct manipulation operations for these parameters. The abstract class *V3DObject* must be overwritten to implement a concrete 3D view.

## 5. Implementation

For the reasons mentioned above, the second approach combining 2D and 3D graphics in the same window was implemented on Silicon Graphics IRIS workstations using the Graphics Library (GL) [SGI91]. GL was chosen because it supports *immediate-mode* rendering. Immediate-mode rendering displays graphical primitives directly into the framebuffer of the screen, where *retained-mode* rendering collects graphical primitives in a database (display list) and redisplays the database every time it is changed. Other 3D graphics libraries like PHIGS+/PEX strongly recommend the use of retained mode rendering. Since most of the 2D graphics libraries support only immediate-mode rendering and the 2D rendering of ET++ is based on this drawing model, an immediate-mode drawing approach was chosen for the 3D graphics, too. This allows ET++ to have full control over all drawings which is important for animations in double buffer mode. It is generally agreed that GL will become an open standard for 3D graphics under the name OpenGL™. OpenGL is announced as a 3D extension for the X Window System and Windows NT on many hardware platforms [Foley92].

In the current version of GL it is not allowed to mix GL rendering with drawing by an additional 2D graphics library in the same window. For this reason all 2D graphics methods of the ET++ application framework had to be implemented using GL. All drawing in ET++ uses methods defined in the abstract class *Port*. The drawing methods of *Port* are specialized for window systems in a subclass called *WindowPort*, and for printing in a subclass *PrinterPort* (see Figure 2). The methods of *WindowPort* are specialized for a specific window system in a subclass of *Window-Port*. These virtual C++ methods are bound dynamically at run-time so that the actual and specialized window or printer port instance can be assigned to a global port variable. There exists for example a *XWindowPort* for the X Window System. This system architecture of ET++ makes it possible to implement a new class *GLPort* inherited from *WindowPort* which implements all drawing routines of ET++ with GL. We use GL in mixed-mode, which means that the input event handling and window management is done by the X Window System whereas the content of the window is rendered by GL. Beside standard drawing routines for line, rectangle, oval, polygon, etc. there exist *Font* and *Bitmap* classes to handle character and image drawing. In the GLPort they are all implemented with routines from the GL graphics library.

For the 3D extension of ET++, the class *Port* was extended by abstract 3D graphics methods which are implemented in concrete terms in the *GLPort*. All 3D rendering is based on 3D methods of the extended *Port* class. This will in the future allow to implement other derivations of the extended class *Port*, e.g. a *PEXPort*.

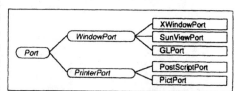

**Fig. 2.** The inheritance hierarchy of the class *Port* which functions as a graphics portability layer.

The class *V3DObject* is a subclass of the abstract class *VObject* which defines the protocols for drawing, automatic layout management, and event handling of all visual objects in ET++. *V3DObject* overwrites the method *DrawAll* of the class *VObject*. The framework calls this method every time a *VObject* should draw itself. In this method, *V3DObject* initialises the 3D drawing mode (e.g. activates the Z-buffer for hidden surface removal), sets the clipping region to the content rectangle, and places the camera and possibly defined light sources. Then it calls the method *Draw*, which should be overwritten in a subclass of *V3DObject* to implement a specific graphical appearance. The method *Draw* uses 3D methods of the class *Port* in order to define 3D graphics. *V3DObject* provides direct manipulation interaction by mouse movements on the *V3DObject* for camera and light positioning. By double-clicking the middle mouse button on a *V3DObject*, a camera/light control window opens which allows the interactive manipulation of the camera and light positions in front, top, side and perspective views in the coordinate system (Figure 3). The change propagation mechanism will automatically update all dependent views of the camera/light control. This functionality is implemented in *V3DObject* and is inherited by all its subclasses.

## 6. Sample Applications

To prove the flexibility of the *V3DObject* approach several reusable classes and applications were written using the new 3D features of ET++. The application shown in Figure 3 visualizes a bone that is sampled by a computer tomograph. The application has various interaction components created with the 2D part of ET++. These sliders, buttons, and menus interact with the 3D model. The view of the 3D data is created by a derivation of the class *V3DObject*. The user can rotate the bone by pressing the middle mouse button and dragging the mouse. These movements are commands and are therefore undoable. By double-clicking the 3D view, a separate camera/light control window appears where the position of the camera and the light can be changed interactivaly. All these features are inherited from the class *V3DObject*. For this application the 3D view only provides the drawing of the polygons. This is done by overwriting the method *Draw* of the super class *V3DObject*.

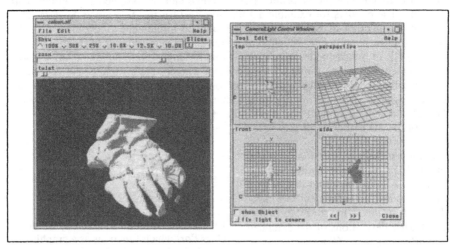

**Fig .3.** An application that visualizes medical data and displays a camera/light editor in a separate window.

The flexibility of objects inherited from *V3DObject* is shown in Figure 4. Since a menu-item in ET++ must be a *VObject* and a *V3DObject* is derivated from *VObject*, it is possible to integrate 3D graphics in menus. Obviously it can also be part of a dialog box. Until now *V3DObject* have not been overlaid by other visual objects. This ability is shown in the extension of the application *draw*, which in its 2D version is shipped with ET++ as a sample application. In Figure 5, 2D and 3D graphics objects are integrated in one view and can be positioned, sized, and arranged in any

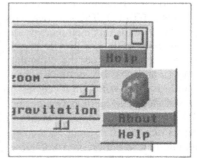

**Fig .4.** A 3D menu item.

order. It is even possible to insert 3D objects in text as shown in Figure 6. While editing, the *V3DObject* will flow with the text, and cut/copy/paste operations are possible. The extent of the 3D object can be expanded or reduced within the text by mouse control while the text layout adopts automatically. The text, including the 3D graphics, can be saved to and loaded from files.

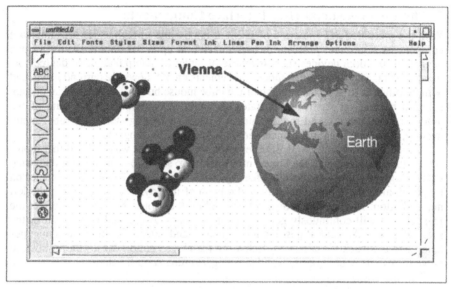

**Fig. 5.** *V3DObjects* can overlay or be overlaid by other *VObjects*.
*V3DObjects* can intersect other *V3DObjects*.

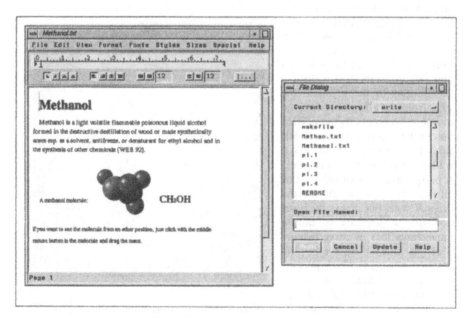

**Fig 6.** A*V3DObject* in a text editor.

All 3D graphics that are seen in Figures 3 to 6 are not images but active objects that can be manipulated in an interactive way with mouse events upon the *V3DObject* or in a separate camera/light control window.

## 7. Three-Dimensional User Interface Components

With the presented 3D extention of ET++ it is possible to realize 3D user interface components. The main problem of user interaction upon 3D data is the use of two degrees-of-freedom devices such as mouse or tablet to manipulate three degrees-of-freedom data. The functions of mouse movements on 3D views are currently switched with modifier keys and pressing one of the three mouse buttons. This is not an elegant solution because of its different states and modi. Depending on the state of the modifier keys and pressed mouse button it means selecting, selecting subelement, moving, stretching, rotating, camera moving, zooming, twisting, etc.

To address this problem, a 3D user interface component was realized that represents a joystick. Although the mouse movements are still two-dimensional, the visual feedback gives a three-dimensional feeling of the interaction. The joystick is selected by positioning the mouse cursor over the knob of the joystick and pressing the left mouse button. Moving the mouse while holding the mouse button will deflect the joystick and will continuosly generate control values. Angle and orientation of the stick relating to the neutral position are computed and considered in the data manipulation and feedback visualization. Releasing the mouse button causes the joystick to move back to its neutral position and to stop generating control values.

The application *etgeoid* visualizes the earth and shows the effect of varying gravitation (Figure 7). The control values of joystick interaction are mapped to camera position changes. Angle and distance of the joystick deflection determine spin orientation and turning speed of the camera rotation. We considered two display possibilities of the joystick: the view from top allows to adapt the mouse movements to the deflection of the joystick (Figure 8, left side). But in its neutral position, it is hardly recognized as a joystick. A perspective view of the joystick allows this recognition in the original state, but makes the reaction of the joystick to mouse movements less intuitive (Figure 8, right side). Until now, no decision was made which joystick view is better suited to interaction and therefore, the user has the posibility to switch the view by pressing the middle mouse button.

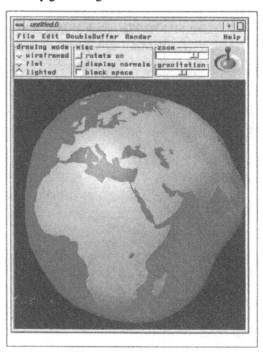

**Fig. 7.** Visualization of the geoid. A joystick changes the camera view point.

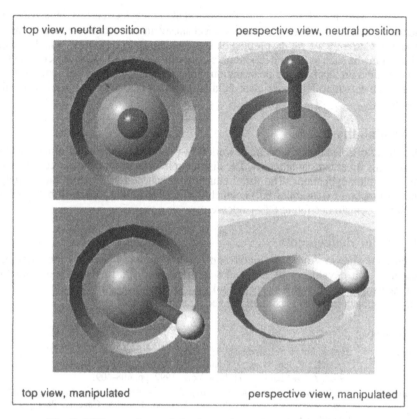

**Fig. 8.** Different views of the *Joystick* user interface component.

## 8. Conclusions and Future Work

The 3D graphics extension of the object-oriented application framework ET++ is seamlessly integrated into the 2D graphics part of the user interface. ET++ gives the opportunity to develop applications which combine interactive 2D and 3D graphics in a general way. Therefore, it can be used as an experimental development environment for new user interface components in order to design intuitive 3D visualization and interaction elements. The presented 3D extension of ET++ still lacks full 3D graphics support, e.g until now there exist no complete 3D modelling facilities and the problem of printing 3D graphics has not yet been addressed. In spite of this, we are satisfied of having proved the applicability of integrating 2D and 3D graphics seamlessly by implementing all drawing methods on a 3D graphics library. The performance of interactive 2D and 3D graphics is reasonably good on workstations such as the Silicon Graphics Indigo. Moreover, we want to emphasize that this kind of 3D graphics extension is extremely open because it will always be possible to enhance its implementation without interfering with the functionality of the application framework. Reusable classes were developed which are based on the 3D extension of the ET++ graphics port.

Future work includes refining of the presented 3D graphics classes, improving the modelling classes, and adding animation mechanisms in order to define time dynamic behavior. Currently we are developing classes for time synchronization, which handle different media such as 2D and 3D graphics, camera, audio, and MIDI objects with the same method protocol. Media presentations are regarded as hierarchical compositions of time objects that define serial or parallel synchronization'of the inserted media objects.

## 9. Availability

The object-oriented application framework ET++ is public domain and distributed by anonymous ftp at iamsun.unibe.ch. The distribution includes all C++ source code and some sample applications. The usual educational and non-profit restrictions apply. The 3D graphics extension of ET++ which is discussed in this paper will be added to the public domain in a future ET++ release.

## 10. Acknowledgements

Thanks are due to André Weinand and Erich Gamma, which are the principal designers and developers of ET++. Peter Stucki and Martin Dürst gave helpful comments on a draft of this paper. Thanks go to Urs Meyer, who has developed an early non-object-oriented version of the geoid application [Meyer89].

## References

[Foley92]      James Foley (chairman): *3D Graphics Standards Debate: PEX versus OpenGL*; Proceedings of SIGGRAPH '92, in: Computer Graphics, 26, 2 (July 1992), ACM SIGGRAPH, New York, 1992, pp. 408-409.

[Gamma88]      E. Gamma, A. Weinand, R. Marty: *ET++ – An Object-Oriented Application Framework in C++*; in Proc. EUUG, pp. 159-174, Cascais, Portugal, 3-7 Oktober 1988.

[Gamma92]      E. Gamma: *Objektorientierte Software-Entwicklung am Beispiel von ET++*; Springer Verlag, Berlin 1992.

[Linton89]     Mark A. Linton, John M. Vlissides, Paul R. Calder: *Composing User Interfaces with Interviews*; in IEEE Computer Vol. 22(2):8-22, Februar 1989.

[Meyer89]      Urs Meyer: *Modellbildung und Animation eines Geoids*; in: M. Paul (Hrsg.), Proceedings GI-19. Jahrestagung I, Computergestützter Arbeitsplatz, pp. 452-459, München, Oktober 1989, Spinger Verlag, Berlin 1989.

[NeXT92]       NeXT Computer Inc.: *NeXTStep Developer's Library*; Addison-Wesley, Reading MA, 1992.

[Scheifler90]  R. Scheifler, J. Gettys: *X Window System: the complete reference to X lib, X protocol, ICCCM, XLFD*; 2nd Edition, Digital Equipment Corporation, 1990.

[Schmucker89]  Kurt J. Schmucker: *Object Oriented Programming for the Macintosh*; Hayden, Hasbrouck Heights, New Jersey 1989.

[SGI91]        *Graphics Library Programming Guide*; Silicon Graphics Computer Systems, Mountain View, California, 1991.

[Weinand89]    A. Weinand, E. Gamma, R. Marty: *Design and Implementation of ET++, a Seamless Object–Oriented Application Framework*; Structured Programming, Vol. 10, No. 2, June 1989, pp. 63-87.

[Weinand92]    André Weinand: *Objektorientierte Architektur für graphische Benutzeroberflächen – Realisierung der portablen Fenstersystemschnittstelle von ET++*; Springer Verlag, Berlin 1992.

# An Experimental Knowledge-Based User Interface Management System

Haishan Huang & Ernest Edmonds

LUTCHI Research Centre
Loughborough University of Technology
Loughborough
Leicestershire LE11 3TU
UK
H.Huang@lut.ac.uk  E.A.Edmonds@lut.ac.uk

**Abstract.** A knowledge-based user interface management system (UIMS) is described, the core component of which is an interface knowledge base that defines the presentation and behaviour of user interfaces. The knowledge base serves as the input to the user interface management system that implements the user interfaces and controls the communication between user interface components and application components. In particular, the interface knowledge base contains two parts: the presentation specification knowledge that represents objects, attributes of objects, object hierarchical structures and relationships in a user interface, and the behaviour specification knowledge that describes the actions and relevant parameters performed on objects in the user interface. User interface design knowledge in the knowledge base can be generated and modified in a direct manipulation manner by the designers using a graphical interface knowledge editor.

## 1  Introduction

We have developed the Knowledge-Based User Interface system (KBUIMS) which is a system to help designers to prototype user interfaces rapidly and easily. The goals of the system are:

• to generate and modify interface knowledge automatically in a graphical, direct manipulation manner.
• to enable the interface designers to have a direct "look and feel" at the effects without delay when the design knowledge of a user interface is being created.

Figure 1 shows the overall organization of the KBUIMS, the heart of which is a knowledge base which describes the presentation and behaviour of the user interfaces in two individual sub-knowledge-bases. These consist of:

• the hierarchical structure of objects in an interface
• the attributes of each object in the interface
• the relationship with other objects in the interface
• actions performed on each object
• parameters required by each action.

The knowledge base can be used for three different purposes:

• to represent the presentation and behaviour design of a user interface
• to simulate and test user interfaces under a user interface management system
• to implement user interfaces via the user interface management system.

This paper focuses upon the structure of the interface knowledge base, presents an overview of the KBUIMS and explains its capabilities.

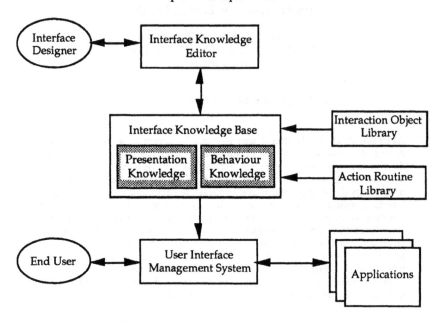

Figure 1. The structure of the KBUIMS

The conventional User Interface Management System (UIMS) [11, 16, 17] requires the interface designer to work at the syntactic and lexical level of design and hence to focus on command names, screen and icon design, menu organization, sequencing rules, and interaction techniques [3]. This tends to very time-consuming and error-prone as the designer has to produce detailed interface specifications, often in cryptic specification languages [14]. To alleviate some of these problems, several UIMSs have been developed, e.g. MIKE [10], UIDE [3, 4], and UofA* [14]. The approaches used in these UIMSs are quite similar. MIKE automatically generates textual interfaces from a description of the semantic commands supported by the application. The designer then adds the graphical interaction facilities to the interfaces generated by MIKE. From a simple and high-level description of the commands and a description of the device on which the user interface will be implemented, the UofA* UIMS automatically produces an initial lexical and syntactic design of the interface. The initial interface is refined by the designer by using a highly interactive and graphical facility. UIDE provides a high-level conceptual design tool in which the designer, by selecting options from menus and by answering prompts, describes the user interface as a knowledge base. After checking the completeness and consistency, UIDE algorithmically transforms the knowledge base into a number of functionally equivalent interfaces. The designer determines which one is most appropriate. The transformed interface definition can be input to a UIMS which implements the user interface.

The KBUIMS described in this paper omits some of steps which are necessary in the systems mentioned above by providing a high-level graphical tool. This tool is used by the designers as an interface knowledge editor to generate the design knowledge that describes the presentation as well as the behaviour of a user interface. The KBUIMS enables the designer to have a direct "look and feel" without delay at the effects of changing the presentation or behaviour of an interface which is being created. This is because the graphical tool provided by the KBUIMS adopts the WYSIWYG (What You See Is What You Get) strategy. A UIMS maps the design knowledge into a user interface when it is required by an application. The KBUIMS significantly shortens the time required to develop an interface, and also avoids the chances of error and the occurrence of incomplete and inconsistent interfaces.

The KBUIMS has been implemented on Sun SPARCstations under the environment includes the UNIX operating system, the Prolog and C programming languages, the X-window system [5] and the OSF/Motif toolkit [12].

## 2 The Interface Knowledge Editor

The central approach of the UIMS described in this paper is to allow the interface designer to generate the design knowledge of direct manipulation interfaces [13, 8] in a visual manner. The designer does not need to do any specification of the lexical and syntactic level and program in the conventional sense required. A graphical interface builder called Interaction Object Editor [7] has been implemented which is used as the Interface Knowledge Editor in the KBUIMS.

As with most of the similar tools, e.g. Peridot [9], OSU [6], and Druid [15], the Interaction Object Editor can be used to create and modify the presentation specification of a user interface easily and rapidly. Similarly, it provides a simple way to create the behaviour of an interface. Accordingly, the Interface Editor is composed of two main components: the presentation editor and the behaviour editor.

The interface presentation editor enables the designer to see the interface appearance exactly as seen by the end user and to have an immediate experience of the look and feel effects when an interface is being edited and modified. As we know, a user interface is the meaningful combination of some basic interaction objects. This editor provides a number of basic interaction objects defined in the Interaction Object Library (Figure 1) which corresponds to all of widgets and menu types supported by the OSF/Motif toolkit for constructing variety user interfaces and menu system. The editor also supports the designer in the use of existing interaction objects in the interface knowledge base by the means of "cut-paste-duplicate" technique to create more complex user interfaces rapidly.

Using the facilities provided by the editor, the designer can instantiate and customise the basic interaction objects by a combination of direct manipulation and form-filling techniques. Attributes such as size, position, colour and font, for basic interaction objects, can be customised by using the direct manipulation techniques. For example, to resize an object, the designer points at the object, presses the button and drags the mouse until the object's size becomes the desirable size. Other attributes such as label string, border width, etc. can be specified by using form-filling techniques in attribute editing sheets. A full report on this editor is available [7]. As shown in the report, the interaction technique adopted in this editor allows the presentation aspects of the interface to be created and modified by non-programmers in a very natural manner. It may even be simple enough for the end users to use it to modify, even to create, their own interfaces. Figure 2 shows the appearance of a user interface called "colour_select" being created.

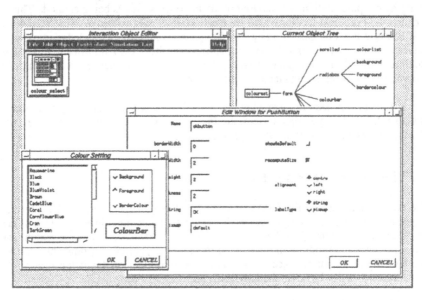

Figure 2. The Presentation Editor in Action

As mentioned above, a user interface is the combination of some basic interaction objects, thus its behaviour is composed of these basic objects' behaviour. A basic object's behaviour is a combination of a series of basic actions. In this editor, we only need to handle the higher level actions, such as getting or changing the current state of an interaction object, sending the current interface state to an application, etc., because the lower level actions, such as highlighting a menu item, leaving and entering an object etc., have been handled in the OSF/Motif widget set. Therefore, the system provides a group of built-in actions defined in the Action Routine Library to satisfy the needs.

The interface behaviour editor provides a behaviour setting window for every basic interaction object. The designer could specify the behaviour in a direct manipulation manner without programming. The designer simply selects a series of actions from the basic action list provided by the editor and gives their parameters according to the system's prompt. The editor will automatically produce an action record for the basic interaction object after the designer finishes its behaviour specification. At any time, the designer can modify the action record using the same method.

To illustrate, we give the behaviour specification of the example shown in the figure 2 which defines a interface called "colour_select". We first specify the behaviour for the colour list's "defaultActionCallback": when the user selects a colour from the list, the background of the "ColourBar" will be set to the correspondent colour. We can specify the following actions to do this task:

getListSelection(colourlist, getColour)
setObjectValues(colourbar, background, getColour).

Next, we specify the behaviour for the "OK" button's "activateCallback", e.g. when the user presses the "OK" button, the message, which includes the selected colour name in the colour list and the selected toggle item in the radio box, will be send back to an application. The designer could specify the actions to do this:

getListSelection(colourlist, getColour)
getRadioboxSelection(radiobox, getSelection)
returnMessage(colour=getColour, selection=getSelection).

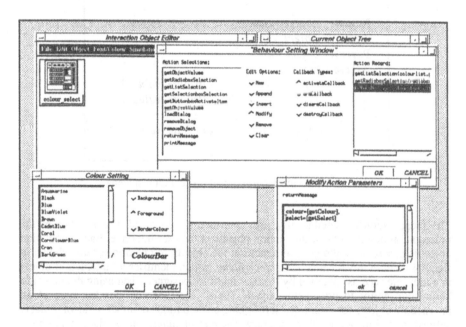

Figure 3. The Behaviour Editor in Action

Figure 3 shows the behaviour of the "OK" button being specified. After specifying the interface behaviour, the designer can send a simulated command to the UIMS to display and to interact with the interface under a real UIMS environment. The main purpose is to enable the designer to have a direct feel for the interface behaviour without waiting for it to be embedded in an application. With experience, the basic action routine library will be extended to allow the designer to specify more complex interface behaviour. Ideally, this basic action library could be extended by the designer but this issue is beyond the scope of this paper. We intend to investigate this issue in the future.

The presentation and behaviour design knowledge of a user interface will be output to the interface knowledge base. In the next section, we will discuss the structure of the knowledge base in detail.

## 3 The Interface Knowledge Base

The interface knowledge base contains two parts: the presentation specification knowledge and the behaviour specification knowledge. The first represents objects, attributes of objects, the object hierarchical structure and their relationships in a user interface. The second describes the actions and relevant parameters performed on objects in the user interface.

```
Name:     object_name
Type:     object_type
Parent:   object_parent
Attributes:
          attribute_name 1 : attribute_value 1
          attribute_name 2 : attribute_value 2
          .......
          attribute_name n : attribute_value n
```

Figure 4. The interaction object presentation schema

The presentation knowledge of a user interface is composed of a number of the presentation descriptions of interaction objects in the user interface. Each interaction object is described in the general structure: the object presentation schema shown in figure 4. Within this schema, the *object_name*, which identifies an interaction object in a user interface, is specified by the user interface designer when using the interface knowledge editor to create the object. The *object_type* defines the type of an interaction object, for example, scroll_bar, push_button, or other kind of objects defined in the Interaction Object Library. The *parent_name* defines the parent object which the described object is laid on. Therefore, the **Parent** field identifies the position of the described object in the object hierarchical structure of an interface and the relationship with other objects. If objects have the same parent, they are at the same hierarchical level. If the *parent_name* is null, the described object is the top level object. The **Attributes** field defines the appearance of the described interaction object, for example, width, height, title, font, etc. are specified in this field. Physically, this presentation knowledge of a user interface is represented as a series of Prolog facts in the design knowledge base. Figure 5 shows the presentation knowledge of the example "colour_select" shown in figure 2.

```
presentation(name: colourset, type: topshell,
 parent: null,
 attributes: [
  title: 'Colour Setting',
  width: 351,
  height: 254,
  allowShellResize: yes
 ]).
presentation(name: form, type: form,
 parent: colourset,
 attributes: [
  width: 351,
  height: 254,
  borderWidth: 0
 ]).
presentation(name: scrolled, type: scrolledWindow,
 parent: form,
 attributes: [
  width: 187,
  height: 203,
  borderWidth: 0,
  scrollBarPlacement: bottom_right,
  scrollBarDisplayPolicy: as_needed,
  scrollingPolicy: automatic,
  topAttachment: attach_form,
  topOffset: 5,
  leftAttachment: attach_form,
  leftOffset: 5
 ]).
presentation(name: colourlist, type: list,
 parent: scrolled,
 attributes: [
  width: 161,
  height: 317,
  selectionPolicy: browse_select,
  automaticSelection: no,
  items: [
  'Aquamarine', 'Black',
  'Blue', 'BlueViolet',
  'Brown', 'CadetBlue',
  'Coral', 'CornflowerBlue',
  'Cran', 'DarkGreen',
  'DarkOliveGreen', 'DarkOrchid',
  'DarkSlateBlue', 'DarkSlateGray',
  'DarkSlateGrey', 'DarkTurquoise'
  ]
 ]).
```

```
presentation(name: radiobox, type: rowColumn,
 parent: form,
 attributes: [
  borderWidth: 1,
  radioBehavior: 1,
  entryBorder: 0,
  topAttachment: attach_form,
  topOffset: 24,
  leftAttachment: attach_form,
  leftOffset: 214
 ]).
presentation(name: background, type: toggleButton,
 parent: radiobox,
 attributes: [
  labelType: string,
  labelString: 'Background',
  indicatorType: n_of_many,
  set: no
 ]).
presentation(name: foreground, type: toggleButton,
 parent: radiobox,
 attributes: [
  labelType: string,
  labelString: 'Foreground',
  indicatorType: n_of_many,
  set: yes
 ]).
presentation(name: bordercolour, type: toggleButton,
 parent: radiobox,
 attributes: [
  labelType: string,
  labelString: 'BorderColour',
  indicatorType: n_of_many,
  set: no
 ]).
presentation(name: colourbar, type: label,
 parent: form,
 attributes: [
  width: 117,
  height: 30,
  borderWidth: 2,
  labelType: string,
  labelString: 'ColourBar',
  topAttachment: attach_form,
  topOffset: 155,
  leftAttachment: attach_form,
  leftOffset: 205
 ]).
.......
```

Figure 5. The interface presentation knowledge

Similarly, the behaviour knowledge of a user interface is composed of a number of behaviour descriptions of interaction objects in the user interface. An interaction object's behaviour is described in a general structure: the object behaviour schema shown in figure 6. Within the schema, the *object_name* in the **Object** field identifies the object on which the behaviours will be performed. The **Behaviour** field defines the object's call-backs, call-back types and their actions. Here, a call-back is a series of actions specified by the designer that are executed when an interaction object is operated by the end user. The *callback_type* in the **Type** field specifies a call-back type which defines what kind of operations are performed on the object and then the call-back will be called. The **Actions** field specifies a series of actions that are performed when the call-back is called. One object can take more than one call-back. For example, the "colourlist" object (see figure 2 & 5), which is a list object instance, has two call-backs defined in the behaviour knowledge base: one is "defaultActionCallback" for when the user double clicks the mouse button on the list object, and one is "browseSelectionCallback" for when the user drags the mouse button on the list object. Physically, the behaviour knowledge of a user interface is stored as a series of Prolog facts in the design knowledge base. Figure 7 shows the behaviour knowledge for the example "colour_select" shown in figure 2.

**Object:**      *object_name*
**Behaviour:**
       **Type:**      *callback_type*
      **Actions:**

           *action_name*   :   *action_parameters*

           ......

           *action_name*   :   *action_parameters*

           ......

      **Type:**      *callback_type*
      **Actions:**

           *action_name*   :   *action_parameters*

           ......

           *action_name*   :   *action_parameters*

Figure 6. The interaction object behaviour schema

```
behaviour(object: colourlist,              behaviour(object: cancelbutton,
behaviour:[                                behaviour:[
 [type: defaultActionCallback,              [type: activateCallback,
 actions:[                                  actions: [
  getListSelection: [colourlist, getColour],  removeDialog: []
  printMessage: [getColour],                 ]]
  setObjectValues: [colourbar, background,getColour]  ]).
  ]],                                      behaviour(object: okbutton,
 [type: browseSelectionCallback,           behaviour:[
 actions:[                                  [type: activateCallback,
  getListSelection: [colourlist, getColour],  actions:[
  printMessage: [getColour],                 getListSelection: [colourlist, getColour],
  setObjectValues: [colourbar, background,getColour]  getRadioboxSelection: [radiobox, getSelect],
  ]]                                         returnMessage: [colour=getColour,select=getSelect]
  ]).                                        ]]
                                            ]).
```

Figure 7. The interface behaviour knowledge

The above design knowledge of an user interface is produced automatically when the designer finishes the creation of the interface using the Interface Knowledge Editor described in the last section. The design knowledge base can be accessed by the Interface Knowledge Editor for modifying the existing interface design knowledge, and by a UIMS for implementing user interfaces on an application's requirement or a simulation requirement from the Interface Editor. A UIMS has been implemented, which accepts the interface design knowledge as input, implements the user interface it describes, and manages the communication with applications.

## 4 The User Interface Management System

A User Interface Management System, called the Harness [1,2] has been developed for knowledge-based front end to existing software systems. The Harness manages communications between the various subsystems. This communication takes place using a clearly defined abstract message structure. When an application or a knowledge-based support module requires the Harness to activate an interaction object, a message has to be sent to the Harness. The Harness, in turn, transforms the design knowledge into the appropriate physical interaction. However, the more complex the interactions are, the larger the messages tend to be. Nevertheless, in the application or knowledge-based support module, the precise information about the user interface must be provided. This could result in the increased complexity of the application module and a poor separation between the user interface and the application. An extended user interface management system has been developed to overcome these problems and is used in the KBUIMS described in this paper to deal with the user interface creation, communication management, etc..

The main extension to the Harness is that the application, or the knowledge-based support module, sends a short message which includes the reference name of an interaction object defined by the developer, rather than a long message describing the interaction object design in terms of the basic provided objects. The latter method would be quite complex.

The communications between the subsystems are under the control of the UIMS, via standard message structures. The basic form of a message is: message(*identifier, content, destination*) [1]. On receiving the message from an application module that requires the implementation of a user interface, the UIMS accesses the interface design knowledge base. The first step is to create the interface presentation, using the basic interaction object described in the Interaction Object Library, and then to attach the interface behaviour actions, described in the Action Routine Library, to the objects in the user interface. When the user operates on a object in the interface, for example pressing a "ok" button, the behaviour attached to the object is performed. Thus, provided that the action "returnMessage" is specified in a object's behaviour definition in the interface, the message about the interface's current state can be sent back to the application module when the user performs the relevant operation on this object. The application module can also change the current interface state by sending an interface update message. For example, to create the interface for which the design knowledge

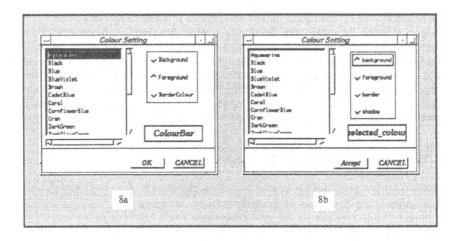

Figure 8. The example interface "colour_select"

is shown in figure 5 & 7, the following message should be sent to the UIMS:

    **message**(message1, **create**(colour1, colour_select, [ ]), **user**).

Here, in this message, the "message1" is the message identifier. The "colour1" is the interface identifier and the "colour_select" is the reference name of the interface prototype in the knowledge base. The bold words are reserved key words. After receiving this message, an interaction object is created and put on the user's screen (figure 8a). When the user presses the "OK" button, the following message which describes the current interaction object state (shown in figure 8a) is sent back to the application module called "example":

    **message**(message1, **return**(colour1, colour_select = [colour = 'Aquamarine',
        selection = 'Foreground', control = [ ok ] ]), example).

Sending following message, the application module can change the current interface state (figure 9a) to the interface state shown in figure 8b:

    **message**(message2, **update**(colour1, colour_select,
        [ radiobox : [toggleButtons : [ background, foreground, border, shadow] ],
        colourbar : [ labelString : selected_colour],
        okbutton : [ labelString : 'Accept']
        ]), **user**).

The interface is removed from the user's screen, if the application module sends the "destroy" message to the UIMS:

    **message**(message3, **destroy**(colour1), **user**).

# 5 Conclusions

We have presented the Knowledge-Based User Interface Management System (KBUIMS). The user interface design knowledge includes presentation and behaviour described in the interface knowledge base. Such design knowledge can be generated and modified by the designer using a graphical interface knowledge editor. The design knowledge of an interface, via an alternate user interface management system, is mapped into a physical presentation under a particular windowing system. This system provides a rapid and easy approach to developing prototype user interfaces.

# References

1. E. A. Edmonds & E. McDaid (1990), An Architecture for Knowledge-Based Front Ends, *Knowledge-Based Systems*, 3(4), 1990, pp. 221-224.

2. E. A. Edmonds, B. S. Murray, J. Ghazikhanian & S. P. Heggie (1992), The Re-use and Integration of existing Software: A Central Role for the Intelligent User Interface. *People and Computers VII*, Cambridge University Press, Monk, Diaper & Harrison (eds.), 1992, pp. 415-427.

3. J. D. Foley, C. Gibbs, W. C. Kim & S. Kovacevic (1988), A Knowledge-Based User Interface Management System, in *Proc. CHI'88 Human Factors in Computer Systems*, Washington, D. C., May 15-19, 1988, pp.67-72.

4. J. D. Foley, W. C. Kim, S. Kovacevic & K, Murray (1989), Defining Interfaces at a High Level of Abstraction, *IEEE Software* 6(1), January 1989, pp. 25-32.

5. J. Gettrs & R. W. Scheifler (1986), The X-Window System, *ACM Transactions on Graphics*, 5(2), April 1986, pp. 79-109.

6. T. G. Lewis, F. Handloser III, & S. Yang (1989), Prototypes from Standard User Interface Management Systems, *IEEE Computer*, 22(5), May 1989, pp. 51-60.

7. H. Huang & E. A. Edmonds (1991), An Interaction Object Editor for the HARNESS UIMS. Ref. 91/K/LUTCHI/027, LUTCHI Research Centre, Loughborough University of Technology, September 1991.

8. E. L. Hutchins, J. D. Hollan, & D. A. Norman (1986), Direct Manipulation Interfaces, *User Centered System Design*, D. A. Norman & S. W. Draper (eds.), Hillsdale, New Jersey, Lawrence Erlbaum Associates, 1986, pp. 87-124.

9. B. A. Myers (1988), *Creating User Interfaces by Demonstration*, Academic Press, boston, 1988.

10. D. R. Olsen (1986), MIKE: The Menu Interaction Kontrol Environment, *Transactions on Graphics*, 5(4), October 1986, pp. 318-344.

11. D. R. Olsen, W. A. S. Buxton, R. Ehrich, D. Kasik, J. Rhyne & J. Sibert (1984), A Context for User Interface Management System, *IEEE Computer Graphics and Applications*, 4(12), December 1984, pp. 33-42.

12. OSF (1990), *OSF/Motif Programmer's reference, Revision 1.1*, Open Software Foundation, Cambridge, CA, 1990.

13. B. Shneiderman (1983), Direct Manipulation: A Step Beyond Programming Languages, *IEEE Computer*, 16(8), August 1983, pp. 57-69.

14. G, Singh & M. Green (1989), A High-level User Interface Management System. In *proc. of the ACM CHI'89 Conf. on Human Factors in Computing Systems*, ACM, New York, 1989, pp. 133-138.

15. G. Singh, C. H. Kok, & T, Y. Ngan (1990), Druid: A System for Demonstrational Rapid User Interface Development. In *proc. of the ACM SIGGRAPH Symp. on User Interface Software*, ACM, New York, 1990, pp. 167-177.

16. P. Tanner & W. A. S. Buxton (1985), Some Issues in Future User Interface Management System (UIMS) Development, in *User Interface Management Systems*, G. E. Pfaff (ed.), Springer-Verlag, 1985, pp. 67-80.

17. J. J. Thomas & G. Hamklin, eds. (1982), Graphics Input Interaction Technique (GIIT) Workshop Summary, June 2-4, 1982, Battelle Seattle, *Computer Graphics*, 17(1) Jan. 1983, pp. 5-66.

# Objects Feeling Objects in a MultiView Object Space

Franz Penz
ERCIM Fellowship Program 1992-93/INESC
Lisboa, Portugal.
e-mail: fp@ani.univie.ac.at

Luís Carriço
Instituto Superior Técnico/INESC
Lisboa, Portugal.
e-mail: lmc@inesc.pt

**Abstract:** User interfaces that allow the direct manipulation of conceptual objects with adequate semantic feedback are not sufficiently supported by the user interface tools of today. We have designed a layered architecture for user interface objects based upon the definition of a three dimensional object space for object manipulation. In this space the usual user centered events are replaced by a logical manipulation "feel" which is symmetrically applied from one object to another. We also consider the consequences of having multiple views of one object in such an object space. An example class definition in C++ gives an example of how to work with our objects.

## 1 Introduction

In the course of trying to implement several of our user interface designs which are all highly based upon the direct manipulation of conceptual objects (objects intended to be in the mind of the user) we discovered several problems with aspects of current implementation platforms. In general, current UI toolkits and tools (especially within the UNIX world), seem to avoid offering much support for direct manipulative interaction and semantic feedback. This is particularly apparent between multiple conceptual objects. In addition, the UI toolkits often constrain interfaces to a set of predefined components which are almost impossible to reconfigure.

The kind of interfaces we are dealing with definitely require a very dynamic approach to the creation, destruction and reconfiguration of UI objects in a flexible object space, as well as an immediate feedback for user interactions. Such UIs provide a high degree of user friendliness to interactive applications and are keys to the success of user-driven interactive programming tools. In general we believe they are becoming more and more important in the next level of user orientation, such as future distributed multiuser-systems.

Contrary to single object manipulation (which can be conceptually managed by the manipulated object itself) the manipulation of objects which simultaneously interact with others requires a more complex manager. This manager must provide the manipulation space and also regulate the object interactions. Based on the requirements of such a world of objects we define the abstract protocol for a direct manipulative 'obget' - an object oriented widget which manages direct manipulative object interaction. In addition we introduce a layered implementation approach to break down the inherent complexity of these UI elements. Each layer provides an interface to the next higher one, specifying the services provided and the possible events.

Our architectural proposal does not limit UIs to a special interaction media or one user, it thus addresses the new requirements for UIs which have been raised by the application areas of CSCW [6] and hypermedia. In addition, the architecture does not necessarily force a closed set of primitives and paradigms of conceptual interaction (although it can be used as such), but instead provides a way to complement existing UIs.

This paper presents ongoing work. The definition and discussion of our architecture are incomplete and subject to change. Our layered model is based on the work presented by Lantz et al [5]. The division of a user interface architecture into layers with an interface consisting of abstract manipulations and feedback functions is a continuation of our work with CommonInteract [12] and the world of objects [13,11], and clearly fits our 4D architecture approach [1,4]. In this paper we concentrate on the definition of the conceptual behaviour of objects in the object space which is realised with the central layer of our architecture, the view system. We think this is the most innovative part of our work and we would like to present the UI community with our requirements and ideas. The other layers will be described in future articles.

After thea definition of the requirements of our system (section 2) and an overview of the object space architecture (section 3) we present the object space (section 4) in detail. We define the behaviour of objects in the space and deal with the problems of multiple views of one object in such a space. Finally, we present a specification of the view system using C++ (section 5) and close with a discussion of our work (section 6).

## 2   Requirements

We want to support the construction of user interfaces for applications with the following characteristics:

**Object Space:** The user is confronted with a conceptual object space. When working with the application, the user has a hierarchy of objects in mind. An object which may contain others is called a container. The user may manipulate single objects and move them to a new location in the object space according to their mental model of the objects. The user may manipulate objects in conjunction with others and freely change the object's container.

**Direct Manipulation:** The object space can be manipulated directly by the user - when users manipulate an object they have the impression of being responsible for the changes occurring in the object space. This is primarily achieved by giving immediate feedback in response to user manipulations so that the manipulation and reaction to the manipulation take place coherently.

**Semantic feedback:** This immediate feedback must take into consideration the "conceptual object" semantics wherever appropriate. For example, if an object is too heavy to be moved then it should not react to a user action, or perhaps move only very slowly. If a container is able to contain only certain kinds of objects (possibly related to the whole conceptual object status), then it should provide feedback only when the user drags these specific objects into the container.

**Multiple Views:** The same object may be present multiple times in the object space. That is an object can be contained more than once in the same container, and can be contained in different containers simultaneously.

## 3 Overview of the Object Space Architecture

Figure 1 shows our implementation architecture which consists of seven layers. Some of these layers are commonly used in UI implementations, so we have included them to explain their role within the overall architecture.

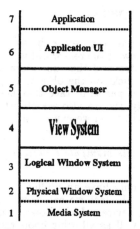

**Fig. 1.** The Object Space Architecture

**Layer 1:** contains the graphic system or media layer, covering not only graphical input and output but also acoustic, haptic and other media specific primitives.

**Layer 2:** is what we call the physical window system. Again this layer is not limited to classical two dimensional graphical windows but should be understood in a broader sense. It provides the services currently given by window systems such as Microsoft Windows, NeWS or X.

**Layer 3:** is the logical window system based on the services provided by the physical window systems. The logical window system provides the services required for multiple users to manipulate multimedia objects in a three dimensional space. This layer already provides an interface to layer 4 which is free of interaction media specific issues, thus mapping that unified interface to the specific physical window system.

The problems to be solved by layer 3 are much more fundamental than the addition of support for multiple users or media in current commercial window systems. In X, for instance, Xlib does not provide an intrinsic function to discover which window is physically below a given one. Thus when one window is moved over another in a direct manipulative way the events go to the moved window. This may be contrary to the aims of the application. If we want to use the next higher X layer, Xt, we face a further problem: in Xt we cannot change the parent of a widget (although it is possible, with unpredictable consequences, to use Xlib to change the parent of the widget's window).

**Layer 4:** is the view system, the "most abstract layer" in the object space architecture. It is independent from both the base hardware and any specific application. Our object space architecture is derived from the functionality of this layer which builds the virtual object space and handles the manipulation of objects within this space.

The view system is also responsible for the management of multiple views of one object if required by an application. At this level therefore, manipulations of the object space are manipulations of views rather than of objects. In its interface to the next layer it provides the events and services necessary to react to abstract user manipulations of the objects, to manipulate the object space and to give object specific feedback.

**Layer 5:** is the object manager which implements a specific object space manipulation dialogue. In this layer, a container manages the contained child objects relying on the protocol and behaviour defined in layer 4. Layer 5 is not only useful in multi-object interaction but may also be used for normal single object manipulations in order to separate the implementation of the object-related manipulation dialogue from the object presentation.

**Layer 6:** is the application user interface layer. It is application specific and adapts an application to the defined object manager layer of the UI environment. This layer emerges from the idea of separating the user interface related code from the functional code in an application implementation.

**Layer 7:** implements the actual functionality of an application.


## 4   The Direct Manipulative Object Space

The usual approach to object manipulation assumes the user is the sole manipulator. This works well as long as a simplified view of the real world is taken, or by assuming that only one object is manipulated and that no interaction with other objects occurs. For example, the user clicks on the objects to perform some action, rather than using another object per se to take that action on the object. Alternatively, and more realistically, we can also see objects as manipulators or "live" entities. Using this approximation we can consider the user as just another object and simply say:

> *In a generalised interactive object space, objects manipulate objects and interact with each other.*

If users are modeled as objects too, we now not only have an unified system but at the same time we gain a lot of flexibility. In fact we can now easily extend our systems to support multiple interaction devices which allow one user to manipulate a multimedia interaction space as well as allowing cooperating users to share a common interaction space.

We will adopt this approach in order to provide an implementation platform supporting our UI requirements. We call the resulting entities 'obgets' in analogy to widgets from common supposedly "object oriented" tools based on window systems such as Xt [10,14]. However, we use a full object oriented approach for design and implementation.

The following subsections discuss the use of our approximation to solve the problems imposed by the adoption of our "users as objects" approach. This will correspond to the "View System" layer of our architecture. We first explain the behaviour of objects in the object space, focusing on the interactions between them. We then address the presentation aspects, focusing on the consequences of allowing multiple views within a hierarchical view model.


### 4.1   The Object Space in the View System

The view system constructs the virtual object space and provides services to allow its manipulation in an abstract way. The object space is a three dimensional model of a world of spatially arranged object views. The positions of all views are measured in a device independent way relative to their container view. Objects in the object space are always contained in at least one container, and are contained once per view.

The view system interface consists of two parts: object manipulations and object feedback (we currently have identified only one primitive manipulation - feel). At any time, an object is defined by a set of shapes related to an object origin. Two shapes are used to define the view manipulation: the "sensitive" and the "active" regions of an object. An additional "children" region is used for object composition. It corresponds to the clipping area of a window in a window system. In simple worlds of objects (such as 2D desktop metaphor based user interfaces) the regions may be restricted to be identical or just a point. Any of the regions of an object may also be empty.

Conceptually, view manipulations are the actions performed by a user or by any object (view) on another object (view). We have reduced the number of possible manipulations to only one primitive - feel - which we hope is sufficient to cover all possible situations. A feel manipulation consists of allowing the manipulated object to feel the manipulating one (which in a simple case may be a user). A manipulation is characterised by the manipulating view, its position relative to the manipulated object, and a "force" vector. Conceptually, during the course of the manipulation, a force is applied by the manipulating view to the manipulated view.

a) Moving objects        b) Lefthand object feels the other    c) Both objects feel each other

**Fig. 2.** Manipulation regions within the object space

If the sensitive region of an object enters the active region of another, it "feels" this object - the object providing the active region manipulates the other. This interaction is not dependent upon which object is moving or which is stationary (both views may even move and feel simultaneously). If the sensitive regions of two interacting views both intersect with the respective active region of the other view, both views are manipulated and both views feel each other.

Figure 2 explains the feel manipulation using two example objects: In 2a) the two objects are shown with their active and sensitive regions approaching each other. In 2b) the active region of the righthand object is just about to enter the sensitive region of the lefthand one. Therefore the lefthand object starts to feel the righthand object and can give some feedback such as changing colour. Note that the intersection of only sensitive regions does not result in a feel manipulation. Note also that the feedback produced by an object is not restricted to the sensitive or active regions, but may also include the children region. In 2c) the sensitive region of the righthand object intersects with the active region of the lefthand one. Both objects can now feel each other. The righthand object in 2c) gives visual and acoustic feedback and also changes its sensitive and active regions in reaction to the feel manipulation.

If the manipulating view or the manipulated view has children and the intersecting active and sensitive regions are covered by the respective active and sensitive regions of the children (which are clipped at the childrens region) then only the children feel or are felt. Only if a child cannot handle a manipulation is it delegated to the parent. Note that the two manipulation regions of a parent can be extended by the respective regions of its children. The manipulation regions of the children are only clipped at the children's region of the parent, not at its manipulation regions.

Figure 3 shows how a normal 2D mouse and window interaction can be mapped to our model. In the figure the mouse cursor - the representation of the user object - is moved over an icon and a mouse button is pressed. The mouse cursor (user) has only one point as its active region. The sensitive region of the user is empty and the children region has no boundary. At the beginning of this manipulation the user has just one child - the image of the mouse cursor. The sensitive region of the icon is the size of the icon image, the children region shows this image, and the active region is empty.

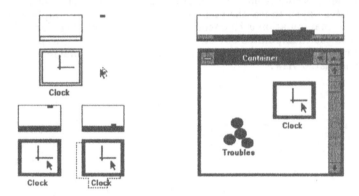

**Fig. 3.** Moving an icon in the object space

Before the mouse button is pressed, the logical position of the user is one unit above the icon. So the icon feels the user entering its sensitive region at some distance. When the mouse button is pressed the user moves down to the icon and the icon feels that the user is closer (see figure 3). Now it can make its decision to move with the mouse pointer and changes from its current container window to become a new child of the user. It then assigns itself an active region at the mouse pointer position (identical to the active region of the user) and removes its sensitive region.

The force of a manipulation is not used in this simple example but may be needed in connection with a mouse to model different keys or multiple key presses. In this example we have made sensitive the objects waiting on the desk and active the moving objects. We could also do the inverse and let the moved object feel the stationary one, or let both objects feel each other.

On the righthand side of figure 3 the icon is moved into a window and the mouse button is released. Analogous to the icon described above, the window has no active region but does have a sensitive one covering its visible picture. If the user now enters the destination window with the icon, the window feels the active region of the icon. If the mouse button is released the position of the feeling changes and the window can make the icon a child of itself. The various window controls (titlebar, menu, scrollbars, resize icon, and so on) and window contents are all children which may themselves feel if a view enters them.

The shapes, positions and containers of an object can be changed by applying feedback functions to its views. Currently we define some spatial feedback functions (which allow changes to the three object regions directly or via a spatial transformation) and one object hierarchy feedback function (to logically change the container of an object). View creation can also be considered as a feedback element but this depends heavily upon the selected implementation model.

## 4.2 Multiple Views

One of our requirements is the support for multiple views of one object - one object may be present more than once in the object space, at the same or at different logical positions, or even be recursively contained in itself. Multiple representations can also be assigned to an object thus enabling different forms (not necessarily visible, but also audible, tactile and so on) to be associated with different views.

The idea of separating abstract (conceptual) objects from their views is not new and is in fact present in many of the current UI architectures such as 4D [1], PAC [2], MVC [3], InterViews [7]. However, when conceptual objects themselves are contained in an abstract hierarchical object space, then these objects' views may also be represented more than once.

Consider for example a two dimensional object space representing one view of a container object showing its children region. A child object is represented twice in that conceptual container (and consequently in the container's view), in different positions and with different forms as shown in figure 4a. These two views roughly correspond to the concept of a view as defined in current UI architectures with the exception, perhaps, that they should "know" that they represent the same conceptual object. If a second view of the container object

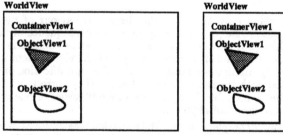
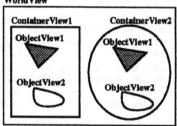

a) Two views of the same object    b) Two presentations of each view

**Fig. 4.** Object views and view presentations

is now created (figure 4b) which also shows the whole children region, then all its children should also appear. Furthermore, as they are in fact the same view they should appear at the same position in that region probably with the same aspect (although possibly geometrically transformed according to the aspect of the container.

The view system must be able to handle these situations transparently. In fact the objects in the object space (or even at the object manager level) have no need to know (and should not know) of the existence of two view presentations. These views are in fact handled automatically and merely represent an exact duplication of the original views. On the other hand, in order to replicate view presentations in different views the view system must know to which view each object belongs. In our example, the container view in figure 4b corresponds to an object in which children already have views, so duplicate presentations of them must be created.

A similar approach was made in Images [8,9]. The major difference is that our view system model, besides handling the two abstraction "levels" of views, provides a higher level even at the view representations. From the user's perspective, a view should behave homogeneously in all its presentations. For example, if the user manipulates one presentation of a view then all presentations of the view should react. This is shown in figure 5 where View1 of Object is moved

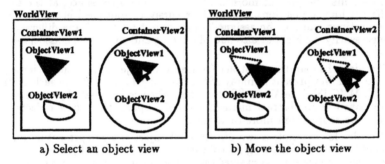

a) Select an object view        b) Move the object view

**Fig. 5.** Interacting with multiple view presentations

inside its container, providing simultaneous feedback. Notice that View2 has not changed, since it is a different view of the same object. Naturally, semantic changes on the object should provide feedback on all its views - if the object is deleted for example.

Although it is relatively easy to define the desired behaviour of multiple views inside a single space, some problems may arise as a consequence of having a hierarchical, graph-like (not simply an inverted tree) set of containers. The following examples illustrate some of the requirements of the view system within a two dimensional directly manipulated object space. For simplification purposes, views are represented with the same shape as long as they correspond to the same object, and a label is introduced to identify different views of one object, for example, V1O2 means view 1 of object 2.

As our first interaction example, consider the situation (see figure 6) in which view 1 of object 1 (V1O1) is grabbed and pulled away from its container object 2. Then V1O1 is moved in both views of object 2 (figure 6a). However, if the user now crosses with V1O1 the border of V2O2, the related presentation of V1O1 in V1O2 is clipped (figure 6b).

Consider now the possibility of associating a "shadow-like" behaviour with a view and suppose that the moved object covers multiple views. If V1O1 is moved over V1O4, V2O4, and V3O4 (see figure 7a), we will see multiple shadows of V1O1 in all three views of object 4. This could happen, for instance, if the active region of V1O1 corresponds to its visible part and the sensitive regions of V1O4, V2O4, and V3O4 coincide with its children regions.

In the final example, suppose V1O4 is moved over V2O4. We now see a recur-

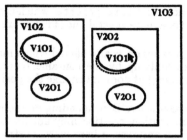 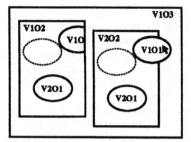

a) Moving a multiply-presented view    b) Changing the container of a view.

**Fig. 6.** Complex behaviour of multiple view presentations

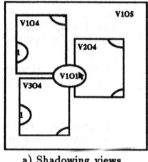 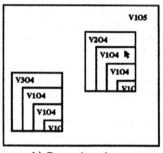

a) Shadowing views    b) Recursive views

**Fig. 7.** Multiple shadows and recursive view presentations

sive presentation of object 4 within itself (figure 7b).

## 5  A C++ specification

This section introduces a C++ example of a specification for the view system layer interface. The example presented is just one implementation possibility; other solutions could for example use separate objects in the view system and object manager instead of basing the connection of the two layers on inheritance or multiple inheritance.

We have identified the need for just one manipulation primitive - **feel**. This should carry as arguments the manipulating object, a position, and a force (position and force are both vectors). This primitive is requested whenever a valid intersection occurs between an active and sensitive region of two views. It is then up to the object-manager to implement the specific behaviour of such a feeling based, for example, on the parameters.

Spatial feedback primitives are also provided in order to allow the object-manager to change the appearance of a view, (that is, the appearance of its active, sensitive and children regions). Besides the three functions to set the three regions (**setActive**, **setSensitive** and **setChildren**) the implementation also provides some simple methods (**move, moveTo, resize, rotate**) which enable the most frequent view manipulations and one more general one (**transform**) to enable a 3D transformation.

An object hierarchy feedback function, **transfer**, is also offered which moves the object within the logical object space built up by the container/contents relationship. It moves a view to a new container but does not change the position of the view.

Views are created from the object-manager layer. Dependending on the view system and/or the object-manager implementation, creation may not be called explicitly thus unbinding these two levels. In any case, a base view constructor should be provided as in our example specification below.

## 5.1 An inheritance based approach

We now present the view system layer interface as a C++ class definition, specifying the methods that the objects provided by this layer offer to the object manager layer above. The class **DMView** defines methods for manipulations and for feedback.

The manipulations have a default implementation in the view system layer and may be redefined in the object manager (a derived class) to react to the corresponding user interactions.

```
virtual void feel (DMView* anObject, Vector position, Vector force);
// anObject is felt with force at position. anObject may be a user.
```

The feedback functions are also implemented in derived classes corresponding to different view system concretisations and are called (virtually) from the object manager component.

```
virtual void setActive    (Region activeRegion);
virtual void setSensitive(Region sensitiveRegion);
virtual void setChildren (Region childrenRegion);

virtual void transfer     (DMView* destinationContainer);
        void move         (Vector distance);
        void moveTo       (Vector position);
        void resize       (Vector scale);
        void rotate       (Vector angle);
virtual void transform    (TransformationMatrix m);
```

The first three functions set the regions of the object; the fourth changes the view container. The **move** function changes the position of the moved view relative to its container view. All (children) views contained in a moved view keep their position relative to the container and therefore move with their container. The **moveTo** function operates in much the same way but moves to an absolute position inside the container. **Resize** changes the size of all three view regions relative to their current size. **Rotate** rotates the view regions around their origin. **Transform** allows an arbitrary spatial transformation of the view.

```
DMView (DMView* container, Vector position, DMObject* me);
```

The constructor should be given its container view, a position, and an identification of the object it represents. Based on this identification, the view system is able to duplicate automatically the presentation of other children views that have already been created for that object.

At the object-manager and view system levels a set of special objects are used in order to distinguish between different logical users and devices: these include objects representing the users (the only objects which may generate events 'by themselves') and views representing disjoint view spaces generated by different independent devices (views without a parent container).

```
DMView *User1, *User2, ...;
DMView *World1, *World2, ...;
```

# 6 Discussion

We have presented our approach to solve a set of problems existing in current UI tools when the direct manipulation of conceptual object spaces is requested by the application designer. We focused the presentation on two major issues:

1. A model for the manipulation of objects with objects, within a multi-user and multi-device paradigm, in a three dimensional hierarchical object space.

2. A model for the representation of one object multiple times in the same or different containers in the object space.

The proposed model is based on the "real world metaphor" which we believe closely conforms to current UI trends. The homogeneity of our model maps to the normal world activities of object manipulation with hands or tools (other objects). Object interaction is based upon the concept of a symmetrical manipulation 'feel'. As a consequence objects may feel each other simultaneously and they are able to immediately give feedback as to their 'feelings'.

The consideration of a three dimensional space also accommodates recent revolutionary interaction devices where three dimensional perception is provided to the user. However, as an open research question, we may extend the model to a fourth dimension which deals with time, or perhaps make a mathematical generalisation of the space into even more dimensions.

The multiple view approach is also based on real world metaphors, such as a room with several windows where the enclosed objects can be seen coherently through all the "views". It is also supported by a more conceptual approach realising that objects can be integrated in different conceptual categories and thus may also be enclosed in different conceptual containers. For example a book on a shelf "container" also belongs to the set (container) of books of its owner.

An interesting example application of the multiple view behaviour could be to show one document in multiple windows, possibly on different screens, manipulated by multiple users simultaneously. The users may not only view different parts of the document, but also use different presentations of the document and/or display window according to their preferences.

# Acknowledgements

The authors remain eternally indebted to Victoria Burrill for proof-reading and English language conversion above and beyond the call of duty!

# References

[1] L. Carriço, N. Guimarães, P. Antunes, A. Pereira, and M. Moreno. Support for Open Tools and Systems. In *Proceedings of the TOOLS'92 Conference*, Dortmund, Germany, March 1992.

[2] J. Coutaz. Architecture Models for Interactive Software: Failures and Trends. In G. Cockton, editor, *Engineering for Human-Computer Interaction*, pages 137-153. Elsevier Science Publishers B.V, North-Holland, 1990.

[3] M. Dodani, C. Hughes, and J. Moshell. Separation of powers. *BYTE*, pages 255-262, March 1989.

[4] N. Guimarães, L. Carriço, and P. Antunes. INGRID: An Object Oriented Interface Builder. In *Proceedings of the TOOLS'91 Conference*, Santa Barbara, California, July 1991.

[5] K. A. Lantz, P. P. Tanner, C. Binding, K-T. Huang, and A. Dwelly. Reference models, window systems, and concurrency. *Computer Graphics*, 21(2), April 1887.

[6] J.C. Lauwers and K.A. Lantz. Collaboration awareness in support of collaboration transparency: Requirements for the next generation of shared window systems. In *Proceedings of the ACM/SIGCHI Conference on Human Factors in Computing*, Seattle Washington, 1990. ACM Press.

[7] M. Linton and P. Calder. The Design and Implementation of InterViews. In *Proceedings of the 1987 USENIX C++ Workshop*, New Mexico, November 1987.

[8] J.A. Marques, N. Guimarães, and L.P.Simões. Images: A User Interface Development System. *Interacting with Computers*, 3, 1991.

[9] J.A. Marques, L. Simões, N. Guimarães, L. Carriço, and M. Sequeira. Images - An Approach to an Object Oriented UIMS. In *Proceedings of the Autumn 1988 EUUG Conference*, Cascais, Portugal, October 1988.

[10] J. McCormack, P. Asente, and R. Swick. *Xtoolkit Intrinsics - C Language Interface, X Window System X11R4*, December 1989.

[11] F. Penz, M. Manhartsberger, and M. Tscheligi. The world of objects - a visual object based interaction language. In Michael J. Tauber, Dirk Mahling, and Farah Arefi, editors, *Cognitive Aspects of Visual Languages and Visual Interfaces Series Human Factors in Information Technology*. Elsevier Science Publishers B.V, North-Holland, 1993.

[12] B. Strassl and F. Penz. Commoninteract - an object-oriented architecture for portable, direct manipulative user interfaces. In *Journal of Object-Oriented Programming*, Vol.6, Nº3, June 1993.

[13] M. Tschelingi, F. Penz, and M. Manhartsberger. N/joy - the world of objects. In *Proceedings of the 1991 IEEE Workshop on Visual Languages*, pages 126-131, Kobe, Japan, October 1991. IEEE-CS Press.

[14] D. Young. *X Window Systems, Programming and Applications With Xt*. Prentice-Hall, 1989.

# HYPER- AND MULTIMEDIA

# ShareME: A Metaphor–based Authoring Tool for Multimedia Environments

Kaisa Väänänen

ZGDV – Computer Graphics Center
Wilhelminenstraße 7
64283 Darmstadt, Germany
email: kaisa@igd.fhg.de

**Abstract.** This paper investigates requirements on tools for the authoring of multimedia information systems. These requirements can be divided into those of the authors who create the information system, and those of the users who interact with these environments. The goal of multimedia authoring tools is to allow the author easily build new information environments, which can subsequently support the user with a variety of interaction methods. It will be recommended that the design and implementation tasks of multimedia environments should be integrated within the authoring tool, and that both the author and users should be supported by the same appropriate user interface metaphors.

The users' and authors' requirements are illustrated with the realisation of the system ShareME (Shared Multimedia Environments). It is argued that ShareME is a new type of authoring tool — a metaphor–based authoring tool — because it exploits real–world metaphors in the user interface to the multimedia environments.

## 1    Introduction

Multimedia is, by definition, the integration of a variety of natural human communication channels. Users of multimedia systems can thus read visually presented text, view graphics and pictures, watch videos, and listen to speech, music, and other sounds. User's input to a multimedia system may consist not only of typed text, but also of selecting and manipulating 2D and 3D objects, using body gestures, and speaking in natural language. Furthermore, it is essential that the multimedia system supports a variety of methods for navigating through its information space. If the juxtaposition of media is carefully designed, multimedia can improve the quality of man–machine communication in many application areas.

Experience has shown that multimedia techniques can improve users' interaction with the application, especially within the areas of information acquisition [1], learning [2], presentation [3], and process control [4]. The tasks that require most effort in the construction of such multimedia systems are the collection of heterogeneous information material, and the definition of interaction possibilities afforded to the users. Interactive authoring tools must support these tasks.

A *multimedia environment* is an information space in which the multimedia information units form a semantically defined collection, and around which the user can "move" using various navigation methods. In a multimedia environment each information unit can be presented as text, graphics, video, animation, sound, or a combination thereof.

The user of an interactive multimedia information system must be provided with facilities to find the information they are interested in. There must be various *interaction* or *navigation methods* with which different users with different goals can find information in the environment. Navigation can be seen as moving through the multimedia information space.

The *authoring* of multimedia information systems consists of the creation of application–dependent multimedia information units, the integration of these units within the application, the construction of information structures, and the provision of interaction methods whereby users can access this information.

Even though it is possible to construct and program such information systems "from scratch", the process of building these systems should be supported by an authoring tool to reduce the author's work load. This should also increase the likelihood of providing a system that is easy to learn and easy to use.

## 2    Use of Multimedia Information Systems

In trying to achieve their goal of finding interesting multimedia information, users of multimedia information systems go through the following process:

1)    Definition of the goal. An example of a *specific goal* is "I want to find a hotel in Rostock which costs less than 50 DM per night". An example of a *vague goal* is "I want to know something about churches in eastern Germany". The goal can also be just to *explore* the information environment.

2)    Developing an understanding about the facilities offered by the system.

3)    Navigation (an iterative process).
    1.    Moving around the information space using the navigation methods.
    2.    Orientation and reorientation (Where am I? Where was I? Where can I go now?) [5].
    3.    Reaching the goal (finding interesting information and identifying it as interesting).

The system should ideally minimise the time spent on phase 2 of the interaction process, and allow selection and use of various intuitive navigation methods for performing the iterative steps of phase 3.

Therefore, to acquire information from multimedia systems, the user needs a set of navigation methods from which they can choose according to their aims (see Fig. 1). These methods and strategies are discussed in [6].

Very few, if any of the current commercial authoring tools offer the user all (or even a large subset) of these navigation methods. Thus, authors must design and implement new navigation techniques as and when they are required and within the limits that the authoring tool sets. This may result in the user having far less choice of interaction and navigation tools than is ideal.

Furthermore, the problem of the user is that learning of the system may take unacceptable long time. To overcome this problem, familiar metaphors should be offered in the user interface to the system. Moreover, whenever possible, the navigation methods should conform to the metaphors.

| Search Strategy<br>Navigation Method Style | Specific | Unspe-<br>cific | Explora-<br>tion |
|---|---|---|---|
| Maps — show visually the structure of information space, e.g. as a chart, index, table of contents | X | X | X |
| Guided Tours — define a path through the information space, possibly added by a "point of view" of the respective guide | — | X | X |
| History — stores the actions, places visited, or other information of the current session | X | X | — |
| Search — allows searching for specific information based on a criteria, e.g. contents or structure | X | X | — |
| Hyperlinks — connect related information allowing direct access to one piece of information to another | X | X | X |
| Random — takes the user randomly to a place in the information space, possibly to one where the user has not been yet | — | — | X |
| Agents — perform some tasks for the user, e.g. collecting interesting information together, or give suggestions to the user about where to go | X | X | X |
| Human Experts — other human users, possibly experts in the theme area, and possibly located elsewhere in the network | X | X | — |

**Fig. 1.** Methods for different navigation strategies (X means very relevant, — means not most relevant for the strategy)

## 3   The Multimedia Authoring Process

The process of authoring a multimedia information system can be thought of as consisting of the following steps:

1) Preparation (collection and editing) of multimedia data
2) Design of information structures
   1. Design of media–dependent representations of information items
   2. Design of media combinations
   3. Design of information structures
3) Design of the user interface
   1. Design of metaphors in the user interface
   2. Design of interaction methods
4) Realisation (programming) of the system
   1. Implementation of methods for integrating information units within the system
   2. Implementation of methods for structuring the information
   3. Implementation of metaphors
   4. Implementation of interaction methods
5) Integration of multimedia information units within the system and the creation of connections (links and groupings) between them

An authoring tool can simplify this process by supporting the various tasks either by automating them, or by offering various predefined options from which the author can choose. Task 1 (collecting data) cannot be supported because the multimedia material is mostly collected from outside of the computer domain. Task 1.2 can be supported by various integrated editors. Task 2.1 is normally supported by predefined low–level interaction techniques to different media (e.g. VCR controls for a video window). The other design tasks of step 2 and step 3 are not normally supported in any way. Furthermore, task 3.1 (design of metaphors) is normally completely ignored. Task 4.1 is supported by all authoring tools. The other tasks in step 4 should be realized in an authoring tool, but are normally done so only partially, or not at all. Step 5 in the authoring process is normally supported by authoring tools for at least a limited subset of media types (normally static but not dynamic media).

### 3.1 Classification of Authoring Tools

Authoring tools can be classified in the following way in terms of the overall authoring style they use [7–9]:

- **Script–based systems:** the author writes short programs ("Scripts") that control the interaction sequences (e.g. ToolBook, HyperCard)

- **Icon–based systems:** the system offers the author "Icons", with which logical control structures can be defined (e.g. Authorware Professional, IconAuthor)

- **Time–based systems:** the author can synchronize the various media and user's actions via time–dependent graphs (e.g. Score module of MacroMind Director, QuickTime)

| | Script–based Systems | Icon–Based Systems | Time–based Systems |
|---|---|---|---|
| 2.1 Design of media representations | Low–level support | Low–level support | Low–level support |
| 2.2 Design of media combinations | No support | No support | No support |
| 2.3 Design of information structures | Simple general structures (e.g. book, stack) | Flowchart | Time charts, overviews |
| 3.1 Design of metaphors for the users | No support | No support | No support |
| 3.2 Design of interaction methods | No support | Little or no support (answer analysis) | No support |
| 4.1 Implementation of methods for inserting information | Supported | Supported | Supported |
| 4.2 Implementation of information structures | Little support within the limits of 2.3 | Logical structures (e.g. "if", "loop") | Little support within the limits of 2.3 |
| 4.3 Implementation of metaphors | No support | No support | No support |
| 4.4 Implementation of interaction methods | Low–level (e.g. hotspots, buttons) | Hotspots, buttons, menus, keyboard | Low–level (e.g. hotspots, buttons) |

**Fig. 2.** Support of authoring tasks in general classes of authoring tools

Script–based methods allow a very flexible design, but the author must normally do a considerable amount of programming to achieve complex information systems. In icon–based systems authors do not need to write any program *code* as such, but they must understand and be able to construct logical flow charts with icons describing the interaction structures. Time–based systems offer advanced possibilities for the synchronization of various (esp. temporal) media, but support for the logical structuring of information and interaction is very limited.

Figure 2 summarizes the support mechanisms of the design (step 2) and implementation (step 3) tasks of the authoring process which the different classes of authoring tools normally offer to authors. (These evaluations are by no means meant to be universal claims; rather, they are generalisations on the types of tools.

### 3.2  A New Class of Authoring Tools: Metaphor–based Systems

A *user interface metaphor* is an analogy modelled upon something that is well–known to its users. Metaphors taken from real–world models are particularly useful for "naive" users. To be effective, user interface metaphors should embody both visual and behavioural aspects of their originating counterparts so as to enable the user to understand the functionality of the system.

The power of metaphors lies in their ability to give cues about the system. Based on a good and consistent metaphor the users can form a correct *mental model* about the system, which helps them to learn the system quickly. Metaphors must be chosen very carefully in order to avoid users forming incorrect mental models [10–12].

Within multimedia information systems, metaphors can be used in two ways:

Firstly, the design of information structures may be supported by an *authoring metaphor* (such as book, flowchart or theatre). These metaphors are used to help the author structure the information and interaction sequences but do not necessarily help the author understand the information structures and interaction possibilities from the user's point of view; these metaphors are, in fact, invisible to the users.

Secondly, the system may be supported by a *user's metaphor*. The user sees the information in a multimedia environment presented via a metaphor, and can interact with this information as if manipulating the originating objects belonging to the metaphor.

It can be concluded based on the discussion in section 3.1 that the major problem with current multimedia authoring tools is in the lack of support mechanisms for design and implementation tasks for structuring information and user interfaces.

The solution suggested here is that the user interface metaphors are offered to both authors and users, and interaction methods should be integrated within the tool. This will allow authors to construct applications based on a predefined (and pretested) user interface design and without having to implement it themselves. The user will then be guaranteed a system that is intuitive and easy to learn and use.

The type of tool based on the concepts presented above is called a *metaphor–based authoring tool*.

# 4    ShareME – Shared Multimedia Environments

The ShareME – Shared Multimedia Environments – system is presented here as an example of system that fulfils many of the requirements stated in chapters 2 and 3. For more information about ShareME, see [13–14]. This multimedia authoring and navigation system illustrates some of the possibilities and limitations of existing multimedia authoring systems.

ShareME is both a tool for authors who wish to build multimedia information systems (environments), and a run–time system for these environments.

The basic concepts of ShareME are:
- direct creation of multimedia environments without programming
- retrieval of information from multimedia structure spaces consisting of units of text, graphics, video, and sound information
- use of metaphors in the user interface
- offering a set of navigation methods that support intuitive interaction in the multimedia environment

Figure 3 shows the structure of the ShareME. The author first prepares the application–dependent multimedia information. Then, the author chooses one of the several metaphors offered by the tool, and then constructs a multimedia environment based on that metaphor. The author does not need to design nor implement navigation methods since they are offered directly by the system.

The user of a ShareME application has access to the information via various interaction techniques. The users then decide which navigation methods they wish to use according to the information for which they are searching. The users (like the author) see the environments "through" the metaphor the author chose during the authoring process.

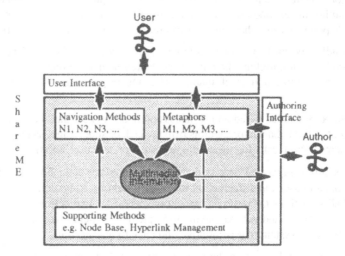

**Fig. 3.** Structure of ShareME

ShareME is implemented on NeXT Workstations connected via Ethernet. The software is implemented using NeXT InterfaceBuilder, Objective–C, and NeXT's Application Kit predefined objects.

## 4.1 ShareME Metaphors

One metaphor offered by ShareME is a house containing a series of rooms in which the information units are organised as nets of multimedia documents and information nodes (see Figure 4). The structure of the house and its structures are presented via the *overview maps* which are visible to the authors and users at all times.

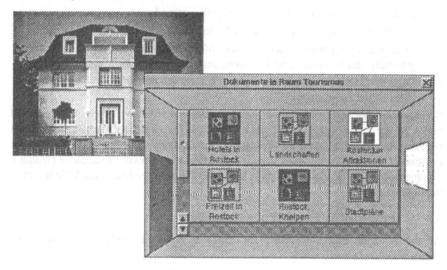

**Fig. 4.** The ShareME entrance to the house, and the overview map of a room

Other metaphors include:
- Library with departments, bookshelves, and books
- Magazine with sections and articles
- Geographical metaphor with mountains, lakes, and other "places" where information can be structured

Interaction within these user interface metaphors follows the model of interaction in their originating objects. For example, a house is entered through its main door, the rooms are entered by "knocking" at the doors; magazine is read by flipping through pages and using a table of contents; and geographical landscape can be visited by "flying" over the scene. The overview maps of each metaphor allow this interaction, and they are represented according to the chosen metaphor.

## 4.2 ShareME Authoring Tool

Authors of multimedia systems are normally experts within the specialist area, but not necessarily in computers. Therefore an interactive authoring tool should allow the construction of multimedia environments without any programming.

Furthermore the tool should offer a metaphor for presentation of information (e.g. a house), and navigation methods which should be intuitive for both authors and users. The author uses these navigation methods (or subset of them) to while inserting information in the system, whereas the user uses them to find information.

The author must create information units (nodes), insert these in the structures (e.g. rooms, documents) of the environment (e.g. house), and finally define connections (hyperlinks) between nodes that should be accessible from one another. All this is done interactively, manipulating the objects directly.

The ShareME authoring process is as follows:

1) Prepare the information base as a collection of nodes.
2) Select one of the metaphors offered by the authoring tool.
3) Design the relationships between the information units in terms of logical grouping and in terms of which nodes must be accessible from one another.
4) Directly manipulate the nodes and insert them in the metaphor–based structures of the environment.

Relationships between information nodes are defined either by arranging the related nodes in the same "place" (such as a room), or by explicitly creating hyperlinks between the nodes. Hyperlinks are created interactively by pointing to the desired position of the link (within the text of a text node) or by drawing a rectangle (within a graphic node). The destination node is then selected from the list of available nodes in the environment.

### 4.3    Navigation in ShareME Environments

At the moment ShareME offers six different ways of navigating through the information space:

1) Navigating by clicking on the overview maps. The navigation is done directly by clicking on the place (represented by an icon) where one wants to go.
2) Traversing hyperlinks between nodes. Hyperlinks can be originated from text and graphic (static) nodes to any type of node[1]. In text the links are shown as icons, and in graphics they are shown as rectangles.
3) Making a keyword search. It is possible to search information in environments with certain keywords. All nodes with the chosen keyword will be fetched, and the user can view any subset of these nodes.
4) Taking a guided tour. Environments can have a set of guides. The guides are virtual experts in a certain theme inside the environment, and they show the user some interesting nodes of their theme area.
5) Revisiting a place using the history list. All nodes visited during a session are inserted into the history list. Later the user can go back to any of these nodes by clicking on the items in the list.
6) Navigation with help of a human expert (cooperation). The users can communicate over the information by pointing to and manipulating items in the structure (via telepointers), and via speech and video channels (see [14]).

These navigation methods can be freely selected by the users, according to the goals and strategy of the user (see section 2, Figure 1).

## 4.4 ShareME: Authoring Tasks Supported by a Metaphor–based Authoring Tool

ShareME is different from other types of authoring systems presented in section 2.1 (Script–, Icon–, and Time–based systems) in terms of how metaphors and predefined interaction methods are used to support both authors and users.

Figure 5 summarises the design and implementation tasks supported by ShareME (see also Fig. 1 for comparison with other types of authoring tools).

| | ShareME: A Metaphor–based Authoring Tool |
|---|---|
| 2.1 Design of media representations | Each media type has a "template" with low–level interaction techniques |
| 2.2 Design of media combinations | Free combination of text, graphic, sound, video, slide show; one media per window (plus textual title) |
| 2.3 Design of information structures | Systems offers various meta–structures based on the metaphors, e.g. hierarchies, groups, lists (visible to the authors via the same metaphors as to the users); hyperlinks |
| 3.1 Design of metaphors for the users | System offers a set of metaphors from which the author can choose |
| 3.2 Design of interaction methods | System offers several navigation methods, with which the user can search for information |
| 4.1 Implementation of methods for inserting information | Supported for text, graphics, video, sound, and slide shows |
| 4.2 Implementation of information structures | The author must decide which information units belong together and which are related |
| 4.3 Implementation of metaphors | The author chooses a metaphor that suits best for the information (a metaphor designer can provide further metaphors) |
| 4.4 Implementation of interaction methods | The author does not need to implement navigation methods; system offers these and the user chooses which ones to use |

**Fig. 5.** Support of authoring tasks in ShareME

Comparing Figure 5 with Figure 2, it can be seen that the benefits of a metaphor–based authoring tool like ShareME lie in

- easy construction of multimedia environments; the design and implementation of user interfaces are integrated in the tool itself

- the pretested user interface metaphors and interaction techniques that guarantee resulting information systems that are easy to learn and easy to use

It is recognised that metaphors do restrict the types of applications that can be constructed using a metaphor–based authoring tool. However, the effects of this disadvantage can be minimised by offering enough different metaphors.

48

# 5 Applications

Areas of application where ShareME can be used include:

- information systems for museums, libraries, hospitals, department stores
- enquiry systems for tourist offices, public service offices, companies
- learning systems for schools, universities, distance learning, open universities
- sales catalogues for drug stores, real estate dealers, computers, houses, cars...
- user manuals for computer systems, for electrical appliances
- advertisement systems and commercials for airlines, tourism resorts, companies, ...
- interactive magazines

The first ShareME environment is an information acquisition system about the former East German states (Bundesländer). It contains multimedia information on tourism, universities, traffic, and geography of these areas.

Figure 6 shows an example of information in this system, in the area (room) of touristic attractions.

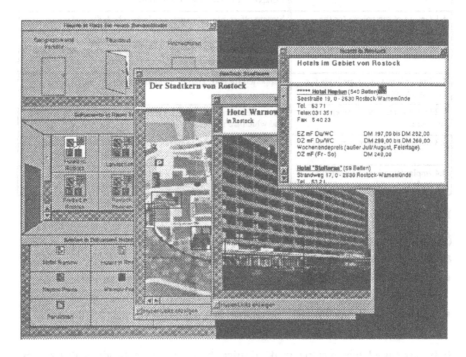

**Fig. 6.** An example interface to a ShareME environment

# 6    Summary and Conclusions

This paper has analysed the authoring and interaction processes of multimedia information environments. It was claimed that the currently existing authoring tools do not support the authoring process in a fully possible way. Especially the tasks in user interface design and implementation are left completely to the author's responsibility. This does not guarantee the best results in terms of usability of the multimedia information systems.

A new class of authoring tool, called metaphor–based authoring tool, was introduced. A tool of this class contains predefined user interface metaphors for both the authors and the users. In addition the tool offers the users wide variety of interaction methods. Using such tool will reduce the work load of the author and improve the usability of the system.

Our experiencing with the ShareME authoring tool shows that the tool is very practical and can be used with very little instruction. It is recognised that the hierarchy provided by the first metaphor (house) of ShareME may not be suitable to all theme areas. This could be helped by letting the author customise the house metaphor, e.g. by defining more levels of hierarchy instead of the three–level structure (rooms, documents, nodes) that is now the only possibility. Ongoing work is implementing a further set of user interface metaphors and navigation methods.

The evaluation of the first ShareME environment shows that the users are able to find the information they are looking for without external help. The user interface is attractive and easy to use to most users and it enables easy understanding of the information structures and interaction options [15]. The metaphors were readily accepted by the users; they were constantly referring to the interface objects with their originating (real–world) names, e.g. by saying "I will now go to this room". The goal of ShareME applications of being easy to learn and to use is (at least at the short–term usage we have observed) fulfilled.

## Acknowledgements

The author is grateful to Prof. Dr.–Ing. José L. Encarnação, Dr. Wolfgang Hübner and Martin Frühauf for their support and encouragement that has made this work possible. Furthermore, the author wants to express very special thanks to Dr. Victoria Burrill for interesting discussions on metaphors, and for invaluable comments on both the language and the contents of earlier versions of this paper.

## References

[1]    Kirste,T. "SpacePicture – an Interactive Hypermedia Satellite Image Archival System", *Proc. of 2nd Eurographics Workshop on Multimedia*, Darmstadt, May 1992 (Technical Report by Springer–Verlag).

[2]    Abmron,S., Hooper,K. "Learning with Interactive Multimedia", Redmond, Washington, 1990.

[3]    Bogaschewsky,R. "Hypertext–/Hypermedia–Systeme – Ein Überblick", *Informatik Spektrum*, No. 15, 1992, pp. 127 – 143.

[4]     Alty,J.L., Bergan,M., Dolphin,C. "Can Multimedia Interfaces be of Benefit to Process Control rather than just provide new Features?", *Proc. of 2nd Eurographics Workshop on Multimedia*, Darmstadt, May 1992 (Technical Report by Springer–Verlag).

[5]     Love, S.J., Chapman, C.M., Connelly, T.G.,J D Ten Haken, J.D. "Design techniques for Ensuring Structure and Flexibility in a Hypermedia Environment". *Multimedia Review*, Summer 1991.

[6]     Encarnação,J.L., Foley,J.D. (Eds.) "Issues and Directions in Multimedia Research", Springer–Verlag, 1993.

[7]     Herzner,W., Kummer,M. "MMV – Synchronizing Multimedia Documents", *Proc. of 2nd Eurographics Workshop on Multimedia*, Darmstadt, May 1992 (Technical Report by Springer Verlag).

[8]     Nickel,T. "The Developer's Dilemma", *Computer Graphics World*, Vol. 14, No. 7, July 1991, pp. 97 – 102.

[9]     Steinbrink,B. "Multimedia–Baukästen", *c't 1992*, Heft 5, pp. 70 – 79.

[10]    Carroll, J.M., Olson, J.R. "Mental Models in Human–Computer Interaction". In Helander,M. (ed.): *Handbook of Human–Computer Interaction*, Elsevier, North–Holland, 1980.

[11]    Erickson, T.D., "Working with Interface Metaphors". In Laurel,B.(ed.): *The art of human–computer interface design*, Apple Computer Inc., 1990.

[12]    Laurel,B. "Interface Agents: Metaphors with Character". In Laurel,B.(ed.): *The art of human–computer interface design*, Apple Computer Inc., 1990.

[13]    Väänänen,K. "Interfaces to Hypermedia: Communicating the Structure and Interaction Possibilities to the Users", *Proc. of 2nd Eurographics Workshop on Multimedia*, Darmstadt, May 1992 (Technical Report by Springer–Verlag).

[14]    Väänänen,K., Hübner,W. "ShareME – Shared Multimedia Environments: Some Issues on Interaction in Distributed Multimedia Information Environments", *Proc. of HCI'92, People and Computers VII*, Monk, Diaper, Harrison (Eds.), Cambridge University Press, 1992.

[15]    Henderson,D., Väänänen,K. "ShareME: A Two–phase Usability Study of a Multimedia Environment – Guidelines for Developers with Limited HCI Experience", *ZGDV –Report* No. 63/92.

# Structured Browsing of Hypermedia Databases

**H. Maurer, F. Kappe, N. Scherbakov, P. Srinivasan**
**Institute for Information Processing and Computer Supported New Media,**
**Graz University of Technology, Schieszstattgasse 4a,**
**A-8010 Austria.**
**Tel.: 43/316/83-25-52/ext.12**          **Fax:43/316/82-43-94**
**E-Mail: fkappe@iicm.tu-graz.ac.at, psrini@iicm.tu-graz.ac.at**

## Abstract

In this paper a conceptually simple hypermedia model focusing on abstract data objects is introduced. The model is based mainly on a basic "node-link" hypermedia paradigm, but concepts from other semantic and object-oriented data models have influenced its features.

While the conventional hypermedia systems have only associative links between "chunks" of multimedia information (i.e., primitive information "nodes"), the hypermedia (HM) data model proposed here can manipulate "entities" and "relationships"; computer-navigable links are also bound between "entities".

The model provides users with a brief structured view to hypermedia databases and considerably simplifies human computer interaction by means of a number of graphical metaphors.

**keywords:** hypertext, hypermedia, browsing, data model.

## 1. Introduction

Hypermedia systems is a generic term for a wide (and ill-defined) class of interactive information systems.

The only common bond is:

(a) the notion that such systems contain various types of information ("multimedia") such as text, graphics, pictures, sounds, software-packages, etc.

(b) that once a user has located a chunk of such information (i.e., primitive hypermedia "node") it is automatically "visualized" (i.e., displayed) by means of a certain procedure; and

(c) that once a node has been visualized there will be a number of references ("links") to other chunks of the information which can be followed (by, e.g., clicking with mouse on one of the link-icons shown).

Thus, we can say that "basic hypermedia paradigm" is a multimedia information structured in accordance with the "node-link" model.

We do not claim that above is a serious "definition" (hence the quotes), yet it will suffice for the purpose of this paper. Maybe hypermedia standardisation work [Newcomb91] will eventually lead to a proper definition! We assume the reader to be familiar with the basic notion of a hypermedia system and refer for details not discussed here to [4, 11, 21] for survey papers, to [1, 16] for books on hypermedia systems, and to [13] for an extensive hypermedia bibliography.

The most serious problems encountered in today's hypermedia systems are well-known "getting lost in hyper space" phenomenon [5, 9, 10, 11, 24] and the "loss of homogeneity or incoherence of obtained information [17, 18, 19, 23, 24].

Both problems are, in fact, problems of human-computer interaction and very closely connected with a so-called "cognitive overhead" (i.e., an additional knowledge about structure and contents of a hypermedia database) needed by users in order to efficiently navigate through the hypermedia database.

There exist methods of simplification of the hypermedia browsing by means of providing users with such a "cognitive overhead" in a particular graphic form. The most well-known methods are:

(i) graphical representation of logical structure of the database (i.e., visualization of a hyper space).

(ii) using a variety of user interface metaphors to assist users in navigation through hyperspace;

The problem has not been solved satisfactorily because in the basic hypermedia paradigm, nodes and links represent very low level of data abstraction and the semantic aspects of the structure are not captured.

We believe that the basic hypermedia paradigm offered by the conventional "node-link" model makes hypermedia systems feel more confusing than they have to be; the notion of a link as something physically existing is potentially limiting our view to a very low, implementation oriented level much like thinking of addresses, pointers or branches has driven many programmers in earlier days too close to implementational details until higher levels of abstraction have made programming easier and more productive.

We feel that the situation may be similar with respect to hypermedia systems: that the notion of a "physical" link is bogging us down, that a higher level of abstraction where links play no or a much smaller role is necessary to obtain better usable hypermedia systems [6, 22].

In this paper we contend that more structured view to hypermedia databases provided by the HM-data model based on abstract hypermedia objects, considerably simplifies browsing, metaphorisation and graphical representation of hyper space.

The rest of this paper is structured as follows: in the next Section 2 we present a brief description of the HM data model (a fuller version is contained in a technical report [15]) and give examples as basis of concrete discussions; in Section 3 we give some further examples and show how alternative graphical based browsing mechanisms can be used in systems based on our approach; The paper ends with a short conclusion and references.

## 2 The HM Data Model

According to the HM-data model, a hypermedia database is a number of abstract data objects called structured collections (abbreviated as S-collections). In contrast to the conventional "node-link" model, links in HM-data model are encapsulated within a particular S-collection. Surprisingly, despite the absence of such "global" links we will see that the recursive structure inherent in S-collection is sufficiently powerful to express all that is usually done using "wild cross-reference" links, in a more orderly and more user-friendly fashion (see fig. 1).

In the HM-data model, each S-collection has a unique identifier (a name) and a so-called *head*. The head in its turn can be a primitive node or another S-collection. A primitive node consists of a *name* and a *data unit*. Both terms are not formally defined any further: this is the task of specific implementations [8, 20] or more detailed papers such as [15]. Whenever a primitive node is accessed, its data unit is executed. The execution of the data unit usually causes the presentation of some information (text, pictures, audio, video-clips), in some cases it can also result in a more complicated interactive dialogue with the user. In fact, any kind of action may happen because of the execution of a data unit. However, the data unit does not support any kind of navigation and therefore is considered to be *atomic*.

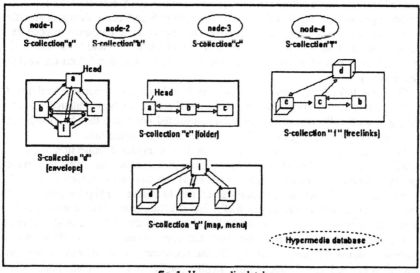

fig. 1: Hypermedia database

Accessing an S-collection results in the visualisation of its head. If the head in its turn is a complex S-collection (i.e., not a primitive node), then the above procedure of visualization is applied recursively.

Each S-collection encapsulates a particular navigable structure. The navigable structure is a set of other S-collections related by a number of computer-navigable links (see fig.1). In the HM-data model the S-collections are linked and not the primitive nodes.

The links are encapsulated within a particular S-collection. Thus, links can be defined only between members of a certain S-collection; and in this sense, they belong to the S-collection, but not to a hypermedia database or to members that are related by means of links. An S-collection devoid of such an internal structure is called a primitive S-collection (see for instance, S-collections "a", "b", "c" and "i" in fig.1).

At any particular moment in time the user can navigate only through one concrete S-collection which is called the *user view*, using the links defined within this particular S-collection. The user view confines the user to a certain navigational paradigm. As we shall see this does not limit the access or scope of information available within the hypermedia database. The navigation consists of a certain number of steps. A concrete S-collection is the current one for each particular navigation step. More precisely, on each navigation step the user can access a certain S-collection within the user view. The S-collection most recently accessed (visualized within the user view) is called *current S-collection*.

For instance, consider the navigation through the previously defined S-collection "d" (see fig. 1). In this case, the user can access the S-collections "a", "b", "c" and "i" by means of links available within the user view (i.e., within the S-collection "d").

More precisely, if the S-collection "a" is a current S-collection, then it is visualized (in this particular case, node-1 is displayed by means of a particular procedure of visualization), and the user has the links to the members "b", "c" and "i" available (i.e., can access the S-collection "b", S-collection "i" or the S-collection "c" on the next step of navigation).

Since the links are encapsulated within an S-collection, they become available (or become activated) for navigation only if the S-collection has been "entered". Such an *entering* of an S-collection to activate the encapsulated links (and thereby changing the current navigational paradigm) will be called the "zoom in" operation.

For instance, if the current S-collection is a complex S-collection (i.e., most recently accessed member of user view is a complex S-collection) then the user can apply the operation "zoom in" in order to make this member new user view (see fig. 2).

Note that the "zoom in" operation gives rise to certain ambiguity problems: the operation is perceived as a substitution of a data structure (consisting of a number of S-collections) instead of a concrete current S-collection. In the HM-data model, only one S-collection can be the current one from the user's point of view. Thus, for the previously discussed example (see fig. 2), the operation "zoom in" can be seen as a substitution of the internal structure of S-collection "e" (i.e., of S-collections "a", "b" and "c") instead of the single S-collection "e". In order to avoid this ambiguity the concept of "head of an S-collection" is applied. That is, a head automatically becomes the current S-collection if the corresponding S-collection (i.e., S-collection which includes this head) becomes user view by means of the "zoom in" operation.

In analogy, the operation "zoom out" is complement to the last "zoom in" action.

More precisely, the operation "zoom out" recovers user view and current S-collection to a state which they had just before the last "zoom in" operation.

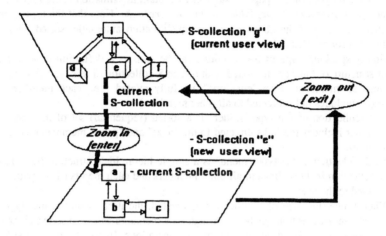

**fig. 2:** "Zoom in" and "Zoom out" operations.

Let us review the basic features of the HM-data model, in particular the notion of an S-collection.

S-collections are main "building blocks" (i.e., abstract data objects) within the HM data model.

On one hand an S-collection can be seen as a primitive object. The S-collections are linked by computer navigable links without taking into consideration their internal structures and can also be visualised independently. The S-collections are the source and target of a link in the HM-data model. These links should not be confused with the case when references lead to the primitive nodes (i.e., cards, pages, etc.) belonging to other collections and are used for referring complex hypermedia objects (stacks, books, etc.) in other hypermedia models [8, 10, 20].

On the other hand the S-collection is a sophisticated navigable structure. An S-collection encapsulates a set of other S-collections and links. Note that links can be defined only between members of the S-collection and, in this sense, the S-collection is a particular context for such encapsulated links. The S-collection is visualised as a whole whenever it is accessed but its internal structure is hidden from the user.

Let us recollect that the links do not belong to the whole hypermedia database as such (i.e., they are not global) but belong to a certain S-collection. This feature deserves a second thought as it represents the crucial idea of the HM-data model. Such an encapsulation of links within an S-collection offers a gross simplification to the otherwise tedious and complicated process of link maintenance within a hypermedia database. The hypermedia database is no more a huge network (or a web) of nodes but a number of S-collections (see fig. 1).

The HM-data model supports a finite number of so-called types of S-collection. The "type" of an S-collection defines a set of properties common to all S-collections of this type. For the purpose of this paper it suffices to explain the situation using four types of special S-collections: *envelope, folder. menu, and freelinks*. Note that the types may be combined and each of the above may have qualification automatic, sorted, annotated etc. (see [15] for more details).

Simply speaking, type of S-collections can be seen as a definition of a particular regular structure of links encapsulated within each S-collection of this type (see fig. 1).

Thus, all members of an "envelope" are fully related (i.e., each member of an "envelope" includes links directed to all other members).

An S-collection of the type "folder" is a sorted (sequential) set of members (i.e., each member includes the links directed to the "next" and "prior" members of the same S-collection).

An S-collection of the type "menu" is a simple hierarchical structure (i.e., head of such S-collection includes links to all other members and each member is provided with link directed to the head).

When a new instance of S-collection is created, the user assigns name, type and head. Once the S-collection has been created, new members can be inserted or existing members can be removed by means of the operations "Insert_New_Member" and "Remove_Existing_Member". Note that all links within S-collections belonging to previously mentioned types, are maintained automatically in accordance with the selected regular structure.

Of course, the previously defined types of S-collections do not restrict us from usage of S-collections in the form of a number of arbitrarily connected S-collections (i.e. members), within a certain S-collection. Thus, we can also apply such an S-collection belonging the type "freelinks" that requires additional edition of link structure by means of the operations "Install link" and "Delete link" and does not include any restriction to the internal structure of links.

In analogy, all primitive S-collections (i.e., primitive nodes) belong to the type "void" where the operation "zoom in" is disabled.

When a certain S-collection (say, "g" from the fig. 2) is entered (it becomes the user view), type determines how the user will be able to work with the structure at issue. Note that the type may be additionally qualified. For instance, if the type of S-collection "g" has been qualified as *automatic* and a particular member (say, "e") is accessed somehow (say, by means of a link leading to "e" within the S-collection "g"), then the S-collection "e" will be entered immediately; if *manual* is specified instead, head of the S-collection "e" (i.e., some information on the contents of "e") will be shown first, allowing the user to enter S-collection "e" by means of the additional operation "zoom in", or else to access some other member of the user view (i.e., of the S-collection "g").

Note also that "type" defines a particular navigational strategy and link maintenance mechanism available within the instances (i.e., the S-collections) of this type, but it does not define a procedure of link visualization (i.e., form of link representation when the user navigates through an S-collection of this type). A particular combination of procedure of data unit execution, procedure of link activation (i.e., visualization) and the form in which the operations "zoom in" and "zoom out" are available for the user, is called an *interface metaphor*. Thus, an interface metaphor is bound to a certain S-collection, and it is valid when the S-collection is a user view.

Observe that S-collections may be nested arbitrarily. This not only permits constructs such as folder of envelopes or folder of maps or maps of menus (and if the intuitive meaning of above is not clear at this point we will explain above by means of examples, shortly), but it also permits an S-collection to be part of a number of other S-collections, and even recursive memberships are possible and very meaningful as we will see below.

Before continuing with a more detailed discussion let us now look at a few concrete examples.

Thus, a particular S-collection may belong to arbitrary many S-collections (i.e. user's view). For example, the S-collection called "The Kiss" (which could e.g. contain a digitized version of that particular picture of Klimt as a head, and a textual description of the picture and another S-collection named "Klimt" describing the artist in some detail as members) could be a member in the S-collection "Modern Austrian Art", in the S-collection "Paintings of the 20th Century" or "Art gallery Belvedere", etc. (see fig.3). It is important to understand that from the user's point of view it is natural that such an S-collection belongs to many other S-collections; this does not mean that in the implementation the data has to be duplicated: it is up to the system to use pointers, or another mechanism instead.

At this moment let us discuss a very interesting property of the HM-data model. Generally, the S-collection "Klimt" also includes the S-collection "The Kiss" as a member (note the recursive membership).

Suppose, the user navigates through the S-collection "Klimt", and enters (i.e. "zooms" in) the S-collection "The Kiss". Hence, the user again has the possibility to enter the same user's view (i.e., the S-collection "Klimt").

Normally, the recursive definition of S-collections is a very important property of the HM-data model which makes it extremely flexible. Thus, for example, the definition (see fig. 3) can be seen as a special navigational strategy which provides users with a possibility to either access the information concerning the picture "The Kiss" during the browsing through the information describing Klimt, or to receive information about the author during the browsing through the hypermedia description of the particular piece of art (the picture "The Kiss" in this particular case).

Of course, the S-collection "Klimt" can be also used as a member of S-collections describing other pictures produced by this author (see fig.3).

Thus, the users who navigate through the S-collection "Spring", have the possibility to enter the S-collection "Klimt" and, hence, access other pictures of the same author(say, "The Kiss").

However, it is important to understand that the HM-data model does not instigate the user to think in terms of links as would be the case in most hypermedia systems. Thus, normally, the information on "The Kiss" would be referred to by means of links from a variety of other nodes, e.g. the nodes "Modern Austrian Art" , "Painters of the 20th century" and "Art gallery Belvedere". If in such an environment "The Kiss" happens to have a link to another picture by Klimt not on display in the Art Gallery Belvedere the user having accessed "The Kiss" from the node "Art Gallery Belvedere" might be very confused ending up with such a picture.

It is exactly this kind of "getting lost" or "incoherence" of hypermedia information because of links that HM-Data model is avoiding by means of flexible "nesting" of complex data objects (i.e., S-collections) (see fig. 3) instead of multiple referring to a unique piece of hypermedia information (i.e., a primitive node).

## 3. A Multi-Metaphor hypermedia browsing

In this section we discuss some "unusual" concepts of the HM-data model, and analyze them from the "Human-Computer Interaction" point of view.

Initially, we wish to contend that the possibility to get lost becomes much less probable if a hypermedia database is structured in accordance with the HM-data model (see for instance, fig. 3).

Since the HM-data model does not support "global" references, all information which is referred within a particular S-collection (i.e., user view) must be inserted into the same S-collection (see, e.g., "references" to the S-collection "Klimt" within the S-collections "The Kiss", "Modern Austrian Art" and "Paintings of 20th Century"). Additionally, the "zoom in" and "zoom out" operations provide users with the possibility to navigate in "orthogonal" direction to the conventional plane of "link-based" browsing. This "additional dimension" of hypermedia browsing gives users a well-defined sense of the current location. We believe that such "local referential integrity" [12] of our data model sufficiently simplifies browsing of hypermedia databases.

In the HM-data model we refer complex data objects (i.e., S-collections) encapsulating particular navigable structures, but not units of hypermedia information (i.e., *not* primitive nodes). See, for instance, references to the S-collections "Klimt", "The Kiss", etc.

Note also that we refer such complex data objects in a particular local context (i.e., as members of a certain user's view). For instance, note the references to the S-collection "The Kiss" in the context of "Paintings of 20th Century", and in other contexts "Klimt", "Art Gallery Belvedere", etc.

We believe that this kind of "context-dependent" references supports "coherence" and "homogeneity" of hypermedia information [17, 19, 2, 3] obtained by browsing. In other words, a hypermedia information is delivered in a proper logical manner even if a freehand browsing is used. Additionally, a number of well-known navigational aids can be adopted by the HM-data model. Thus, so-called overview diagrams [16, 4] are used in a number of hypertext/hypermedia systems. The obvious situation when a hypermedia database cannot be depicted as a single diagram, necessitates some kind of multi-level structure of overview diagrams.

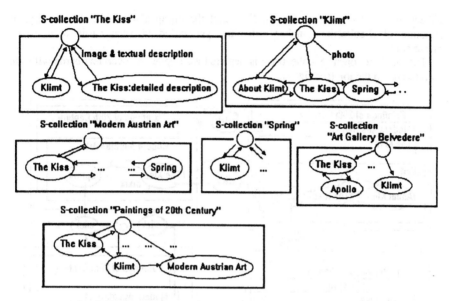

**fig. 3:** Section of hypermedia database corresponding to the example

A variety of questions remains open and unanswered in relation to application of such overview diagrams, namely:
- how many diagrams should be used in order to provide users with exact information of the current location?
- how one could generate multi-level diagrams including "global" links?
- how one could automatically share an integral hyperweb between diagrams (i.e., identify nodes and links to be included in each diagram)?

Alternative method is a so-called "fisheye" view [7] where the user is shown a whole hyperweb in the form of one diagram, but a "closer neighbourhood" of the current user's position is depicted in more details than remote parts of the hyperweb. In this approach, the user is provided also with the possibility to "resize" a particular part of the current fisheye view in order to dynamically generate a new fisheye view and so forth. Actual implementation of the "fisheye views" concept raises even more questions than the "overview diagrams". Normally, both the strategies are efficiently applicable in hypermedia databases that are structured hierarchically [7, 16].

In the HM-data model, both concepts are combined into a rather powerful mechanism for "graphical browsing" called manipulation with "overview cards". Let us recollect that at any particular moment in time, the user can navigate through a certain S-collection (i.e., user view) and a current stack of "open" (or previously "entered" but not "exited") S-collections exist. Thus, the current stack of "open" S-collections and current S-collection are the exact position of the user within a hyperweb. This situation can be easily represented in a graphic form. Thus, there are a number of so-called "overview cards", each card is a screen-sized graphic image of internal structure of a particular S-collection (see, for instance, fig. 4). Note that the encapsulation of links and regular structure of S-collections makes automatic generation of such cards quite easily mastered.

The stack of "open" S-collections is depicted as a "pile" of overview cards with the current one on the top (see fig. 4).

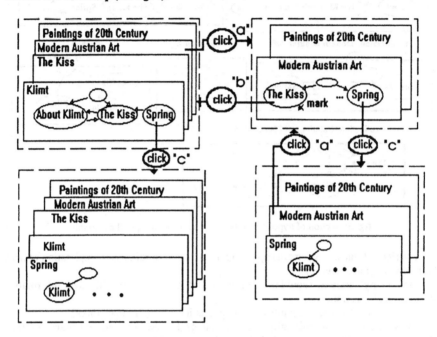

fig. 4: Overview cards

Note that we distinguish between "content-based" browsing and "graphical browsing". Thus, the terms "current stack" and "user view" belong to "content-based" browsing, but the terms "pile of cards" and "overview card" are used in "graphical browsing". At any point, the user can switch to "graphical browsing". In this case, the current user's position is just visualized in the "graphical" terms, but further manipulation with overview cards do not affect current user's position, which, generally, allows the user to continue "content-based" navigation applying additional knowledge i.e., "cognitive overhead", obtained as a result of the manipulation with overview cards.

Thus, the user can click on a particular overview card within the current "pile" in order to "put it on the top" (see action "a" in fig. 4). Hence, the click on a card within the current "pile" results in popping of all previous items (see fig. 4).

Additionally, all previously "zoomed in" S-collections are pointed out with a special mark on each overview card. Note that one of such cards belongs to the current stack, but others have been "popped out" by means of "zoom out" operations (i.e., the corresponding S-collections have been traversed in downward and upward directions by means of "zoom in" and "zoom out" operations respectively).

The user is allowed also to click on the image of any S-collection within the current (i.e., top) overview card.

In this case, there exist three different situations which should be distinguished:

- if the user clicks on a currently "open" S-collection (i.e., the graphical image which is marked as belonging to the current stack), then the system recovers graphical image of the current stack (see action "b" fig. 4);

- if the user clicks on an S-collection which has been traversed (i.e., "closed" by means of the "zoom out" operation during the user's session), then the corresponding card is pushed down (i.e., put on the top) including all marks;

- if the user clicks on an S-collection which has not been "zoomed in" during the session, then a new overview card is generated and pushed down (see action "c" in fig. 4). This action recovers an initial "graphical" meaning of the "zoom in" operation.

## Summary

In this paper we contend that the multitude of links available in ordinary hypermedia systems are often more confusing than helpful for users of such systems.

We discuss our approach for the reduction of links called HM data model in this paper in general terms and explain how the model can be used to obtain powerful yet easy to use hypermedia systems.

## References

[1]     Berk, E., Devlin, J. (Eds.): Hypertext/Hypermedia Handbook; McGraw Hill Software Engineering Series, New York (1991).

[2]     Botafogo, B.A, Shneidermann, B.:Identifying Aggregates in Hypertext Structures; Hypertext'91(1991)

[3]     Boy, G.A.: Indexing hypertext documents in context; Hypertext'91 (1991).

[4]     Conklin, E.J.: Hypertext: An Introduction and Survey; IEEE Computer 20 (1987), 17-41.

[5]     Conklin, J., Begeman, M.: gIBIS - A Hypertext Tool for Exploratory Policy Discussion; Proc. CSCW (1988), 140-152.

[6]     De Young, L.: Links considered harmful; Proc. ECHT, Versailles 1990, Cambridge University Press (1990), 238-249.

[7]     Furnas, G.W.: Generalized fisheye views: In Proc. of the ACM CHI'86 (Conf. on Human Factors inComputing Systems) (1986) pp. 16-23.

[8]     Goodman, D.: The complete Hypercard Handbook. Bantam books, New York (1987).

[9]     Halasz, F., Moran, T., Trigg, R.: NoteCards in a Nutshell; Proc. ACM Conf. Human Factors in Computer Science (1987), 45-42.

[10]     Halasz, F.: Reflection on Notecards: seven issues for the next generation of hypermedia systems; C. ACM. 31, 7 (1988), 836-852.

[11]     Kappe, F.: Aspects of a Modern Multi-Media Information System; IIG Report 308, Graz (1991).

[12]     Kappel, G., Schrefl, M.: "Local referential integrity"; Proc. Entity-Relationship Approach - ER'92, Karlsruhe, Germany, LNCS 645, Springer Pub. (1992), 41-57.

[13]     Maurer, H., Tomek, I.: Hypermedia Bibliography, J.MCA 14, 2 (1991), 161-216.

[14]     Maurer, H.: Why Hypermedia Systems are Important; Proc. ICCAL'92, Wolfville, Canada, LNCS 602, Springer Pub. (1992), 1-15.

[15]     Maurer, H., Scherbakov, N.: The HM Data Model; IIG Report, Graz (1992).

[16]     Nielsen, J.: Hypertext and Hypermedia; Academic Press (1990).

[17]     Nielsen, J.: The Art of Navigating through Hypertext. C. ACM 33, 3 (1992), 247-310.

[18]     Stotts, P.D., Furuta, R. : Adding browsing semantics to the hypertext model. Proc. ACM Document Processing Systems Conf., Santa Fe, NM (1988), 43-50.

[19]     Thuring, M., Haake, J.M., Hannemann, J.: What's Eliza doing in the Chinese Room? Incoherent Hyperdocuments-and How to Avoid Them; Hypertext'91 (1991).

[20]     Using Toolbook , Version 1.0, Asymmetrix Corporation, Bellevue, WA (1989).

[21]     Tomek, I., Khan, S., Muldner, T. Nassar, Novak, G., Proszynski, P.: Hypermedia - introduction and survey; J.MCA 14, 2 (1991), 63-103.

[22]     Van Dam, A.: Hypertext'87 Keynote Address, C.ACM 31, 7 (1988), 887-895.

[23]     Yankelovich, N., Haan, B., Meyrowitz, N., Drucker, S.: Intermedia: The concept and the construction of a seamless information environment, IEEE Computer, 21, 1(1988),81-96.

[24]     Zellweger, P.T.: Scripted Documents: A hypermedia Path Mechanism, Hypermedia'89 (1989), 1-14.

# Object-Oriented Dialog Control for Multimedia User Interfaces

Rainer Götze[1], Helmut Eirund[2], Roland Claaßen

Universität Oldenburg, Fachbereich Informatik
Postfach 2503, D-26111 Oldenburg
goetze@arbi.informatik.uni-oldenburg.de

**Abstract.** The incorporation of continuous media like audio and video in multimedia user interfaces poses new requirements on user interface development tools especially the simultaneous execution of continuous output operations and user interactions. Therefore, we have developed an object-oriented dialog control model which facilitates the recognition and processing of user defined interactions by object hierarchies. Furthermore, the model incorporates object classes for the definition and synchronization of complex multimedia actions represented as directed acyclic graphs. Concurrency between interactions and continuous output actions can be modelled by synchronization operators. The presented dialog control model supports the development of common graphical user interfaces as well as multimedia user interfaces releasing the dialog developer from programming difficult synchronization operations by offering abstract operators. It builds the basis of an object-oriented User Interface Toolkit (UIT) which has been implemented and will be applied to an interactive development environment for multimedia presentation applications.

**Keywords:** multimedia user interfaces, user interface tools, complex interactions, synchronization, object-orientation

## 1 Introduction

Tools for the development of multimedia user interfaces have to support common discrete media like graphics and text as well as new continuous media like audio and video. Discrete media imply a transitional model of dialog control. Each event caused by user inputs or internal messages is processed by a particular action that will be terminated before the next event is processed. However, the integration of continuous media causes this model to become inadequate because actions like presenting a video or playing an audio possess a duration. In order to facilitate user interaction simultaneously to continuous output actions, e.g. manipulation of volume or resolution, a dialog control model has to incorporate concurrent execution and synchronization of output actions and interactions.

In the last years, there have been published several approaches to the management of continuous media in user interfaces. Nearly all approaches to multimedia presentation encompass concepts for defining the temporal relations of time-variant output actions.

Gibbs [9] presents a framework for the composition of multimedia objects. Composite multimedia objects manage a collection of component multimedia objects and define their temporal relations by composite timeline diagrams.

---

[1]   This work is funded by "Stiftung Volkswagenwerk" (ref. 210-70631/9-13-14/89).

[2]   OFFIS e.V., Westerstraße 10-12, D-26121 Oldenburg.

A technique for the formal specification and modelling of multimedia composition with respect to intermedia timing and synchronization is presented in [16]. This technique is based on a modification of Timed Petri Nets and temporal intervals. The augmented Petri Net model defines two additional mappings which assign duration and resource usage to the places and thereby supports the synchronization of concurrently presented temporally related multimedia objects.

Other approaches have enhanced formal document structures by concepts for the definition of temporal relations. Hoepner [14] proposes a synchronization model for ODA ("Open Document Architecture") [24] based on events and actions. The synchronization of the presentation of multimedia objects is specified by path expressions including path operators which define the temporal relations of output actions and control their corresponding synchronization. Another approach to the standardization of representing multimedia, hypertext, hypermedia, time- and state-based documents is HyTime ("Hypermedia / Time-based Document Structuring Language") ([18], [25]). In HyTime the temporal scheduling of multimedia objects is expressed in terms of "finite coordinate systems" which define a specific measurement domain and a reference time unit. Another currently developed standard supported by ISO is known as MHEG [4] ("Multimedia and Hypermedia Information Coding Experts Group") and focuses on multimedia synchronization, hypermedia navigation and object-orientation. In [17] a hypermedia object model and presentation environment based on MHEG is proposed. This model uses composite objects for the definition of temporal relations between subordinate objects and additionally supports synchronization at internal reference points which are modelled as timestone events and propagated to other objects. Timestone events may coincide with video frames, audio samples or animation scenes and facilitate the implementation of more sophisticated synchronization mechanisms than parallel or sequential start and end.

The Ttoolkit [11] represents an approach to the integration of time management into an existing user interface toolkit for the development of graphical user interfaces. It has been implemented as extension of the Xt toolkit [19] by defining a new branch of the Xt class hierarchy. In order to achieve an isomorphic treatment of time and space the new classes conform to the Xt model for spatial composition.

Timelines present another approach to the implicit specification of temporal relations by specifying the starting time and duration of continuous output actions in physical or logical time units. They are used in the multimedia construction tools Muse [13] and MAEstro [7]. Because or their user-friendliness they have also been adopted by many commercial multimedia design tools, e.g. Director [22] and MediaMaker [23].

All these approaches use temporal relations only for the synchronization and composition of multimedia presentations and either do not consider user interactions at all or only incorporate predefined standard user interactions like in [4] and [17]. The object-oriented dialog control model presented in this paper not only supports the composition of multimedia output actions but also their synchronization with interactions. Thus, it especially supports the implementation of interactive multimedia applications.

The description of complex interactions has already been considered in other approaches. Especially the interaction model [15] and the AIT model [5] are concerned with this problem and have incorporated ideas from Anson´s device model [3] which uses hierarchically arranged logical devices for the description of complex user inputs. These models apply the paradigm of interaction hierarchies [5] by modelling user interfaces in terms of complex interactions. However, in contrast to our dialog control model, actions in the interaction and AIT model are tightly coupled to events since they are executed before or after an event occurs. Thus, they do not facilitate a synchronization of continuous actions and interactions which is the main feature of our dialog control model.

In the next chapter we first describe the main principles of the COMMAND model ("COntrol of MultiMedia output ANd multi-threaded Dialogs") ([6], [21]), an object-oriented model for event handling and output synchronization in multimedia user interfaces. Afterwards, temporal operators supporting the synchronization of concurrently executed actions and interactions are defined. The implementation of the COMMAND model is briefly discussed in chapter four. In chapter five we present concepts for the incorporation of the COMMAND model into an interactive development environment for multimedia presentation applications.

# 2 Basic Concepts of the COMMAND Model

The COMMAND model is an extension of the interaction model [15] that facilitates the recognition and processing of user-defined complex events (interactions) by object hierarchies containing basic events as leaves. The model integrates dialog control into the event handling process and supports a strong connection between input and output processing. Complex multimedia output actions are defined as composition of discrete and continuous output actions.

In the COMMAND model events are recognized by so called event-sensitive objects which supervise their occurrence and inform other interested objects. Complex events composed of basic and other complex events are recognized bottom-up by hierarchies of event-sensitive objects. Each event-sensitive object announces interest in the events recognized by its subordinate objects and will be informed about their occurrence. Basic events are received and propagated by an object-oriented device interface to the underlying window system and the application consisting of so called device objects. Besides the events of the window system the COMMAND model also supports temporal and application-specific events. Fig. 2.1 shows the main tasks of the event-sensitive objects, event recognition and propagation.

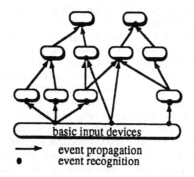

basic input devices

→ event propagation
• event recognition

Fig. 2.1 Event recognition and propagation

## 2.1 Complex Events and Dialog Operator Objects

Fig. 2.1 already elucidates that event-sensitive objects can be informed about events recognized by multiple other objects. They aggregate the information about several events and define a complex event which is propagated to all interested objects. Complex events represent combinations of basic and other complex events and are supervised by so called dialog operator objects which support the definition of event hierarchies. A dialog operator object defines the recognition order of subordinate events and the conditions for the occurrence of the corresponding complex event. By distinguishing four classes of dialog operator objects (AND, OR, SEQUENCE, REPEAT), the COMMAND model employs concepts from the interaction model [15].

- SEQUENCE-operator:
  The subordinate events are supervised sequentially. Thus, the operator terminates supervision after all subordinate events have occurred in the specified order.
- REPEAT-operator:
  Subordinate events are divided into a repeat event sequence and an abort event. The repeat event sequence is processed repeatedly until the abort event occurs. The operator object terminates supervision after the abort-event has occurred.
- AND-operator:
  The subordinate events are supervised simultaneously. The operator object makes no requirements on the order of event occurrence and terminates supervision after all subordinate events have occurred.
- OR-operator:
  The subordinate events are supervised simultaneously until one of them has occurred. After an subordinate events has occurred supervision of the other subordinate events is stopped.

The first two dialog operators (SEQUENCE and REPEAT) restrict the order in which subordinate events may occur and thereby implement the integration of dialog control into the event handling.process.

## 2.2 Integration of Event Processing and Recognition

Since interactions also incorporate the processing of basic and complex events, the COMMAND model supports actions and conditions implemented as host language statements to be integrated into the event recognition process. Conditions can check necessary properties of events whereas actions can output prompts or process events, e.g. by sending messages to presentation and application objects (call-backs). In contrast to conditions, actions do not return any value. Actions and conditions are incorporated at any level of the event hierarchy (i.e. for basic and complex events) by using them as subordinate objects of SEQUENCE and REPEAT-operator objects. Thereby, the COMMAND model supports an event processing at different levels of abstraction and a strong connection between input and output processing which is suited to the implementation of direct feedback. Since the AND- and OR-operator logically combine complex events to more complex ones, they do not permit action and condition operands however.

The upper part of fig. 2.2 presents a control panel for the simultaneous presentation of video and audio clips consisting of two buttons and two sliders. The object hierarchy for implementing the dialog control with the COMMAND model is shown below. The SEQUENCE-operator on the left is controlling the start of the demonstration. The REPEAT-operator on the right facilitates the iterated manipulation of volume or resolution until the presentation is finally terminated by clicking on the Stop-button. Manipulation of volume and resolution is implemented by two SEQUENCE-operators used as operands of the OR-operator.

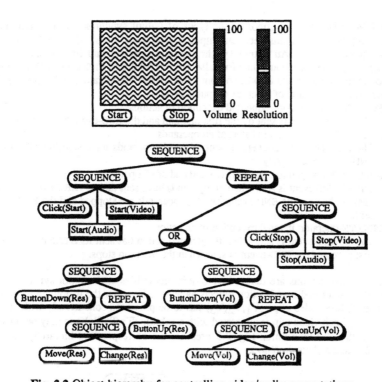

**Fig. 2.2** Object hierarchy for controlling video/audio-presentations

## 2.3 Composition of Complex Multimedia Output Actions

Generally, multimedia output actions are composed of several actions according to the different types of media involved. Since the included continuous output actions possess a duration, their composition has to consider their temporal relations, i.e. the synchronization of output operations. In order to facilitate synchronization of continuous output actions, we have introduced START and END-events which are sent at the start and end respectively. Based on these events, operators for the definition of temporal relations of continuous output actions are defined. The COMMAND model distinguishes two different types of continuous action objects:
– Timer actions: INTERVAL[n]
  A timer action lasts exactly the number of time units specified as parameter and will be used to restrict the duration of concurrent continuous actions.
– Present actions: PRESENT (output-object)
  A present action controls output of time-invariant or time-variant media by communicating with an output object. For presenting time-variant media they send start- and stop-messages to so called active objects that encapsulate output processes of continuous media. Active objects indicate the start and end of their output process by sending START- and END-events to present-actions. Discrete output actions are treated as continuous output actions with infinite duration and must be stopped explicitly.

The COMMAND model supports four types of output synchronization operators that model the temporal relations between output actions using the START- and END-events sent by action objects. An output synchronization operator and its operands define a complex continuous action and therefore also send START- and END-events. Thus, they can be used in turn as operands of other output synchronization operators and thereby support the hierarchical definition of complex output actions.

- SEQUENTIAL-operator: sequential execution of actions
  The START-event is sent by the first operand and the END-event by the last operand.
- PARSTART-operator: parallel start of all operands
  The START- or END-event is sent when all operands have sent their START- or END-event, respectively.
- PARSTARTEND-operator: parallel start and end of all operands
  The START-event is sent when all operands have sent their START-event. After one operand has sent its END-event the other operands are stopped and the END-event is sent.
- ITERATE-operator: iterated execution of an action
  The START-event is sent when the iterated action has sent its START-event for the first time and the END-event is sent when the iteration stops.

Complex output actions are defined by object hierarchies with output synchronization operators as inner nodes and action objects as leaves. Consider the following example: A sequence of three video clips $(V_1, V_2, V_3)$ has to be presented concurrently with an audio sequence A. Each video clip is annotated with a subtitle $(T_1, T_2, T_3)$ and may be presented no longer than 30 time units. Fig. 2.3 presents the corresponding hierarchy of output synchronization and action objects.

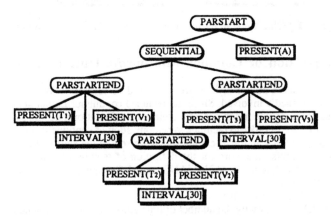

**Fig. 2.3** Composition hierarchy of a complex output action

Other approaches to the synchronization of multimedia output actions like Timed Petri-Nets [16] and Path Expression [14] can model more complex relations than those that can be modelled by object hierarchies. In order to increase the modelling power of the COMMAND model we have defined two additional output operators called ANDTRIGGER and ORTRIGGER that facilitate the definition of output actions started after the termination of multiple other ones which are called trigger actions.

- ANDTRIGGER-operator: start of an output action after all trigger actions have sent their END-event,
- ORTRIGGER-operator: start of an output action after one of the trigger actions has sent its END-event.

Thus, the COMMAND model facilitates the definition of complex multimedia output actions by direct acyclic graphs. Each complex output action must have exactly one action object without a preceding output synchronization or trigger operator object. By starting and stopping this root object, the complex output action is started and stopped respectively. This approach to modelling multimedia output actions does not directly support synchronization at internal reference points (see [17], [20]) because synchronization events are only generated at the start or end of continuous output or timer actions. However, internal reference points can be modelled by timer actions started concurrently with continuous output actions. The START- and END-events of these timer actions can be used for synchronizing them with other continuous output actions. Hence, the COMMAND model supports the functionality of internal reference points without dealing with the quanta of continuous media like video frames, audio samples or animation scenes.

The underlying run-time system is based on a logical time system ([2], [9]) which ensures the continuous synchronization [20] of timer and continuous output actions, i.e. their precise temporal alignment, and copes with synchronization problems caused by different presentation speeds. Thereby, it supports the functionality of internal reference points. This approach to modelling internal reference points is similar to the cue-concept used in the MM-Viewer [12].

# 3 Concurrency of Interactions and Actions

The dialog control model presented in the previous chapter incorporates concurrency in the definition of interactions (AND- and OR-operator) and complex output actions (PARSTART- and PAREND-operator). For the introduction of concurreny between interactions and continuous actions we first have to define a common basis for their synchronization. Therefore, we extend the COMMAND model by introducing START- and END-events for interactions, i.e. associating a duration with them.

For the basic events START- and END-events are sent immediately after the event has occurred, i.e. basic events have no duration. START- and END-events of an interaction (complex event) are sent when certain subordinate events have sent their START- and END-event, respectively. If one of the subordinate events is in turn a complex event, the above definition is applied recursively. The start of an interaction can be defined as the time of either its first relevant event or prompt output. Analogous the end of an interaction can be defined as the time of its last relevant event or the time when its processing has terminated. This definition can be described using two functions start and end which map interactions to their START- and END-events respectively. Let $e_i$ denote a basic or complex event and $c_i$ denote an event, action or condition.

- start(SEQUENCE $(c_1, ..., c_n)$) = start($c_1$)
  end(SEQUENCE $(c_1, ..., c_n)$) = end($c_n$)
- start(OR $(e_1, ..., e_n)$) = start($e_i$) with $e_i$ as the event first sending its START-event
  end(OR $(e_1, ..., e_n)$) = end($e_j$) with $e_j$ as the event which occured last
- start(AND $(e_1, ..., e_n)$) = start($e_i$) with $e_i$ as the event first sending its START-event
  end(AND $(e_1, ..., e_n)$) = end($e_j$) with $e_j$ as the event which occured last

- start(REPEAT $c_1, ..., c_n$ UNTIL $e_{n+1}$) = start($c_1$) for the first occurrence or execution of $c_1$
- end(REPEAT $c_1, ..., c_n$ UNTIL $e_{n+1}$) = end($e_{n+1}$)

Since the COMMAND model describes the duration of interactions and continuous actions by intervals delimited by their START and END-events, the definition of their concurrency has also to be based on intervals. Generally, we do not only want to define concurreny but the temporal relations of interactions and continuous output actions. Therefore, we have considered Allen's interval calculus [1], a well-known approach to temporal reasoning with time intervals which has also been considered for the definition of the output synchronization operators. The interval calculus defines the thirteen possible mutual exclusive relations of two time intervals. Considering that the duration of interactions and continuous actions is described by START- and END-events, we choose only those relations that can be mapped to equality relations of their start and end points. Thus, we introduced the synchronization operators MEETS, STARTS, ENDS and EQUALS.

## 3.1 Synchronization of Actions with Interactions

In graphical user interfaces, actions are mainly executed in response to events caused by user inputs. However, with the integration of multimedia, continuous actions have to be executed while event handling is still going on. Synchronization operators satisfy this requirement by facilitating actions (timer and output actions) to be executed concurrently with interactions.

- STARTS(interaction,action)
  The action operand is started immediately after the interaction operand has sent its START-event.
- EQUALS(interaction,action)
  The action operand is started immediately after the interaction operand has sent its START-event. Either of the operands will be stopped immediately after the other one has sent its END-event.
- ENDS(interaction,action)
  Either of the operands will be stopped immediately after the other one has sent its END-event.
- MEETS(interaction,action)
  The action operand is started immediately after the interaction operand has sent its END-event.

Synchronization operators control the duration of one operand dependent on the duration of the other one, i.e. the start and end of one operand are synchronized with the start and end of the other one by evaluating START- and END-events. Yet they are passive operators because they start or stop operands only after having received appropriate START- or END-events (control events) i.e. they are triggered by the control events of their operands. Thus, they neither conform to the bottom-up modelling of event recognition nor to the top-down modelling of complex output actions. However, they offer a flexible approach to the temporal composition of these two paradigms.

In order to point out the advantages of synchronization operators we once more consider the example of fig. 2.2. Its presented implementation has three main disadvantages:

- Since the presentation of audio and video has been implemented without using output synchronization operators, the implementation takes no care of exceptions like audio

terminating before the video and vice versa.
- The association between start- and stop actions is not an model-inherent feature but has to be programmed by the dialog designer. Therefore adding and removing of output actions requires changes at multiple parts of the object hierarchy.
- Furthermore, the implementation takes no care of exception situations, e.g. when the video and audio presentation terminate before the user clicks at the St op-button.

All these disadvantages can be avoided by using an appropriate synchronization operator. Fig. 3.1 presents the improved implementation which separates the output operation from the interaction and synchronizes them by the EQUALS-operator. When the control panel interaction sends its START-event, the EQUALS-operator will immediately start the complex output action. After one of the operands has sent an END-event, the other one is stopped immediately.

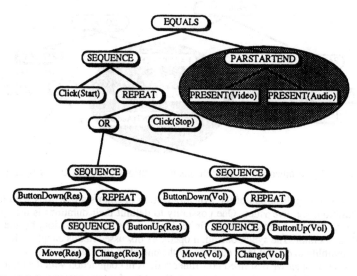

**Fig. 3.1** Synchronization of actions with interactions by the EQUALS-operator

## 3.2 Synchronization of Interactions with Actions

The synchronization operators for actions and interactions are polymorphic, i.e. they can also be applied the other way around for the synchronization of interactions with actions having the corresponding semantics.
- STARTS(action, interaction)
- EQUALS(action, interaction)
- ENDS(action, interaction)
- MEETS(action, interaction)

The START-event of the action operand will cause the start of the interaction operand. This kind of synchronization makes sense if it is the action whose start has to be synchronized with the start of the interaction. Synchronization of interactions with actions is especially suited to combining interactions with continuous output actions included complex output actions.

Suppose that the video/audio action of the control panel example is included in a complex output action but that we still want to ensure to have access to the control panel when the video/audio action is executed. The dialog control will start the root object of the complex output action and will have no direct influence on the start of single component output actions. Therefore, it cannot decide when the control panel interaction has to be started. By combining the video/audio action and the control panel interaction with the EQUALS-operator, we ensure their synchronization while still being able to use the video/audio action as component output action of a complex output action. Fig. 3.2 depicts this concept by a concurrent combination of the video/audio action with a second output action presenting a subtitled video for a restricted duration.

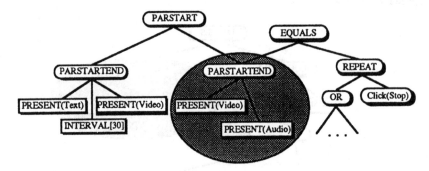

**Fig. 3.2** Synchronization of interactions with actions by the EQUALS-operator

Other convincing applications of the synchronization operators are actions with a priori infinite duration, e.g. live video. One possiblity to delimit their durations is the synchronization with another action having a finite duration, e.g. a timer-action, by the PAR-STARTEND-operator. The synchronization operators discussed in this chapter additionally offer the possiblity to delimit their duration by the end of an user interaction.

In the previous chapter we described how timer actions in conjunction with the logical time system of the run-time system support the functionality of internal reference points. Since synchronization operators can also be applied to the synchronization of timer actions and interactions, the COMMAND model supports the integration of interactions in complex multimedia output actions at arbitrary reference points, i.e. at the start or end of continuous output actions as well as at internal reference points.

# 4 Implementation of the COMMAND Model

The COMMAND model has been implemented as a class hierarchy (see fig. 4.1) in the object-oriented programming language C++ as part of the object-oriented XFantasy-UIT [10] which is based on the X Window System. The class hierarchy can be subdivided into classes for the implementation of interactions (abstract base class FEventGuard), classes for the implementation of complex output actions (abstract base class FContinuous-Action) and classes for the synchronization of interactions and actions (abstract base class FSyncOperator). The interface between dialog operator objects and their component objects is defined in the abstract base class FComponent. Hierarchies of dialog operator objects defining complex interactions are supported by allowing that instances of the class FEvent reference subordinate dialog operator objects.

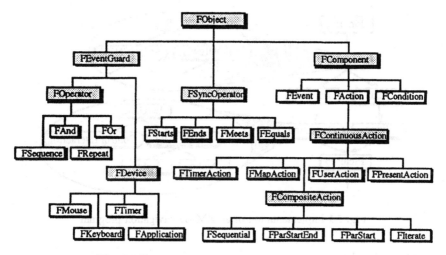

**Fig. 4.1** Class hierarchy of the COMMAND model

# 5 Multimedia Presentation Applications

The presented dialog control concepts supports an abstract modelling of interactions and complex output actions by hierarchically arranged objects. The interactive tool XMAD [8] applies these concepts to a visual programming environment for interactive multimedia presentation applications. This kind of applications is characterized by predefined interaction techniques supporting the navigation through a set of singlemedia objects (SMOs) and are suited to the evaluation of the COMMAND model.

In XMAD the schedule of an interactive presentation is specified by a directed graph, i.e. navigation paths are represented by graph structures defined interactively with a graph editor. Within these graphs edges represent the control flow (order of presentations) whereas nodes represent either presentation objects or special control objects that facilitate the specification of branching and choice. SMOs are selected from a set of presentation objects that is retrieved by filter mechanisms based on object descriptors. XMAD encompasses only a few generic control object types that can be parameterized and flexibly combined and thereby offer a big modelling power:

- CHOICE-objects are used when navigation depends on user interaction, i.e. when a graph node has multiple outgoing edges. However, by choosing appropriate parameter values, CHOICE-objects can also control the iterated presentation of all of its successor nodes.
- COLLECTION-objects model complex presentations since they facilitate the concurrent presentation and synchronization of multiple SMOs. Furthermore, they support the integration of interactions into complex presentations.

Fig. 5.1 present a small example of a XMAD navigation program. The control flow of XMAD navigation programs is implemented by the COMMAND dialog operator and output synchronization objects as indicated for the CHOICE- and COLLECTION-object.

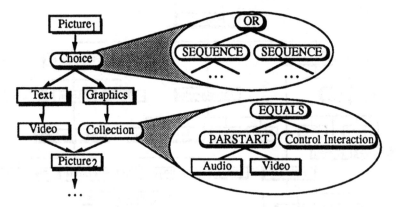

**Fig. 5.1** Implementation of an XMAD navigation program

# 6 Conclusion

The COMMAND model represents an extended dialog control model especially adapted to the requirements of interactive multimedia applications. It facilitates the definition of interactions and complex multimedia output actions. Interactions are defined by hierarchies of dialog operator objects whereas complex output actions take the form directed acyclic graphs including output synchronization operators. In order to support the concurrent execution and synchronization of interactions and continuous output actions the model encompasses special synchronization operators Thereby, the COMMAND model goes beyond the scope of other approaches to multimedia development tools which have mainly focused on the synchronization in multimedia presentations.

# References

[1]    Allen, J.F.: Maintaining knowledge about temporal intervals. – Communication of the ACM, Vol. 26., No. 1, pp. 832-843, 1983.

[2]    Anderson, D.P., Homsy, G.: A Continuous Media I/O Server and Its Synchronization Mechanism. – IEEE Computer, Vol. 24, No. 10, pp. 51-57, 1991.

[3]    Anson, E.: The Device Model of Interaction. – Computer Graphics 16 (3), pp. 107-114, 1982.

[4]    Bertrand, F., Price, R.: Edition ISO/IEC JTC1/SC/WG12, MHEG Working Document S.6, "Coded Representation of Multimedia and Hypermedia Information Objects", May 1992.

[5]    van den Bos, J.: Abstract Interaction Tools: A Language for User Interface Management Systems. – ACM Transactions on Programming Languages and Systems 10 (2), pp. 215-247, 1988.

[6]     Claaßen, D.: Synchronization Mechanisms for the Event Handling of the XFantasy-UIT (in German). – Master thesis, University of Oldenburg, Department of Computer Science, 1993.

[7]     Drapeau, G.D., Greenfield, H.: MAEstro – A Distributed Multimedia Authoring Environment. – Proceedings of the 1991 Summer USENIX Conference, 1991.

[8]     Eirund, H., Götze, R.: Modelling Interactive Multimedia Applications. – Proceedings Eurographics Workshop on Object-Oriented Graphics, Champery, pp. 229-245, 1992.

[9]     Gibbs, S.: Composite Multimedia and Active Objects. – Proceedings OOPSLA´91, pp. 97-112, 1991.

[10]    Götze, R. et al : Final Report of the XFantasy Project Group. – Report No. IS-13 (in German), University of Oldenburg, Faculty of Computer Science, 1992.

[11]    Guimarães, N.: Programming Time in Multimedia User Interfaces. – Proceedings UIST´92, ACM Press, pp. 125-134, 1992.

[12]    Herzner, W, Kummer, M.: MMV – Synchronizing Multimedia Documents. – Proceedings of the Second Eurographics Workshop on Multimedia, Darmstadt, Eurographics Technical Report, pp. 107-126, 1992.

[13]    Hodges, M.E. et al: A Construction Set for Multimedia Applications. – IEEE Software 1 (1989), pp. 37-43, 1989.

[14]    Hoepner, P.: Sychronizing the Presentation of Multimedia Objects – ODA Extensions. – Kjelldahl, L. (Ed.): Multimedia - Systems, Interaction and Application, Springer-Verlag, pp. 87-100, 1991.

[15]    Hübner, W.: An Object–oriented Interaction Model for the Specification of Graphical Dialogs. – PhD thesis (in German), Zentrum für Graphische Datenverarbeitung, Darmstadt, 1990.

[16]    Little, T.D., Ghafoor, A.: Synchronization and Storage Models for Multimedia Objects. – IEEE Journal on Selected Areas in Communications, Vol. 8, No. 3, pp. 413 427, 1990.

[17]    Marchiso, P., Panicciari, P., Rodi, P.: A Hypermedia Object Model and its Presentation Environment. – Proceedings Third Eurographics Workshop on Object-Oriented Graphics, Champery, pp. 335-353, 1992.

[18]    Newcomb, S.R., Kipp, N.A., Newcomb, V.T.: The "HyTime" Hypermedia / Time-based Document Structuring Language. – SGML SIGhyper Newsletter, Vol. 1, No. 1, pp. 10-44, 1991.

[19]    Nye, A., O´Reilly, T.: X Toolkit Intrinsics Programming Manual. – O´Reilly & Associates, Sebastopol, CA, 1990.

[20]    Steinmetz, R.: Synchronisation Properties in Multimedia Systems. – Technical Report, IBM European Network Center, 1989.

[21]    Tiemann, D.: Modelling of Interactions and Object Relations in an Object-Oriented System. – Master thesis (in German), University of Oldenburg, Department of Computer Science, 1991.

[22]    West, N.: Multimedia Design Tools. – Macworld, pp. 194-201, November 1991.

[23]    Yager, T.: Build Multimedia Presentations with MacroMind's MediaMaker. – Byte, pp. 302-304, September 1991.

[24]    ISO/IEC: Information Processing – Text and Office Systems – Office Document Architecture (ODA) and Interchange Format (ODIF). – International Standard 8613, 1988.

[25]    ISO/IEC: Information Technology – Hypermedia/Time-based Structuring Language (HyTime). – International Standard Draft, JTC1/SC18 N3190, 1991.

# SUPPORTING THE USERS

# Contextsensitive Help-facilities in GUIs through Situations

Friedrich Strauss

Institut für Informatik und Gesellschaft
Abt. 1, Modellbildung und soziale Folgen
Albert-Ludwigs-Universität Freiburg
Friedrichstr. 50, D-79098 Freiburg, Germany
e-mail: strauss@modell.iig.uni-freiburg.de

### Abstract

Standard Graphical User Interfaces (GUI) or User Interface Management Systems (UIMS) fail to supply a user with sufficient information about its usage. These systems usually provide a uniform representation of interfaces for different applications but lack the possibility to represent the application specific context and functionality adequately. Help in these systems is typically limited to the explanation of the GUI and a separate explanation about the functions of the application.

We introduce SUSI a 'Situation-oriented USer Interface model' which is a knowledge representation designed to represent both the functionality of the GUI and of the application. An important characteristic of this account is the explicit representation of contexts and the effects of user-actions in a current context. It will be briefly demonstrated how useful help-tools for application *and* GUI can easily be build upon this knowledge representation.

Keywords:   Help facilities, context, Graphical User Interfaces (GUI), self-descriptiveness, transparency.

## 1   Introduction

User Interface Management Systems and Interface Builders allow the programmer to implement the GUI of an application and the application independently. This separation between application and user interface makes it difficult to build help-facilities which provide information about GUI *and* application. Within the GUI there is no information about the functionality of the application and within the application there is only little information about the GUI. Though application and GUI are separated from each other, we want to address both the interaction-problem and the content-problem, i.e. the system should be able to give help-information about GUI *and* application. The following questions should be answerable by the system to enhance self-descriptiveness and transparency[1] as basic help-features: Which functions does the GUI serve to change the presentation of information? How can the functions of an application be invoked through the GUI? Which effect has a certain command? All these help-functions should take into account the context of the application at a specific point in time to be useful to the user.

Besides these questions about the functionality we also address some help possibilities regarding the history of actions. A GUI presents the current state of the application but it does not allow a user to inspect the history of his/her actions or even recreate the state of the system at some point within the history.

To illustrate the dependencies between GUI and application and different help features, we present a fileviewer as a small but illustrating example which will be used throughout the paper: Among other features, fileviewers of unix-systems have the capability to move files from one folder to another by dragging the file-icon with the mouse. Some fileviewers differentiate between files and folders that are owned by the user and those that are owned by other users. For example they copy the file if the user has not the permission to move the file or if the target folder is not owned by the user. This context-dependent functionality is explainable if we represent the possible actions and their conditions for appropriateness and the state of the system with regard to the properties of the files and folders. A help-system using this knowledge may explain i.e. make explicit why it has moved one file and copied another file.

If we are able to explain the current and the general behaviour of an application as in the example of the fileviewer we provide the means to make the functionality of the application transparent. We do not try to anticipate the users goals and give him advice about how to reach these goals within this framework. This would make it necessary to make a plan of the users tasks. We believe that this is today only possible within highly constrained domains. It is doubtful that such a tool is valuable if we assume that the advice given may be wrong and mislead the user from time to time. [Suchman 1987] shows the problems of establishing intelligent behaviour through building plans. She presents a 'view of communication and action as situated' as an appropriate basis to solve complex tasks. In this sense we want to provide systems with some (basic) features to explain their situation or context and possible actions or 'situated actions' as Lucy Suchman calls it, but we are not going to provide the user with goal oriented help within our approach.

---

[1]For a definition and discussion of self-descriptiveness and transparency see [ISO 9241 Part 10] and [Opperman, et. al. 92].

In the following we discuss how to incorporate context-sensitive knowledge about the GUI *and* the application into a UIMS. The notion of contextual knowledge seems important to us as a basis for an adequate description of applications with GUIs and will be discussed further. We have developed a 'Situation oriented User Interface model' called SUSI which allows to describe possible actions and contexts within GUIs and applications. SUSI describes an application by programmer-defined types of contexts which represent the different states of the application as it is presented to the user. In section 3 we introduce SUSI and illustrate it by a description of a fileviewer application. We show how adequate help-functions for the questions discussed above can be realized within SUSI and conclude with information about our current and future activities in developing and evaluating SUSI.

# 2   User assistance within UIMS

User Interface Management Systems and Interface Builder simplify the construction of building complex Graphical User Interfaces. They are gaining increasing importance as a high level tool in the field of Human Computer Interaction (HCI). We will show in this section how application specific knowledge can be incorporated within a UIMS to serve as a basis for enhancing the explanation capabilities. This knowledge representation has to take into account the different contexts in which the system might be. Information about the current context allows the system to explain the possible actions and their effects. This enables the user to establish a refined plan for his current task without any recognition of the user's plan or task by the system.

We start with a brief description of the structure of classical UIMS and show how knowledge about GUI and application can be added. We will then discuss the important notions of context and current context which should guide the representation of the knowledge.

UIMS need some application specific information about how to control the dialog between user and application. Classical UIMS therefore consist of three parts as represented in Figure 1 [Edmonds 82].

The Presentation Component handles physical input and output such as keystrokes or mouse clicks, the Dialog Control knows about when to demand the user for input and recognizes user actions such as activating an icon by a mouse click which are passed to the application. The Application Interface couples the application with Dialog Control and transforms the data into a suitable format.

Application specific knowledge in UIMS is restricted to a purely syntactic level.

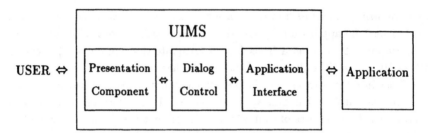

Figure 1: Architecture of an UIMS.

The UIMS has (implicit) knowledge about the presentation of visible objects, the structure of the dialog and the set of possible commands to the application. For example, it 'knows' which commands are possible in a specific situation or which parameters are needed to invoke a specific command.

Providing help in an environment such as discussed in section 1 is impossible without adding knowledge about the functionality of GUI and application and an explicit representation of the dependencies between user commands and the change of the state of application and GUI. Therefore the Dialog Control and the Application Interface should comprise a description of possible user actions and their effects within the GUI and within the application relative to the current context. This description should be user oriented and should abstract from implementation details.

In our fileviewer-example we have to represent the different effects of dragging a file-icon to another place. The system has to know about the ownership of files and folders and under which circumstances the files are moved or copied. If the system has to explain the possible actions in a current context it has to take into account the current working directory of the fileviewer and the selected files within this directory. This information is part of the context which constraints the actions with regard to the effects within the filesystem.

It seems important to us to combine this knowledge with the current state of the application. The current state of an application allows us to focus on those parts of the knowledge base which are applicable in the current situation and are therefore useful to enhance the explanation. Using knowledge in its context is a difficult task. It is in general not clear what constitutes a context and when contexts change. In the field of GUI we are dealing with a somewhat simpler case. The applications have a finite set of clearly typed contexts which are given through the different interfaces (or states of the interface) of the application.

For a broad discussion of different notions of context see [Shoham 91] and [Brezillon 1993]. A notion of context is also introduced for the special problem of Office Automation Systems. The Esprit project IWS and the successor project Ithaca have constructed an end-user context management system

[Ader, Tueni 87], [Marke, Jonckers, Daelemans 87].

According to Suchmans critique, IWS tries to understand or know about the tasks of the user and the plans to solve them. It supports the user with information about the application belonging to an activity. IWS allows the user to start relevant applications locally from the current application for example to gather important information in a database while editing a text. It therefore knows that the database lookup is done in the context of the text editing. Whether it is possible to anticipate all useful plans a user can have to solve a specific task depends strongly on the offered features. For example the user might want to lookup an address not in the database but get it from an e-mail because (s)he knows that the address is included there. IWS can not anticipate all such possibilities to lookup an address in a nonstandard way.

However, the system does not to support the user with features which 'explain' the current situation and possible actions of the application. It only explains which applications belong to the same activity.

# 3  SUSI as a Modeling Language for Transparent Applications

In this section, we will first give a short overview of our concept of context called situation which is loosely coupled with the 'situations' from 'Situation Theory' (see [Barwise, Perry 83], [Cooper, Mukai, Perry 90]). Possible contexts of applications can be divided into several types where each type has some invariant characteristics. This leads to our 'situation-types' (see section 3.2) which are the elementary concept to model contexts within SUSI. A situation-type consists of a logical description of possible actions which a user can invoke and a logical description of the dependencies between these actions and their effects within the application. We illustrate SUSI by our fileviewer-example and we briefly show how different enhancements can easily be build upon the situation oriented representation of knowledge.

## 3.1  Situations

A situation is a collection of facts about a restricted part of the world. A situation describes which information holds within a scene. This information is a set of basic facts (called infons) and constraints which relate different infons (formulas about infons). Action-rules describe the possible actions within this situation by stating the pre- and post-conditions of an action. They describe actions in a way that the action may change the current situation or that the action leads to another situation. A situation may contain information about other situations. This means, situations are allowed as arguments of facts. In

Situation Theory, there is no means to model the dynamic change of a situation. The action-rules introduced here for that objective have no counterpart within Situation Theory.

The distinction between action rules and constraints is synthetic because all constraints are in some way related to some user commands and hence to some action-rules (otherwise they are useless). But this distinction has to be made carefully during the design of the situation oriented description of the GUI: The designer's implicit model of an application during the programming constrains the possibilities of an adequate description of contexts.

In our fileviewer-example a situation corresponds to a current state of the application with a current working directory, some icons representing the files in this directory etc. The constraints describe relations between the icons on the screen and the corresponding files, they describe the knowledge about ownership of files etc. The action-rules represent the effects of actions like dragging a file with the mouse to another place, selecting a file, activating a menu and also asynchronous output from the application.

To describe situations of an application systematically, we introduce situation types which combine our notion of situations with the fact that the contexts in GUIs have a predetermined set of actions and invariant constraints.

## 3.2   Situation-Types

Possible situations in GUIs are usually bound to windows, icons or other mouse-sensitive areas of the screen and their constraints and action-rules do not change within this 'context'. Therefore we describe each context by a *situation-type* which collects all invariant knowledge. Situation-types[2] consists therefore only of action-rules and constraints. The action-rules describe how the commands construct a new situation of some type from the current situation or alter the current situation.

We can now define the notion of a *current situation* as a situation-type with some additional facts specifying the current context in detail. A fact is *derivable* in a current situation if the constraints and the additional facts suppport it.

The system handles a user action by adding the facts representing the action like mouse-click on an icon dragging some icon etc. If the preconditions of an action-rule are all derivable in the current situation the action-rule is activated.

We will represent a situation graphically by a box with the name and the type of the situation in the top left corner. The current facts are displayed within the

---

[2] Our situation-types are only loosely coupled with situation-types as introduced by Barwise & Perry [Barwise, Perry 83]. The latter form a different situation-type for every set of infons (elementary facts) while I will distinguish between situation-types only if the constraints or action-rules are different.

box. The constraints and action-rules of the situation are already determined by the situation-type. Sometimes we will add them to the representation to make it more legible. A situation of the type 'fileview' is represented in Figure 2.

$$
\begin{array}{|l|}
\hline
s : \text{fileview} \\
\hline
window(s,x,y) \\
icon(obj_1,x,y) \\
selected(obj_1) \\
cwd(obj_2) \\
\hline
\end{array}
$$

Figure 2: A situation of situation-type 'fileview'.

Some of the constraints of the situation-type 'fileview' are listed in Figure 3. They describe dependencies between facts of the GUI and also dependencies between facts of the fileviewer. For example, the fileviewer is able to recognize different types of files and offers special actions for each type of file. These constraints state if it is possible to view, edit, execute, or compile the file and how to do it. The effects of dragging files to another folder also depend on these constraints. Constraint$_1$ represents the conditions for 'movable files' which the deciding factor whether a file is moved or copied.

constraint$_1$ (which files are movable):
  $owner(*dir) \land same\text{-}part(*files, *dir) \rightarrow movable(*files, *dir)$
constraint$_2$ (what object can be selected):
  $selected(*obj) \rightarrow file(*obj) \lor directory(*obj)$
constraint$_3$ (display utilities for file of type dvi):
  $dviFile(*obj) \rightarrow display\_utility(*obj, *xdvi)$
constraint$_4$ (which files are of type dvi):
  $file(*obj) \land filename\_ending(*obj, '.dvi') \rightarrow dviFile(*obj)$
constraint$_5$ (which icons in a situation are visible):
  $icon(*obj, *s) \land not\ overlap(*s, *t) \rightarrow visible(*obj)$

Figure 3: Some constraints of the situation-type fileview.

The action-rules in figure 4 describe the dynamic behaviour of the fileviewer. They formulate the changes in situations which happen through user actions or asynchronous output from the application. An action-rule describes the transition from one situation-type to another situation-type (those types may be equal): If a given situation matches an action-rule (i.e. each of the infons of the left hand side of the action-rule are derivable within the situation) a new or altered situation will be constructed from the right hand side of the action-rule. The right hand side of the action-rule determines the situation-type of the new situation and the facts constructed by instantiating the variables are specifying the new situation. Information flow between old and new situation is provided by using variables on the right side, which are instantiated on the left side. Some action-rules of the situation-type *fileview* are listed in Figure 4.

*select(\*icon): fileview: cwd(\*obj), window(\*s,\*x,\*y)*
$\qquad$ *⇒ fileview: cwd(\*obj), window(\*s,\*x,\*y), selected(\*icon)*

*activate(\*icon): fileview: directory(\*icon), cwd(\*obj), window(\*s,\*x,\*y)*
$\qquad$ *⇒ fileview: cwd(\*icon), window(\*s,\*x,\*y)*

*drag(\*icon,\*t): fileview: file(\*icon), movable(\*icon,\*t), cwd(\*obj₁), window(\*s,\*x,\*y)*
$\qquad$ *⇒ fileview: window(\*t,\*x,\*y), cwd(\*obj₁), exec(mv,\*obj₁,\*icon,\*t)*

*activate(\*icon): fileview: file(\*icon), postscript(\*icon), cwd(\*obj), window(\*s,\*x,\*y)*
$\qquad$ *⇒ preview-PS: window(\*t,defx,defy), cwd(\*obj), show-obj(\*obj,\*icon)*

Figure 4: Some action-rules for situations of the type Fileview. (* marks the variables)

## Hierarchies of Situations in a GUI

The situation-types as introduced represent one kind of context. To describe a GUI completely within SUSI, we have to combine the different situations which can occur simultaneously on a screen. This combination can be made hierarchically through the inclusion of situations. If situation *a* creates a new situation *b*, then *b* will be a subsituation of *a*. This enables also the representation of dependencies between different situations. Constraints and action-rules may contain facts with situations as parameter and therefore are facts referable in constraints and action-rules which belong to other situations. We can now define a *current context* which describes the current state of the GUI and consists of the set of the current situations and subsituations describing all interface objects visible on the screen.

For example, starting a session in a GUI corresponds to establishing an initial situation of type screen. This situation handles the (user dependent) establishing of login windows and is responsible during the whole session for context focus which is usually provided by the mouse pointer or clicking with the mouse in the appropriate window. Action-rules and constraints which describe this behaviour are included in all situations. Figure 5 is a description of the current context in a session with fileviewer and mailtool present. With the 'front-of' predicate there are some facts described which state dependencies between different situations. The situation₂ is in front of situation₄ and. This information is useful to derive which part of situation₄ is visible from this fact and some constraints which describe the invariant knowledge about visible objects.

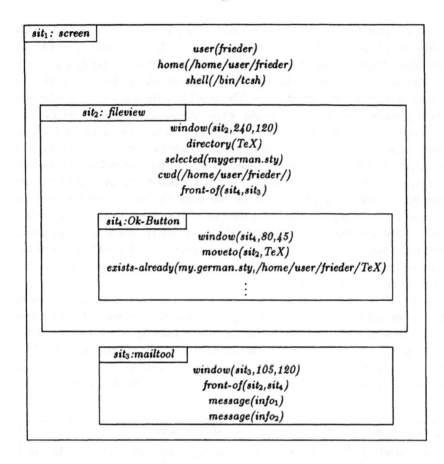

Figure 5: Hierarchy of situations of a current context with Mailtool and File-viewer activated. Within the Fileview situation, there is a subsituation representing an OK-button. Not all infons of the situations are explicitly represented.

## 3.3 Applications of situation oriented GUIs

SUSI as introduced here is a good basis for the enhancement of GUIs. We will demonstrate with the fileviewer-example how some of the questions from the introduction can be answered by using the situation oriented representation of the current context.

The current situation describes all possible actions of a user within this situation-type. Presenting the mouse-sensitive regions together with a representation of the corresponding action-rules helps to show the possible actions of the GUI. This can be realized by highlighting or flashing the region or by inverting the mouse-pointer when it enters the region.

It is also desirable to present the dependencies and effects of an action. This information is provided through the action-rule and the constraints of the current situation. Together with the current facts of the situation we can give not only general help about the functionality but also help about the functionality of the application in the current state. The possible actions in a current situation are represented by those action-rules whose preconditions are consistent with the current situation. This corresponds to the fileviewer-example in the way that the user can get information about all possible actions within this type of situation or (s)he can ask for the specific actions possible within the current situation. If the user has selected a file, the presented actions would take into account the ownership of the file. If the user is not the owner of the file, then the action-rule about copying the file in the case of dragging it to another place is a possible valid action. The action-rule about moving the file is not a consistent action because the selected file is not a movable file and therefore one of the preconditions of the action-rule is inconsistent with the current situation. See figure 6 for an example help text.

The situations and the consistent actions within these situations support us with the contextual knowledge which can represented in different ways. In figure 6 we have represented the constraints and the action-rules by text-templates. Each constraint, each fact and each action-rule has an associated text-template where the parameters are instantiated by the current situation. This allows for an adequate representation of the action-rules and constraints to the user.

| Your current context is: | Possible Actions: |
|---|---|
| – current working directory is */usr/include/sys/*<br>– Following files are selected: *stdio.h*<br>– Owner of the current directory is *root* | – Dragging the icon to another place to get a copy of the file.<br>– Dragging the icon to another place to move the file is impossible because the file is not *movable*.<br>– Selecting icons to drag multiple icons.<br>– Double click to open the file for *edit*.<br>– Activate a menu function on the file: *edit, view, print*. |

Figure 6: Help-screen describing the current situation and the possible actions in this situation.

The successive actions and the corresponding situations define a history of the current situation. Storing these actions and the current facts of the situations may serve as a source for a history browser. The user has the opportunity to browse his action and their effects and may return to a previous situation.

However, returning to an earlier state of the application strongly depends on the application and the possibilities of undoing actions or re-establishing certain contexts.

A situation oriented description may serve as the front end of a language describing application interface and dialog control within an UIMS. Establishing this situation oriented description together with the implementation part of a UIMS during the design would be the best way to incorporate a user oriented view (through functions relying on situations) into the software.

# 4 Conclusion

We have shown how the functionality and the current context of an application with a GUI can be adequately represented by situations in SUSI. The integrated description of an application and a GUI built upon situations (as demonstrated by the fileviewer example) are a good basis for enhancing transparency and providing context-sensitive explanations. Possible user actions in a situation are represented by action-rules. They 'explain' under which conditions an action can be activated and which effects it has. In this sense SUSI provides an explicit representation of 'situated actions'. This is a profound basis according to Suchman on which users are able to build and modify their plans to solve a task. Establishing a representation of an application with SUSI is nevertheless a non-trivial task. Concepts like the fact 'movable' in the fileviewer example which are not explicitly given by the application itself have to be defined within SUSI. A formal description of the user's view of the application has to be established which is informally presented within the manual or only implicitly exists as the user's application-model in the view of the designer.

Our current work is the completion of a prototype interpreter for SUSI and the enhancement of a small application such that it explains its contexts by the SUSI model. Different tools will be integrated which visualize situations and include explanation facilities. This prototype will serve as the basis for a first evaluation of the SUSI knowledge representation and its usefulness for presenting the user with the functionality and the current context of an application.

The integration of a SUSI-model into the software-development process is a worthwhile task to minimize the overhead in designing the model. To reach this goal, SUSI has to be expanded by low level primitives which directly implement the different components of a Graphical User Interface. This step leads to a UIMS where the dialog-control and the application interface are based on top of SUSI-description. One goal is to develop SUSI in a way that we are able to build a self-descriptive and transparent UIMS with an (expanded) SUSI-language as its basis. Another goal is to show the importance and possible benefits of an explicit representation of contexts (based on situations) in a GUI.

# References

[Ader, Tueni 87] Ader, M., Tueni, M.: An Office Assistant Prototype Using a Knowledge-Based Office Model on a Personal Workstation, in [ESPRIT 87], p. 1205-1225.

[Barwise, Perry 83] Barwise Jon, Perry John: Situation and Attitudes, MIT 1983.

[Brezillon 1993] Brezillon, Patrick (ed.): Proceedings of the IJCAI-93 Workshop on 'Using Knowledge in its Context', Laforia 93/13 University Paris 1993.

[Cooper, Mukai, Perry 90] Cooper Robin, Mukai Kunaiki, Perry John (eds.): Situation Theory and its Applications, Volume I, CSLI Lecture Notes 22, Stanford, 1990.

[Edmonds 82] Edmonds E. A.: The man-computer interface – a note on concepts and design. International Journal of Man-Machine-Studies, 16, 1982, p. 231-236.

[ESPRIT 87] ESPRIT Results and Achievements, North-Holland, Amsterdam, 1987.

[ISO 9241 Part 10] Ergonomic Dialogue Design Criteria, Version 3, Committee Draft, December 1990.

[Lu, Vanneste, Ader 90] Lu, Gang, Vanneste, Claude, Ader, Martin: End-User Dialogue Context Management of Office Automation Systems, in: Human-Computer Interaction - INTERACT 90, Diaper, D. et. al. (eds.), Elsevier, Amsterdam 1990, p. 535-541.

[Marke, Jonckers, Daelemans 87] von Marcke, K., Jonckers, V., Daelemans, W.: Representation Aspects of Knowledge-Based Office Systems, in [ESPRIT 87], p. 1226-1238

[Opperman, et. al. 92] Oppermann, Rinhard, Murchner, Bernd, Reiterer, Harald, Koch, Manfred: Softwareergonomische Evaluation – Der Leitfaden Evadis II, de Gruyter, Berlin 1992. An older report in english is available as GMD-Report No. 169: Evaluating of dialog systems (EVADIS), St. Augustin, Gesellschaft für Mathematik und Datenverarbeitung mbH, 1989.

[Shoham 91] Shoham, Yoav: Varieties of Context, in: 'Artificial Intelligence and Mathematical Theory of Computation: papers in honor of John McCarthy', Vladimir Lifschitz (ed.), Academic Press 1991.

[Strauss 1992] Strauss Friedrich: Situationen in der Mensch - Computer - Interaktion. In: Proceedings of the 3rd International Symposium for information science, Man and Machine - Informational Interfaces of Communication, Zimmermann (eds.), Universitätsverlag Konstanz, 1992.

[Suchman 1987] Suchman Lucy A.: Plans and Sitated Actions, The problem of human machine communication, Cambridge MA, 1987.

# User-Adapted Hypertext Explanations

Fahri Yetim

Dept. of Information Science, University of Konstanz
Box 5560 D87/88, D-78434 Konstanz

yetim@inf-wiss.uni-konstanz.de

**Abstract:** Explanations should be adapted to the user's need. Therefore, a good explanation facility should offer an alternative if a given explanation is not clear or complete. This paper describes how this purpose can be achieved through a combination of user modeling, adaptive explanation generation, and hypertext techniques. First, we describe how to generate menus of questions which are adapted to the working context and the explanation situation, so that selections can be made. The user-tailored question-answering facility described next produces a first, short answer to the question asked according to what the user probably needs. However, assumptions about the user's need are open to various sources of uncertainty, and therefore may be incorrect. Therefore, our system offer the user the option of accessing other, possibly important, pieces of information through a hypertext facility. Thus, the advantage of this approach is that it reduces difficulties in user modeling and in interpreting requests for further information

## 1. Introduction

Explanation is one aspect of user interfaces for knowledge-based systems. Explanations are needed so that the user understands the actions of the system and knows what to do next. Explanations should be adapted to the user's background and needs. Recently there has been a considerable amount of research concerned with improving the explanation facilities of knowledge-based systems. Because of the view that improvements in explanation will come from improvements in the user model, considerable effort has been expended in representing a detailed model of the user - including the user's goals, the user's domain knowledge, how information should be presented to the user, and so forth [9]. The focus of these efforts is on how to take advantage of a user model to generate the "best" explanation in one shot [13]. However, following Winograd and Flores

[19] and Sparck Jones [18], detailed user models are difficult to obtain and may be application-dependent. Therefore, the knowledge captured about the user could not be sufficiently rich for a system to be able to offer a user a full and appropriate explanation in every situation. A further problem arises when the hypotheses of the user model are not correct, and therefore the explanation provided does not fully correspond to user expectations. The user must have the opportunity to ask follow-up questions and receive further elaboration of an explanation [13,14].

The approach to explanation described in this paper combines user modeling, adaptive explanation generation and hypertext/hypermedia techniques, and thus will allow a flexible use of the system and will overcome many of the problems evident in earlier explanation facilities. One important contribution of the hypertext methodology for improvement of the explanation facility is that it allows the flexibility for structuring and organizing explanation texts in a non-linear way as well as for presenting them e.g. using multimedial facilities [10,23]. Thus, hypertext allows providing alternative explanations, if a given explanation is not clear or complete; "making oneself understood often requires the ability to present the same information in multiple ways or to provide different information to illustrate the same point" [14, p.1505]. Hypertext follow-ups gives the users the freedom to escape from the system's assumptions about their information needs. The users are able to have acces to other, possibly important, pieces of information, by the hypertext facility.

Before presenting the explanation facility, we provide a brief discussion of some related work on explanation.

## 2. Related Work

There have been a number of attempts to add intelligent explanation facilities to knowledge-based systems. The one problem addressed is how to interact with the system. Using natural language as a medium for interacting with users is critical for the effective use of knowledge-based systems [6, p.921]. Input of user user requests through natural language, or some restricted form of it, has difficulties quite appart from problems such as misspellings or ambiguity. Users do not like having to type long strings of characters. The system has difficulty recognizing the intent of the request even when using a user model and speech-act-oriented analysis of the dialog. Another approach is to generate menus of possible question which seem to suit the working context and the user's knowledge, so that selections can be made [7]. The system presented here uses the classification of the user questions and their assignment to explanation situations to generate the best menu of questions and to recognize the intention of a question from the situation in which it is asked by the user.

Concerning the generation of explanation texts, many systems have employed a user model or are capable of making inferences about the user's current goals and plans, or about the user's preferences in order to provide relevant explanations to the user [1,11,13,14,15,16,24]. Most of them use rhetorical predicates to generate definitions. For example, Maybury [11] uses rhetorical predicates to represent the utterance classes. The rhetorical predicates used here are of a different nature; they are used to retrieve semantically distinct kinds of information from an underlying knowledge base to answer complex user questions.

Finally, most research efforts concentrate on exploiting a user model to improve responses. As Moore and Paris [13] pointed out, these systems were thus atempting to generate the "best" answer in one shot, given an appropriate user model. To compensate for an unreliable user model and to be able to react to feedback (follow-up questions) from users, some researchers emphasize the importance of dialogue capabilities in explanation systems, where the content of the explanation may be negotiated [1,11,13,14,]. Moore and Paris [13] argue that to interact with the user and to achieve the communicative goals, the system must 'understand its own explanations' in order to be able to answer follow-up questions. To address this problem, their system represents explicitly the 'design' of the explanations it produces. However, the explanation modul will be more complicated than the system which this modul is intended to explain to the user. This raises the question whether we need a meta-explanation component for explaining the reasoning of the explanation component itself. More dangerously, information may result in misconceptions on the part of the user which lead to bad decisions or invalid conclusions, which may have costly or even dangerous implications [23]. This problem is especially relevant for problem-solving applications such as the WISKREDAS system [3] to which an explanation model is required which should be simple and direct applicable.

## 3. The Explanation Module

WISKREDAS [3] is a knowledge-based system which has been designed to support a complex decision-making process by cooperative knowledge processing. WISKREDAS consists of five modules. One of them is the explanation module which we describe in this paper. To present the explanation facility we first describe the system's knowledge base. Next, we describe how menus of possible questions can be provided to the user in a way which is adaquate for the given explanation situation and which can help the user to express his or her need of explanation. Then, we address the user-tailored question answering facility, which is employed only to produce a first, short explanation to a question according to the likely needs of the user. Finally, we present hypertext follow-ups, which enable the user to have acces to other, possibly important pieces of information.

## 3.1. The Knowledge Base

The basic unit of knowledge representation in WISKREDAS is the so-called *macro-frame* where the complete static knowledge about cases has been modeled in a frame-like structure. The macro-frame is the prototypical structure for the representation of individual cases; it is the unique skeleton of each individual case. Hypertext and knowledge based methods are integrated in the knowledge base of the system [6,23]. One can consider the macro-frame as a network whose nodes represent concepts (*frames*) and whose links (*relations*) express interrelationships between concepts. Concrete cases are *instances* of the macro-frame whose structure has been filled with values, i.e. case-specific data.

Explanation texts are organized in a flexible way which is inherent to hypertext and allows flexible text generating capabilities. These texts are associated with concepts of the macro-frame. Each text associated with a specific concept is organized in different levels of abstraction so that the relation '*is-detail-of*' between text exists. Some texts are static texts, others are text structures (*templates*) in which current values or concrete concept names etc. can be entered. Static texts can be substituted by other texts called *stretchtexts*[1]. They permit variation of the details of an answer in order to determine the content in a flexible way, according to what the user needs. This can be carried out both by the system considering the information about the user (e.g. user model)[2] and by the user asking for an elaboration of the first explanation provided by the system.

## 3.2. Determining Relevant Questions

Determining possible questions which are relevant for the given explanation situation and can help the user to express his or her need

---

[1] Similar as used by [5]

[2] Our system has no user model, but we use stereotypes of users for our explanation module.

of explanation, require the definition of the relationships between question types or categories and explanation situations.

**Question Categories.** There are many question categories which are necessary for the interaction with knowledge-based systems and especially for their explanation components. We use the question categories proposed by Hughes [8], which are hierarchically ordered. The hierarchical structure of these question categories allows the system to handle them flexibly: it enables the user to browse in the question hierarchy if the question menu offered by the system does not meet her need. Inheritance possibilities along the hierarchy can be used as well.

Hughes distinguishes between *temporal* and *atemporal questions*: A sub-category of temporal questions is *result-seeking questions* (questions like: "Why did you ask me that question"). Another sub-category is *cause-seeking questions* (questions like: "Why did you conclude that?"). Both sub-categories are characterized by a movement of attention away from the question concept in the causal chain towards a resultant state or enabling act. *Atemporal questions* may be *intraconceptual* (e.g. "What is cash-flow?") or *interconceptual* (e.g. "Which has higher value, entity A or entity B?"). All this have further sub-categories, as discussed in [20]; however, these are not of interest here, but the relationship of the question categories to explanation situations.

**Explanation Situations.** We can distinguish situations in which a user needs an explanation:

- *Presentation of a final or preliminary result by the system (S1):* In this situation, the user's reaction might be, for example: to test whether the system has taken into consideration the knowledge that the user considers relevant; to check whether the system's problem-solving strategies are satisfactory; or to check whether all data which the system has taken into consideration are relevant for the stage of the problem;

- *The system asking questions (S2):* The user requests an explanation of a question, for example, he wants to know why the system asked the question, or wants to know beforehand how his answer will be used, or wants to find out what alternatives for the input exist, etc.

- *User's lack of domain-specific knowledge (S3):* In this situation, the reaction of the user can come from his lack of domain-specific knowledge, which requires explanations concerning static knowledge (rules or concepts), independent of concrete problem situations.

- *System's lack of menu options (S4):* The situation can arise in which the system's question-menus do not meet the user's needs, in this case the user can navigate in the knowledge base.

As mentioned above, the same question asked by the user in different situations can have different intentions (e.g. the 'Why'-Question). Both enabling the system to present the questions relevant to the situation and recognizing the intention of a question from the situation in which it is asked by the user requires a meaningful assignment of questions to these explanation situations. As shown in the following, the types of explanations in situations S1 and S2 relate to explanations about dynamic knowledge, whereas Situation S3 requires explanations concerning static knowledge.

S1 <--> cause-seeking
S2 <--> result-seeking
S3 <--> atemporal
S4 <--> further system facilities to browse

Determining the relevant question is not only based on the explanation situation, but also on the user activities. In WISKREDAS, there are several activity spaces for user activities, such as 'analysing the case data', 'computing the case' etc. They are also assigned to the question classes discussed above. Formal definitions of the rules determining relevant questions and detailed information to the aspects of the representing questions in Frames is provided in [20,22].

### 3.3. Answering Questions

The first step to answer a question is to determine the relevant pieces of information. To carry out this task, several researchers (as discussed in section 2) have used rhetorical predicates. The predicates used here relate information about the entity being defined to the entity itself. Each predicate can be handled as a question or as a tool for getting some pieces of information about an entity. However, answering complex user questions such as *what*, *why* or *how* questions, requires the combination of such predicates.

For the modeling of such combinations of predicates, scripts [17] are used. Using scripts for the modeling allows also the definition of the pragmatic aspects of answering questions. Scripts are used for answering questions for both statical and dynamical knowledge. In the following example (Fig. 1), the script contains strategies for answering a what question such as "what is an *entity*?".

Like text plan operators, each script defines the *Preconditions* that must hold before it applies and the refinements or *Decompositions* into subgoals of the action, as well as its intended effects (*Actions*) in the knowledge base, i.e. the creation of a hypertext card. We distinguish between *essential* preconditions (e.g. entity descriptions apply only to entities) and *desirable* preconditions (e.g. assumtions on the userøs knowledge about the entity)[3]. The *decomposition* part of the script contains optional components, which are called sub-scripts. The optional elements of the script for a *what question* provide various aspects of an answer to such a question, and thus they build together a complete answer to the question, i.e. definitions by identification, synonym, constituents or property of an entity etc.

*Script-name:* what_is(User, Entity)
*Preconditions:*
    *essential:* is_entity (Entity)
    *desirable:* not know_about (User, Entity)
*Decompositions:*
    define_by_identification (User, Entity) ∧
    define_by_synonym (User, Entity) ∧
    define_by_constituency (User, Entity) ∧
    define_by_property (User, Entity) ∧
    define_by_function (User, Entity) ∧
    define_by_analogy (User, Entity) ∧
    define_by_example (User, Entity)
*Actions:* create_explanation_card(what_is(User, Entity))

**Fig. 1.** An example for a script[4]

The optional components in the *decompositions* of a script can be primitive predicates or sub-scripts. In the latter case, a hierarchical organisation exists. The application of some of the predicates could be dependent on the application or failure of the other. For instance, if the sub-script 'define-by-identification' fails then the system may attempt a synonymic definition. The order of the predicates reflects the preferred sequence of the aspects of a definition.

At the bottom of the text plan hierarchy, there are primitive predicates, which provide the relevant text by matching the text fragments to the corrospending variables. Some of these primitive predicates contain procedures as arguments which provide *templates* with concrete values. Some texts fragments are assigned to specific user types, whereas others have variables and therefore are appropriate to all user types.

When the decomposition of a script succeeds, the activated and non-activated sub-scripts are stored. Recording any selected subscripts, untried sub-scripts (whose essential preconditions were succesful), failed subscripts (whose essential preconditions failed) enables the system to provide the user some kind of follow-up as discussed later.

---

3 This is inspired from the work of [11].
4 Arguments to predicates include variables

## 3.4. Presenting Answers

Explanation texts provided by the scripts constitute the content of an explanation. These texts are presented in the format of a hypertext card. Assembling the texts and presenting them on the card is carried out by the predicate *create-explanation-card* which is activated by the script mentioned above. The predicate 'create_explanation_card' determines all sub-scripts (or predicates), which were succesful and provide different aspects of an answer, and presents each of them in a separate field on the card. It also presents those predicates which were not used because of pragmatic considerations (e.g. considering the assumptions of the systems). They are further possibilities and can be handled as follow-ups.

| | |
|---|---|
| *define_by_identification* | The concept 'extended cash flow' is the economical definition for ... |
| *define_by_function* | 'extended cash flow' can be computed from the sub-parameters 'turnover' and 'costs'. |
| *dictate_how* | using the mathematical formula: $extended\text{-}cash\text{-}flow = turnover - costs$ |
| *define_by_alternative* | the value of 'extended cash flow' can be entered by the user as well |
| *dictate_how* | the value for 'extended cash flow' must be an integer within the range: *10,000 and 10,000,000 DM.* |

**Fig. 2.** An example for an explanation

To give an example of an explanation, we consider a what question, e.g. "What is 'extended cash flow'?" (fig. 2). We assume further that this question is asked in the explanation situation in which a computation is performed, and the system asked the user for the value of the 'extended cash flow' which it needs to continue the computation process. The above question is then asked by the user to understand what the concept means. First of all, the identification of 'extended cash flow' as a concept and its definition is provided (*define-by-identification*). Secondly, the functional dependency of this concept to other concepts is shown, i.e sub-parameters from which the value of this concept is computed (*define-by-function*). Further, the exact formula is given (*dictate-how*). Finally, an alternative way of getting the value needed is shown (*define-by-alternative*) and the user is informed about the value scale (*dictate-how*).

The exact formula (*dictate-how*) given in this example might not be provided in another situation and instead be represented by a button which the user might activate or not. This reduces the information on the card, yet makes further information accessible in case it is reqiured. Thus, it serves as a kind of follow-up question. Because each field of the card (a specific aspect of an explanation) is considered a semantically closed units, it allows the user to ask further questions concerning a specific aspects of an explanation, as well as to vary the content or the presentation of it, as discussed in the following.

### 3.5. Hypertext Follow-up

The explanation generation facility presented produces only a first, short explanation. Determining what is relevant and which form is appropriate depend on the user characteristics and explanation situations. However, as mentioned in the introduction, where the hypotheses about which information the user needs to receive are not correct, the explanation provided does not fully correspond to the user's expectations, and the user must be able to easily acces the information he or she needs. The user must be able to ask follow-up questions.

Hypertext follow-up gives the user the freedom to escape from the system's assumptions about her information needs. The hypertext facility gives the user access to other, possibly important pieces of information. We distinguish two kinds of hypertext follow-up: (1) *object links* which provide (or lead to) more information about a specific object (or entity) mentioned in the first explanation; (2) *explanation links* which lead from a start explanation (in most cases it is the first explanation) to further possible explanations e.g. to the elaboration or refinement of an explanation etc.

**Object Links.** By these facilities, users may obtain more detailed information to an object and therefore can extend the content of an explanation in the following directions:

- *detail-info-on-object:* These links provide detailed texts on objects (e.g. attributes or concepts mentioned in the explanation) by substituting the text first provided with a more detailed one. By applying these links several times the user can successively expand the text.

- *alternativ-media:* This link provides a result in another form (e.g. tables, graphics) that permits easier understanding of the data.

- *historical-info-on-entry:* This link provides historical information on an entry which informs about the temporal development of certain entries, and its corresponding resources. By using it, the user can test whether information of any resource has been considered yet.

**Explanation Links.** Links between explanations allow the user to navigate from the first explanation to an alternative explanation concerning the same question; for example, to abtract or to refine the first explanation as well as to look for similar explanations. The definition of such links is based on the internal structure (conceptual properties) of the starting explanation, i.e. objects and relations between them. These objects are either concepts of the macro-frame (conceptual model) or instances of it (see chapter 3.1).

The first explanation is called *instantiated explanation* if it consists of instances, whereas it is called *conceptual explanation* if it consists of concepts of the macro-frame. The following links are defined[5]: *Abstraction (conceptualization) of an instantiated explanation*, by the substitution of instances by their concepts in the macro-frame; *instantiation of a conceptual explanation*, by the substitution of the concepts of the macro-frame by their instances. Because there exists more than one instance of a specific object, there could be more than one variation of the instantiation of an conceptual explanation. Instances of the same conceptual explanation are called *brother explanation*. A further link is the *refinement link*, which refines an explanation by providing more details.

These links are useful not only because they lead to alternative explanations, they are also helpful for testing the knowledge base. For example, the existence of a conceptual explanation and simultanously the non-existence of an instantiated explanation could inform the user about the absence of case specific data.

## 4. Discussion and Conclusion

The explanation facility presented provides an alternative approach to explanation by combining user modeling, adaptive explanation generation, and hypermedia techniques. This approach allows the system to generate menus of possible questions which seem to suit the working context and the situation that led to the need for an explanation, so that selections can be made. Another advantage of this approach is that it reduces difficulties in user modeling and in interpreting requests for further information. Hypertext follow-ups allow the user the freedom to escape from the system's assumptions about her information needs. They offer the user alternative information to explain the same point, and thus aid him or her in a better understanding of the problem.

---

5 The definition of such relations is inspired from the work of Cordier and Reynaud [2]; for detail information see [22].

The explanation links are only defined, but not realized yet. Therefore, at this stage of system development, we can make only some general asumptions about their usability in real explanation dialog, but not give any practical results or evaluations.

# Literatur

1. Cawsey, A. (1992): Adapting Explanations to the User. In: Proc. of the Workshop on User Adapted Interaction, Bari, Italy 1992.
2. Cordier, M. O.; Reynaud, C. (1991): Knowledge Acquisition Techniques and Second-Generation Expert Systems. In: Applied Artificial Intelligence, (5), 1991, 209-226.
3. Dambon, P.; Glasen, F.; Kuhlen, R.; Thost, M. (1989): WISKREDAS: Ein Wissensbasiertes Kreditabsicherungssystem; Informationswissenschaft, Universität Konstanz, Bericht SFB 221/B3-3/89.
4. Dambon, P.; Yetim, F. (1990): Integration of Hypertext into a Decision Support System. In: Herget,J.; Kuhlen, R. (eds.): Pragmatische Aspekte beim Entwurf und Betrieb von Informationssystemen. Konstanz: Universitätsverlag, 64-77.
5. Encarnacion, A. O. ; Boyle, C. D. B. (1991): A User Model based Hypertext documentation system. In: Kay, J; Quilici, A. (eds.): Proc. of the IJCAI Workshop Agent Modeling for Intelligent Interaction, Sydney, 1991, 44-65.
6. Finin, T. W.; Joshi, A. K.; Webber, B. L. (1986): Natural Language Interactions with artificial experts. In: Proceedings of the IEEE 74 (7), July 1986, 921-938.
7. Hartley, J.R.; Smith, M.J. (1988): Question answering and explanation giving in on-line help systems. In: Artificial Intelligence and Human Learning. London: Chapman & Hall Computing, 1988, 338-360.
8. Hughes, S. (1986): HOW and WHY: HOW far will they take us, WHY should we need any more?. In: Proceedings of a Workshop on Explanation. London: Alvey. 1986, 69-82.
9. Kobsa, A. (1992): User Modeling: Recent Work, Prospects and Hazards. In: Proceedings of the Workshop on User Adapted Interaction, Bari, Italy, may 22-23, 1992
10. Kuhlen, R. (1991): Hypertext - ein nicht-lineares Medium zwischen Buch und Wissensbank. Berlin et al: Springer Verlag.
11. Maybury, M. T. (1992): Communicative acts for explanation generation. In: Int. J. Man-Machine Studies, (1992) 37, 135-172.
12. McKeown, K. R. (1985): Discourse Strategies for Generating Natural-Language Text. In: Artificial Intelligence 27 (1985), 1-41.

13. Moore, J. D.; Paris, C. L. (1992): Exploiting User Feedback to Compensate for the unreliabity of User Models. In: User Modeling and User-Adapted Interaction 2: 287-230, 1992.
14. Moore, J. D.; Swartout, W. R. (1989): A Reactive Approach to Explanation. In: Proceedings of IJCAI'89, 1504-1510.
15. Paris, C. L. (1989): The Use of Explicit User Models in a Generation Systems for Tailoring Answers to the User's Level of Expertise. In: Kobsa, A.; Wahlster, W. (eds.): User Models in Dialog Systems. Berlin et al: Springer, 200-232.
16. Sarner, M. H. ; Carberry, S. (1992): Generating Tailored Definitions Using a Multifaceted User Model. In: User Modeling and User-Adapted Interaction 2: 181-210, 1992.
17. Schank, R. C. & Abelson, R. (1977). Scripts, plans, goals and understanding. An inquiry into human knowledge structures. Hillsdale: Lawrence Erlbaum.
18. Sparck Jones, K. (1989): Realism About User Modeling. In: Kobsa, A.; Wahlster, W. (eds.): User Models in Dialog Systems. Berlin et al: Springer, 341-363.
19. Winograd, T; Flores, F. (1986): Understanding computers and Cognition: A new Foundation for Design. Norwood, New Jersey: Ablex Publishing, 1986
20. Yetim, F. (1991): Eine Hypertext-Komponente zu einem Expertensystem: Benutzerfragen für Erklärungsdialoge. In: Maurer, H. (ed.): Hypertext/Hypermedia '91. Berlin et al: Springer, 1991, 286-298.
21. Yetim, F. (1992): Ein Ansatz zur flexiblen Gestaltung benutzergerechter Antworten für Erklärungsdialoge. In: Zimmermann, H.; Luckhardt, H.; Schulz, A. (eds.): Mensch und Maschine - Informationelle Schnittstellen der Kommunikation. Konstanz: Universitätsverlag, 1992, 338-353.
22. Yetim, F. (1993): Integration von Hypermedia- und Wissensbasierten Methoden für Erklärungen in Informationssystemen. Universität Konstanz, Informationswissenschaft (Doktorarbeit, in Vorbereitung).
23. Yetim, F.; Dambon, P. (1991): Can Hypermedia improve the Acceptance of Knowledge-Based Systems? In: Bullinger, H.-J. (ed.): Human Aspects in Computing: Design and Use of Interactive Systems and Information Management. Elsevier Science, 1991, 889-893.
24. Zuckerman, I. (1992): Content Planning based on a Model of a User's Beliefs and Inferences. Report, Dept. of Computer Science, Monash University, Australia.

# From Conflict to Dialogue:
# On Attack and Defense in On-line Assistance

Peter W. Fach, Maria Bannert, and Klaus Kunkel

Department for Computational Linguistics
University of Stuttgart, Germany
fach@adler.ims.uni-stuttgart.de

Center of Empirical Educational Research
University Koblenz-Landau, Germany
bannert@sun.rhrk.uni-kl.de

**Abstract.** A survey of the literature concerning user assistance of software products reveals that the working environment of a user is hardly taken into consideration, although direct manipulation user interfaces and the respective metaphors have conquered the market of personal computing. We argue that ignoring a user's working environment in the context of on-line assistance will end up in a deterioration of the Task-Artifact-Cycle which leads on-line assistance into a dead end. However, when taken into account (e.g. as a scenario of representative user tasks), a small set of dialogue rules, so-called "game rules", may establish a "critical dialogue" between users and on-line assistance. Such a critical dialogue is based on rights of attack and obligations of defence.

## 1 Introduction

User assistance for the use of software products is becoming an increasingly important design topic within the development process. This is partly due to the fact that in case of damage caused by the use of faulty or defective computer documentation, the respective manufacturer will be liable. To date one can distinguish two contrasting approaches for user assistance: the system-oriented one, which focuses on how the respective software works, and the task-oriented one, in which such information is structured along user tasks [1].

According to this work, task orientation is preferable in respect to computer-documentation. Several empirical studies provide evidence for this approach [2,3]. Some problems are still unsolved in task-oriented user assistance, e.g. the selection of appropriate and representative tasks, as well as how to present them [4]. On the one hand, it seems impossible to ensure that all problems are covered which can possibly occur during system use [5]; on the other hand, it is not clear how to structure a task-oriented documentation [6]. Should one describe a single, complex and comprehensive task or present a specific, narrowly-defined task in each section?

Our main concern in this paper is to present a framework addressing these problems in on-line user assistance. We presume that a task-oriented design approach is insufficient for documenting computer systems. Furthermore, we presume that ignoring a user's working environment results in a continuously developing discrepancy between the user's actual task and the artifact (i.e. on-line assistance[1]) documenting the user task.

## 2 The Task-Artifact-Gulf

The *Task-Artifact-Cycle* developed by Carroll and colleagues shows that artifacts created to manage a task will influence and change the task itself: »In HCI the important objects are user tasks, designed artifacts, and the Task-Artifact-Cycle through which both develop« [7]. In expanding upon the types of artifacts presented by Caroll and colleagues, namely hardware, systems, applications and interfaces, our approach also embraces user assistance, e.g. "Training Wheels"[2] [8], as an artifact which can drastically influence the course of the Task-Artifact-Cycle and which is simultaneously exposed to the impacts of the cycle. Thus, in general, we regard user assistance as such an artifact which leads to the assumption that user assistance can also have repercussions on the task for which it was designed.

For example, in writing a business letter, the user may get the idea that he should design a graphic layout of the letterhead or reference pages for serial letters if unnecessary information is presented in the documentation. In the opposite case, i.e. when provided information is insufficient, the user may leave aside some aspects of the original task [5]. Based on our assumption that user assistance tends to modify a user's task, we propose to also consider the working environment where task and artifact are anchored, since in most cases the artifact is designed in a working environment different from the one in which a user carries out a specific task. Thus, help systems, either active or passive ones, context related or not context related, frequently originate from a situation in which, at best, an abstract user's working environment is assumed. In Figure 1 such a design situation is contrasted with a working environment in which a user task is anchored. A different perspective on the task and the artifact arises in each of the two environments. And, in turn, each perspective has its particular impact on the relationship between task and artifact. A divergence between task and artifact results, and the "Task-Artifact-Gulf" is born. Thus, in order to bridge these differing perspectives and to make use of the convergence of the Task-Artifact-Cycle (as intended by the "Training Wheels"), we argue that it is insufficient to develop documentation from a task-oriented design approach, as proposed by Wright [5], but it seems indispensable to also consider the working environment, a requirement which has been formulated elsewhere [9].

---

[1]This paper is intended to cover on-line user support in general. Thus, in this context we will use "user assistance", "user support" and "documentation" in a synonymous fashion.

[2]The "Training Wheels" concept is a reduced-function training environment which prevents problematic user actions.

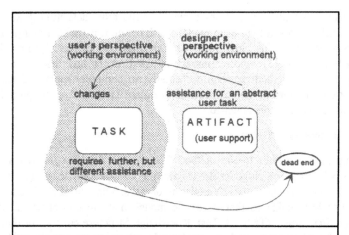

**Fig. 1. The Task-Artifact-Gulf.** Divergent working environments lead to deterioration of the Task-Artifact-Cycle because user assistance (artifact) does not meet a user's requirements and thus alters his task. This altered task, in turn, calls for modified assistance. The Cycle runs into a dead end.

## 3 Role Conflicts

In the following we refer to these perspectives (i.e. the user's and the designer's one) as *roles* shaped by the respective working environment. Further, we refer to the gulf (see Figure 1) as a *role conflict* due to different role expectations. As shown by the Task-Artifact-Gulf in the case of divergent working environments, the expectations of one role towards the other are misleading ones: the world of objects, concepts or terms is necessarily different. Or worse: tasks which are self-evident for one party do not even exist for the other one, and therefore, cannot be anticipated or made available (e.g. be documented) to the opposite party. Bridging such conflicts which originate from different "working-worlds" is the center of our attention in the following section.

### 3.1 Close Attention to Original User Tasks

So far, we argued that diverse working environments create conflicts which confront designers when developing user assistance for computer systems. Methodologically, we attempt to grasp the working environment through a collection of typical and representative tasks ("scenarios" in the terminology of Carroll and colleagues) before such a task has been transformed into a computer-supported one. Not only the positive experiences we made earlier[3] lead us to apply the method "*Knowledge Analysis for Tasks*" (KAT) [10] and its extension [11] to individualize, analyze and describe such user tasks. Another reason is because KAT supports us in realizing our

---

[3]The authors worked on a usability-project at the Heidelberg Scientific Center of IBM Germany [14].

goal to ensure that the working environment is the most determining key to user assistance: this method allows us to model a task before it is transformed into a computer-supported one. This close focus on "original user tasks" distinguishes our approach from others [3], whose approach is based on the task description method GOMS [12]. This method concentrates chiefly on computer-supported tasks, and therefore these authors do not consider the original task, not yet supported by the software which is being documented.

### 3.2  Task Knowledge Structures ...

In our approach we refer to the method "*Knowledge Analysis for Tasks*" (KAT) [10,13]. KAT consists of three levels: (1) analysis of task knowledge, (2) identification of task characteristics, and (3) modeling of tasks. The aim of KAT is to identify a user's task knowledge so that it can be modelled by means of so-called "*Task Knowledge Structures*" (TKS). A Task Knowledge Structure consists of objects and their internal structures, procedures, goals and goal-structures and their relations to other TKSs. For example, a clerk may have the following TKS about writing a business letter: The major *goal*, of course, is writing a business letter. A possible *object* is a business letter whose internal structure is composed of a list of items such as "typical instance" (e.g. private check), "centrality" (of the object relative to the entire task), "associated actions" (e.g. switch on type-writer), "related objects" (e.g. correction fluid), "features" (e.g. high quality paper) etc. A *goal structure* shows the relation of such objects, and may be broken down into subgoals. *Procedures* coordinate the actions (e.g. switch on type-writer, insert paper, etc), which are associated with the objects to achieve the desired goal. The use of the method will be presented in more detail in the example provided in the last Section.

### 3.3  ... to Predict Role Conflicts

Up to this point, KAT allows us to model the major source of conflicts between users and assistance-systems. When we model both working environments (i.e. the designer's and the user's one as we will demonstrate in the last Section) by a collection of tasks, (i.e. scenarios), we have a means to predict or at least to estimate how the Task-Artifact-Gulf might come into effect, and where possible conflicts may appear. For this reason, we understand conflicts as the point where to tackle the problem. In the following, we first give a more precise characterization of the kind of conflict on which our approach is based, and second lay the foundations for an interaction form which should overcome the effects of the Task-Artifact-Gulf.

## 4  From Conflict to Dialogue

In the context of this paper a conflict involves two parties: the *proponent* (a designer of a help system) and the *opponent* (the user of the help system). A conflict denotes every situation in which a user is given a piece of advice or help which does not meet his needs. We will speak of a *non-constructive* conflict if neither party has detailed knowledge about the other's working environment. If at least one party has detailed knowledge about it (e.g. by means of a scenario of modelled tasks as proposed in the preceding Section), we will call this kind of conflict a *constructive* one. In the following we will only be referring to constructive conflicts. Thus, we suppose that a task analysis (e.g. by KAT) of those aspects of a user's working environment which are relevant to the design of the documentation has been carried out.

## 4.1 Attack and Defense Guides Conflict Resolution

Our approach to resolving constructive conflicts makes use of so-called "critical dialogues". The aim of critical dialogues or rational debates is to study how conflicts can be resolved by verbal means. »A "dynamic" theory of how to solve them (..) becomes an instrument for bringing about and for speeding up a flux of opinions (..). This speeding up is achieved by the "aggressive" character of critical dialogues in the sense that they involve systematic attacks on statements made by other persons« [15].

In the context of a specific help-giving or advice-giving system, this means to facilitate a critical dialogue between the user (the critic or opponent) and the system. The former can systematically attack the "statements" made by the latter (the proponent) who, in turn, is obliged to defend or justify his own statements against the attacks of the opponent. Rights to attack and obligations of defense are granted as "game rules", which both the proponent and the opponent should have agreed upon in advance. To put it briefly, we suggest a set of rules guiding and pushing forward a kind of discussion based on the theory of critical dialogues.

Since we are basically interested in advice-giving systems for complex software products with direct manipulation user interfaces such as WORD FOR WINDOWS we favor a "discussion" similiar to a CBT-program[4] for the respective software product. But instead of mere animated demonstrations showing a user how a sample task can be carried out in a fixed task-oriented manner, we invite the user to attack the steps of such a demonstration, thus forcing the on-line system to "defend" or justify its own statements (i.e. its steps). It is very important to note that both parties must strictly obey the rules established for attack and defense so that the framework of the resulting interaction, the rational debate, becomes predictable for both parties. In more linguistic terms one can say that we use "game rules" as the interaction-syntax of an advice-giving system and TKSs as a semantic representation of potential users' tasks being "under discussion".

## 4.2 "Game Rules" for Conflict Resolution

To show how rights and obligations actually work, our first assumption is that a user-task-based scenario has been extracted from the user's working environment as proposed in the preceding Section. User tasks, then, are available in terms of goals, subgoals, objects, actions and relations among them. In accordance with our understanding of conflicts, only constructive conflicts are allowed to arise in the course of a help session. Furthermore, we assume that a help system is available which always works in the same way: (a) A help topic $G_0$ selected by a user corresponds to a TKS-goal. (b) The system answers by splitting up the goal into two subgoals $G_1, G_2$ (each available as TKSs, too), which are regarded as prerequisites to reach $G_0$. In Figure 2

---

[4]The CBT-Program delivered with WORD™ FOR WINDOWS or animated demonstrations as studied in [16] serve as examples.

| opponent | proponent | rule | associated action |
|---|---|---|---|
| | $T: G_1, G_2 \Rightarrow G_0$ | | Help topic selected by the user |
| $aT:$   $G_1, G_2$ | | RIIa | user manipulates the interfaces achieving the subgoals $G_1, G_2$ |
| **(1)** | $G_0$ | RI | help system's obligation to demonstrate the necessary steps |
| $aT:$   $G_1, G_2$ | | | user does not succeed in achieving one of the two subgoals (Task-Artifact-Cycle ceases to work; typical conflict situation) |
| | $aG_1$ | RIIb | help systems's attack (asks the user to carry out $G_1$) |
| ca | | RIII | user's counter-attack (his non-acceptance or inability) |
| | $G_1$ | RI | help system's defense prompts the user to achieve the subgoal in reponse to his counter-attack |
| **(2)** | $G_0$ | RI | the help system now can defend itself against the user's first attack by showing how to achieve the initial goal $G_0$ |

**Fig. 2. Assistance Control by attack and defense.** Box (1) demonstrates a help situation that works because the user know how to "use" the help. Box (2), however, reveals that the user cannot understand the piece of help given and therefore cannot go ahead. The help system pushes forward the "discussion" by launching an attack ($aG_1$) towards the user

we refer to such a help topic $T$ as: $G_1, G_2 \Rightarrow G_0$. This is the basis for the formulation of the following sample dialogue rules[5]:

(I) *The obligation of defense (RI).* The help system advocates $T$ (the piece of assistance given) and therefore must defend $T$ against attacks of the user.

(II) *The user's right of attack (RIIa).* Suppose the user is able to perform both subgoals which have been proposed as a piece of help, but does not see how to reach the desired goal $G_0$. The user, now, may attack the statement $T$. This is done by manipulating the interface of the software product in such a way that the user achieves both subgoals $G_1$ and $G_2$. In other words, he challenges the help system by creating the necessary task context. Now, by means of *(RI)* the help system has the obligation of

---

[5]The rules (RI),...,(RIII) have their roots in [15].

defense in showing how to reach $G_0$. This might be implemented as a unit in a CBT-program which prompts the user to carry out the necessary manipulations. In box (1) of Figure 2 we refer to an attack towards a statement $T$ by writing $aT$.

(III) *The help system's right of attack (RIIb)*. Assume the opponent (the user looking for help) is not able to create the task context (i.e. to achieve either $G_1$ or $G_2$) and therefore the help system is unable to demonstrate how to reach $G_0$. This, indeed, is a typical situation encountered in a help session where the user may not understand how to apply the piece of advice given to his own problems. In most cases, this breaks off the help session. The Task-Artifact-Gulf emerges. In order to facilitate the "flux of opinions", the help system is now granted the right of attacking the user. This attack can be understood as a challenge towards the opponent to manipulate the interface so that, for example, $G_1$ is achieved. Since in this case the opponent does not know how to achieve $G_1$, he can launch a counter-attack.

(IV) *The user's right of counter-attack (RIII)*. Whenever the user is attacked by the help system, he has the right to launch a counter-attack. The help system, by virtue of rule *(RI)*, must show the opponent how the respective subgoal can be achieved. In box (2) of Figure 2 we refer to a counter-attack by writing $ca$.

We hope that this short scenario (see Figure 2) has given the reader an idea of how "critical dialogues" can be implemented when used as on-line assistance. In addition we sum up how conflict resolution is managed by a set of sample dialogue rules:

- By rule *(RI)*    the user can always be sure that the on-line assistance will provide a "justification".
- By rule *(RIIa)* the user becomes actively involved in conflict resolution by creating the necessary context.
- By rule *(RIIb)* the user is challenged to achieve a specific subgoal prerequisite to reach the major goal.
- By rule *(RIII)* the user requests the justification of what has been proposed by the on-line assistance.

Whenever the user is prompted by virtue of rule *(RI)*, the "Training Wheels" come into effect. Whenever it becomes necessary to apply rule *(RIIb)*, the "Training Wheels" must have failed due to a discrepancy between task and artifact. However, it is important to note that rule *(RIIb)* can successfully be applied only under the condition of a constructive conflict. In this case, one can be sure that - if the user launches the counter-attack *(RIII)* - the justification given by the system corresponds to a real user task thereby avoiding the effects of the Task-Artifact-Gulf.

## 5 Constructive vs. Non-constructive Conflicts: An Example

In the following scenario "user" stands for a role occurring in a dentist's office. "Documentator" stands for a role taking place in a commercial documentation center. On the basis of intuitive expectations concerning the user's role, the documentator creates a task-oriented documentation for the following task.

The task is to write a business letter by means of a text processing program making use of reference pages. Such reference pages determine the layout of an entire class of documents so that data, such as address, date, subject, etc, is entered via dialogue boxes and automatically placed within the document to be written.

Comparing the Task Knowledge Structures of both roles clearly reveals a non-constructive conflict situation. The goal structure of the documentator (role $A$ , see upper right-hand box of Figure 3) reflects a primarily product-oriented point of view, whereas the user's goal structure (role $B$, upper right-hand box of Figure 4) originates from a traditional typewriter-based working environment. For role $A$, the object "address" only serves the purpose of demonstration. In the environment of role $B$, however, "address" is a structured object, which already is a component of another software application. The most striking discrepancy, however, is caused by the absence of the user's object category "input" (see lower left-hand box of Figure 4), which is nevertheless anticipated and therefore documented by role $A$ (lower left-hand box of Figure 3). In this case it is obvious that the Task-Artifact-Gulf will lead the documentation into a dead end. This conflict will be regarded as a constructive one, if one of the parties has a TKS-description of the other party at its disposal. If the user's TKS-structures are available, a documentator can develop a task-oriented documentation in form of a "critical dialogue" with respect to the user's goal and object structures.

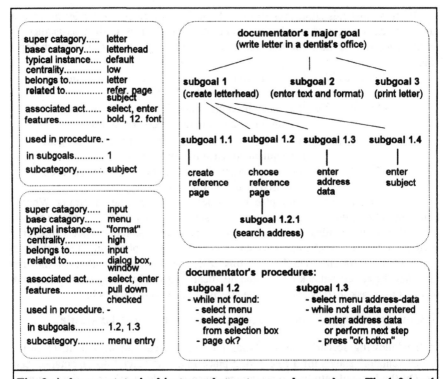

**Fig. 3. A documentator's objects, goal structures and procedures.** The left-hand boxes show two objects extracted from the documentator's working environment. The right-hand boxes show the documentator's goals and the corresponding procedures.

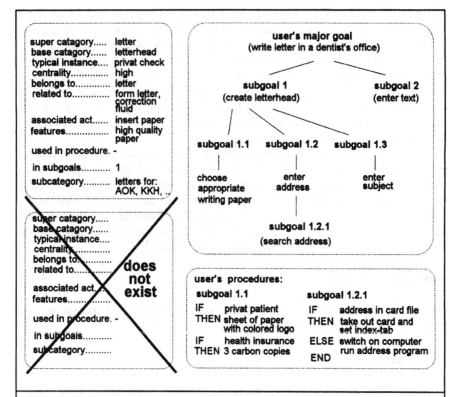

**Fig. 4. A user's objects, goal structures and procedures.** The left-hand box shows one object extracted from the user's working environment. The right-hand boxes show the user's goals and the corresponding procedures. Although both parties talk about the same objects, they are completely different. Notice that the user is not familiar with any object comparable to the documentator's "menu"-object (see left-hand boxes of Fig. 3).

# 6 Discussion

In retrospect, we can now attempt to give an answer to the issues posed in the introductory Section: (1) selection of appropriate, representative tasks and their presentation and (2) description of a single, complex and comprehensive task vs. presentation of a specific, narrowly-defined task in each section of the documentation.

To start with the first issue on how to present user tasks, our answer is to establish a set of "game rules" upon which both parties have agreed beforehand. These "game rules" should be chosen in such a way that a dynamic discussion is facilitated thus pushing forward the "flux of support" between user and on-line system. In particular, we accentuate the on-line system's right to attack the user. Together with the user's right of counter-attack, this rule helps the user to resume a help session in which he has lost his orientation.

The second question that is posed in the introduction, whether to present a single and complex task rather than a narrowly defined one, is circumvented through the argument that a task should be a real, original user task which is extracted from a user's environment prior to the computer-system which is being documented. This argument emerges directly from what we called the Task-Artifact-Gulf: a possible divergence of task and artifact. Last but not least this argument is also supported by our way of presenting such tasks. By means of critical dialogues it is, apriori, not necessary to present an entire task. The portion of the task presented is determined only by the way the critical dialogue proceeds.

In conclusion, the combined application of KAT for modelling user tasks and the environment in which they have to be performed, and critical dialogues for moderating user assistance offers a promising way to meet the goal of producing appropriate on-line user support. However, we must stress that the entire construction will only work if the conflicts which are critically discussed are constructive ones. The game rules can serve the purpose of clarifying the expectancies linked to the roles, but they cannot avoid the effects of the Task-Artifact-Gulf.

## Ackknowledgements

The authors would like to thank Eleonore Hertweck for fruitful discussions and comments on earlier drafts of this paper.

## References

1. S. Rosenbaum, R.D. Walters: Audience Diversity: A Major Challenge in Computer Documentation. IEEE Transactions on Professional Communications 29, 48-56 (1986)
2. E.K. Odesalchi: Documentation is the Key to User Success. IEEE Transactions on Professional Communications 29, 16-18 (1986)
3. R. Gong, J. Elkerton: Designing a Minimalist Documentation Using a GOMS-Model: A Usability Evaluation of an Engineering Approach. In: C. CHEW, J. Whiteside (eds.): Proceedings of the CHI'90 Conference: "Empowering People". New York: ACM Press 1990, pp. 99-106
4. D. Watts: Creating an Essential Manual: An Experiment in Prototyping and Task Analysis. IEEE Transactions on Professional Communications 33, 32-37 (1990)
5. P. Wright: Issues of Content and Presentation in Document Design. In: M. Helander (ed.): Handbook of Human-Computer Interaction. Amsterdam, New York, Oxford: North-Holland 1988, pp. 629-647
6. S.K. Partridge: So what is Task Orientation, Anyway? IEEE Transactions on Professional Communications 29, 26-32 (1986)
7. J.M. Carroll, W.A. Kellog, M.B. Rosson: The Task-Artifact Cycle. Research Report RC 15731 IBM Watson Research Center. IBM T. J. Watson Research Center.Yorktown Heights, NY 10598 (1990)

8. J.M. Carroll, Carrithers: Training Wheels in a user interface. Communication of the ACM 27, 800-806 (1984)

9. J.S. Brown, S.E. Newman: Issues in Cognitive and Social Ergonomics: From Our House to Bauhaus. Human-Computer Interaction 1, 359-391 (1985)

10. P. Johnson: Supporting System Design by Analysing Current Task Knowledge. In: D. Diaper (ed.): Task Analysis for Human-Computer Interaction. Chichester: Ellis Horwood Limited 1989, pp 160-185

11. L. Reichert, K. Kunkel, R. Gimnich, R. GARBO: A Graphical Tool for Modelling User Tasks in Human-Computer Interface Design. IBM HDSC TR.75.92.01 June 92, Heidelberg: IBM Scientific Center (1992)

12. S.K. Card, T.P. Moran, A. Newell: The Psychology of Human-Computer Interaction. Hillsdale, NY: Erlbaum 1983

13. P. Johnson, H. Johnson, H.: Knowledge Analysis of Tasks: Theory, Method, and Suggestions for Application to System Design. In: A. Downtown (ed.): Engineering the Human Interface. Chichester, New York: McGraw Hill (1991)

14. K. Kunkel, R. Gimnich, R.: Task Analysis with TAKD/TKS: Method, Application, Experience. IBM HDSC Technical Note 91.11, December 91, Heidelberg: IBM Scientific Center (1991)

15. E.M. Barth, E.C.W. Krabbe: From Axiom to Dialogue. Berlin, New York: Walter de Gruyter 1982

16. S. Palmiter, J. Elkerton: Animated demonstrations vs. written instructions for learning procedural tasks: a preliminary investigation. International Journal of Man-Machine Studies 34, 678-701 (1991)

# STUDYING THE USERS

# Toward Deep Modelling and Control of Human Activity at the Microscope

A. Derder and C. Garbay

Equipe SIC
Lab. TIMC / IMAG - Université Joseph Fourier
CERMO BP 53X - 38041 Grenoble Cédex - France
Tél : 33 76 51 48 13 - Fax : 33 76 51 49 48 -
Email : derder@imag.imag.fr / garbay@imag.imag.fr

**Abstract.** The purpose of the paper is to present a system able to supervise the activity of cytotechnicians and pathologists, as performed under the HOME workstation. The HOME workstation provides a set of computerized tools facilitating specimen examination ; human activity may thus be approached through a set of parameters, such as the specimen exploration strategy or observation time. A deep model of human activity is progressively elaborated by our system, based on these parameters, in terms of three contextual factors : case factors, task factors, and human factors. Such model allows to consider the mutual effect of these factors on work quality. A navigation system is designed and presented, which offers easy access and navigation through these informations. The model is also used in alarming mode, to notify a deviation from reference behaviour : further information may then be gained by questioning the navigation system.

## 1 Introduction

The examination of microscopic specimen is a tedious task, performed routinely for diagnosis and prognosis purposes by trained personal. The HOME system [1] [Brugal 92] has been designed to assist routine screening and reviewing tasks : it provides a set of tools supporting various activities such as marking, relocation and analysis of cells. It is based on a PC connected to a microscope equipped with a camera and offering built-in video text and graphic mixing with the optical image. This system is currently developed in our laboratory in the framework of the IMPACT European Project (AIM initiative). Our purpose is to design a system able to supervise the work performed under the HOME apparatus, thus providing higher level assistance to human activity.

Such objective implies an original view on man machine assistance. Up to now in fact, the aim of classical approach in Artificial Intelligence has been to built automated system able to replace human in the performing of various tasks (diagnosis for example). Expert systems have been designed to this end, handling knowledge about the domain under study and the task to be performed [2]. Such approach has been used to design KIDS (Knowledge-based Image Diagnosis System) [3], a multi-agent system devoted to cytological image interpretation and using a distributed approach to model medical reasoning in cytology. Our purpose is different, since it is to design a system able to supervise a human agent in the execution of a complex task ; to reach such purpose, it appears necessary to develop not only knowledge-based but also behaviour-based modelling, that is a technology able to model and control human behaviour in front of a task.

## 2 The HOME Microscope Workstation

### 2.1 What is Cytopathology

Clinical cytopathology is the study of the morphological features of the cells of human body, that are spread, fixated and stained on a slide. It represents the routine work of cytotechnicians and pathologists and involves the visual observation of various cellular structures, and their description in terms of quantity, size, shape, colour, opacity or texture. Cytotechnicians are responsible for assuming the first phase of cytological examination, so-called screening phase, while the second phase, so-called reviewing phase, is assumed by a trained cytopathologist. The aim of the first phase is to select and mark a few fields and/or cells of interest, to be reviewed by the cytopathologist for final diagnosis. Microscopic examination implies handling a variety of informations, including patient clinical records, sample type and staining quality, previously selected fields and current diagnosis hypothesis ; it further implies a rigourous approach to specimen investigation.

Growing attention is now focused on the quality of cytopathological examination, which takes priority over speed, especially in routine work such as screening for cervical cancer [4, 5]. The development of computer technologies has led to a growing number of information processing and management tools : image analysis tools have been introduced in cytopathology to complete morphological analysis with quantitative information [6] ; patient data may also be accessed and managed through dedicated information systems. A growing number of qualitative and quantitative information are therefore available, which is a matter of increasing the cognitive efforts that are necessary to handle, retrieve and fuse them mentally. There is thus a need for dedicated information systems able to assist the user in the processing and management of information.

### 2.2 HOME System Design [1, 7]

A number of image analysis systems are commercially available for measurement on biological specimens. The acquisition of diagnostically relevant information with these systems is often labour-intensive, time-consuming, and poorly correlated with the conventional pathologist's knowledge and practice : the user must switch permanently from microscope to computer, to locate relevant information and then to carry out the required measurement operations. Usually, this cycle must be repeated many times to obtain a statistically representative value for the overall specimen. The feasibility of direct interfacing between microscope and computer has been studied in the framework of the HOME project, in order to bridge the gap between conventional practice in pathology and sophisticated cytometry and histometry technology : the purpose is to combine human observation at the optical microscope and any computer facility in a single interactive microscope workstation.

The appearance of the HOME prototype workstation is that of a conventional microscope : the attached mouse is the only device suggesting the presence of a computer, no conventional computer keyboard nor video monitoring is necessary to work under HOME. The microscope is equipped with a video input at the entrance of camera lucida optical pathway to project a high-resolution computer display onto the image seen through the microscope eyepieces. The hand-driven stage is equipped with encoders that enable the computer to read the current position of the stage at any time ; a dedicated slide clip is provided to ensure the accuracy and reproducibility of slide positioning and repositioning. A magnetic objective turret encoder enables the computer system to automatically adapt the display scale to the objective in use and to record, whenever useful, which objective has been used and where during observation of a slide. HOME functions are accessed by clicking on appropriate dialogue boxes and icons displayed in the observation field : there is no need for the observer to look up from the microscope.

### 2.3 Screening and Reviewing Assistance

Examining a cytologic specimen through the HOME workstation may be divided into general purpose and specific screening and reviewing tasks. User code and case reference are entered first, which makes patient's clinical information available to the user. Screening and reviewing functions are accessed afterwards by clicking on the corresponding icons in the menu.

During screening, the cytotechnician examines the slides as usual, changing magnification and marking objects of interest whenever necessary. The marking of objects is performed simply by clicking with the mouse : different kinds of marks may be used, and marking style may be customized for each laboratory. Any mark can be deleted by double clicking. A double click elsewhere calls up an icon of the slide providing a global view on mark locations, which allows the user to control scanning completion ; any marked field may then be relocated at any time under the objective. The diagnosis is entered at the end through specific dialogue boxes. Reviewing is performed by the pathologist on cases submitted by the cytotechnicians. Pathologist's work is not different in nature from that of cytotechnicians : the specific difference is that informations about the cytotechnician's examination may be accessed at any time by clicking on a specific icon. The work of cytotechnicians and pathologists is stored separately in the system file.

During recent years attention has been focused on screening quality. Many kind of errors can occur, at any step, in the complex sequence of sampling, preparing, observing and reporting about a case. The HOME workstation addresses the mere observation and reporting steps. Such system should potentially increase the effectiveness, consistency and standardization of the reporting process.

## 3 Background

The aim of our work is to supervise the activity of a human operator at a computerized workstation. Such work lies at the frontier between cognitive ergonomy and qualitative reasoning, since it has to deal with modelling and control of user behaviour.

### 3.1 Cognitive Ergonomy

The objectives behind the design of sophisticated man-machine interfaces are twofold : to reduce the distance between men and machines, while encouraging the human creativity and motivation. Preliminary efforts have concentrated on requirements such as behaving friendly to the user, or revealing easy to use : the challenging issue in other words was to reduce the distance between men and machines. More recent work promotes the concept of "autonomy", by conceiving computer systems as agents able to adapt dynamically to the user needs, and even to predict the needs and intentions of the user.

Various models for man-machine interaction have been considered during the last decades : modelling human as information processing systems, from a very physical point of view, has early been introduced through the Model Human Processor [8]. Other attempts have been to model the mental activities and physical actions that are involved in the process of communication as a succession of states to be reached, or in other words to model human as a sequential automata. A major attempt has then been made to model communication as a distance to be covered, thus coping with potential user difficulties. Modelling communication as a model-based process [9] has been one major contribution in this area, by proposing to distinguish between the user's conceptual model (user's interpretation of the system image) and the system's model (model of the user that is built by the system). Modelling the interaction as a knowledge-based process has also been considered : to transmit a mental concept, any "actor" willing to communicate has successively to transcribe it into semantical, syntactical and lexical representations, before executing the action that yields the physical transcription of that concept onto the screen [10]. The notion of cognitive compatibility has finally been introduced [11], thus pointing out the necessity to care about the profile, current knowledge or mental state of a user, as well as to display a coherent set of functionalities, regarding the user expectations.

Recent lines of research address the notion of adaptivity : it is claimed in fact that computer systems should be responsive and adaptive to the changing needs of the user, and that adaptability should be differentiated from customisation. Embedded user models have been proposed as a way to design systems offering adaptive functionality [12] ; they are a class of user model holding information about user characteristics or about the behaviour of an individual when using an interactive computer system. In contrast to other "mental" models or "designers" models, which are intangible and implicit, EUMs are explicit representations of user features and decisions, and can be considered as part of system software. While attempts are made to use "classical" mental models to predict user performance and user preference with different interaction techniques [13], EUMs allow the dynamic adaptation of the system interface to the user needs. Plan recognition may also be used as a further technique to identify the user's intention by means of a formal method for analyzing actions [14]. The computer, according to this of approach, is considered as an intelligent agent, a collaborator able to assist the user in performing a task.

The aim is then to design a system able to assist the user in the execution of a task, and able to adapt dynamically to its needs. Our purpose is to go further in man-machine assistance, since it is to design a system providing simultaneously low level tools to assist task execution and high-level supervision of human activity. Low level tools are provided by the HOME system, in terms of facilities to mark, locate and analyze cells. High level supervision is supported by the so-called "Watch Dog" system, a system controlling the quality of human activity in a transparent way. The Watch Dog system moreover offers high-level modelling of human behaviour, together with navigation tools to access the various features of its activity. The navigation tool plays the role of an "auxiliary memory", which is used to recover missing information, thus reducing the cognitive load of the user by offering a synthetical presentation of all activities and results.

## 3.2 Qualitative Reasoning

The aim of research in qualitative reasoning is to understand and reproduce the human reasoning on physical systems. The basic establishment underlying this work is that neither mathematic model nor precise numerical values are used by human to understand the global functioning of systems ; mere "qualitative reasoning" on the contrary is used by him to predict, control or adjust system behaviour [15]. The fundamental issue in qualitative reasoning is the derivation and use of understandable models of system functioning, that have to take into account the essence of a phenomena, while preserving effective predictive power.

Microscopic and macroscopic modelling levels are usually distinguished in Physics. Microscopic level is made of a set of variables : the elementary entities of the model. Macroscopic level is meant to describe the system structure and determine how the elementary variables interact. As in Physics, qualitative variables are introduced as basic entities for qualitative modelling : such variables however take their values in finite symbol sets. Qualitative structural descriptions are proposed for macroscopic modelling.

There are three principal approaches to qualitative structural description [15, 16]. In the first, represented by B. Kuipers, the description is issued from a simple transcription in qualitative language of the differential equations driving the system running. In the second, represented by J. De Kleer, the system is viewed as an assembling of interconnected components; system functioning is deduced from the description of these components and their interconnecting. For F. Forbus finally, the physical world is driven by processes that act on objects and can potentially modify their characteristics, and even provoke the appearing / disappearing of objects.

Such model may help understanding human behaviour at the microscope : a variety of objects are to be handled in fact, such as slides, fields, cells, marks, or diagnosis hypotheses, to which various properties are attached. The objects are viewed at a given time in a given state : an event may be seen as informative, or a diagnosis hypothesis as consistent. Actions finally modify the objects, by giving rise to new events (specimen exploration) or new diagnosis hypotheses (diagnosis formulation).

Other objects, and other actions should however be considered to model the human behaviour and functioning "deeply", in its complexity : various contextual factors in fact play a role in increasing or decreasing the human ability to process the objects correctly, by blurring or not its perception of reality. Deep cognitive modelling has to be proposed to this end.

# 4 Towards a Deep Modelling of Human Activity

## 4.1 Deep vs Shallow Task Models

The GOMS model [8] has been introduced to analyse tasks of human-computer interaction in the field of text editing : it provides a designing methodology but remains an approach restricted to performance evaluation. A cognitive activity is described by four terms: goal, operator, method and selection. A goal is defined as a hierarchical symbolic structure (set of states), while an operator represents an elementary action (cognitive, perceptual, or motor) applied sequentially to change the system or user state. A method allows to define how to reach a state by means of a conditional action plan and a selection provides a mean to select among methods achieving similar goals. GOMS may thus be considered as a purely behaviourist model, modelling the human activity merely as a linear and error process. Main criticism to the approach is that it refers to natural language theory rather than modelling cognitive processes [17].

A growing interest is devoted to deep cognitive modelling : it is defined as involving causal knowledge at increasing levels of detail, together with information about the underlying structure and behaviour of the system, and pointers to other types of knowledge associated with causal knowledge [18]. Such model would represent a deep understanding of human behaviour, rather than reducing to a collection of "pattern-action" rules [19].

### 4.2 Toward a Deep Task Model

The purpose of this paragraph is to examine the task model that is needed to model and control work performed under HOME by cytotechnicians and cytopathologists. Screening and reviewing tasks, as already mentioned, are submitted to a variety of contextual factors that may influence the way the input data is viewed and processed by the human. A new task model is thus proposed (figure 1), so-called "Deep Task Model", which takes into account not only the input and output to a task, but also considers three Contextual Factors : Case Factors (diagnosis hypothesis, or slide quality), Working Factors (time spent per event, or specimen exploration strategy) and Human Factors (individual background, or daily workload).

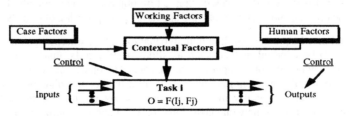

**Fig. 1.** Deep Task Model.

Some of these factors act positively by contributing to the creation of a powerful mental context, resulting in a facilitation of work, while others act negatively by provoking mental confusions or omissions, thus impairing work quality. To be more precise, negative influence may be considered to eliminate relevant informations from the working memory of the individual, or modify their appearance, confidence degree or truth value, thus resulting in a shift of the mental model at hand. "Positive" parameters act by enhancing the mental model available to process a situation, while "negative" parameters act by blurring this model. The apparent "distance" between mental model and reality is reduced in the first case, and augmented in the second situation.

Our purpose may now be stated more precisely : it is to derive a contextual representation of human activity that would allow context-based analysis of work performance as well as context-based assistance, by refreshing contextual informations as often as necessary.

## 4.3 Toward a Deep Modelling of Human Activity

Such approach is based on the assumption that problem solving may be seen as the process of finding the mental model closest to reality. It is proposed that such model be seen as the combination of case, task and human models, as described below. These models are defined as object-based hierarchies, sharing a common root node. These hierarchies are interrelated, to support flexible navigation processes. Some redundancy may however be introduced, to avoid swapping too frequently from one hierarchy to the other.

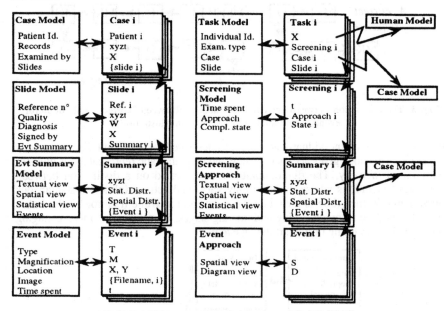

**Fig. 2** : Rough sketch of (a) the case model hierarchy and (b) the task model hierarchy.

A rough sketch of the case model hierarchy is provided in figure 2a. The root node (Case Model node) provides general information about the case under interest and gives access to the corresponding slide set. The Slide Model node involves features describing each slide (quality, diagnostic, detected events). The Event Summary Model node entails global properties about event sets, under textual, statistical or spatial form. Each event may then be accessed through the Event Model node, which describes its type, location, magnification used and time spent. Access to an external image file may also be provided.

A rough sketch of the task model hierarchy is provided in figure 2b. The root node (Task Model node) gives access to case-based or slide-based activities, for given individuals ; either screening or reviewing activities may be explored. In case of screening activity, the Screening Model node gives information about the time spent, approach (how the slide has been examined) and completion state (percentage area effectively explored for example) of the activity. Approach as well as completion state may be examined under textual, statistical or spatial representations, as specified by the Screening Approach Node.

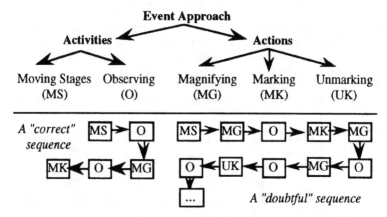

**Fig. 3.** The distinction between activities and actions, between "correct" and "doubtful" event examination approaches : an illustration

Each event may be individually accessed, as described by the Event Approach node (figure 3). This node gives access to spatial and diagrammatic representations of event exploitation activity. The diagrammatic view is based on a distinction between activities (operations whose duration may vary) and actions (almost instantaneous operations). In fact, time is meaningful for the former, while it is not for the latter. By activities, we mean observing and moving stages. By actions, we mean changing the objectives, marking or unmarking an event.

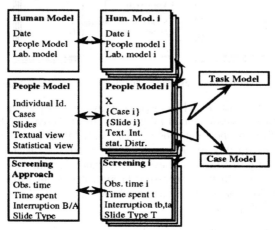

**Fig.4.** Rough sketch of the Human Model hierarchy.

A rough sketch of the Human Model hierarchy is provided in figure 4. The root node (Human Model node) gives access to the date, and to two sub-hierarchies, describing respectively the People and Laboratory Models. People Model node gives information about individual workloads, in terms of cases and/or slides examined. These informations may be accessed in textual or statistical form. Each slide may then be accessed separately, through the Slide Workload node : this node gives information about the time of observation, the time spent, the slide type and the interruptions that have preceded or followed its examination.

Interrelations between hierarchies are outlined in figure 2(b) and figure 4 : referring to any slide number, for example, gives access to any of its description in the Case, Task or Human Model hierarchies. Instances of these models are shown on the right part of the figures. These instances may be used to describe current observations of the Watch Dog Supervisor, but also to store reference models, specifying working standards at the laboratory or individual level.

## 5 Navigation System : Design and Functions

### 5.1 System Design

The system architecture is displayed in figure 5. The Watch Dog system is implemented in C and runs under UNIX on a SONY workstation. Graphical programming is performed under Motif/X11 environment. Communication in delayed time is currently implemented with the HOME system by means of structured files. Real time communication will be realized in a near future, by means of RS232 interface in a first step ; communication through Ethernet network will be used in a second step.

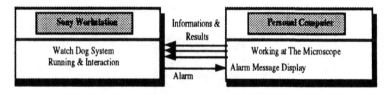

**Fig. 5.** Watch Dog system architecture.

### 5.2 System Functions

The role of the Watch Dog function is to transparently model, and control, the work being done by a cytotechnician or pathologist. It may be operated in two different modes : the quiet mode or the alarm mode. A detailed work model is elaborated under the first mode, in a transparent way ; this model may then be exploited by various functions, from mere navigation to intelligent tutoring. When placed in alarm mode, the system has moreover the ability to compare the model that is currently elaborated to reference models, previously stored under the Archiving function. Alarms are triggered in case of detected differences. Current model as well as reference models may be accessed at any time, in any mode, to recall current contextual elements.

The role of the Navigation function is to serve self validation purposes by assisting the exploration of current or reference working models. Various ancillary tools may be accessed, if necessary to modify the presentation style : graphical or textual appearance, level of detail of the presentation, for example. Other tools allow the computation of a variety of characteristics, among which statistical description, thus providing the possibility to synthetic information over several working models, and eventually compare them. Interaction style is illustrated in figure 6 and 7 : a Hypercard metaphor is used as a mean to facilitate navigation. Three card hierarchies are implemented, called namely Case, Task and Human hierarchies.

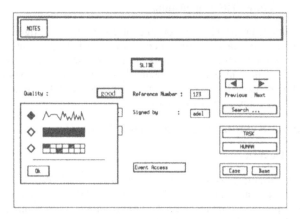

**Fig. 6.** The navigation system ; (a) a view of the Slide card (Case hierarchy)

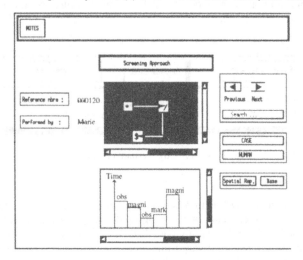

**Fig. 7.** The navigation system ; a view of the Event Approach card (Task hierarchy).

A "Slide" card is shown in figure 6 : this card belongs to the Case hierarchy, and gives information about the slide quality and diagnosis. A button allows to access the event summary. This card may be presented according to one of the three presentation style : statistical (statistics about event type frequency for example), textual (short comment), or graphical (visualization of the events location and type). Various means are provided to navigate among informations : other slides may be accessed in a sequential way (previous and next buttons), or through associative retrieval (search button) ; the root of the case hierarchy, as well as the base card may be accessed at any time ; corresponding information in the task and human hierarchies may also be obtained (slide exploration strategy, or global observation time, for example).

The "Screening Approach" card is shown in figure 7. It gives a view of the screening approach, at the event level. The event location on the slide is represented in the middle window, together with the preceding and succeeding events that have been observed. Each of these events has been denoted by a different mark type. The diagrammatic representation below gives a view of the sequence of activities and actions that have been undertaken, together with the time spent on each.

# 6 Conclusion

This paper has described current research on computerized assistance to cytological specimen exploration, as performed under the HOME workstation. The purpose is to design a system able to supervise the human expert in the execution of specimen exploration task. Deep cognitive modeling of human behaviour has been proposed to this end, based on a context-sensitive task model. The model involves three interrelated hierarchies describing case factors, working factors and human factors. A navigation system has been presented, which allows the easy access to information stored in these hierarchies. Such approach is currently extended for quality control purposes. It will also be applied in a near future to the design of an intelligent tutoring system for cytopathology.

Tutoring system would act as a superset of Watch Dog system, its role being basically to model the trainee's work, and facilitate its evaluation. The alarm mode would be used to alarm dynamically the trainee, in case of deviation from reference behaviour, while quiet mode would be used for self-evaluation purposes. Two different tutoring modes would then be distinguished, namely supervised and unsupervised. The first mode would correspond to the trainee being shown the way to approach a task, giving rise to the progressive elaboration of a reference model. This reference model may then be used in supervised mode, as if repeating several times the same exercise. In unsupervised mode, on the contrary, the work is performed in quiet mode, and evaluated afterwards.

### Acknowledgements

The project was partially funded by the Commission of the European Communities under its Advanced Informatics in Medicine (AIM) action, contract A 1007. The authors wish to express their indebtedness to the members of the HOME consortium, and particularly to Pr. G. Brugal, Dr. B. Krief, Dr. A. Morens and D.Adelh (Grenoble, France), Pr. G. Slavin (London, United Kingdom) and Pr. Vooijs (Nijmegen, the Netherlands), Pr. Tucker and Dr. Duvall (Edinburgh, United Kingdom), Dr. Faltermeier and Dr. Kohlhaas (Oberkochen, Germany).

# References

1. G. Brugal, R. Dye, B. Krief, J.M. Chassery, H. Tanke and J.H. Tucker : HOME : Highly Optimized Microscope Environment. Cytometry, Vol. 13, pp. 109:116 (1992).

2. Bartels & al. : Expert Systems in Histopathology, AQCH 11(1):1-7 (1989)

3. Ovalle, A. & Garbay, C. : KIDS, a Distributed Expert System for Biomedical Image Interpretation. 12th International Conference on IPMI, pp. 419-433. Colchester et Hawkes (Eds), Springer-Verlag (1991)

4. Cowan, D.F. : Quality assurance in anatomic pathology : an information system approach, Arch. Pathol. Lab. Med. 114:129-134, (1990).

5. Travers, H. : Quality assurance indicators in anatomic pathology, Arch. Pathol. Lab. Med. 114:1149-1156, (1990).

6. Baak, JPA : Quantitative pathology today, A technical reiew. Pathol Res Pract 182 : 396_400, (1987).

7. Morens, A., Krief, B. & Brugal, G. : The HOME Microscope Workstation : a new tool for cervical cancer screening, AQCH Vol. 14(4):289-294, (1992).

8. Card, S., Moran, T. & Newell, A. : The Psychology of Human Computer Interaction, Lawrence Erlbaum Associates Publish., (1983).

9. Norman, D.A. & Draper, S.W. : User Centered System Design. Lawrence Erlbaum Assiocates Publ. (1986).

10. Schneiderman, B. : Designing the User Interface : Strategies for Effective Human-Computer Interaction. Addison Wesley Publishing Company, 1987.

11. Streitz, N.A. : Cognitive compatibility as a central issue in human-computer interaction : theoretical framework and empirical findings. In "Cognitive Engineering in the Design of Human-Computer Interaction and Expert Systems", (G. Salvendy, eds), Elsevier Science Publ., pp. 75-82, (1987).

12. Murray, D. : Modelling for Adaptivity, In "Mental Models and Human-Computer Interaction 2", (M.J. Tauber & D. Ackerman, eds), Elsevier Science Publishers B.V., (North Holland), pp.81-95, (1991).

13. Metzler, C., Wetzenstein-Ollenschlager, E. & Wandke H. : How to predict user performance and user preference with different interaction techniques, In "Mental Models and Human-Computer Interaction 2", (M.J. Tauber & D. Ackerman, eds), Elsevier Science Publishers B.V., (North Holland), pp. 201-224, (1991).

14. Desmarais, M.C., Giroux, L. & Larochelle S. : Plan recognition in HCI : the parsing of user actions, In "Mental Models and Human-Computer Interaction 2", (M.J. Tauber & D. Ackerman, eds), Elsevier Science Publishers B.V., (North Holland), pp. 291-311, (1991).

15. Page, M. : Systèmes Experts à Base de Connaissances Profondes -Application à un Poste de Travail "Intelligent" Pour le Comptable, Thèse de Doctorat de l'Institut National Polytechnique de Grenoble, (1990).

16. Raoult, O. : Diagnostic de Pannes Des Systemes Complexes, Thèse de Doctorat de l'Institut National Polytechnique de Grenoble (France), specialité Informatique, Février (1989).

17. Udo Arend : Analysing Complex Tasks with an Extended GOMS Model, Mental Models and Human Computer Interaction 2, M.J. Tauber and D. Ackermann, Elsevier Science Publishers B.V. (North Holland), pp 115-133, (1991).

18. Chandrasekaran, B., Smith, J.W. and Sticklen, J. : Deep models and their relation to diagnosis. Artificial Intelligence in Medicine, 1/29-40, (1989).

19. Chandrasekaran, B. and Mittal, S. : Deep vs compiled knowledge approaches to diagnostic problem solving. Int. J. Man-Machine Studies, 19:425:436, (1983).

# Locating the primary attention focus of the user

Matthias Rauterberg & Christian Cachin

Work and Organisational Psychology Unit, Swiss Federal Institute of Technology (ETH)
Nelkenstrasse 11, CH-8092 ZURICH
rauterberg@ezrz1.vmsmail.ethz.ch

**Abstract.** First, a signal detection experiment was carried out to estimate the maximal distance between the primary attention focus of users and the screen position of visual feedback (e.g. messages). The results indicate that the maximal distance between the primary attention focus and the position of visual feedback should not exceed 3". Second, to pinpoint the location of the primary attention focus we carried out an eye movement recording experiment. The results indicate that if the task solving process requires mouse operations and the visual feedback of the results of these mouse operations appears close to the mouse cursor, then the visual focus and the mouse cursor position on the screen are highly correlated: between 76% and 95% correspondence.

**Keywords:** primary attention focus, visual focus, mouse control, visual feedback, user interface, design.

## 1  Introduction

One important problem in interface design is making appropriate design decisions regarding the positioning of visual feedback on the screen (e.g. messages, alert boxes, hints, pop up menus, icons, etc.). While highlighting techniques can aid the user in locating important messages, it is not always possible to predict what may be important to the user at a given time.

The traditional solution is a mask layout that allows the user to" easily" find any of the information on it by adopting a consistent format for all masks of a character user interface (CUI). Following the guidelines of [1] and [2] the screen layout looks as follows:
(1) the top line contains the screen title, time of day, and product name;
(2) the second line contains a command input field;
(3) the third line contains a list of the commands that are currently valid;
(4) the middle part of the screen contains the work area (e.g. output area for menus, data lists, data entry forms, etc.);
(5) messages appears in the bottom two lines.
This mask layout has been empirically "verified" (e.g. [10], [11]). One problem with these kinds of empirical studies is the experimental control group condition: both studies compared structured and consistent mask layouts on the one hand with accidentally arranged mask layouts on the other hand. Under these specific circumstances it is very probable, that each kind of 'structured' conditions is better than a total 'unstructured' condition.

The following design decision tries to overcome this problem in the context of the design of graphic user interfaces (GUIs): important messages appears in the centre of the screen (see [8]). This solution minimises the distance between the unknown locus of the primary attention focus of the user and the locus of the message on the screen.

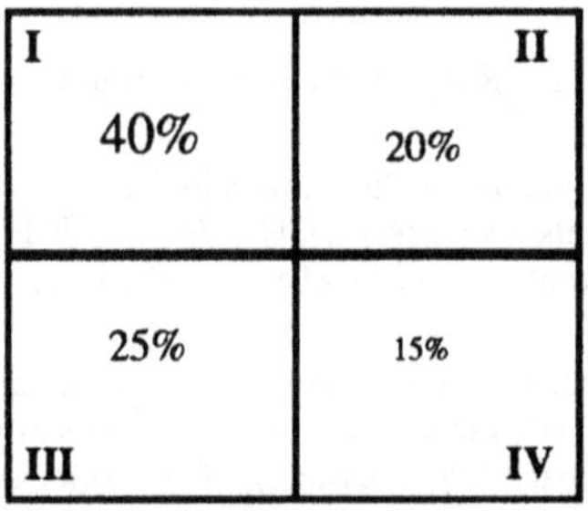

| I         |          | II     |
|-----------|----------|--------|
| 40%       | 20%      |        |
| 25%       | 15%      |        |
| III       |          | IV     |

Figure 1. The relative ratios of the user's visual focus looking expectantly on one of the four quadrants of a dark and unstructured screen [9].

What is an *optimal* screen layout is till now the open and unanswered question. Where is the *best* place to put messages on the screen? How far away from the primary attention focus should the message be? To answer these questions, first we carried out a 'signal detection experiment'. From the literature [9] we know that the main area of expectation (40%) is in the left upper quadrant I of a dark and unstructured screen. The visual focus is further on shared by quadrant III (25%) and quadrant II (20%). In 15% of observation time the attention focus is in quadrant IV (see Figure 1). First, we carried out a signal detection experiment to estimate the maximal distance between the primary attention focus of users and the screen position of visual feedback (e.g. messages) regarding to the four screen quadrants. Second, we investigated the eye movements to pinpoint the actual location of the primary attention focus of the user on the screen regarding to different task's types.

## 2 Signal Detection Experiment

One major determinant of both the context and the quality of perception is *attention*. Foley and Moray [4] present a list that at least the following variables play a role in controlling dynamic visual attention:
(1) the rate at which the display varies: the greater the bandwidth, the more frequently is the display sampled;
(2) the value of the information: the more the information is worth, the more frequently the display is sampled;
(3) the cost of observation: the more costly an observation, the less frequently is the display sampled;
(4) forgetting: as time elapses since the last observation, the user becomes less certain of the value of the observed information even if it varies only slightly or not at all;
(5) the coupling between displays.
We proved aspect (2) and (3) with the dimension 'signal type' as a value indicator and with the dimension 'distance' as a cost indicator in this signal detection experiment.

## 2.1 Subjects

Eleven women and 8 men took part in the experiment (mean age: $33 \pm 14$ years). 12 subjects were students of computer science at the ETH.

## 2.2 Tasks

Subjects were introduced to solve two tasks: the primary task was 'counting a small set of circles' (6 – 10 elements) presented in one of the four screen corners (visible: 1000 ms; area: 2.5" x 2.0"), and the secondary task was 'detecting an X' (see Figure 2).

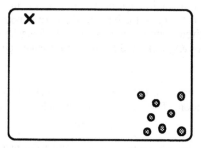

Figure 2. An example screen with 8 circles in quadrant IV and an X signal in quadrant I in the 'large distance' condition.

To control the perception of the semantic of the signal we presented two different signs: an X and a square of the same size. One of the two signals appeared after 500 ms of circle presentation time and was visible for the duration of 500 ms along with the circles (see Figure 3). The subjects were requested to respond only to the X signal. The attention focus of the users was controlled by the primary task.

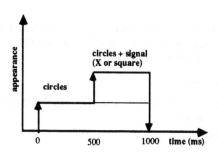

Figure 3. The time structure of the signal presentation.

## 2.3 Procedure

We have a nested test design, because the factor A and C are only possible for the signal type 'X' and 'square':

Factor A 'distance' (D) between primary attention focus and signal (inside 0",
small 0"-3", medium 3"-6", large 6"-9") – the factor A was only varied
for the signal type 'square sign' and 'X sign';

Factor B 'signal type' (19 masks with 'no signal'; 19 masks with a 'square' sign [8
mm x 8 mm]; 19 masks with an 'X' sign [8 mm x 8 mm]);

Factor C 'screen quadrant' of circle output (top left [tl], top right [tr], bottom left
[bl], bottom right [br]).

Each user saw overall 682 different masks (individual session).

## 2.4 Material

We ran the experiment on an IBM compatible PC (Olivetti M386) with a colour
screen (VGA, 14"). A special program was developed in MacMETHModula to
present the signals on the screen. Each subject saw 16 masks with circles and an X
sign, 16 masks with circles and a square sign, and 16 masks with circles only. We
randomised the order of all masks and number of presented circles.

## 2.5 Measures

Three dependent measures are used in this study: (1) 'signal deviation', (2) 'error
ratio', (3) 'circle deviation'. The signal detection table (see Table 1) is the basis of
measure (1) and (2).

Table 1. The 'signal detection table' with the 'a', 'b', 'c' and 'd' as names of the four
different cells.

|  |  | NO X SIGN (nothing or square) | X SIGN PRESENTED |
|---|---|---|---|
| answer of the subject | NO | a | b |
|  | YES | c | d |

The investigator protocolled the number of counted circles and the subjects' answer
whether he or she had seen an X. The 'signal deviation' (XD) estimates the quality
of the secondary task ('detection of an X'):

$$XD = |\#X_{detected} - \#X_{presented}| \qquad (1)$$

XD is zero for all cases in cell 'a' and 'd'. The 'error ratio' (ER) is based on the 'signal
detection table' (see Table 1).

$$ER = (b + c) / (a + d) * 100\% \qquad (2)$$

Cell 'b' contains the number of 'overlooked signals'; cell 'c' contains the 'false alarms'
and/or 'misinterpretations' of the 'square sign'.

The 'circle deviation' (CD) rate is a measure of the accuracy of the primary task
('counting of circles'):

$$CD = |\#CIRCLES_{counted} - \#CIRCLES_{presented}| * 100\% / \#CIRCLES_{presented} \qquad (3)$$

CD is an independent measure of the absolute number of presented circles. With CD we can control the extent to which the users concentrate on the primary task solving process.

## 2.6 Results and Discussion

To analyse the data with a full factorial analysis of variance we computed the analysis only for masks with an X or a square sign (N=608). No detection errors ('false alarms') occurred at all in the signal type condition 'no signal' (N=76). We decided to exclude these data from the analysis of variance of XD. So, the results of XD are based on a full factorial analysis of variances.

The factor A 'distance' of the dependent variable XD is significant (N=152, $XD_0$"= 6%; N=152, $XD_3$"=11%; N=152, $XD_6$"= 27%; N=152, $XD_9$"= 43%; p≤.001, see Table 2). It is interesting to note that the factor B 'signal type' is not significant (N=304, $XD_x$= 23% 'overlooked'; and N=304, $XD_{square}$=20% 'misinterpreted'; p≤ .343, see Table 2). This result indicates that users have on average the same problems to detect an X independent of the semantic of the signal type.

Table 2. Results of the full factorial analysis of variance of the dependent variable XD (all masks of signal type 'no signal' are excluded).

| Source | df | $\Sigma$ of $^2$ | means$^2$ | F test | p |
|---|---|---|---|---|---|
| A distance | 3 | 12.847 | 4.282 | 29.001 | .001 |
| B signal type | 1 | .133 | .133 | .902 | .343 |
| C quadrant | 3 | .176 | .059 | .397 | .755 |
| A x B | 3 | 1.308 | .436 | 2.952 | .032 |
| A x C | 9 | 1.410 | .157 | 1.061 | .390 |
| B x C | 3 | .926 | .309 | 2.090 | .100 |
| A x B x C | 9 | .923 | .103 | .694 | .714 |
| error | 576 | 85.053 | .148 | | |

Table 3. Results of the full factorial analysis of variance of the dependent variable CD (all masks of signal type 'no signal' are excluded).

| Source | df | $\Sigma$ of $^2$ | means$^2$ | F test | p |
|---|---|---|---|---|---|
| A distance | 3 | 251.12 | 83.73 | 1.063 | .364 |
| B signal type | 1 | .75 | .75 | .010 | .922 |
| C quadrant | 3 | 611.02 | 203.67 | 2.585 | .052 |
| A x B | 3 | 74.46 | 24.82 | .315 | .815 |
| A x C | 9 | 898.18 | 99.80 | 1.267 | .252 |
| B x C | 3 | 119.16 | 39.72 | .504 | .680 |
| A x B x C | 9 | 267.31 | 29.70 | .377 | .946 |
| error | 576 | 45387. | 78.80 | | |

The factor C 'screen quadrant' of the dependent variable XD is not significant, too (N=152, $XD_{tl}$=22%; N=152, $XD_{tr}$= 19%; N=152, $XD_{br}$= 24%; N=152, $XD_{bl}$=21%; p≤.755, see Table 2). The interaction term (A x B, see Table 2) is significant (N=76, $XD_{0'',X}$= 4%; N=76, $XD_{0'',square}$= 8%; N=76, $XD_{3'',X}$=13%; N=76, $XD_{3'',square}$= 8%; N=76, $XD_{6'',X}$=24%; N=76, $XD_{6'',square}$=30%; N=76, $XD_{9'',X}$= 51%; N=76, $XD_{9'',square}$=34%; p≤.032, see Table 2). This result is primarily caused by the difference between the average $XD_{9'',X}$=51% and $XD_{9'',square}$=34% in the large distance (9") condition. The user's have significantly more problems to detect an X sign in the large distance condition than to misinterpret a square sign as an X.

The significant effect 'quadrant' of the variable CD (p≤.052, see Table 3) means that the primary task 'counting circles' is differently influenced by the secondary task 'detecting an X'. One can observe the greatest relative deviation between presented and counted circles (CD) in quadrant II and III (see Figure 4). In quadrant II the user must look 'left-down', in quadrant III he has to look 'right-up' to detect an X. Quadrant IV contains the lowest deviation of CD. It seems to be the easiest way for the user to look 'left-up' to detect a small signal (e.g. see Figure 2).

| I | II |
|---|---|
| CD=6.1% | CD=6.8% |
| CD=6.9% | CD = 4.4% |
| III | IV |

Figure 4. The average of CD of each screen quadrant (see the significant effect 'quadrant' in Table 3).

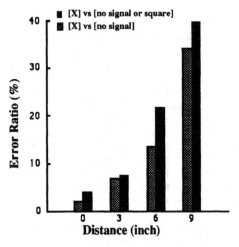

Figure 5. The error ratio (ER) plotted against the distance (D).

Overlooking an X or misinterpreting a square as an X (see Figure 5) causes the maximal detected perception errors (ER). As we can see in Figure 5 and Table 4, the error rate increases rapidly with the distance. The number of overlooked X's (cell 'b') increases between distance 0" and 3" by a factor of 3. The number of misinterpreted squares and false alarms (cell 'c') increases between distance 3" and 6" by a factor of 4.

Table 4. Contents of the cells of the 'signal detection table' and the 'error ratio' (ER). Cell 'a' and 'c' contain all cases with 'no signal' or a 'square signal'.

```
            +-----+----+----+-----+------+
            |  a  |  b |  c |  d  |  ER  |
------------+-----+----+----+-----+------+
distance 0" | 146 |  3 |  6 | 73  | 4.1  |
------------+-----+----+----+-----+------+
distance 3" | 146 | 10 |  6 | 66  | 7.5  |
------------+-----+----+----+-----+------+
distance 6" | 129 | 18 | 23 | 58  | 21.9 |
------------+-----+----+----+-----+------+
distance 9" | 126 | 39 | 26 | 37  | 39.8 |
------------+-----+----+----+-----+------+
on average  | 319 | 70 | 61 | 234 | 23.7 |
------------+-----+----+----+-----+------+
```

Compared with XD (see Table 2) the values of ER are slightly different. The reduced sample for the analysis of variance of the dependent variable XD causes this difference.

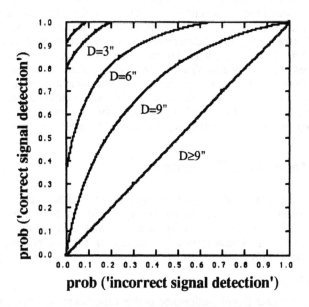

Figure 6. The 'receiver operating characteristics' (ROC) diagram regarding to Table 4. The ROC depends of the distance D.

The 'receiver operating characteristics' (ROC, see [3] and [7]) of the average user as a 'receiver' is based on the content of the 'signal detection table' (see Table 4). The probabilities prob('incorrect detection')=c/(a+c) and prob('correct detection')= d/(b+d) are calculated for each distance condition. If the 'receiver' ignores the signal and guesses, then the point describing his behaviour will fall on the diagonal running ('chance line') from the origin to the upper right-hand corner. The quality of the detection task can be estimated with a ROC diagram (see Figure 6). If different signals are easily discriminated by the 'receiver', the ROC will leave the origin with a steep slope, and it will deviate considerably from the chance line. The closer the signal is to the attention focus of the user, the better is the discriminating power.

Table 5. Contents of the cells of the 'signal detection table' and the 'error rate' (ER). Cell 'a' and 'c' contain all cases with 'no signal'; only 'false alarms' were possible.

```
              +-----+----+----+-----+------+
              |  a  |  b |  c |  d  |  ER  |
--------------+-----+----+----+-----+------+
distance  0"  | 76  |  0 |  3 | 73  | 2.0  |
--------------+-----+----+----+-----+------+
distance  3"  | 76  | 10 |  0 | 66  | 7.0  |
--------------+-----+----+----+-----+------+
distance  6"  | 76  | 18 |  0 | 58  | 13.4 |
--------------+-----+----+----+-----+------+
distance  9"  | 76  | 39 |  0 | 37  | 34.5 |
--------------+-----+----+----+-----+------+
on average    | 76  | 70 |  0 | 234 | 22.6 |
--------------+-----+----+----+-----+------+
```

Most perceptual errors are false alarms (see Figure 5 and Table 5). If the signal appears 6" far away from the attention focus of the user, then the error ratio of 'false alarms' is 13.4% (see Table 5). The error ratio for 'false alarms' and 'misinterpretation' is 21.9% (see Table 4). The difference between these both error ratios is 8.5% and is caused by 'misinterpretations'. To reduce the perceptual uncertainty, the user moves his eyes ('focus of attention') to the screen place, where the appearance of the signal was assumed. What we now need, is a good indicator, which gives the interactive program the information, where the primary attention focus is actually on the screen. If we could find such an indicator, then we are able to present the actual message, feedback, etc. left above of the actual focus on the screen.

## 3 Eye Recording Experiment

In this eye movement recording experiment we have proofed the hypothesis that eye movements correlate with mouse cursor movements. To do this we carried out an eye movement recording experiment. The main assumption is that the visual focus measured with eye movement recording is an indicator for the primary attention focus of the user [5] [6].

### 3.1 Subjects

A total of six subjects (N=6) participated in this experiment: 2 women and 4 men with the average amount of 2175 hr's ± 1742 hr's of experience with mouse control operating a GUI. Five subjects were students of computer science at the ETH. One subject studied psychology.

## 3.2 Experimental Setting

To overcome the low accuracy using the NAC Eye Mark Recorder IV we projected the PC output with an overhead display on a screen of size 1.1 m x 1.4 m (see Figure 6). The subject with the eye mark recorder sat 1.5 m away from the projection screen. Using this special setting we could reduce the size of the visual angle and by that we increase the solution accuracy of the NAC Eye Mark Recorder. The subject was looking at the projection screen during the whole task solving period; to avoid a decalibration of the NAC camera the subject was instructed not to look down to the mouse device.

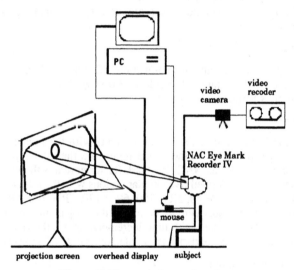

Figure 7. The experimental setting.

## 3.3 Tasks

Subjects were instructed to solve three tasks using the mouse:
- (1) computer game: Reversi (N=4) or Solitaire (N=2);
- (2) text processing (N=6): formatting a given piece of text with the text processing system Write (Windows 3.0); the subject had to read the text to get the right orientation, to select text and appropriate menu options, to press dialogue buttons and to scroll along the 70 lines of the text document;
- (3) hypertext navigation (N=6): the subject had to answer five questions by navigating and searching in the help system of the Microsoft Work program.

Analysing subjects' behaviour solving the three tasks we identified the following sub-tasks:

(1) HYPER     read in hypertext; 'long' click on words or other symbols (≥ 1 s).

(2) ICON     click on icon on the desktop or on button in a dialogue box; click on window frame or ruler.

| | |
|---|---|
| (3) MENU | open a pull down menu, select a menu option and click. |
| (4) POINT | point to dialogue object; double click on icon; set a Reversi stone. |
| (5) SCROLL | scroll in a text window with button or slider. |
| (6) SEARCH | search and look around; all other not classified sub tasks. |
| (7) SELECT | select a piece of text. |
| (8) SOLI | play the game Solitaire. |
| (9) TEXT | normal text reading ($\geq 1$ s). |

### 3.4 Procedure

A one-factorial test design was used. Factor A was the sub task type (HYPER, ICON, MENU, POINT, SCROLL, SEARCH, SELECT, SOLI, TEXT). All subjects had to solve the same three tasks in the same fix order (1. computer game, 2. text processing, 3. hypertext navigation). 135 min. overall task solving time was recorded. 75 min. of this material is appropriate for an evaluation, an average of 12.5 min. per subject.

### 3.5 Material

The experiment was run on an IBM compatible PC (Olivetti M386) with a colour screen (VGA, 14"). The standard Windows 3.0 environment was used with the delivered programs Write and Works.

### 3.6 Measures

To calculate the correlation of the eye movements with the mouse cursor movements the distance (d) between the visual focus and the mouse position on the screen must be measured. The NAC Eye Mark Recorder marks the visual focus as a hooklet on the video. We defined five circular regions with the following radius: 1R = 20, 2R = 40, 3R = 60, 4R = 80, 5R = 100, 6R = 120, 7R = 140, 8R $\geq$ 160 screen pixels. A radius of 1R is equivalent to 50 mm on the projection screen, or 9 mm on the VGA monitor. We counted with time increments of 1 s the frequencies of the mouse cursor in any of these regions (4521 data points over all subjects).

### 3.7 Results and Discussion

The evaluated time of each sub task and the percentage of the total evaluated recording time will be presented first. As we can see in Table 3, the sub tasks HYPER (28.2%), POINT (18.0%) and TEXT (17.5%) are the sub tasks with the largest portion of evaluated task solving time. The number of data points per sub task is equivalent to the number of seconds of the recorded part.

The content of each sub task requires more or less mouse control. Since the subjects could not use a keyboard for task solving, we can only distinguish between (1) mouse operations with visual control, (2) mouse operations without visual control, and (3) visual scanning behaviour without any mouse operations. The following sub tasks incorporate reading and looking around on the projection screen with minor mouse operations: HYPER, SEARCH, and TEXT. These three sub tasks characterise the task solving process during 48.2% of evaluated time. The other sub tasks contain intensive mouse operations: ICON, MENU, POINT, SCROLL, SOLI, and SELECT. These sub tasks are used during 51.8% of evaluated time.

For the sub tasks without mouse operations we found only a low interdependency between eye scanning behaviour and mouse movements: between 24.7% and 69.4% of the data points show the mouse cursor in the region d $\leq$ 4R (see Table 4).

On the other hand, for the sub tasks with mouse intensive operations we found a close correlation between the visual focus and the mouse position: 48.6% - 95.6% of the data points showed the mouse cursor in the region d ≤ 4R (see Table 4).

Table 3. Absolute and relative portions of the sub task's time of total time.

| sub task | eval. time [min. : s] | percentage [%] | number of data points |
|---|---|---|---|
| HYPER | 21:13 | 28.2 | 1273 |
| SEARCH | 1:52 | 2.5 | 112 |
| TEXT | 13:12 | 17.5 | 792 |
| ICON | 2:22 | 3.1 | 142 |
| MENU | 7:28 | 9.9 | 448 |
| POINT | 13:30 | 18.0 | 810 |
| SCROLL | 5:13 | 6.9 | 313 |
| SELECT | 4:09 | 5.5 | 249 |
| SOLI | 6:22 | 8.4 | 382 |
| total | 75:21 | 100.0 | 4521 |

Table 4. The distance between visual focus and mouse cursor position.

| sub task | distance [R] (mean ± SD) | % with d ≤ 2R | % with d ≤ 4R |
|---|---|---|---|
| HYPER | 4.7 ± 4.3 | 42.9 | 69.4 |
| SEARCH | 7.6 ± 5.1 | 21.4 | 37.5 |
| TEXT | 8.5 ± 4.5 | 15.7 | 24.7 |
| ICON | 2.3 ± 2.4 | 73.2 | 92.2 |
| MENU | 2.1 ± 1.4 | 78.6 | 94.2 |
| POINT | 3.0 ± 2.0 | 54.8 | 81.9 |
| SCROLL | 6.6 ± 5.1 | 41.6 | 48.6 |
| SELECT | 2.1 ± 1.3 | 76.3 | 95.6 |
| SOLI | 3.8 ± 3.1 | 42.4 | 76.2 |
| total | 4.7 ± 4.3 | 44.7 | 67.8 |

The sub task SCROLL seems to be an exception because only in 48.6% of the data points lay the mouse cursor nearby the visual focus. If we assume that users observe the content of the text window during 'scrolling' to control the success of the scrolling activity, then we can explain this low dependency; they do not primarily match the slider bar.

# 4 General Discussion and Conclusion

We can conclude from the results of the signal detection experiment' that the position of visual feedback on the screen must be very closed to the primary attention focus of the user. A distance over 3" should be avoided. On large screens (>14") the designer must solve the problem of estimating the actual position of the user's attention focus to avoid many unnecessary eye movements.

The results of the 'signal detection experiment' lead directly to a general design principle: the position of visual feedback must be as close as possible to the primary attention focus of the user. If the interface designer follows this principle, then he can minimise the visual scanning behaviour. The results of the 'eye recording experiment' indicate, that the mouse position is a reliable and valid indicator for the visual attention focus on the screen during mouse operations or mouse intensive tasks. We found that eye movements correlate with mouse cursor movements. If the user works with the keyboard, then we can assume, that the attention focus of the user is nearby the input cursor on the screen. This is probably true for expert users with blind typing ability. If there is no input activity, then the user reads, thinks, etc. For most of these cases the user is in an eye scanning mode, so that feedback in the centre of the screen or in reserved regions gives the user the necessary information without the feeling of being disturbed.

# References

[1]    Burroughs Corporation: InterPro (TM) user interface standards, Version E (March 20, 1986).
[2]    DIN 66 234, Teil 3: Bildschirmarbeitsplätze – Gruppierung und Formatierung von Daten. Beuth Verlag GmbH, Berlin 30, 1981.
[3]    J. P. Egan, F. R. Clarke: Psychophysics and Signal Detection. in: Experimental Methods and Instrumentation in Psychology, J. B. Sidowski , Ed., New York: McGraw Hill, 1966, pp. 211-246.
[4]    P. Foley, N. Moray: Sensation, perception, and systems design. in: Handbook of Human Factors, G. Salvendy, ed., New York: John Wiley, 1987, 45-71.
[5]    R. Groner, P. Fraisse, Eds., Cognition and Eye Movements. Amsterdam: North-Holland, 1980.
[6]    R. Groner, G. d'Ydewalle, R. Parham (Eds.): From Eye to Mind: Information Acquisition in Perception, Search, and Reading. Amsterdam: North-Holland, 1990.
[7]    W. Lee: Decision Theory and Human Behavior. New York: Wiley & Sons, 1971.
[8]    OSF/Motif Style Guide: Open Software Foundation. Englewood Cliffs: Prentice Hall, Revision 1.1, 1991, p. 4/44.
[9]    M. J. Staufer: Piktogramme für Computer. New York: de Gruyter, 1987.
[10]   R. Teitelbaum, R. Granda: The effects of positional constancy on searching menus for information. in: Human Factors in Computing Systems, Proceedings of the CHI'83 Conference, A. Janda, Ed., New York: ACM, 1984, pp. 150-153.
[11]   T. Tullis: The formatting of alphanumeric displays: a review. *Human Factors* 25, 12 (December 1981), 657-682.

# MODIFIER: Improving an End-User Modifiable System Through User Studies

Andreas Girgensohn

NYNEX Science and Technology
500 Westchester Avenue
White Plains, NY 10604, USA
andreasg@nynexst.com

**Abstract.** End-user modifiability allows different users to tailor a system to pursue different tasks, to have different preferences, and to adapt it to changing needs over time. User studies were performed with a system called MODIFIER, an end-user modification component for design environments. These studies helped refine previously hypothesized principles of end-user modifiability and identify new principles. The studies provided new insights about the requirements for system explanations. It also became apparent that system-maintained task agendas and critics can guide users through modification tasks. Unsolved problems were discovered and will be used as a guideline for future research.

## 1 Introduction

End-user modifiable systems support user modifications of systems according to the users' needs. End-user modifiability is necessary because different users pursue different tasks, have different preferences, and have evolving needs or requirements due to changes in the world. The intended users of end-user modifiable systems are knowledgeable in the application domain but unwilling or unable to modify a system at the programming language level.

MODIFIER is the end-user modification component of JANUS, a knowledge-based design environment for kitchen design [4]. Knowledge-based design environments consist of a construction kit that provides a direct-manipulation interface and a domain-oriented palette of design units and critics that critique suboptimal construction situations. JANUS supports the construction of kitchens from domain-oriented building blocks such as appliances. Critics [3] in JANUS apply their design knowledge to critique the designer's partial solutions.

User studies were helpful in improving several prototypes of MODIFIER. General principles for achieving end-user modifiability have also been refined and extended in these studies [2, 6, 7]. The studies provided new insights about the requirements for explanations that are given during modification tasks. It is also apparent that system-maintained task agendas and critics can guide users through modification tasks. Unsolved problems such as the need for a clear indication for the supported scope of modifications have been found. The principles and methods developed during the research on MODIFIER have been used in other application domains, most recently in an application for Business Marketing Operations at New York Telephone.

## 2   End-User Modifiability

Users must be in control of the interaction designed to achieve their goals. Otherwise, they have to put up with an unsatisfactory state of affairs, or they may not use a system at all if it does not fit their needs. Users of computer systems want to be independent of computer specialists. Therefore, tools should be usable directly by those who need them rather than indirectly by intermediaries. But more control is not always better. Users should be able to delegate their tasks, but it must be possible for them to intervene if such delegation does not work.

End-user modifiable environments will free designers of tools from the impossible task of anticipating all possible uses of a tool and all people's needs. However, making systems modifiable by their users does not mean that the responsibility for good design of the system is transferred to the users. In fact, normal users may not be capable of building tools of the quality a professional designer would. Grudin and Barnard [8] report that command names designed by naive text-editing users were much less effective than those supplied by skilled designers. The goal of end-user modifiable systems is that only if the system does not satisfy the needs and preferences of the users, the users should be able to adapt it.

Enabling the user to customize menus, screen layout, or similar properties is important but does not go far enough. The user should be able to change the *behavior* of the program and to extend the model of the problem domain with which the program operates. Users should be supported more than simply in the mechanics of the changes. For example, users might not have a good understanding of the consequences of the changes or whether the changes are the best solution for their problems.

One might think that automatic programming will make end-user modifiable systems unnecessary. Rich and Waters [12] give a "cocktail party" description of automatic programming:

> There will be no more programming. The end user, who only needs to know about the application domain, will write a brief requirement for what is wanted. The automatic programming system, which only needs to know about programming, will produce an efficient program satisfying the requirement. Automatic programming systems will have three key features: They will be end-user oriented, communicating directly with the end user; they will be general purpose, working as well in one domain as in another; and they will be fully automatic, requiring no human assistance.

They point out that this description is based on a number of myths. It is not possible for end users to communicate with an automatic programming system that knows nothing about the application domain, a point that is discussed in detail by Barstow [1]. Requirements cannot be complete because there is no practical limit for details in a specification. Creating a program is not a two-step process in which first an end user creates a requirement and than the automatic programming system makes a program. Since requirements are not complete, a dialog must be established for clarifying them, and in addition, the requirements of users change with the feedback of the growing program. End-user modifiability is an answer to some of the problems with automatic programming systems. End-user modifiable systems have

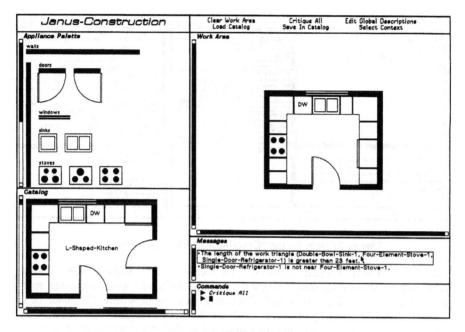

**Figure 1:** JANUS

domain knowledge, and instead of requiring detailed and complete specifications they provide immediate feedback and support users in finding a solution.

Knowledge-based systems, such as expert systems, are becoming widely used for both large and small tasks. The difficulty of the knowledge acquisition process for such systems has been documented by McDermott [10] and by Mittal and Dym [11]. This process is costly in both the time and money required to develop the knowledge base. This work focuses on minimizing the need for knowledge engineers in the knowledge acquisition process by providing tools and representations that allow end users to make modifications to the knowledge base of the system they are using. Besides making existing knowledge-based applications more affordable to create and maintain, we believe these techniques allow for a new range of applications of knowledge-based systems, which were previously insupportable due to limitations in existing knowledge acquisition techniques.

## 3 An Example of End-User Modifiability: JANUS and MODIFIER

JANUS is a design environment that allows designers to construct residential kitchens. The system enriches traditional design practice by augmenting the designer's creative and analytical skills. JANUS is a knowledge-based system supporting the construction of kitchens from domain-oriented building blocks called design units.

JANUS contains knowledge about how to distinguish "good" designs from "bad" designs and can explain that knowledge. The system knows how to combine building blocks into functional kitchens. Its knowledge includes design principles [9] based on three areas: building codes, such as "the window area shall be at least 10% of the

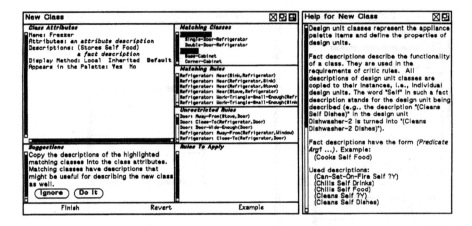

**Figure 2:** Help for the "Descriptions" Field of a New Class

floor area" (Such a critic could not be formulated in JANUS because only relationships between individual design units can be critiqued.); safety standards, such as "the stove should not be installed under a window or within 12 inches of a window"; and functional preferences, such as "the work triangle should be less than 23 feet." Critics in JANUS apply their design knowledge to critique the designer's partial solutions. The critics display messages, such as "the refrigerator is not near a stove" in a critic window (see Figure 1).

JANUS employs several knowledge representation strategies; the goal is to support end users in modifying all these representations. The system is used as a test case for the end-user modification component MODIFIER. MODIFIER implements methods for achieving end-user modifiability in knowledge-based, domain-oriented design environments. These methods are not restricted to the domain of kitchen design; they can be and have been transferred to other domains.

### 3.1 A Scenario

This scenario gives an overview of the features of MODIFIER. It shows how a user would add a new appliance to the palette. A designer wants to design a kitchen with a freezer in it. She discovers that the palette does not include a freezer. She decides to add one to the palette. A window with several subwindows represents a form for describing the new class (see Figure 2). MODIFIER suggests entering a name for the new class and explains that the name is used for identifying classes. The corresponding field in the "Class Attributes" window is highlighted. After the user enters the name "Freezer." MODIFIER suggests entering descriptions for the new class. The user clicks on the "Descriptions" field and presses the HELP key. The help window explains how descriptions are used and provides a list of descriptions already used in MODIFIER. The user picks the description "(Stores Self Food)" from the list. Selecting a description from the list of used ones requires only that the user can decide whether a description seems fit to the new class. If the new class is described with existing descriptions instead of new ones, it is possible for MODIFIER to list classes in the "Matching Classes" window that might have related useful descriptions and later to classify the new class in relation to existing ones. MODIFIER

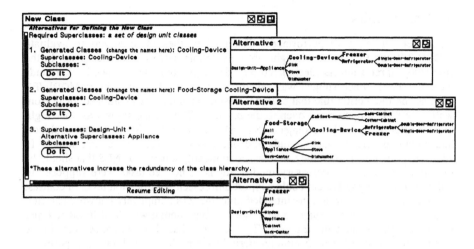

**Figure 3:** Suggestions for Embedding a New Class into the Inheritance Hierarchy

suggests copying the remaining descriptions of the matching classes because they might be useful for describing the new class as well. The user follows the suggestion by clicking on the "Do It" button and gets all local and inherited descriptions of the classes "Refrigerator" and "Cabinet," which both have the description "(Stores Self Food)." Now the user removes descriptions that are inappropriate for a freezer such as "(Stores Self Dishes)" and adds the new description "(Freezes Self Food)."

The next step is to decide which critic rules should apply to the new class. MODIFIER supports that decision by listing rules whose requirements are fulfilled by the description of the new class in the "Matching Rules" window as likely candidates for rules for the new class. Instead of following the suggestion to copy some of the matching rules, the user executes the command "Copy All Rules" from the menu of "Refrigerator" in the "Matching Classes" window that copies all rules applicable for refrigerators. The rationale for copying all these rules is that refrigerators are similar to freezers so that most of the refrigerator rules should be applicable for freezers as well.

MODIFIER suggests three different alternatives for embedding the new class in the hierarchy of existing classes (see Figure 3). For each alternative a window shows in a graph how the class hierarchy would look if that alternative were chosen. These graphs use a fisheye view in which classes are printed smaller if they are farther away from new classes and classes that are too far away are not shown at all. By suggesting how the new class could be embedded into the class hierarchy, MODIFIER frees the user from the burden of locating related classes, changing super class fields appropriately, and moving descriptions and rules around. In order to understand these alternatives better, the user gives the generated classes meaningful names. The user selects the second alternative and the class "Freezer" and the two generated classes "Food-Storage" and "Cooling-Device" are installed.

# 4   User Studies

Two user studies were performed. The goal of these studies was to evaluate MODIFIER and to gain new insights on how people perform modifications. In the first study, three subjects (designated S1 - S3) with computer science backgrounds were observed. Each subject was asked to complete different tasks in MODIFIER such as "define a critic rule that critiques design units that are positioned away from walls," or "add a microwave oven to the palette." The second study was done eight months after the first. Nine subjects (S4 - S12) were tested. Seven of these subjects had computer science backgrounds and one had also been in the first study. In addition to the given tasks, they were asked to identify a part of JANUS that should be modified and to do the necessary modifications. The free tasks were supposed to indicate how well the system could support unforeseen modification tasks in contrast to the other tasks for which the intended outcome was completely known. The first study had shown that the subjects were not familiar enough with MODIFIER in order to do the tasks without any training. To overcome that obstacle, the subjects in the second study had either a 15-minutes period to read the manual and to experiment with the system or they were given a 15-minute demonstration of the system.

The intended users of MODIFIER are regular users of JANUS. Because JANUS has not been used by anybody on a regular basis, it was not possible to find subjects who were familiar with JANUS. Many of the problems were related to the interaction style of a SYMBOLICS LISP machine. Many of the subjects had not used a SYMBOLICS LISP machine at all or at least not on a regular basis. Problems caused by the lack of familiarity with either JANUS or a SYMBOLICS LISP machine are not discussed below. The focus is on MODIFIER.

Many insights for the directions of future research were gained from the free tasks in the second user study. The impossible tasks made the limits of the current implementation of MODIFIER apparent. The remaining free tasks showed how users would approach modification tasks that had not been foreseen in the design of the system and what kind of support tools would be necessary to support these tasks.

## 4.1   Impossible Tasks

Three subjects tried to do modification tasks that were impossible to perform in the implementation of MODIFIER. That shows that MODIFIER does not give its users a sufficient model of its scope and limitations. This is an important issue for end-user modifiable systems that needs to be looked into in the future.

S4 wanted to define tall freezers that could not provide set-off space for sinks. Set-off space is used for putting down items next to the sink. He proposed to add a height attribute to the class "Freezer" that could be checked in the requirement of the critic rule that would watch for set-off space around sinks. This modification was impossible because attributes could not be checked in the requirements of critic rules. A plausible solution would have been a LISP expression such as the following:

```
(> (height freezer) (inches 30))
```

That solution or a similar one could not be used because at the time of the study the requirements could contain only references to fact descriptions and no LISP expressions. After being told that the proposed solution was not possible, the subject used a description that distinguished tall freezers from others.

S8 wanted to add a grid or a ruler to the work area. Extensions of the system in that direction are not supported at all so that such a task had to be done completely in LISP.

S10 wanted to define a critic that checked whether the kitchen has a door. That would have required changing the representation of critic rules and the mechanism that applied rules because all critic rules check the relationships between design units in the work area in the current implementation. Such a mechanism cannot check for the existence of a door because no critic rule for a door would fire if no door existed in the work area.

The main problem with these three failures was not that the subjects could not do the intended tasks but that they could not tell that the tasks would not be possible. In general, it was almost impossible for the users to judge the limits of the end-user modification component. Future research will have to find methods to represent these limits and to communicate them to the users. This problem is discussed in more detail in Section 6.2.

## 4.2   Free Tasks

The subjects were asked to define their own modification tasks for parts of JANUS that needed improvements. Some of these tasks were impossible to do as already discussed above. The remaining tasks uncovered problems that did not appear in the given tasks. Free tasks are the real test for an end-user modification component because the purpose of such an component is to allow users to make additions to a system that are not part of the original system.

S4 wanted to define tall freezers that could not provide set-off space for sinks because they are too tall to have a counter top. He realized that he should start with modifying the class "Freezer," but he did not know whether he should modify the attributes or the descriptions of that class. The conceptually better solution would have been to add an attribute "Height" to the class "Freezer" but it was impossible to access attributes in the requirement of a critic rule. After learning that, the subject decided to use a description that would represent whether a freezer could provide set-off space. First he looked through the existing descriptions and decided to use "(Affords Self Set-Off-Space)" because that was similar to the existing descriptions "(Needs Self Set-Off-Space)." He then proceeded with defining a new critic rule "Not-Next-To(Freezer,Sink)" that had "(Not (Affords Freezer Set-Off-Space))" as its requirement.

S6 wanted to add a microwave oven to the appliance palette. He only had a few problems during the definition of the class but did not recall immediately all the steps he had done in task 1. This might indicate that the system should provide more guidance for the modification task. The subject defined a critic rule for microwave ovens. Like a few of the other subjects, he tried to start the definition of the critic rule by manipulating a design unit in the work area. After getting past that mistake, he used an example during the definition of the critic rule.

S10 wanted to add to the appliance palette a detached cabinet that must not be surrounded by appliances or other cabinets. He wanted to copy and edit an existing cabinet and was told to look in the menu of a palette item after he asked the study supervisor about it. He discovered the "Copy & Edit" command and started to define the new class as a copy of the class "Base-Cabinet" without problems. He had a few difficulties changing the appearance of the new class in the "Graphics Objects" field but succeeded with it. After completing the definition of the new class, the subject started to define a critic rule that would check the constraints for detached cabinets. He knew that he wanted a relation such as "Not-Next-To" as the condition of the critic rule but overlooked it at first in the help window for the rule condition. He put too many classes into the parameter field because he wanted both cabinets and appliances to be checked with respect to detached cabinets. A critic told him that the rule had too many parameters and he realized that he had to define two rules in order to accomplish his goal. After filling the parameters field, the subject wondered whether he needed a requirement and decided against it. He used the "Example" button to decide which value to choose for the "Apply To" field and would have liked to see an example of a rule that had "Not-Next-To" as its condition. The algorithm for finding an example did not consider the condition field the most important and showed a different example. The subject decided to leave the value at "One" and to test the rule. After some testing the subject realized that the value for "Apply To" should be "All" and changed it accordingly but did not remember at first how to locate the new rule. When the subject defined the second critic rule that checked appliances, he did not use "Copy & Edit" but defined the rule from scratch. After the subject filled the fields of the second rule, the system suggested merging the two rules and replacing the two classes "Cabinet" and "Appliance" by "Design-Unit." The subject did not like the suggestion because it was too general and would have included walls and windows as well.

### 4.3   Discussion

These studies point out some problems with the MODIFIER approach. First, it is necessary to provide rationale for the existing critic rules in order to aid the users in deciding which rules to copy. The requirements of critic rules were another source of confusion. A few subjects did not understand the concept of an applicability condition and many subjects had some problems with the LISP-like format of the requirement field and its relationship to the descriptions of objects. The improved help windows used in the second study and the use of modification critics reduced these problems but could not eliminate them.

In addition to pointing out how the system had to be improved, the studies also helped to refine and extend the principles for making systems end-user modifiable. The first study already showed that providing a list of possible values is not enough of an explanation for a field in a property sheet. The second study confirmed that explanations for the purpose of the object and field being modified increased the understanding of the subjects. But the second study also indicated that verbose explanations are as bad as no explanations at all because most subjects did not read them. Examples are often the preferred form of explanations. System-maintained task agendas seemed to be very helpful for guiding users through modification tasks. However, system developers have to be very careful in designing the actions suggested by the system because some of the subjects followed them almost blindly.

Modification critics proved to be very valuable in immediately pointing out misconceptions to the subjects. The combination of system-maintained task agendas and critics seems to be well suited for guiding users through a variety of modification tasks. The need for domain orientation became apparent during the studies. S12, who had an architectural design background, especially had problems with concepts used in the system such as classes, rules, and relations. Representations have to be found, at least for the top layer of a layered architecture, that hide the system concepts better.

Visualization seems to be a good way for dealing with inheritance hierarchies. None of the subjects in the second study had problems in understanding the suggestions of the system for embedding the new class into the inheritance hierarchy. The "fisheye" view [5] used for reducing the size of the shown hierarchies did not seem to trouble the subjects at all, so that this method should scale up nicely to larger hierarchies. In some cases the subjects did not understand why the system had come up with a certain set of suggestions. That indicates the need for an explanation for the suggestions of the system.

# 5 Future Research

Although the current version of MODIFIER was successful in enabling the subjects to complete their tasks during the user studies, there are areas for future research that promise improvements. In order to assess the potential of new and existing principles for achieving end-user modifiability, more formal user studies have to be performed that can tell whether the improvements are statistically significant.

## 5.1. Domain-Oriented Representations

The user studies showed that although subjects without a computer science background were able to complete the tasks, they felt uncomfortable with representations that were too far from the problem domain. These subjects commented that concepts such as classes, rules, and relations were too far from the kitchen domain. In order to overcome these problems, representations have to be found that are more familiar to the users.

The inheritance hierarchy of classes could be simplified by using the results of Rosch's [13] research on categories. She observed that there are basic level categories which are the least-specific categories for which prototypes can be envisioned. An example of such a category is a chair. Super ordinate categories such as furniture do not have prototypes and subordinate categories such as a recliner do not add much knowledge compared to the basic level categories. A system that emphasizes basic level categories should make it more natural for users to deal with an inheritance hierarchy. In the kitchen domain, examples for basic level categories are stoves, sinks, and refrigerators. Subordinate categories can be represented by a catalog of concrete appliances from different manufacturers and descriptions such as "three heating elements" or "two doors." Super ordinate categories such as appliances can be represented by grouping basic level categories.

The representation of critic rules in JANUS proved to be difficult to understand for many of the subjects in the user studies. The applicability condition that relates a critic rule to descriptions of design units such as "(Cooks Self Food)" was a major source of problems. The LISP-like format of descriptions and the use of keywords such as "Self" was a part of these problems. A representation has to be found that is more familiar to users and, at the same time, constrained enough for the system to reason with it. Another source of confusion was the mechanism for specifying how many combinations of design units had to be tested. For example, a stove has to be near to only one refrigerator but it should be away from all windows. In many cases this distinction is of no importance because most kitchens contain only one stove and one refrigerator. A related problem is that critic rules that check for the absence of design units cannot be formulated in the current representation. For example, it is impossible to check whether a kitchen has a door or whether the window area is at least 10 percent of the floor space.

Spatial relations in JANUS use LISP predicates as their conditions. Users need to use only a very small subset of LISP consisting of arithmetic and comparison functions in addition to the provided library of spatial functions. But the use of LISP is unfamiliar to most domain experts. An infix notation might be a slight improvement but the problem remains that many end users might not be able to formulate appropriate predicates. Fortunately, most users will not have to define new spatial relations because most new critic rules can be defined just by using existing relations. Minor adaptations of relations can be done by copying existing ones and by changing conditions by textually replacing parts of it, such as a number that represents a distance. However, this is not satisfying in a spatial domain. Most spatial relations could be specified with a direct-manipulation interface.

## 5.2 Indicating Limits

As part of the user studies, subjects were asked to choose a modification task of their own. This part of the study showed that it was difficult for the subjects to assess the limits of the end-user modification component. Some of the subjects chose tasks such as adding a grid or a ruler to the work area that were far outside of the scope of the system. If users do not have a good understanding of the limits of the system, they might waste much time in looking for a solution that does not exist or they might give up prematurely although a solution could have been found. In order to be able to notify a user if an intended task is outside the scope of the system, the system needs to have a representation of the task the user wants to perform. The user could specify such a task or the system could try to infer it and ask the user for confirmation. If the scope of the task representation component is significantly broader than the scope of the modification component, the system will be able to tell the user which tasks are impossible. Users can be prevented from giving up prematurely if the system guides them through a task with a task agenda and critics. The current implementation of these support tools proved to be very helpful in the user studies but they need to be extended so that they cover the full range of possible modification tasks.

## 5.3 Adaptive Component

End-user modifiable systems belong to the category of adaptable systems, but they can benefit from adaptive mechanisms [14]. In order to achieve adaptivity, a user model has to be maintained. Such a model collects information about a user such as knowledge about certain topics, command usage, and preferences. A user model can be used for providing minimalist explanations; that is, the system adapts the information provided in an explanation to the user. In order to adapt the interface of a system to a user two models are needed in addition to a user model. An interaction model represents the available interaction objects such as windows and menus and a task model represents the tasks a system can perform and on a lower level commands and their results. These models are already needed for a demonstration component and a tool for indicating the limits of the system discussed in the previous sections. If all these models are being used by the system, it can adapt the interface of the system to different users by hiding commands and providing different views of the system. Different views can support the transition from the system model to different situation models of different users.

# 6 Conclusions

Two user studies were performed with twelve subjects to identify problems with MODIFIER and to learn more about the conceptual framework of end-user modifiability. Several conceptual problems were observed that led to new principles for the design of end-user modifiable systems. Explanations were discovered to be insufficient and the importance of concise explanations that describe the purpose and use of a parameter was recognized. Examples were discovered to be a preferred form of explanation. Modification critics proved to be effective in pointing out misconceptions of the subjects immediately. A system-maintained task agenda was successful in guiding the subjects through modification tasks. Several problems still existed by the time of the second study. Most of these problems were related to system concepts such as classes or rules that were confusing to some of the subjects. This shows the importance of domain orientation.

The representations used in MODIFIER were not close enough to the application domain. Several promising approaches for simplifying the inheritance hierarchy, the critic rule mechanism, and spatial relations need to be tested and refined. In the second study, the subjects were asked to perform one task of their own choice. Several of the subjects chose tasks that were impossible to perform with MODIFIER. The subjects had no indication that these tasks were outside the scope of the system, a problem that needs to be addressed in the future. An explicit representation of the kinds of tasks an end-user modification component can perform can be used for indicating the limits of the system to the users. An adaptive component of an end-user modifiable system can adapt explanations to different users, provide different views, and hide certain commands. A serious shortcoming of MODIFIER has been that it was tested only in laboratory settings. That will be overcome by integrating MODIFIER in an application for Business Marketing Operations at New York Telephone and deploying the system in a real-use situation.

# Acknowledgments

I would like to acknowledge the support of Gerhard Fischer. As advisor and dissertation committee chairman he has been a source of advice and constructive criticism that has served to guide my research. I thank Mike Atwood for his comments that improved this paper greatly and for giving me the time to work on the paper. The research was conducted at the University of Colorado and supported by grants No. IRI-8722792 and No. IRI-9015441 from the National Science Foundation.

# References

1. Barstow, D.R., *A Perspective on Automatic Programming.* AI Magazine, 1984. **5**(1): p. 5-27.

2. Fischer, G. and A. Girgensohn. *End-User Modifiability in Design Environments.* in *Human Factors in Computing Systems, CHI'90 Conference Proceedings (Seattle, WA).* 1990. New York: ACM.

3. Fischer, G., *et al.*, *Critics: An Emerging Approach to Knowledge-Based Human Computer Interaction.* International Journal of Man-Machine Studies, 1991. **35**(5): p. 695-721.

4. Fischer, G., R. McCall, and A. Morch. *JANUS: Integrating Hypertext with a Knowledge-Based Design Environment.* in *Proceedings of Hypertext'89 (Pittsburgh, PA).* 1989. New York: ACM.

5. Furnas, G.W. *Generalized Fisheye Views.* in *Human Factors in Computing Systems, CHI'86 Conference Proceedings (Boston, MA).* 1986. New York: ACM.

6. Girgensohn, A., *End-User Modifiability in Knowledge-Based Design Environments.* 1992, Department of Computer Science, University of Colorado:

7. Girgensohn, A. and F. Shipman. *Supporting Knowledge Acquisition by End Users: Tools and Representations.* in *Proceedings of the Symposium on Applied Computing (SAC'92).* 1992. New York: ACM.

8. Grudin, J. and P. Barnard. *When Does an Abbreviation Become a Word? And Related Questions.* in *Human Factors in Computing Systems, CHI'85 Conference Proceedings.* 1985. New York: ACM.

9. Jones, R.J. and W.H. Kapple, *Kitchen Planning Principles - Equipment - Appliances.* 1984, Urbana-Champaign, IL: Small Homes Council - Building Research Council, University of Illinois.

10. McDermott, J., *R1: The Formative Years.* AI Magazine, 1981. **2**(2): p. 21-29.

11. Mittal, S. and C.L. Dym, *Knowledge Acquisition from Multiple Experts.* AI Magazine, 1985. **6**(2): p. 32-36.

12. Rich, C.H. and R.C. Waters, *Automatic Programming: Myths and Prospects.* Computer, 1988. **21**(8): p. 40-51.

13. Rosch, E., *et al.*, *Basic Objects in Natural Categories.* Natural Categories, 1976. **8**: p. 382-439.

14. Totterdell, P.A., M.A. Norman, and D.P. Browne. *Levels of Adaptivity in Interface Design.* in *Proceedings of INTERACT'87, 2nd IFIP Conference on Human-Computer Interaction (Stuttgart, FRG).* 1987. Amsterdam: North-Holland.

# THE USE OF SPECIFICATION

# Handling interaction in software specification

Christian ATTIOGBÉ, Jean-Louis DURIEUX
IRIT-Université Paul SABATIER
118, Route de Narbonne
31062 Toulouse Cédex
e-mail:  attiogbe@irit.fr

## Abstract

A specification approach for interactive and graphical systems (IGS) is presented. Considering IGS as a system involving interactive cooperation between a software and a user, changing its state according to external events, we elaborate a convenient method which takes account of this cooperation. The background of the method consists of organizing information through three concepts : State, View and Memory around which the notions of *Configuration* and *Transaction* are defined to express the evolution of the system as a transition system. Algebraic specification techniques are used to deal with information representation. Specifications are expressed as semantic rules where specific symbols are introduced with their semantics, to enhance the simplicity of writing and to increase expressiveness. The whole specification can be viewed as a set of so called *transactions*. Formal reasoning issues are handled with dynamic logic, thus offering means for studying the specification.

## Key words

Interactive and graphic system – User participation – Formal specification
– Interaction – Dynamic logic – behavior modelling

# 1 Introduction

We attempt to specify Interactive and Graphic Systems (IGS) by taking account of interaction with the user through visual objects. A formalism is proposed for this purpose.

Following some works in Software Engineering, our motivation is to find a way to help the development of robust, maintainable and reusable systems or applications. A way to achieve this goal is to make a formal specification of the desired application and to derive software from this specification, manually or automatically. We are interested here by the first step of this process, that is, specification techniques. In this area many works must be underlined : [8],[7],[2],[12],[15],[1].

We focus our study on IGS, typically software dealing with data manipulation (creation, consultation, transformation) in reaction to user's operations on input/output devices. So the specification of such software is specific and can differ from one system to another. We face the problem by developing a specification technique based on system behavior according to user participation, that is, by formalizing the evolution of the system with the time. To formalize the state of the system before and after an evolution, we need three concepts: *State*, *Memory* and *View*. These concepts were found when considering the main characteristics of IGS. Indeed, we consider an IGS as a system in interdependency with users, one waiting for the other to achieve its task. User participation in this process can be expressed as key pressure, mouse moving, etc and the effect is to start some internal operations in the system. The result of these operations are expressed by a modification of the external aspect of the system through a display device. Then, the user can act again according to the new aspect of the system which, gives a graphical overview of objects manipulated and available actions.

So, operational behavior of an IGS is a succession of situations, and going from one to the other is done by user contribution through what we call *external events*, that is, clicking on button, clicking on object pictures or entering commands, all this depending on the graphical environment of the system.

Two main facts can be stated : first, we deal with the internal and dynamic behavior of the system; second, we deal with the external and modifiable aspect which summarizes the internal one and allows users to interact opportunely with the system.

Our approach follows these operational and dynamic aspects, by characterizing each of them and involving the graphical environment and the external events which leads modifications. The aim is to give simple and powerful means to formally specify the behavior of interactive software in a graphical environment. The formal aspect is important and we try through the semantics of transactions to establish a formal reasoning area, by using *Dynamic Logic* which seems to us an appropriate one.

Our approach is a completely new direction. We have not found closely related works in the literature.

In the work of D. Harel on statecharts [11], emphasis was on reactive aspect rather than on interaction through graphical objects. The same remark can be made for the work of D. Clément and J. Incerpi [3], they dealt with the specification of reactive graphical objects using Esterel.

In section 2), we will present the background of our approach and the concepts introduced for modelling and evolution. Section 3) will describe the main steps of the specification and in section 4) we will present a new formalism through its syntax and semantics. In section 5), an example will be presented. Section 6) will evoke formal reasoning issues with dynamic logic and in section 7) the link with transactions will be established.

## 2 Background of the approach

In our approach, specification of the evolution of a software is essentially based on *Configurations* and *transactions*. To make them clear, we must explain the concepts of *Memory*, *State* and *View* we introduced earlier. The main idea is to consider the system behavior over time and according to the external events it receives from users. This behavior can be described by a set of rules which characterize the transition from one situation to another. These transitions are the result of applying external events which express user's action on the system.

Then, we need a modelling of a situation (global state of the system) and the expression of the evolution from one situation to the resulting situation.

### 2.1 Modelling

Several software specification techniques deal with modelling: abstract data types, logics, set theory, etc; but to formally handle the graphical aspect and interaction we need to add some features related to graphical objects and their relationship with the internal objects manipulated by the system. So we introduce three concepts to model any situation of the system:

**2.1.1 State** The state ($S$) of an IGS in the specification process, is the set of information which characterizes its global aspect, both internal and external, at any time during its evolution. The state includes the environment objects such as windows, menus, mouse position, etc.

**2.1.2 Memory** The memory ($M$) of an IGS in the specification process is the part of the State (as defined above) that concerns the data used in the system. That is the materialization of objects manipulated by the user and those of the environment, especially those involved in the interaction. Here we use algebraic techniques, and objects are represented by abstract data types [7].

**2.1.3 View** The view $(V)$ for us is a partial snapshot of the system. It characterizes the external aspect of all objects belonging to the system and concerned with direct manipulations.

We can say that it is the visual part of the Memory plus some particular graphical objects in the current State. Interactions are made possible through the elements of View.

With these three concepts, we can completely express any situation in which the system is waiting for an input or a signal. Let us define an *entry point* as such a situation in which external events can be considered by the system.

**2.1.4 Configurations** A *Configuration* (noted $C = \langle S_M, V \rangle$) is a stable situation of the IGS, a situation in which the system is on an *entry point*. That means, the complete description of the system when it is waiting for *external events* to continue its evolution.

## 2.2 Expressing the evolution

The evolution of an interactive system is a consequence of user action. Depending on the system environment user action can take different forms.

**2.2.1 Preliminaries** User operations are activated by input/output (I/O) devices, especially by acting on the mouse, since we deal with a graphical environment. These I/O devices are the source of events received by the system, so external events are used to characterize user actions or operations during the evolution of the system.

Simple mathematical objects such as transition systems are appropriate to formalize the evolution of a system.

Configuration changes after the execution of an operation. This means that, the effect of an external event is to start an internal operation on objects, when the system is on an entry point. The results will be modification of objects or generation of new objects, so modification of Memory and consequently that of View. In addition, an operation implies a transition from one configuration to another, which is defined as a *transaction*.

**2.2.2 Transactions** A *transaction* is the expression of the change from one configuration to another according to the impact of the application of an external event to the initial configuration. We note

$$\langle S_M, V \rangle \rightarrow_{ee} \langle S'_M, V' \rangle$$

where

$ee$ is an external event,

$\langle S_M, V \rangle$ is the system configuration before the event $ee$ and

$\langle S'_M, V' \rangle$ characterizes the system configuration after the event $ee$, the result of applying $ee$ on $\langle S_M, V \rangle$.

We can then claim that an IGS can be completely specified by a set of transactions, since IGS behavior generally consists of going from one configuration and reaching another after performing some operations. We must clarify now, how to build configurations and transactions, and how to express the whole IGS specification with these concepts.

# 3 Building specification

A good specification requires properties like communicability [9],[13], understandability, testability, maintainability [1]. To meet these requirements a convenient specification is required. We then need precisely defined syntax and semantics to build the specification. From this point of view, our approach includes existing techniques like algebraic (abstract data types) and logic ones.

Since it is first a software system, an IGS can be specified as a mixture of different components acting together to achieve some goals. Each component can be specified as a simple or a complex data item with related manipulation functions. The new aspect to be handled is the interaction with user.

## 3.1 Description of system components

In the specification, the components appear in the *State*. Each component identified in the system should be described in an algebraic term using *abstract data types* [15],[6]. Then the entire system is the set of these abstract data types. In this way, all computation and transformation on objects will be performed through appropriate operators. Thus, to manipulate objects in the specification we use abstract syntax terms. In order to express construction, transformation and computation of objects in the specification, we adopt the following Prolog-like notation which will also be used to write formulas of the specification. All abstract syntax terms will be written in the form *operator* ($argument_1$, $argument_2$, $\cdots$, $argument_n$).

## 3.2 External forms of data

Interaction implies that users act on external forms of objects, then referring and consulting objects appear as requirements in the interactive environment. A step in this direction is to associate external forms to the desired objects and to allow selection of these external forms in order to have access to objects they represent.

In the specification, the external forms must be formalized too. This can be done by using *signature morphisms*[15],[6] (morphisms that transform a signature to another equivalent one) on identified initial objects, or simply *algebra-morphism* to express graphical interpretation of objects.

We consider here, both textual and graphical form as external representations of objects. We distinguish graphical forms depending on the application itself i.e. those obtained by graphical interpretation of application objects, and those depending on the environment i.e. windows, buttons, panels, etc. An object can have many graphical forms according to its interpretation.

However, in a current view, only one graphical form is available, it means there is a bijection between internal form and external form. This is very important for the designation of objects; it means the object pointed by the user is unique. For objects depending on the graphical environment, representation conventions can be made to fix both internal and external forms.

As external forms establish the link between objects and users, they are the main elements for the interaction and, therefore, are very important when specifying IGS.

### 3.3 Interaction

In an IGS, the user participates in the execution of applications. This participation is done with I/O devices.

As I/O devices help to characterize the graphical environment and are used by systems, they must be considered in the specification process. Graphical aspects are characterized by Window systems, bitmap screen, pointing and selecting devices. In our approach we deal with all these notions by taking them as part of the graphical environment and grouping their actions in a *class of external events*. In general, every environment of IGS includes at least a Window system with bitmap screen, keyboard and mouse.

Then, we must describe the interaction through these graphical elements, windows, graphical cells, data pictures and the external events. Designation and selection of these elements enable users to interact with the system.

When considering the graphical environment in the specification process, we meet principle 4 of the list of "good specification principles", enumerated by [1] : *"A specification must encompass the environment in which system operates".*

### 3.4 System behavior

The major step when building a specification is the description of the system behavior, using all the information previously defined.

The main idea is to express, using transactions, the system behavior for each external action. All external events corresponding to a particular operation of the system must be described. The result is a set of transactions.

A transaction like $C_i \rightarrow_{ee} C_f$ defines the operational semantics of the computation which leads from the initial configuration $C_i$ to the final $C_f$. According to this, the whole specification of a system is the set of such transactions defining the entire behavior of the system. That is a kind of transitions system. Here, configurations replace states and transactions define labelled transitions between configurations.

The way the system deals with each operation is not important, we must express just what will be done. From one configuration to another, we express the operations involved and the objects on which they act.

We then obtain a set of transactions which defines the operational semantics of the system evolution. However the new problem is : how to express the transactions with precise semantics ?

# 4 Formalism of transactions

Following the idea that *"a specification is formal if it is written entirely in a language with an explicitly and precisely defined syntax and semantics."*[13], we define the basic syntax and semantics of transactions.

## 4.1 Syntax

At this stage we can say that a configuration is a triplet made of a collection of expressions denoting elements of State, elements of Memory and elements of View. According to the definition of transaction in section 2.2.2), we shall have an expression made of two main parts, one for each configuration of the transaction. The difference between the two parts is the modifications on objects appearing in the initial configuration and affected by the event that leads to the transaction. The other objects stay unchanged.

We notice here that all objects that are not affected by the transaction will be in the final configuration. It may be sometimes unpleasant to repeat the same expression in the two parts of a transaction. To avoid this unpleasantness and in the same way to simplify transaction writing, we introduce appropriate notations as follows.

We consider the metasymbol $\vdash$ as Sintzoff [14] with same wide semantics.

The notation $a \vdash b$ expresses that $b$ can be deduced from $a$ or more generally that $b$ is a consequence of $a$ and there is no implicit rewriting of elements of $a$. The second notation $\left|\frac{a}{b}\right.$ expresses that if we have $a$, then we can conclude $b$ and here there is an implicit rewriting of all unmodified elements of $a$ in $b$.

## Using $a \vdash b$

Assume we have a collection $O$ of *definitions*, i.e. objects (in an abstract syntax form), each of them identified by a name. To evoke a definition $def_i$ related to the collection without writing the whole, we write $O \vdash def_i$. According to the specification method we call this an *abstraction* and every abstraction on S, M or V is a *formula*.

Then from S, M and V we have respectively $S\_formulas$, $M\_formulas$, $V\_formulas$ i.e. formulas of the form $S \vdash s\_element$ , $M \vdash m\_element$ , $V \vdash v\_element$ . Consequently a configuration $C = \langle S_M, V \rangle$ is a conjunction of formulas :
$$S \vdash st\_element \wedge M \vdash m\_element \wedge V \vdash v\_element$$

## Using $\left|\frac{a}{b}\right.$

This stands for transactions. When we write $\left|\frac{C_i}{C_f}\right.$, we explicitly mean that from the configuration $C_i$ one can reach the configuration $C_f$.

Now to meet the definition of transaction, it is important to notify the event which induces it, so we extend the notation in this direction, meaning : the lower part must have the following syntax $\models_{\overline{C_f}}^{ee}$ if $ee$ is the event concerned. This is correct only in a transaction.

### 4.1.1  Basic syntax for transaction

Assume $ee$ an external event, $C_i$, $C_f$ configurations, the notation :

$$\left\| \frac{C_i}{\left\| \frac{ee}{C_f} \right.} \right.$$

stands for the transaction yielding $C_f$ when the IGS specified is in a configuration $C_i$ and the event $ee$ occurs.

### 4.1.2  Expressiveness

### Disjunction

*Disjunctive transactions* can be used to simplify multiple transactions. For this purpose we need the operator *or*, also noted $|$.

To express situations where, from a given configuration, one can have many events and consequently reach many final configurations, we write

$$\left\| \frac{C_i}{\left\| \frac{ee_1}{C_{f_1}} \right| \left\| \frac{ee_2}{C_{f_2}} \right| \left\| \frac{ee_3}{C_{f_3}} \right.} \right.$$

instead of three transactions

$$\left\| \frac{C_i}{\left\| \frac{ee_1}{C_{f_1}} \right.} \right. \qquad \left\| \frac{C_i}{\left\| \frac{ee_2}{C_{f_2}} \right.} \right. \qquad \left\| \frac{C_i}{\left\| \frac{ee_3}{C_{f_3}} \right.} \right.$$

### Conditional

In some cases, one can reach a configuration only if specific criteria or conditions are satisfied (computation results, resource availability, etc), these conditions must be specified as premises for the final configuration; for this purpose we write

$$\left\| \frac{C_i}{\left\| \frac{cond}{\left\| \frac{ee}{C_f} \right.} \right.} \right.$$

Implicitly if conditions (premises) are not satisfied the system stays in the initial configuration.

## 4.2 Semantics

Informally, a transaction expresses the fact that, when receiving an external event, the system does some internal operations which act on the system objects, modifying thus its state, so the system goes to a resulting configuration. The modification of the system and consequently that of its objects must be described in the configurations before and after the event.

### 4.2.1 Handling the evolution
To express the evolution of the system, we need a semantic function, say $\mathcal{E}ffect\_of$ such that

$$Cf = \mathcal{E}ffect\_of(C_i, ee)$$

where $\mathcal{E}ffect\_of$ is the mapping which computes $C_f$ by applying $ee$ effects on all formulas of $C_i$. The following three rules explain how this works:

*i*) If ee is the external event corresponding to mouse pressure and the mouse cursor is on a selectable object, then this object becomes the current object or the selected object.

*ii*) If ee is the external event corresponding to mouse pressure and the mouse cursor is on a button, then apply to the current object the operation associated to the button.

*iii*) If ee is an operation of the system, then apply this operation to the current object.

By applying these rules we obtain a new configuration which defines another entry point. Thus, $\mathcal{E}ffect\_of$ defines the semantics of transactions.

### 4.2.2 Properties
According to the broad semantics of the metasymbol ⊢ we obtain some interesting properties for transactions:

**P1** There is *no formula consumption*, i.e. we can use formulas of $C_i$ many times in $C_f$. That means, formulas in $C_i$, which are not modified are implicitly rewritten in $C_f$. It works like the implicit Girard's "Biensur" operator in Linear Logic (see [5]).

**P2** There is *formula conservation*, i.e. we do not have to write all formulas in $C_i$. Since in a given specification process we deal with the same configuration of a system in a dynamic way, all configuration information stays valid (once defined) if no modifications are specified.

## 5 A working example

We consider here a transaction which specifies the application of an operation to an object. The object appears in a window through its external aspect i.e. an image.

The mouse pressure activates the associated operation. The object associated to the button is then modified by the operation.

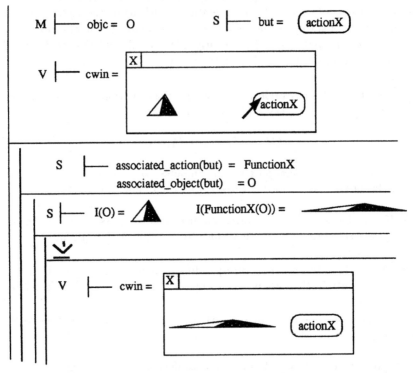

The arrow indicates the position of the mouse cursor, it is an operator, here applied to the external representation of the button *but*. In the View (V) we have an image in a window identified by *cwin*. I is a function which indicates the graphical representation of an object and $\stackrel{\vee}{-}$ is a constant which denotes the mouse pressure.

Notice that the transaction works only if an event occurs, otherwise the system stays in the same configuration.

The mouse behavior and the operation involved are then completely specified. So, given the characteristics of the graphical development environment, we can specify, using transactions, the behavior of graphical objects. To state the correction of such a transaction, we must introduce a convenient process.

## 6 Formal reasoning issues

To handle formal reasoning like proof, correctness, consistency and testability which emphasize qualities of good specification, one needs a formal support.

Some specification techniques use, to resolve this question, a formal language to write the specification; algebraic specification techniques are the most used with mathematical formalisms.

With our approach, we have two solutions to resolve the question: first, elaborate a formal method for the transaction formalism to reason about formulas, second, match the transaction formalism into an existing one which allows formal reasoning.

We adopt the second solution. Our investigation turns around formalisms that allow reasoning about dynamic situations. Presently, Dynamic Logic seems to be a good direction.

## 6.1 Transactions and Logic

A *formula f* is *true* in a configuration $C$ if $f$ is an *S_formula* or an *M_formula* or a *V_formula* of $C$. Notice that the validity of a formula is linked with its syntactic presence, either in an initial configuration or in a final configuration by deduction mechanism.

We define *compatible formulas* as two (or more) formulas concerned with the same definition, that is, the same object (maybe with some modifications in its abstract syntax form as a result of a transformation or a computation).

*Example* :
$M \vdash m\_element \wedge V \vdash v\_element$ are not compatible formulas.
$M \vdash obj = (+ a (+ b c)) \wedge M \vdash obj = (+ (+ a b) c)$ are two compatible formulas.

## 6.2 Dynamic Logic

Dynamic logic [10] provides a way of studying assertions about dynamic objects. Dynamic objects in this point of view are programs, and assertions are termination, equivalence, correctness.

Research in Dynamic Logic and related topics can be viewed as providing tools for reasoning about general dynamic situations by extending modal logic[10]. So we have good motivations to explore this direction. We summarize here the main characteristics of Dynamic Logic which are important for our approach. For more information and details on Dynamic Logic see [10] and for Modal Logic see [4].

Dynamic Logic adopts the $(W, \rho)$ scheme of Modal Logic, and $W$ is taken to be the set of all possible execution worlds corresponding to the programs considered, and $\rho$ the accessibility relation among these worlds. An accessibility relation $\rho(\alpha)$ over $W$ is associated to any program $\alpha$ such that $(s, t) \in \rho(\alpha)$ iff $t$ is a possible final world of $\alpha$ with $s$ an initial world.

In dynamic logic, modal operators qualify the accessibility relations they stand for. For the accessibility relation $\rho(\alpha)$ one must write $[\alpha], \langle \alpha \rangle$ in place of $[], \langle \rangle$ (modal operators) because of the diversity of accessibility relations.

Three levels of reasoning are distinguished in dynamic logic: propositional, first-order uninterpreted and first-order interpreted.

We are concerned here with the propositional reasoning and accordingly with Propositional Dynamic Logic (PDL).

*The syntax of PDL* is based on two sets of symbols : $\phi_0$, the set of atomic (or basic) formulas, sometimes called propositional symbols, and $\pi_0$, the set of atomic programs. The sets are, respectively, abstraction of properties of worlds and of basic instructions such as assignment statements, that transform one world to another.

*The semantics of PDL* is defined relative to a given structure (or model) $U$, of the form : $U = (W, \tau, \rho)$ where

$W$ is a set of worlds,

$\tau : \phi_0 \to E^W$ the mapping which assigns to each proposition $p \in \phi_0$, the set of worlds in which $p$ is true, and

$\rho : \pi_0 \to E^{W*W}$ the mapping which assigns to each atomic program $\alpha$ some binary relation with intended meaning $(s, t) \in \rho(\alpha)$ if execution of $\alpha$ can lead from world $s$ to world $t$.

### 6.3 Matching the formalism of transactions to dynamic logic

The question is : how can we move to Dynamic Logic formalism after specifying with the method we described i.e. with transactions? To answer this question, two conditions must be established: first, the correspondence of transaction formulas with dynamic formulas, second, the meaning of the accessibility relation. According to the semantics of transactions, we can deal with the two points. Dynamic formulas can be extracted from transactions and the meaning of accessibility relations is here, not the execution itself but an idea of what it will be during the execution of the specified system.

We stay in the propositional case since we never have variables in external events. Now let us clarify the syntax and the semantics of PDL in our case. We shall use the same terminology as in [10].

**Syntax : Defining W, $\phi_0$, $\pi_0$**

We define W as the set of possible configurations of the IGS being specified.

$\phi_0$ is taken to be the set of basic formulas used to define a configuration (formulas used to describe $S, M, V$ ).

$\pi_0$ is taken to be the set of external events (events that start internal operations and consequently modification of configuration)

**Semantics :** Analogously, we define a structure over $\phi_0$ and $\pi_0$ with the same meaning. i.e. a structure $U = (W, \tau, \rho)$ where :

$\tau : \phi_0 \to E^W$ assigns to each proposition $p \in \phi_0$, the set of configurations in which it is true, and

$\rho : \pi_0 \to E^{W*W}$ assigns to each event $ee$ some binary relations $(C_i, C_f)$ with the meaning, $(C_i, C_f) \in \rho(ee)$ if the taking to account of $ee$ can lead from configuration $C_i$ to configuration $C_f$.

Then according to this, we can build the structure corresponding to a given specification and use the axiom system of the dynamic logic (see [10]) to reason about it.

## Computing dynamic formulas

To get dynamic formulas from transactions, let us define a function $\mathcal{D}f$ such that $\mathcal{D}f\left(\left|\begin{array}{c} C_i \\ \hline \frac{ee}{C_f} \end{array}\right.\right)$ yields a collection of *dynamic formulas*.

That is, formulas of the form $f_i \to \langle ee \rangle f_j$, which mean that if we have $f_i$ true, after the event $ee$ we have $f_j$ true. Considering $C_i$ and $C_f$ as conjunctions of *formulas* we can write $C_i \to \langle ee \rangle C_f$. $f_i$ and $f_j$ are compatible formulas.

For disjunctive transactions like $\left|\begin{array}{c} C_i \\ \hline \frac{ee_1}{C_{f_1}} \mid \frac{ee_2}{C_{f_2}} \end{array}\right.$ we have

$$C_i \to \langle ee_1 \rangle C_{f_1} \ \lor \ \langle ee_2 \rangle C_{f_2}$$

# 7 Transactions and formal reasoning

## 7.1 About the working example

In 5) we gave an example of transaction without a proof of correction. To handle such a proof, we introduced dynamic logic since we were dealing with a dynamic situation. The transaction can be noted as follows:

$$\left|\begin{array}{c} C_1 \\ \hline \begin{array}{c} \overline{Cond1} \\ \overline{Cond2} \\ \underline{\mathsf{v}} \\ C_f \end{array} \end{array}\right.$$

To prove this transaction comes down to proving that : if an event occurs when, in the current configuration, the mouse cursor is on a button, apply the associated operation of the button to the current object.

But according to the semantics of transactions, this is always true. So what we have to do is to write formally this semantic rule as an axiom system. We do this by fixing some button characteristics and the button's behavior.

**7.1.1 Button characteristics** Let *graph_env* be the graphical environment (a collection of graphical objects) of the system and let us note b : BUTTON to define a button as a graphic object.

The main characteristics of a button are the following : it has a name, an action, and an associated object on which the action is applied when the button is activated. Every button has two external representations, one when the mouse is pressed on it and the other if the mouse is released. Formally we write :

S ⊢ graphenv = (...; b : BUTTON; ...)

associated_name(b) = ActionName

S ⊢ norm_repr(b) = ( ActionName )

activ_repr(b) = ( ActionName )

Graphical objects representing the button are formal terms too, we can write them by defining the appropriate operators, for example *button (ActionName, ExternForm)* to get a button with a given external form, but we prefer the visual formalism.

**7.1.2 Button behavior** A button changes its external representation when the mouse is pressed and activates the associated operation when the mouse is released. Assume we have a variable $obj_c$ to designate the current object of the system. The following two transactions formalize the behavior of the button.

S ⊢ graphenv = (...; but : BUTTON; ...)

V ⊢ but = ( ActionName )

V ⊢ but = ( ActionName )

V ⊢ but = ( ActionName )    M ⊢ $obj_c$ = O

V ⊢ but = ( ActionName )

M ⊢ $obj_c$ = Opcall(ActionName, O)

This latter expresses that, after releasing the mouse, the action is applied to the current object ($obj_c$). According to the operations used in the example and in the preceding transactions $\pi_0 = \{^\searrow, ^\vee\}$.

From these transactions we get the axiom system stating the axioms needed for the proof.

## 7.2 The axiom system and the proof

The advantage of dynamic logic is, for us, its ability to support reasoning with dynamic situations. Here we use this particularity to deal with the correction proof of the transaction defined above. Let us define $\varphi_0$. According to the above transactions, $\varphi_0 = f_1, f_2, f_3, f_4, f_5, f_6$ such that:

$f_1$ is $S \vdash graphenv = (\cdots; but : BUTTON; \cdots)$
$f_2$ is $V \vdash but = MouseCursor(button(ActionName))$,
$f_3$ is $V \vdash activ\_repr(but)$,
$f_4$ is $V \vdash norm\_repr(but)$,
$f_5$ is $M \vdash obj_c = O$
$f_6$ is $M \vdash obj_c = Opcall(ActionName, O)$

According to the previous transactions, the axiom system we need is just:

$$a1 : (f_1 \wedge f_2) \rightarrow \langle \overset{\vee}{-} \rangle f_3$$

$$a2 : (f_3 \wedge f_5) \rightarrow \langle \overset{\vee}{-} \rangle (f_4 \wedge f_6)$$

Then, the proof is :

*i)* apply $a1$ from the initial configuration $C_1$ by considering $V \vdash activ\_repr(button(actionX))$,

$$C_1 \rightarrow \langle \overset{\vee}{-} \rangle (V \vdash activ\_repr(button(actionX)))$$

*ii)* then using $a2$, we get, according to $Cond1$, the application of $FunctionX$ to the object $O$ which is associated to the selected button. This implies that $obj_c$ has changed in the Memory and we have $M \vdash obj_c = FunctionX(O)$

$$(C_1 \wedge Cond1) \rightarrow \langle \overset{\vee}{-} \rangle (M \vdash obj_c = FonctionX(O) \wedge V \vdash norm\_form(button(actionX)))$$

*iii)* combine this result with the information about the graphic representation of $FunctionX(O)$ in $Cond2$ i.e. $I(FunctionX(O))$,

$$(C_1 \wedge Cond1 \wedge Cond2) \rightarrow \langle \overset{\vee}{-} \rangle (M \vdash obj_c = FunctionX(O) \wedge V \vdash I(FunctionX(O)))$$

*iv)* we obtain $V \vdash I(FunctionX(O))$ since $M \vdash obj_c = FunctionX(O)$; in *ii)* we obtained $V \vdash norm\_form(button(actionX))$. Now put all this information back in *cwin*. It is exactly what we have in the final configuration $C_f$. We conclude that the transaction is correct.

# 8 Concluding remarks

We deal with an approach for software specification. It aims to include in the specification process, the requirements of software specification techniques and the behavior of an IGS according to the graphical environment. We attempt to consider, in the specification process, the different and specific aspects of the IGS, i.e. graphical environment and interaction through I/O devices. This leads us to define new concepts, those of configuration and transaction, which enable us to manage the different levels of software components. These levels are those depending on the application itself, those depending on the graphical environment of the application and those inherent in interaction or cooperation with the user. The approach is sufficiently precise to restrict the semantics aspects to a single and unambiguous interpretation, guaranteeing that the specification can be a good communication medium for designers, users and implementors, and to allow formal reasoning about specifications or more generally about systems. We show that Dynamic Logic can be used to reason about IGS specification. We are continuing investigation in the direction of dynamic logic and related works in order to find a systematic environment for formal reasoning about IGS specification.

# References

[1] R. Balzer and N. Goldman. *Principles of good Software Specification and their Implications for Specification Language*, pages 25–39. Software Specification techniques. International Computer Science Series, 1986.

[2] R. M. Burstall and J. A. Goguen. *An Informal Introduction to Specification using CLEAR*, pages 363–390. International Computer Science Series, 1986.

[3] Dominique Clément and Janet Incerpi. *Specifying the behavior of graphical objects using Esterel.* In Proceedings of the International joint conference on Theory and Practice of Software Development. TAPSOFT'89. LNCS Vol. 352, 1989.

[4] E. Audureau & P. Enjalbert and L. Farinas Del Cerro. *Logique Temporelle.* Masson, 1990.

[5] J-Y. Girard. Linear logic. *TCS*, Vol. 50, 1987.

[6] J. A. Goguen and R. M. Bustall. Some fundamentals algebraic tools for the semantics of computation. part 1: Comma categories, colimits, signatures and theories. *The Journal of the EATCS*, Vol. 31(Num. 1– 2), 1984.

[7] J. A. Goguen, J. W. Thacher, E. G. Wagner, and J. D. Wright. Abstract data types and initial algebra and the correctness of data representations. In *Proceedings of conference on computer Graphics, Pattern recognition and Data structures*, 1977.

[8] J. A. Goguen, J. W. Thacher, E. G. Wagner, and J. D. Wright. Initial algebras, semantics and continuous algebras. *Journal of ACM*, 24:68–95, 1977.

[9] Guttag. *Notes on Types Abstractions*, pages 55–74. Software Specification techniques. International Computer Science Series, 1986.

[10] David Harel. *Dynamic Logic*, volume II, pages 497–604. D. Reidel Publishing Company, 1984.

[11] David Harel. Statecharts: A visual formalism for complex systems. *Science of Computer Programming*, 8:231–274, 1987.

[12] C. B. Jones. *Systematic Program Development*, pages 89–110. Software Specification techniques. International Computer Science Series, 1986.

[13] B. H. Liskov and V. Berzins. *An appraisal of Program Specifications*, pages 3–23. Software Specification techniques. International Computer Science Series, 1986.

[14] M. Sintzoff. Expressing program developments in a design calculus. *Nato ASI Series – Springer Verlag*, F36:343–365, 1987.

[15] M. Wirsing. Structured algebraic specifications : A kernel language. *TCS*, Vol. 42(Num. 2), 1986.

# Dialogue Design Through
# Modified Dataflow and Data Modelling

**Søren Lauesen & Morten Borup Harning**

Copenhagen Business School
Howitzvej 60, DK-2000 Frederiksberg
E-mail: {sl.iio,mbh.iio}@cbs.dk

**Abstract**. Structured methods based on dataflow diagrams and data modelling are widely used for system analysis and design, but they are not suited for dialogue design. This paper shows a method for dialogue design that is based on modified data modelling and dataflow diagrams: The usual datamodel is complemented with a forms-based or picture-based model. This model is later extended with function bubbles representing dialogue actions.

The method consists of a number of steps that lead to a final dialogue, for instance in the form of a prototype. The method allows a high degree of user participation, especially in the first steps, where the major design decisions seem to take place.

## 1. Introduction

Many system development methods are variations of structured analysis and design [DeMarco, 1978; Yourdon, 1989]. They are based on dataflow diagrams and data modelling (e.g. entity modelling). These methods are widely used today. Originally they were used for business administration systems, but today they are also coming into use with more technical systems, e.g. real-time systems [Hatley & Pirbhai, 1987]. However, the methods are not well suited for dialogue design, especially if we want a high degree of user participation. But since the methods are that well received, it is interesting to try adapting them for dialogue design.

What are the current methods for dialogue design? Roughly, they fall into two groups: The formal methods and the prototype-based methods. These two groups are extremely different, but at present very little exist in between.

The formal methods use mathematical or program-like definitions of the dialogue [Harrison & Thimbleby, 1990; Kieras & Polson, 1985; Moran, 1981]. As far as we know, none of them are in regular use for dialogue specification. Furthermore, they are not suited for direct user participation since few users are able to understand such specifications.

The importance of user participation in various ways is well-known [Grudin, 1991; Greenbaum & Kyng, 1991], and prototypes are important to achieve that. With the prototype-based methods, a series of prototypes are constructed. Each prototype is tested with users and modified until we have an acceptable result. [Gould & Lewis, 1985; Bailey, 1993].

Prototyping is fine for user participation, but lacks the necessary structure and consistency for use in larger systems: The prototypes are often constructed based solely on intuition, possibly with some guidelines on screen design (layout). Even if some structured analysis has been done already, the step from dataflow diagrams and datamodels to prototypes is left to intuition or trial and error. For larger systems this leads to unstructured dialogues that are difficult to make correct, consistent, and maintainable.

The situation can be compared to programming: It is well-known that without proper programming techniques, we end up with messy programs that cannot be made correct no matter how much we test and correct them.

Very little has been done to use dataflow and data modelling for dialogue design, but [Sutcliffe & McDermott, 1991] show an attempt. Their approach seems to be heavily dataflow-oriented, while the datamodels play a minor role. One observation is that the step from dataflow to dialogue is far from simple, because functions must be reorganized to match the dialogue, and because the subtasks are performed in an unpredictable sequence. Another observation is that although some data modelling was made, it was not used directly in the screen design.

In this paper we will show a method that uses modified datamodels and dataflow diagrams to make a more user-centered conceptual and functional design.

We assume that an initial analysis of the current system has been made and that some ideas exist about the area to be computerized. This is often a major effort, but our method does not try to cover that.

However, the method will guide us through the rest of the development through a number of steps. As with all stepwise methods, there will often be a need to go back one or more steps to revise some decision in light of knowledge gained in a later step. We will just take that for granted below.

## 2. Example: A Hotel Booking System

The method is suitable for design of many kinds of systems: business administration, software tools, devices with buttons, etc. Below we will illustrate the method with a simple hotel booking system. We assume that the area to be computerized consists of room administration, checking in and out, etc. Thus, we will not consider accounting functions, personnel, purchase, etc.

We will illustrate the method by an example: a simple hotel booking system. We will focus on room administration, checking in and out, etc. Thus, we will not consider accounting functions, personnel, purchase, etc.

We will first show a traditional datamodel for the system. Within the booking domain there are a number of objects (entities) that the system has to handle: Guests, rooms, and various kinds of breakfast selections. Figure 1 shows a traditional datamodel that reflects this. It shows the three basic classes of objects (the boxes) and two classes of relationship objects (the diamonds) which show booking/occupation of rooms, and breakfast servings.

This datamodel is a conceptual design of a rather technical nature. The concepts are the objects and their attributes. Such a model is rather precise and a good basis for development. However, it is difficult to have a deeper discussion with users about it - unless they are trained well in data modelling. On the other hand, it is important to receive the users's comments on the data to be stored in the system. This is what the first step of the method accomplishes:

## 3. User Datamodel

A user datamodel is a way to present the system data to users. The basic idea is to show the data as "forms" or other pictures of the data. Figure 2 is a possible user datamodel for the hotel booking system. The first form shows the data that the

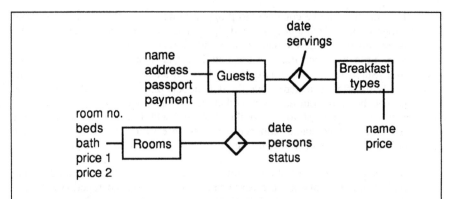

Figure 1. A traditional datamodel for a hotel booking system. There are three basic object classes (rectangles) and two connection object classes (diamonds).

system has on a guest (name, address, passport number, payment form) and the relationships to rooms and breakfast selections. We are able to see on which dates a guest has occupied or booked which rooms, and on which dates a guest has received breakfast. We should imagine that the system stores a pile of these forms - as suggested in the figure.

Note that we have filled out a form with realistic data. For instance, we have included an important, but somewhat special situation: a guest changes his room and becomes two persons. Such examples are essential to encourage user participation.

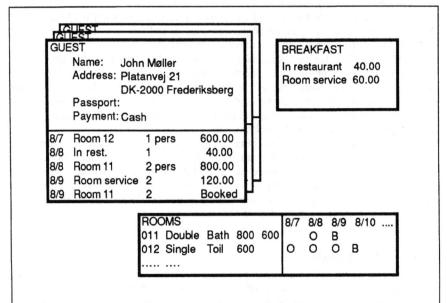

Figure 2. A user datamodel with the same information as the traditional datamodel. This example is based on a forms metaphor.

The bottom form shows the rooms and part of their relationships to the guests. We can see the room attributes and on which days they are booked (B) or occupied (O). This form will be useful when the receptionist has to find a vacant room.

The last form shows the breakfast types and their attributes. This form will be useful, for example when we have to change prices or add other types of services.

Note that we use two metaphors for repeated data: The card metaphor corresponding to a pile of index cards (for example the guest file). And the list metaphor corresponding to a list of information on a single form (for example the room form).

### User Participation

We can discuss these forms with the users. For instance, can they see a similarity to what they use at present? Can they understand what the fields mean? Is any information lacking? Are there any difficult situations that we have not considered?

As an example, the first version of the user datamodel for hotel booking did not contain two prices for each room, nor did it include change of room. This would not have been revealed by merely discussing the technical datamodel with the users.

Naming things is another important issue that should be discussed with the users. For instance, in the hotel system the field "bath" constitutes a problem. "Bath" may be a bath, a lavatory or nothing. Is it reasonable to call it "bath"? After a discussion with the users, it became clear that the term "bath" was a reasonable choice.

Names of fields etc. will appear in many places in the operational system. In order to achieve consistency we must, at an early stage, establish the right user-oriented names. It should be in the form of a user datamodel with all fields carefully named. It should be supplemented with an authorized name list to be updated throughout the lifetime of the system (a data dictionary with non-technical terms).

The way in which we have illustrated the data has two significant qualities:

### Similarity to Screen Pictures

The forms resemble something we might later show on the screen. In fact, we can make the later, real screen pictures by "cutting" large pieces out of the user datamodel. For the time being, however, we will imagine a giant screen, on which, for example, room bookings can be shown for several months.

### Similarity to Familiar Papers/Forms

The forms resemble something the user already knows. For instance, the guest form resembles quite well the invoice received by a guest, and the room form resembles the reservation book which is normally found in small receptions.

Obviously, it makes it easier for the user to understand the system if the screen pictures resemble something he knows. However, keeping to something that the user knows also has its drawbacks. It makes it difficult to produce something that is completely different (and perhaps much better) than what the user is familiar with. For instance, we may not think of using graphics, curves, pictures, etc.

However, we can also deliberately try to be creative already with the user datamodel and use graphics, curves, etc. For instance, we could show the rooms as a map of the hotel. This would be an advantage when we have to choose a room with a view - or a quiet room. Probably, we should include both forms in the system. We will then, together with the user, have to verify that it is, in fact, a better model.

### Relation to the Traditional Datamodel

What is the connection between the traditional data model and the user datamodel?

First of all, the user datamodel is not normalized. A form may contain repeated groups of data and it may contain data from several datamodel objects. Second, the same information may appear in several forms. The booking state of a room, for instance, appears on both the guest form and the booking form.

These issues would make the user datamodel unsuitable for a thorough technical design. In practice, we suggest to make both a traditional datamodel and a user datamodel, as they support different aspects of the development process. We could also imagine CASE tools that assist in mapping one to the other.

## 4. Task List

In this step we first list the key user tasks for the system. In the hotel booking system, the list could start like this:

- Booking a guest per telephone, telex, or letter.
- Checking in with booking.
- Checking in without booking.
- Checking out.
- Change of room.
- Entering the breakfast list from the kitchen.

How large or small should the tasks be? It is difficult to give a general answer, but a task must not be so small that it becomes meaningless. For instance, it is not a task to choose *checkout* from the main menu (that is an *action*). The tasks should be small, but complete, i.e. a closed task.

How do we know if we have included all the tasks? Unfortunately, it is also difficult to give a general answer here, but we must rely on the expert users for advice. Besides, we can conduct a systematic check against the traditional datamodel as follows:

- Do the tasks allow the user to see and change all attributes? If not, some tasks are probably missing.

- Do the tasks allow the user to create and delete all the entity types? If not, some tasks are probably missing.

These questions will often cause further tasks to be added to the list. In our example, it is easy to see that some tasks are missing on our list. For instance, the user cannot change or delete bookings. We would have to add these tasks.

In reality, there is a very large number of task variants, which are impossible to write down in detail. But in the task list we try to include all the tasks we believe will require special dialogue actions. Luckily, it turns out that with a limited number of dialogue actions it is possible to cover a very large number of tasks and task variants: The user performs the tasks by combining the dialogue actions in his own way.

If we have made our check against the technical datamodel thoroughly, we are sure that the user in principle can do "everything" with the system. However, we cannot be sure that he will know how to do it, or that it can be done in a convenient way. We cannot analyze all the tasks and task variants one by one, but we believe that the selection of key tasks make us focus on the most essential dialogue functions.

## 5. Information Demand Diagrams

The next step is to take the tasks one by one and identify the parts of the user datamodel that have to be visible at some point during the task. We also identify additional data needed temporarily during the task. Figure 3 shows this for the *booking* task.

When a guest books a room, the receptionist must be able to see an empty guest form. On this form the name and address have to be entered. The empty guest form is shown with dotted lines. It should remind us that this data item is not stored by the system, but only used temporarily during the dialogue.

Upon the guest's acceptance, the room must be booked and the guest created in the system. When the receptionist "creates" the guest, the temporary form will become a real guest form, now included in the guest file.

In the figure we have shown the guest file as a pile of forms. The top form is shown in heavier lines to suggest that this is the form we imagine the user will look at (i.e. the form "chosen" by the system).

The receptionist must of course be able to see which relevant rooms are vacant in the period requested. Presumably, the hotel has so many rooms that assistance from the system is necessary in order to find the relevant rooms.

To guide the search, the receptionist must be able to specify the search criteria: the desired period, number of persons, and bathroom facilities. The data to guide the search are also shown with dotted lines since they are temporary.

The room form is very large, as it covers all rooms for a long period. In the form we have marked a frame suggesting the data that the user looks at (i.e. the result of the search).

Finally, it may be necessary to print a confirmation and send it to the guest.

Note that most of the information demand diagram consists of parts of the user datamodel, the exception being the search criteria. The empty guest form and the confirmation are just variants of the regular guest form.

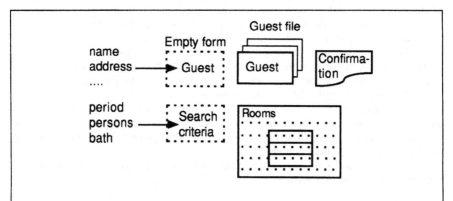

Figure 3. An information demand diagram for the booking task. Most data are parts of the user datamodel. Dotted lines show temporary data, which exist only during the dialogue.

**User Participation**

It is easy to discuss the information demand diagram with the users. They usually have a good understanding of the information necessary to perform a task.

# 6. Function Diagram

In this step we take the information demand diagrams and add functions to them. Each function corresponds to a dialogue action, i.e. a "button" that the user can press. On the diagram we show the "buttons" as function bubbles. At this stage we need not care whether the "button" corresponds to a function key, a menu selection, or a real button (as in computer controlled devices). In order to perform the task, the user will in general have to push several "buttons".

Figure 4 shows the function diagram for the booking task. When the receptionist has filled out the empty guest picture, he uses the *Create* button, which will make the empty picture become a form in the guest file.

The arrows to and from *Create* show that the Create function takes the whole dotted form and places it at the top of the guest file. Note that we use a notation where the arrows go to or from the *border* of the forms in order to show that the entire form is moved.

Another notational detail is the arrows without a function bubble. They indicate that the user is changing or looking at a data field. We can place names on an arrow to specify which data fields the function is using.

When the receptionist has to find the rooms that may be of interest to a guest, he uses the function *Find Rooms*. The arrows to and from *Find Rooms* show that the function takes data from the search criteria and makes a frame around the corresponding parts of interest on the rooms form.

Note that the arrow goes from *inside* the search criteria in order to show that we use the contents of the search form, in contrast to doing something on the entire form. Likewise the arrow goes to the border of the frame on the rooms form in order to show that we create the frame.

If the customer wishes to book one of the rooms, the receptionist selects the room and pushes *Book*. The arrows from *Book* show that the function changes the booking status on the room form and places a booking line on the guest form.

Finally, the receptionist can push *Confirm*. This function takes the contents of the guest form and prints a corresponding confirmation letter.

In practice, we should add a mini-spec (pseudo-algorithm) for each "button" to specify in a bit more detail what it is supposed to do.

Note that the function diagram does not specify a sequence for pushing the "buttons", although there might be an implicit sequence because the necessary data must be available for a button to operate. Apart from such implicit sequence restrictions, the user is actually free to choose the action sequence.

This freedom is in contrast to the formal dialogue specifications, where sequences and their variations are the key specification technique. (A more free specification technique is shown by Howes and Payne [1990]. Their sequences are determined by the display contents.)

Below we will see how sequence variations make it possible to handle several tasks with the same buttons.

**Checking the Dialogue**

We have now introduced the necessary functions ("buttons") for booking. For

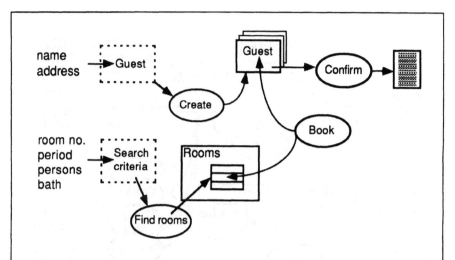

Figure 4. A function diagram showing the "buttons" to be used during the booking task. A "button" is a single dialogue action. It is shown as a function bubble. Arrows show the data needed and produced by the function.

each function we have shown which data it uses, and which data it changes. In principle, the functions are sufficient, but is the dialogue convenient from a user's point of view?

It is difficult to give an answer without testing the dialogue in practice. We have tried to go through the function diagrams with potential users, and our current experience is that some users (expert users) readily understand the diagrams and give valuable comments on them. But with other users, the dialogue is too abstract at this stage.

With the hotel booking system, we have observed that the expert users notice some problems. For instance, according to the diagram, we must have created the guest before we can use *Book*. It may well be that the receptionist finds this procedure inconvenient, because he has not yet received the customer's full name and address.

It is possible to change the diagram to address the problem, but we will not show that here.

### Including Other Tasks

We could handle other tasks in the same way: Make the information demand diagram and add the functions.

But in many cases it will pay to continue working on one of the previous function diagrams. In this way we can reuse many functions, and the dialogue will become more uniform from task to task. Figure 5 shows the result of including four more tasks into the function diagram: Checking in with booking, checking in without booking, change of room, and checking out. A total of five bubbles had to be added to handle these tasks.

### Checking in with Booking

When a guest has made a booking and arrives at the hotel, the receptionist has to find the right guest from the file.

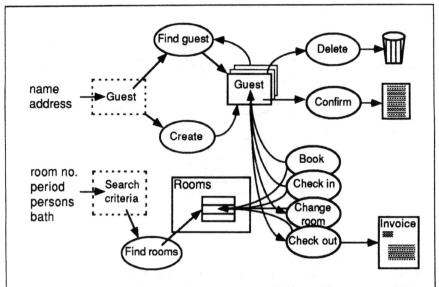

Figure 5. The function diagram with 5 buttons added for handling four more tasks, each involving several buttons. Most buttons can be used meaningfully during several tasks.

A typical way in which to handle this task would be to fill in something on the empty guest form, for instance the name of the guest. Then the receptionist must use a new function, *Find Guest*. The function will take a guest form with a matching name from the file and place the form at the top of the pile so that it is visible.

If it is not the right guest, the receptionist can use *Find Guest* once more, and the function will now take the next matching form from the file. The guest's room appears on a booking line of the guest form.

When the right guest has been shown, the receptionist can use another new function, *Check In*, which registers the guest as moved into the room and marks the room as occupied.

All in all, we had to use two new functions, but the forms (and thus the screen pictures) are the same.

**Checking in without Booking**

When a guest arrives and asks for a vacant room, we are in fact able to handle the situation with the functions we have now: The receptionist uses *Find Room* (as during booking), then creates the guest, and finally uses *Check In*.

**Change of Room**

When a guest wants to change his room, we can use most of the diagram again. However, it would be convenient, if we were able to find the guest form by means of the room number. It requires that we also include the room number as a search criterion on the empty guest form.

Once more, we must use the search criteria for rooms in order to find a new room. Finally, we must have a new function, *Change Room*, which cancels the remaining booking of the old room and marks the new one as occupied.

### Checking Out
When a guest wishes to check out, we must find the guest by means of the name or room number. Next, we must be able to enter the form of payment and finally choose a new function, *Check Out*.

Check Out prints the invoice on the basis of the information on the guest form. Moreover, it will cancel any remaining booking the guest might have.

If the guest is not a regular costumer, we must be able to remove the guest from the file. This is handled by the *Delete* function, which takes the guest form out of the file and puts it in the waste paper basket.

### Breakfast List
The remaining task on the task list is to register breakfast servings. When the breakfast list arrives from the kitchen, it has to be entered and registered under the individual guests. This is best done using an auxiliary form for batch-like entry of the data. The corresponding function diagram is straightforward, but not shown here.

## 7. Screen Outlines and State Diagram
The next step in the dialogue design is to fit forms or form parts into screen pictures. The aim is to display all information needed for a task in one or a few pictures. To achieve this, it may be necessary to combine several form parts into a single picture, and divide large forms into several pictures or scrollable regions. For simplicity, we have assumed in the example that we have a traditional screen without windowing and with 25 lines of 80 characters.

Figure 6 shows which screens we could then design for the booking system. In total, we need three screens:

(1)     The *New Guest* screen contains an empty guest form and search criteria for rooms. In addition, there is space for showing a selection of rooms corresponding to the search criteria.

(2)     The (registered) *Guest* screen is almost similar to the first screen, but instead of an empty guest form it shows the form for a registered guest.

(3)     The *Breakfast* screen is the special form for entering breakfast servings.

The system can thus be in three main states: it shows either screen 1, 2 or 3.

A function ("button") can be used in connection with certain screens, but rarely in connection with all of them. When we use the function, it can change the state to show another screen. To get an overview of the situation we have made the diagram as a state transition diagram.

For instance, the *Create* function can only be used when *New Guest* is shown. When we use the function, we should end up with a *Guest* screen  - unless there are some errors in the fields.

In order to switch between the screens we have had to add a couple of functions: *Breakfast* brings us to the *Breakfast* screen. *Return* brings us from a *Guest* screen to the *New Guest* screen. *Terminate* can be used from the *New Guest* screen and will just erase the screen.

There is no initial screen with a main menu, although it could have been made. Instead, we use *New Guest* as the initial state, since it will almost always be the first screen that is needed in a task.

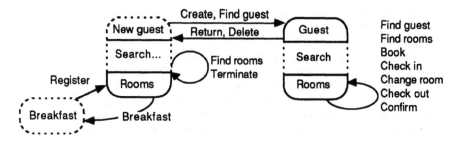

Figure 6. Screen outlines and state diagram. The hotel booking system needs three screens (two of them almost identical). It has three main states and state transitions as shown. A few buttons had to be added to navigate between screens.

## 8. Syntactical Design

The last step in the method is to make the syntactical design, for instance in the form of a prototype, and test it with prospective users.

The syntactical design is rather straightforward. If we have made a careful user datamodel, we can "cut out" parts of it and combine them to make the screen layouts. A lot of attention is still needed to provide a good layout, phrase error messages properly, provide help screens, etc.

An important point is to keep the parts from the user datamodel recognizable from one screen to another. In that way it is much easier for future users to infer the proper user datamodel from the screens.

The function diagrams and state transition diagrams tell us what "buttons" to provide for each screen. At this stage we will of course have to make a choice of how to represent a "button": As a function key, a menu point, etc. However, there will usually be a standard for this, depending on the software platform used.

Validation of this prototype is still essential in order to catch and repair the "bugs". Usability testing, heuristic evaluation, etc. can be applied here as usual. However, the whole aim of the method is that rather few problems should be found here and that they should be easy to correct. Our current experience suggests that this actually is the case.

## 9. Results

At present we have only limited experience with the method. We have designed a few small systems with it, and we have given several courses where users and programmers cooperated to make a design by means of the method. Our observations on user participation in the various steps stem from that.

We have been surprised to learn that the major design decisions are embodied already in the conceptual design, i.e. the user datamodel. This step calls for a lot of imagination, and user participation is easy to achieve.

The function diagram is the most technical step, and real user participation is more difficult here. For instance, many users have troubles seeing the difference between the function diagrams and the state transition diagrams.

Another observation is that the dialogue ends up with rather few screens compared to typical dialogues in similar applications. Finally, the usability of the dialogue is high already with the first syntactical design.

Validating the method in a larger context is a current, big task. One barrier we have met is that professional software groups use CASE tools and insist that our method should be supported or coordinated with their current tool.

## References

Bailey, G. (1993): Iterative methodology and designer training in human-computer interface design. (To appear in proceedings of InterCHI'93).

DeMarco, T. (1978): Structured analysis and system specification. Yourdon Press, New York, 1978.

Gould, J.D. & Lewis, C.H. (1985): Designing for usability: Key principles and what designers think. Comm. of the ACM, 28, pp300-311.

Greenbaum, J. & Kyng, M. (eds.): Design at Work: Cooperative design of computer systems. Lawrence Erlbaum Associates, Hillsdale, N.J. 1991.

Grudin, J. (1991): Interactive systems: Bridging the gaps between developers and users. IEEE Computer, April 1991, pp59-69.

Harrison, M. & Thimbleby, H. (eds.): Formal methods in human-computer interaction. Cambridge University Press, 1990.

Hatley, D.J. & Pirbhai, I.A. (1987): Strategies for real-time system specification. Dorset House Publishing, New York, 1987.

Howes, A. & Payne, S.J. (1990): Display-based competence: Towards user models for menu-driven interfaces. University of Lancaster.

Jeffries, R., Miller, J.R., Wharton, C., and Uyeda, K.M. (1991): User interface evaluation in the real world: A comparison of four techniques. ACM 0-89791-383-3/91/0004/0119..0124.

Jeffries, R. & Desurvire, H. (1992): Usability testing vs. heuristic evaluation: Was there a contest? SIGCHI Bulletin, Oct 1992, pp39-41.

Kieras, D.E. & Polson, P.G. (1985): An approach to the formal analysis of user complexity. Int. J. of Man-Machine Studies, 22, 365-394.

Moran, T.P. (1981): The Command Language Grammar: A representation scheme for the user interface of interactive systems. Int. J. of Man-Machine Studies, 15, pp3-50.

Sutcliffe, A.G. and McDermott, M. (1991): Integrating methods of human-computer interface design with structured systems development. Int.J. Man-Machine Studies (1991) 34, pp631-655.

Yourdon, E. (1989): Modern structured analysis. Yourdon Press, New York, 1989.

# Deriving the Functional Requirements
# for a Concept Sketching Device : a Case Study

## Raghu Kolli and Jim Hennessey

Delft University of Technology
Faculty of Industrial Design Engineering
Jaffalaan 9, 2628 BX Delft, The Netherlands
Fax: +31 15 784956
e-mail: r.kolli@io.tudelft.nl

**Abstract.** Paper-and-pencil still remains the favourite tool for designers, especially in the initial ideation phase. Computer-based tools are not considered suitable for this phase because of their lack of intuitivity. We are attempting to develop a new sketching tool based on an understanding of the traditional work practices of designers. This paper presents our understanding of sketching practices in industrial design domain and describes how we derived the functional requirements for a new sketching device using the contextual inquiry method.

**Keywords**: sketching, conceptual design, user interface, industrial design, CAD, contextual inquiry

## 1. Introduction

The IDEATE Project at our Faculty is an umbrella for research in several areas related to the conceptual phase of industrial design (Hennessey, 1992). Our goal is to provide the industrial designer with more intuitive and useful computer tools that eventually lead to better product design. For more than a year, we focussed our efforts in obtaining a clear understanding of the conceptual phase of product design, mainly through interviews with practising industrial designers. Based on our observations, we identified several aspects related to user behaviour and work practices that are characteristic for the initial ideation phase (Kolli et. al., 1993). Subsequently, we formulated a schematic user environment in which several devices and systems support the various functions of ideation phase. In this paper, we describe the functional requirements for one such device, namely a sketching device which plays a critical role in the design process. Currently, we are in the process of building the initial prototypes for this device.

This paper is organized as follows: Section 2 describes the importance of sketching in the design process. Section 3 briefly reviews various computer-based sketching tools for suitability for the idea generation phase. Section 4,5 and 6 describe the background, application and observations of contextual inquiry methodology, a method for understanding user requirements for product development purposes. The functional requirements for the new sketching device are discussed in section 7.

## 2. The Importance of Sketching in Conceptual Design

Inspite of the fact that sketching is a predominant activity in most creative and engineering professions, it is only recently that researchers have begun to investigate the sketching process. The motivation for their research is the unexploited potential of computers to aid the sketching and visual idea generation process. Design methodologists are now studying mechanical engineers, architects, graphic designers and industrial designers from various perspectives of design education, artifact design, group communication, and development of new tools (Radcliffe and Lee, 1990). Based on the work of prominent researchers : Ullman, Goldschmidt, Athavankar and Scrivener, we will try to describe the role of sketching in the visual thinking process.

Scrivener describes a sketch as 'a special kind of sparse drawing, usually produced quickly in a manner peculiar to its creator' (Scrivener and Clark, 1993). Sketching is closely associated with the problem solving or ideation phase of design and can be considered as a means of externalization of ideas. We recognize sketches as those figures containing any of the following representational forms or combinations:

> *Visual notes* - quick documentation of a form or detail in a situation study or during a client's briefing.
> *Textual notes*- brief jottings of main points or verbal descriptors to visual depictions, annotations
> *Doodles* - scribbles or squiggles without attempting to represent any concrete idea.
> *Explanatory notations* - schematic notations made during a discussion to augment the oral explanation ( a direction map, for instance).
> *Schematic representations* - abstract notations of an idea or concept represented using certain accepted symbols or methodology, for example flow charts, block diagrams etc.
> *Storyboards* - a sequence of pictures that depict a temporal activity.
> *Collages* - combinations of photographs and hand drawn graphics.
> *Idea sketches* - pictorial representations of ideas depicting certain detail, form or function in a series of explorations
> *Geometric or measured drawings* - precise scale representations in context of solving a detailing problem.
> *Concept renderings* - idea sketches with a high level of detail and visual resemblance to final product.

In dealing with complex design situations, designers can perform only limited transformations in the mind (Goldschmidt, 1991). Ullman et. al. (1990) state that it is necessary to externalize ideas because of the limitations in storage capacity of the human Short Term Memory system (STM). During protocol studies of mechanical engineers, they observed that sketching is the most preferred way and 100% of the drawings made during conceptual stage were sketches.

Sketching is the most natural and fastest way of externalizing form concepts. Based on studies of individual industrial designers, Athavankar described a typical ideation scenario of 'cycles of intense brooding followed by spurts of rapid sketching' (Athavankar, 1992). Scrivener and Clark (1993) also confirm bursts of sketching activity stating that 'cessation of drawing surface activity is followed swiftly by the onset of further sketching'. Their empirical studies of designer dyads on use of a drawing surface showed that 61% of intervals between drawing acts were less than 12 seconds with 33% of these being less than 3 seconds. In their studies, Ullman et. al. (1990) observed that the average length of sketch is about 8 seconds. Therefore, it is clear that sketching is a very rapid process and any use of instruments or complex controls will severely impair the underlying cognitive functions.

Sketching is an intuitive and effortless activity. Athavankar (1992) observed that designers totally switched off from the physical environment around them during the creative act and stated that 'the sketch-book, pencil and the hand act like extensions of mind'. Schenk (1991) quoted a graphic designer as saying 'your hand is part of your brain, it is as though your brain is drawing'. Considering such views, there is a close one-to-one intimate bond between the designer and the tools/materials used for sketching.

The marked property of a free-hand rapid sketching is that 'one can read off a sketch more than was written into it ' (Goldschmidt,1991). According to her, 'new and unexpected relationships among shapes on paper harbour numerous clues to potentially useful information'. Radcliffe and Lee (1990) argue that sketching alone is not sufficient to realize concepts and that a designer needs creative strategies to get the most from sketching.

Work done in this area so far is still not adequate to explain how exactly sketching supports the creative design (Scrivener and Clark, 1993), but there are few insights which have bearing on computer tools. For instance, Fish and Scrivener (1990) found indeterminacies in sketches : incomplete contours, wobbly lines, accidental smudges, energetic cross-hatchings, blots and scratch marks. They state that 'deliberate or accidental indeterminacies may trigger innate recognition search mechanisms that generate a stream of imagery useful to invention'. Goldschmidt (1991)cites an example from a protocol study where tacit clues from early sketches lead to a successful design solution using manipulation of visual information through sketching. She states that 'though sketches are always produced in a series, the insight processes are not necessarily sequential'. Athavankar (1992) observed that the process of sketching also included 'reconsidering and rebuilding' it several times. He argues that the process of representation must necessarily offer an 'on-line feedback' to react to allow quickly reversible changes.

It is beyond the scope of this paper to construct a cognitive model of sketching. However, descriptions of models can be found in Radcliffe and Lee(1990), Fish and Scrivener (1990) and Goldschmidt(1991).

Understanding the role of sketching alone is not sufficient to develop devices to support sketching. Additional information regarding current practices of designers and usage of traditional tools/materials is necessary. In our case for instance, we need to know: what should be the size of sketching surface, what tools are needed, where do people sketch and if they sketch alone or together. Before we report on our studies to elicit such information, we will review some of the currently available computer-supported sketching systems.

## 3. Computer Tools for Sketching

Computer supported sketching is not entirely a new activity. We will briefly describe computer-based sketching tools as found in different domains: graphic arts, CAD, collaborative work and mobile computing.

The last decade has seen a large number of commercially available paint and draw graphic programs running on the personal computers. The paint programs support free form sketching using metaphors based on conventional tools like pen, pencil, eraser, brush etc. The draw programs on the other hand, make use of primitive geometric objects like circles, rectangles, lines etc. and provide features for intuitive manipulation. Normally, users sketch or draw using a mouse or a stylus connected to a digitizer tablet. These graphic programs are primarily intended for making high quality illustrations and not for evolving a conceptual idea iteratively. Also, these programs do not have any features for image management ie. indexing and retrieval.

CAD systems on the other hand, treat sketching as an input activity to generate surface or solid models (Dohmen, 1992). Examples of such systems are Design Capture System (Hwang and Ullman, 1990), Fast Shape Designer (Van Dijk and Mayer, 1992) and 3-Draw (Roberts, et. al., 1990). Typically, a two dimensional sketch is generated on the screen using a stylus and a digitizer tablet. In the case of 3-Draw, users sketch directly in 3D in real time using hand movements in space. Since these systems mainly aim to interpret the sketches into wireframe or surface models for flexible manipulation, they impose certain notational constraints on the user. Some commercial CAD systems instead of supporting sketching activity, use the scanned image of a paper sketch as an underlay to create free form lines from the scratch (Emmett, 1991). Obviously, this is an intermediate solution to transfer paper sketches into 3D computer models.

Due to a growing interest in collaborative design activity, several researchers are experimenting with drawing tools for supporting group or pair communication. Examples are : Teampaint (Ishii et.al, 1992), We-Met (Wolf and Rhyne, 1992) and Conversation Board (Brinck and Gomez, 1992). These tools are very similar to the paint programs but have additional functionality for annotation, recording and playback of sessions. The emphasis understandably in such systems is on real time interpersonal communication through audio or video link rather than creative sketching or drawing.

Another approach to supporting sketching has been in form of electronic note books. Lakin et. al. (1989) prototyped a system called *vmacs* which supports text and graphic input in a free wheeling style. The system however, uses a mouse for graphic input and a keyboard for touch typing. *vmacs* permits multiple representation languages like bar charts, rigid body diagrams and FSA diagrams etc. on the same page. In addition, a selected screen area is processed at users command by spatially parsing the arrangement of the graphics and performing appropriate semantic interpretation. The system is primarily aimed to serve as an engineer's note book. The NPL Electronic Paper project (Brocklehurst, 1991) uses transparent digitizer placed on a flat panel display and a stylus to mimic the pen-on-paper feeling. The display is connected to a Sun workstation for providing the computational power. Like *vmacs*, the NPL project also focuses on system recognition of hand written text and graphic data like lines, circles etc. for further operations. A true portable wireless device termed as ScratchPad was prototyped at Xerox PARC using a transparent digitizer and a flat panel LCD display (Weiser,1991). A multi-button stylus is used to write or perform operations on the screen. ScratchPads augment the conventional computer screen with the main advantage of portability.

Currently, a new breed of portable devices, namely, the notebook computers and personal digital assistants (PDAs) are making their entry into the business market. These portable devices (for example, Personal Communicator from EO machines, Newton from Apple, PenMaster from Samsung, GridPad from Grid Systems) support direct stylus-based writing and sketching on a LCD display (Baran, 1992) ( Linderholm et. al.,1992) (Bortman, 1993). These devices are designed to meet the requirements of mobile executives: taking notes, form filling, faxing, language translation, maps, documentation etc. and are likely to become affordable in the near future.

We are particularly encouraged with the developments in portable computing and we see the possibilities for building a specialized sketching device for industrial designers. Our research is also motivated by the views expressed by the industrial design professionals that most of the current computer systems do not fulfil the needs of idea sketching phase (Tovey, 1989) (Emmett, 1991) (Rosenthal, 1993). Hence, in order to design a usable system, we needed to derive the functional requirements for sketching based on user studies.

## 4. Methodology

Our motivation in studying sketching habits of designers is the necessity to make timely design decisions in the development of new product and not as much to validate a scientific theory. In view of such requirements, we choose the contextual inquiry method advocated by Wixon et.al. (1990) of Digital Equipment Corporation.

The contextual inquiry method has been developed because of the fact that the traditional empirical research methods do not provide direct input for product development and design decisions. This method is reported to have been practiced widely in the high-technology engineering community. The method relies on direct observation of users at their own work environments in context of real life tasks. Because of the short time available for such studies, the sample base of users is relatively small. In order to make up for this deficiency, users are selected for maximum differences. Typically, experimenters talk with the users while they are working. If the work occurs over months, then artifacts that are used or produced during the course of work are used as props for the discussion. The data comes from interpretation of the observations by the experimenter rather than 'measured' results. Even the observations are not bounded into pre-defined categories. During the talk, users are engaged as partners and user's interpretations, language, and the structure of their work activities are gathered. The structure of users' work is revealed in users' thoughts, intentions and how they orient to their work tasks. Having practiced the method, Wixon et. al (1990) state that the key to the success of the method is to develop a shared understanding of these thoughts.

In our adaptation of the contextual inquiry method to our domain ie. conceptual phase of industrial design, we asked the individual subjects (in our case, industrial designers), to choose one of their recent projects to form the basis for discussion.

## 5. Data Sources

To derive the functional requirements for a sketching device, we mainly used three sources of qualitative data, each with its own characteristic information : 1. Interviews with industrial designers 2. Video tapes of concept sketching sessions and 3. Project sketchbooks of one designer.

*Interviews*
Our user base consisted of eight practicing industrial designers belonging to different industrial design studios in The Netherlands. Each designer has atleast 2 years of design experience. By coincidence, rather than arrangement, seven of them have graduated from Delft University of Technology as it is the only graduate design school in the country. For practical reasons, we accepted the sample base to be sufficiently representative for our purpose. However, the design projects handled by each of them are quite different (coffee machine, lamp, radio safety device, electronic key, air-heater, information booth, measuring tape etc.).

A typical interview session lasted 60-90 minutes at the designer's work place. During the session, the designer was encouraged to describe the conceptual design phase of a recent project, showing the relevant artifacts (sketches, mock-up models, product samples, competitors products ) from the project folder or archives. The designer was interrupted from time to time to talk about the techniques and tools used to make a particular sketch, or to state his or her personal preferences. The discussion was recorded on audio tapes and photographs were taken from time to time documenting the artifacts as well as the general studio environment. Since, in our case, the experimenter is also the developer for the new product, we placed emphasis on getting a first-hand experience of industrial designers' contextual needs rather than meticulous documentation.

*Video of sketching sessions*
Sketching sessions of four senior industrial design students were recorded using video cameras fitted above the sketching area. The students were individually generating conceptual ideas for new cars for an automobile design competition. No time limits were

set for the sessions but the students were requested to use thicker marker pens in order to capture legible sketches on the video. The video tapes yielded a rich source of temporal data related to build up of sketches, particularly the hand positions at various stages and constant movement of paper. Such a data is not available normally when examining completed sketches.

*Sketchbooks*

We also examined seven elaborate sketchbooks maintained by an individual designer who was exploring new forms for street furniture as part of his graduation project. The sketchbooks spanned several months of his project and included a variety of form explorations, doodles, verbal descriptions and conceptual ideas. These sketchbooks also gave us an insight into the organization of sketches based on individual concepts and the moods of the designer over time as revealed by the choice of pens and the nature of strokes.

The contextual inquiry method proved to be practical and useful. Even though the interviews were conducted at work places of designers, the setup was unobtrusive. We did not find the need for video recording. Sometimes we sat around the designer's desk. Other times, we talked in a conference room, but were later shown around the design studio. As also experienced by Wixon et. al.(1990), we got a fairly reasonable picture by the time we finished collecting the data. Later, we spent about a week summarizing our observations based on the audio recordings and photographic documentation. A summary of observations from all these data sources is described in the following section.

## 6. Observations

*Use of artifacts*

Designers in general, showed a marked preference for sketching on A3 (297mm x 420mm) sheets of paper in horizontal format. Though loose sheets are commonly used for flexibility (easy to spread them out on the table), some designers use A3 sketchbooks or occasionally, a scroll. The loose sheets are later filed into a project folder. For initial sketching only fineliners, pencils and colour marker pens are used. We did not see use of any paint brushes. Sometimes, a ruler is used to draw straight lines. Sketches are seldom erased, though they are frequently overwritten. Designers expressed a need to retain all thoughts drawn on paper, however inaccurate. Though the use of overlays (tracing an image using a translucent paper) is known in design professions, we have not seen much use of such medium. We have seen many instances of clever use of plain paper to reduce or enlarge sketches and to get mirror images (using a transparent sheet). Quite often designers make a number of copies of a sketch and explore different colour combinations. Also collages are made of product environments in combinations with sketches. For example, an image of a factory worker is cut out from a magazine and a safety-device is sketched on it roughly to give the impression that the guard is holding the device. Or, in some cases, forms are sketched on copies of floor plan drawings.

*Contents of sketches*

Sketchbooks contained a variety of representations and notations in a free-wheeling style: textual descriptions, annotations, perspective views, plans, incomplete markings, and even some scale drawings. Sometimes pictures or related data are pasted in the book similar to a scrapbook. The sketchbooks are labelled serially. Since sketchbooks are replaced over a period of time, it is not uncommon to find a collection of different sizes or types of books and all sorts of loose sheets in the project folder. Colour is used to mark or highlight certain components or area of sketches. Some designers are trained to rapidly produce colour sketches which resemble highly realistic renderings. We were surprised to see that such highly quality illustrations could be produced in a few minutes simply using colour marker pens. We observed that the size of a sketch usually is about the size of maximum wrist stroke. The empty space on a sheet is filled up, if necessary by scaling down the later sketches. A new idea is normally started on a fresh page. All the sketches on a given page are some what linked to the main concept on the page in some fashion ie. variation of form, enlargement of detail etc., unless some sketches are drawn later.

*Temporal activity*
It is fascinating to see how sketches are built up over time in the video. We noticed that the paper is constantly adjusted with the one hand (or the wrist) to facilitate access to the empty space while the other hand holds the writing tool. Also there is a high frequency of pen swapping while making colour sketches. Often, commonly used markers (black, for example) are held in one hand, or sometimes, the pen caps are also held habitually in the non-active hand. As the paper gets filled up, the wrist or even the elbow is rested on the paper to sketch properly. Sometimes, a blank paper is placed on the sketched areas so as not to soil the area with sweat from the wrist. While sketching, previous sketches (often the most recent one) are placed in view for constant reference. From time to time the previous sketches are referred either by spreading them out on the table or by flipping through the pages of the book. There are a number of breaks during the sketching activity: to get new pens or tools, to get coffee or to discuss progress with a colleague. In the video, we observed that during the discussions centered around the sketch, colleagues point out certain areas on the paper but show a reluctance to draw on it, especially if it looks neat.

*Archiving and re-use*
Selected sketches are made into slides for later presentation purposes. Despite shortage of storage space, many designers keep an archive of all their sketches for historic or nostalgic reasons. Old sketches are almost never re-used though they are browsed through occasionally. Also, once a page is used, it is rare that it is used again at a later stage for sketching. Designers casually reach out for a fresh page to start a sketch.

These qualitative observations of current work practices helped us to evolve the initial set of functional requirements for a device to support sketching. These are described in the next section.

## 7. Discussion: Functional Requirements

We derived the functional requirements for the concept sketching device based on several sources: 1. cognitive requirements of sketching as described in literature 2. qualitative observations during contextual inquiry 3. our own needs as practising designers and design educators and 4. current developments in portable pen-based devices.

Contrary to the wide-spread belief that computer-supported sketching must necessarily result in recognition of textual and graphic input, we find that it is not necessary for the ideation sketching. The reason being that these sketches are drawn for designer's own externalization of ideas and do not follow any decipherable conventions. Any slightest imposition of representational structure will defeat the very cause of sketching as an imagery aid. We believe that a computer can best support sketching by following an image-based approach rather than object-oriented approach or recognition-based approach. In other words, the system has no sensitivity to the contents of a sketch whether text, graphics or annotation marks but merely facilitates writing or sketching and creative manipulation at an image level. However, some transparent recognition mechanisms may be useful. For instance, since designers create a number of sketches on a page over a period of time, it may be possible to recognize 'chunks' of images based on an analysis of temporal activity.

The main requirement of the sketching tool is to facilitate rapid capture of ideas as they occur. The tool should match in pace and respond as quickly to designer's natural motor actions. Undoubtedly, there are no tools currently, which can match the pen-and-paper performance in this aspect. Even the state-of-art LCD tablets and stylus suffer a fractional time delay and unsatisfactory visual quality of lines due to resolution of screens.

A second requirement is to permit casual use of the tool. While it doesn't seem necessary for the tool to be portable, because the most intensive sketching is almost always carried out at the work desk, a user should be able to place the tool on the desk and shift it around during sketching. The tool should be able to support postural habits like resting of wrists, palms or elbows. Also, since designer's share an intimate feeling for their customized tools, a designer should be able to carry the tool around casually and plug in during a meeting.

The size of sketching area plays an important role and designers have repeatedly expressed a need for a visual size that they find inviting. The preferred size is A3. Again current LCD tablets are severely limited to a maximum size of 150mm x 200mm.

Paper being an inert medium, most designers have trained themselves to manipulate mentally the images drawn on paper. The only physical manipulation possible on paper is overwriting or cutting and pasting parts of sketches (or copies of sketches) using a pair of scissors and glue. Or at another level, reducing the size of images using a copier. The potential for manipulation of images is immense in computer medium. Besides facilities for cropping of pictures to make a collage, duplication, reduction and enlargement, marking and colouring, we did not find any other specific requirements for manipulation.

During the interviews, we learned that most industrial designers work in teams of 2 or 3 within the company. Informal communication across the tables is quite common. Very often an idea is developed across table with everyone sketching furiously on a common paper or in their own sketchbooks. Hence, it seems that the sketching tool need to support such acts of group communication as well.

A last area which needs to be considered is the integration of video with sketching. Similar to sketching forms, there is a great need for producing quick animations of sketches, especially while designing user interfaces or adjustable products (a couple of designers expressed difficulties in trying to visualize the moving mechanisms of products. eg. a dentist's chair). A related requirement is the possibility of annotating videos or animations in real time.ie. intuitively making simple marks on dynamic information accompanied by audio comments. We have explored this possibility and found it to be not only feasible but also provocative.

An area where a computer tool can support ideation is by providing or facilitating visual stimuli that lead to new ideas. A designer may realize new possibilities by bringing together parts of sketches from different pages in a collage fashion. Or selected images on a page may be highlighted using colour or by increasing the intensity of lines to facilitate visual comparison while the other images recede into the background in grey form. Or it may be possible to continuously display the sketched images randomly in a corner of the screen to help the designer benefit from tacit clues. Such features however, because of their innovative nature have to be evaluated empirically to assess their usefulness.

We have benefited immensely from our study of users. Besides, obtaining clear answers for some of our questions (for instance, designers mostly work in teams of 2 or 3, they sketch mostly in office at their desk etc.), we are also able to anticipate some key design issues (the need to support the palm on sketching surface, for example). Once, these requirements are interpreted into concrete design specifications, these need to be further validated by users. We hope to follow the suggestion of Wixon et. al.(1990) to continuously share our assumptions and interpretations with users by inviting them to comment on our initial designs.

## 8. Conclusion

Sketching plays an important role as an imagery aid in evolving new ideas during the conceptual phase of design. Inspite of the advancements in computer technology, there are still no devices that provide meaningful support to the sketching activity. We are attempting to develop innovative concepts for a new sketching tool based on an understanding of the ideation phase of design. In order to derive the functional requirements for such a tool, we used the contextual inquiry method, a method developed by Wixon et. al. to provide direct input for product development. We found the method to be practical and useful in understanding the sketching requirements of industrial designers. This understanding with users is proving to be valuable in evolving new design ideas for our sketching tool. We hope that other researchers will benefit from our description of functional requirements.

194

## 9. Future Plans

We are currently in the process of translating the functional requirements into concrete design specifications. The concept prototype for our sketching device called IDEATOR will be completed by summer of 1993 and we plan to evaluate the concept with industrial designers. We are also looking for research partners and corporate funding to build a functional prototype and to carry out further testing.

## 10. Acknowledgements

We would like to thank Wim Muller and Mick van Ooy for making available the video tapes of their workshop; Gert Pasman for his assistance in conducting the interviews; and Matthijs van Dijk for providing his sketchbooks for our study.

## 11. References

Athavankar, U.A., Rediscovering the Act of Sketching: Implications of its Support to the Creative Thought Process, *Design Researche*, September, 1992, 45-60.

Baran, N., Rough Gems: First Pen Systems Show Promise, Lack Refinement, *Byte*, April, 1992, 212-222.

Bortman, H., Personal Communicators, *MacUser*, February, 1993,249-252.

Brink, T. and Gomez, L.M., A Collaborative Medium for the Support of Conversational Props, In *CSCW'92 Proceedings*, ACM, 1992, 171-178.

Brocklehurst, E.R., The NPL Electronic Paper Project, *International Journal of Man Machine Studies*, 34, 1, 1991, 69-95.

Dohmen, M., Shape Modification Using Simulated Gestures, Internal Report, Faculty of Industrial Design Engineering, Delft University of Technology, The Netherlands, 1992.

Emmett, A., Guardians of Style, *Computer Graphics World*, June 1991, 30-40.

Fish, J. and Scrivener, S., Amplifying the Mind's Eye: Sketching and Visual Cognition, *Leonardo*, 23, 1, 1990, 117-126.

Goldschmidt, G., Visual Clues; Tacit Information Processing via Sketching, In *Proceedings of 3rd International Symposium on Systems Research, Information and Cybernetics*, Baden-Baden, 1991.

Hennessey, J.M., The IDEATE Project: Exploring Computer Enhancements for Conceptualizing, In *Automation Based Creative Design*, White, T. and Tzonis, A.(Eds.), Elsevier, Amsterdam, 1992 [In Press].

Hwang, T.S. and Ullman, D.G., The Design Capture System: Capturing Back-of-the-envelope Sketches, *Journal of Engineering Design*, 1,4,1990,339-353.

Ishii, H., Kobayashi, M. and Grudin, J., Integration of Inter-personal Space and Shared Workspace: ClearBoard Design and Experiments, In *CSCW Proceedings*, ACM, 1992, 33-42.

Kolli, R., Pasman, G. and Hennessey, J.M., Some Considerations for Designing a User Environment for Creative Ideation, In *Proceedings of INTERFACE'93*, The Human Factors & Ergonomics Society, Santa Monica, 1993, 72-77.

Lakin, F.,Wambaugh, J., Leifer, L., Cannon, D. and Sivard, C., The Electronic Design Notebook: Performing Medium and Processing Medium, *The Visual Computer*,5, 1989,214-226.

Linderholm, O., Apiki, S. and Nadeau, M., The PC Gets More Personal, *Byte*, July 1992. 128-138.

Radcliffe, D.F. and Lee, T.Y, Models of Visual Thinking by Novice Designers, In *Proceedings of Design Theory and Methodology'90*, ASME, September, 1990, 145-152.

Roberts, A., Sachs, E. and Stoops D., 3-Draw: A Three Dimensional Computer-aided Design Tool, In *Computers in Engineering*, Proceedings of the ASME International Computers in Engineering, ASME, 1990, New York, 299-307.

Rosenthal, L., Can You Sketch on a Computer, *Industrial Design*, January-February, 1993,82.

Schenk, P., The Role of Drawing in the Graphic Design Process, *Design Studies*, 12,3, July 1991, 168-181.

Scrivener, S.A.R. and Clark, S.M., How Interaction with Sketches Aids Creative Design, in *Proceedings of the International State-of-the-Art Conference, Interacting with Images*, National Gallery, London, 10-11 February, 1993.

Tovey, M., Drawing and CAD in Industrial Design, *Design Studies*, 10, 1, January 1989, 24-39.

Ullman, D.G., Wood, S., and Craig, D., The Importance of Drawing in the Mechanical Design Process, *Computer & Graphics,* 14, 2,1990, 263-274.

Van Dijk, C.G.C. and Mayer, A.A.C., Sketch Input for Conceptual Surface Design, submitted to *Computer Aided Design Journal*, 1992.

Weiser, M., The Computer for the 21st Century, *Scientific American* September, 1991, 66-75.

Wixon, D., Holtzblatt, K. and Knox, S., Contextual Design : An Emergent View of System Design, In *Proceedings of CHI'90*, ACM, 1990, 329-336.

Wolf, C.G. and Rhyne, J.R., Communication and Information Retrieval with a Pen-based Meeting Support Tool, In *CSCW'92 Proceedings*, ACM, 1992, 322-329.

# SUPPORTING COOPERATION

# Theory-Based Negotiation Frameworks for Supporting Group Work

Beth Adelson
Rutgers University
adelson.chi@xerox.com

## Abstract

In this paper we begin by presenting a taxonomy of impasses in group work situations[1]. The taxonomy includes factors such as goal conflicts and resource limitations. We then present a prescriptive theoretical framework designed to support negotiation during these impasses. We also describe NegotiationLens, a system which embodies the framework by supporting the actions prescribed by the theory. We then analyze the adequacy of the framework which stresses a collaborative form of negotiation. From this analysis we suggest a line of research which would lead to an expanded taxonomy. We hypothesize the expanded taxonomy would include interpersonal factors such as inequalities in the power of negotiating parties. We then discuss the framework and tools which would be useful given this expanded view of causes of group work impasses. Lastly we suggest the relevance of these factors to other classes of groupware.

**Keywords:** Computer Supported Cooperative Work, Task And User Analysis, Negotiation as a Support for Group Work

# 1 Impasses in Group work: The Need for Negotiation

The growing body of literature on cooperative work describes a number of tasks in which, increasingly, multiple actors come together with multiple goals and complex sets of constraints. These tasks include collaborative engineering and design; writing; research; and strategic planning and decision-making[21, 9, 14, 15, 12, 19, 20, 8]. However, these tasks, at a minimum, require the coordination of goals, actors, and constraints[21, 9, 20], making their completion vulnerable to deadlocks. This leads us to ask how can collaborative negotiation restart the process of group work when it stalls?

---

[1] This work was made possible by a Henry Rutgers Research Fellowship and by the generous intellectual and financial support of Tom Malone at MIT's Sloan School Center for Coordination Science.

We begin by describing a taxonomy of situations in which groups working together to solve complex problems can reach deadlocks. We then present a prescriptive theoretical framework for collaborative negotiation. In the framework, negotiating parties are asked to make their usually implicit needs and resources explicit. This has several effects. First, making needs explicit allows their incorporation into mutually beneficial solutions. Second, making resources explicit allows their full utilization and so can lead to solutions which are better than ones developed through traditional non-collaborative bargaining. Third the collaborative stance taken during this process has been found to foster better working relationships[25, 10, 11, 1, 2, 3].

It needs to be noted that our initial framework assumes that collaborative workers can without too much difficulty enter into a negotiation and state the needs and resources which they bring to the situation. Work on conflict resolution done in the last decade has shown that negotiating parties can make their needs and resources known[25, 10, 11, 1, 2, 3]. However, in Section 5.2 we examine at some length the cases in which collaborative negotiation is difficult to achieve.

Note that we are putting forth a mechanism which is meant to restart the process of group work when it stalls. In this sense our work differs from work on design rationale in that it is meant to support group work during the initial rather than later stages of documentation, maintenance, etc.[19, 8]. It does however form companion research, in that the pressures operating during a negotiation may also operate during the creation of a design rationale (Section 5.2).

## 2   A Taxonomy and Examples

Our taxonomy consists of six elements of group work which are central to its success, prone to conflict and amenable to negotiation. The taxonomy builds on the work of Malone and Crowston on coordination theory [21, 9].

*The elements of the taxonomy are:* Goal Selection, Goal Decomposition, Goal Reformulation, Allocation of Limited Resources, Role Interdependencies and Role Conflicts. Below we define and illustrate a conflict relevant to each element.

*Coordination conflicts:*

1. *Goal Selection:*
   Goal selection problems can arise when two groups with differing roles and therefore differing agendas work jointly on a project within an organization.

   In this example[2] a disagreement arose in a research group when a visiting researcher told her manager that she wanted to start up two new projects and the manager replied that she should not do so until she had completed the one project she had already started.

---

[2]Here and below, the names or task domain of the examples have been changed to ensure the anonymity of the participants.

Behind each position lay a set of legitimate concerns. However, neither side felt able to express them in the context of the tension which suddenly sprang up as a result of their opposing positions. The researcher's goal was to finish, by previously established deadlines, a set of talks on works-in-progress. She needed to start the new projects in order to meet the talk deadlines. Further, she had handed the first project off to her research assistants and she wanted to keep working while she waited for their results. On the other side, the group manager was worried that the researcher's desire to start new projects signaled a loss of interest on the part of the researcher and so he was worried that his goals would not be met: The current project would not be finished; the work done so far would be lost; and the time invested in training the researcher on the lab's equipment would turn out to have been wasted. In his experience, some visitors were very productive although others left projects unfinished and he found it hard to tell into which category this visitor would ultimately fall.

The relationship which previously had been strongly positive became tense.

## 2. *Goal Reformulation*:

Often as work progresses groups decide that their original goals are not in their own best interests and need to be reworked. Consider a case in which management had given a multi-media and a curriculum development group the task of working together to develop a line of multi-media educational software. Each group saw this collaboration as an opportunity to create a breakthrough product, but only within its own sphere[7]. That is, although initially the two groups had the goal of collaborating, they also had implicit conflicting goals concerning what they wished to accomplish. As a result, a deadlock was reached during the initial design phase and little was accomplished for several months. Eventually, as the deadline grew near, the multi-media group withdrew from the project, deciding that it would gain a more secure position in the company if it worked on some other project in which multi-media played a more central role. Although this left the curriculum development group to proceed freely, it also placed them under a great deal of time pressure.

## 3. *Goal Decomposition:*

The goal decomposition process entails making decisions about how a task should be accomplished and who in a team should have responsibility for each sub-task. In the kind of multi-disciplinary effort described in the above example (point 2) this is another likely candidate for debate.

## 4. *Allocation of Limited Resources*:

These conflicts may involve constraints on funding, time, personnel and/or facilities. Here we present an example concerning funding constraints.

An educational institution had, not unconventionally, divided its computer-based activities into two interdependent organizational entities; a Computer Science department and a Computer Services center. Although the roles of the groups forced them into some cooperative endeavors, the alliance was forced, rather than freely entered into. For example, the computer science department maintained electronic mail service for all of the university's computers and the computer services center provided computational facilities for courses taught in the computer science department. Additionally, the university had, at the time, very limited resources for new projects. The Computer Science department had been approached by a computer company and been offered a 'matching grant', an arrangement under which the company would sell the department $40,000 worth of equipment for $20,000. The Computer Science department (without notifying Computer Services) got the administration to agree to this outlay of money and made arrangements with the computer company to proceed with the deal. At this point Computer Services heard about the arrangement and became concerned that the outlay would eat up the administration's entire computer budget for some time to come. Computer Services therefore persuaded the administration to cancel the arrangement (without notifying Computer Science). Shortly after this the computer company representative who had initiated the arrangement both with Computer Science and internally with his management called the Computer Science department to tell them that the administration had reneged on its half of the funding. He also told them the university had put the company to a lot of trouble and had in the process made him and his manager look bad. He informed computer science that, as a result, the company had decided that in the future they would not be willing to offer matching funds to any part of the university. Adding jealousy to frustration, he explained that another local university had instead been chosen for the matching fund program.

5. *Role Interdependencies*:

Conflicts can arise when two interdependent organizational entities with different goals have occasion to deal with a third party. An aspect of the 'matching fund' dispute between Computer Science and Computer Services (point 4) serves as an example. When the representative for Computer Science was informed that the department was no longer eligible for the matching grant program he responded adversarially to the situation. His goal was to try and diminish the perceived inter-group interdependency and get the computer company to separate its opinion of computer science from its opinion of computer services in order to regain computer science's eligibility. Basically he said that the ill-advised behavior of computer services was not to be taken as a predictor of the behavior of computer science. He further stated that now that he was aware of the type of behavior that might be expected from computer services he would in the future take action to prevent a situation like the current one from arising. In effect he was casting aspersions on another part of his organization in order to preserve the reputation of his own group.

6. *Role Conflicts*:

One situation in which role conflicts can arise occurs when two individuals in different groups each feel that they must individually complete a given piece of a joint project. The following example is provided by [13]. Typically on large software projects the functional design specifications are produced by the software engineers. Eventually these specifications are turned over to a group who is also responsible for producing the user interface. This can create a situation in which the software engineers and the user interface designers both feel a need to produce and receive sole credit for the user interface. As Grudin,[14] points out there can be many reasons underlying this feeling. One, of course is professional pride, but others include questions concerning who actually is the person best qualified to do the work and attempts by one group to establish dominance over another.

In the following section we describe a framework for negotiation which was designed to support cooperative work situations. In Section 5.2 we discuss the fit between the framework and the above examples.

# 3    A Framework for Collaborative Negotiation

In this section we present a prescriptive framework for managing group conflict. The framework is intended to help groups, like the collegial but diverse groups typically involved in large projects, find optimal solutions to conflicts. It is also intended to move these groups away from impasses and back into collaborative relationships. This is accomplished by having the groups make explicit their needs and resources and then allowing them to jointly construct mutually acceptable solutions. This has the effect of solidifying and improving existing working relationships.

The underpinnings of our framework derive from theoretical and empirical work on negotiation which has accumulated over the last decade[24, 17, 25, 6, 22, 23, 10, 11, 16, 1, 2, 3]. We begin with a description of the framework. We then describe the tool which embodies it.

1. *Making Needs Explicit:*

In this part of the negotiation the parties are asked to state what they need in order to reach a successful resolution of the situation. Part of this process includes: i. Making implicit desires explicit. This allows both sides to better understand their own needs and the needs of the other party. When needs are made explicit it is more likely that they can be focused on and therefore incorporated into conflict solutions. ii. Providing explanations as to the importance of each need. This allows each party to feel that the other has well-motivated rather than simply arbitrary needs. iii. Developing objective criteria concerning the legitimacy of each need.

This will aid both parties in deciding which positions or parts of their positions are reasonable as they work towards a resolution.

2. *Making Resources Explicit:*
Here the parties state what they can offer each other in their collaborative endeavor. This stage makes clear the boundaries of the situation. Additionally, it can make each party feel that the other is making a good-faith effort.

3. *Matching Needs to Resources:*
This is a process by which the parties look for opportunities for mutual gain. But, the discovery of these opportunities has in practice been markedly difficult without computer support. However, using our software, the parties are easily able to systematically compare a given need against the currently listed resources. This process is illustrated in Section 4, point 4.

4. *Developing Joint Solutions:*
Here the parties are encouraged to: i. Initially develop a variety of solutions which might accommodate the needs of both sides equally; and ii. Iterate through this process by evaluating emerging solutions until a mutually agreeable one is found. (See point 6 and Section 4, point 5.)

5. *Developing Alternatives:*
In addition to developing possible negotiated solutions the parties are also asked to individually examine their alternatives to working together. This serves several functions. When good alternatives to working together do exist, knowing these alternatives can increase the parties confidence in their own resources, allowing them to approach the negotiation with a mind-set which has been found, empirically although perhaps counter-intuitively, to foster flexibility[3]. However, it can also allow the parties to quickly decide that the current collaboration should be abandoned. The interesting point here is that this kind of determination, when made early on, often preserves the collaborative relationship, allowing future joint efforts to succeed.

In the case where good alternatives are not found, it can increase the parties' commitment to the negotiation process, thereby motivating the parties to construct a joint solution.

6. *Respecting the Other Side:*
A central part of this framework is that it asks the parties to commit to respecting each other. This aspect of the framework acts as a global constraint on the others: Part of respect entails giving both the parties the opportunity to make their needs, resources and rationales explicit. It also takes the form of having the parties treat the needs of the other side as seriously as if they were their own and so manifests itself in the development of mutually beneficial alternatives. Additionally, it means the parties not only commit to the negotiation as a whole but also to the agreements which result.

# 4 Using NegotiationLens to Illustrate the Framework: Walking through a simple negotiation

In this section we present a description of NegotiationLens, a system developed to embody the framework presented above. The software embodies the framework in that the actions available to the user reflect the actions that the framework suggest are useful for collaborative negotiation.

We begin by giving the reader an overview of the user's experience of NegotiationLens. As to what users see: Figure 1 shows a window from the resolution of the 'Visiting Researcher' example (Section 2, point 1). This window, which lists the needs and resources of the parties represents a typical NegotiationLens window. There is a menu bar across the top of the window which allows the user, via a mouse-click, to open each item and see further related actions or through a double mouse-click to directly perform the action associated with the menu item's name. Below the menu bar there is a set of rows or "fields". To interpret each row read along the colums from left to right. The top two rows associate the window with a proposed solution for a particular negotiation. The next set of rows list the parties' needs and then resources (second column of each row), along with how well those needs and resources are respectively being satisfied or utilized by the current solution, the name of the party who entered them, and, in the case of needs, its importance to the party. As to how this window was created: NegotiationLens has a root level window with a menu which via a double mouse-click allows users to create Needs and Resources, Problem Statement or Problem Solution windows. These windows are all writeable. As to facilities: Through these windows, NegotiationLens allows users to keep track of the information on the table throughout a negotiation. And because the windows are writeable they provide appropriate workspaces at appropriate times. Further, a piece of text in a Problem Solution or Problem Statement window can be selected and then, via a mouse-click, be made to appear as a resource in a Needs and Resources window. This can significantly decrease the amount of typing users have to do; an important factor in determining whether a piece of groupware will be used (Carroll, personal communication). A full description of NegotiationLens is presented in [4] but it should be noted here that the system is implemented on top of and integrated with Object Lens[18]. Users of NegotiationLens therefore have full access to all of the facilities of Object Lens, again increasing the probability that NegotiationLens will be accepted in that it can be used a part of a daily working environment[14].

In what follows we walk the reader through the system by describing its use in the context of the Visiting Researcher goal selection conflict ( Section 2, point 1). Recall that in this example a disagreement arose when the visiting researcher (Rebecca) told her manager (Jose) that she wanted to start up two new projects and Jose replied that she should not do so until she had completed the one project she had already started. Eventually, Rebecca and Jose (along with Ursula the researcher who had been collaborating with Rebecca on the first project and

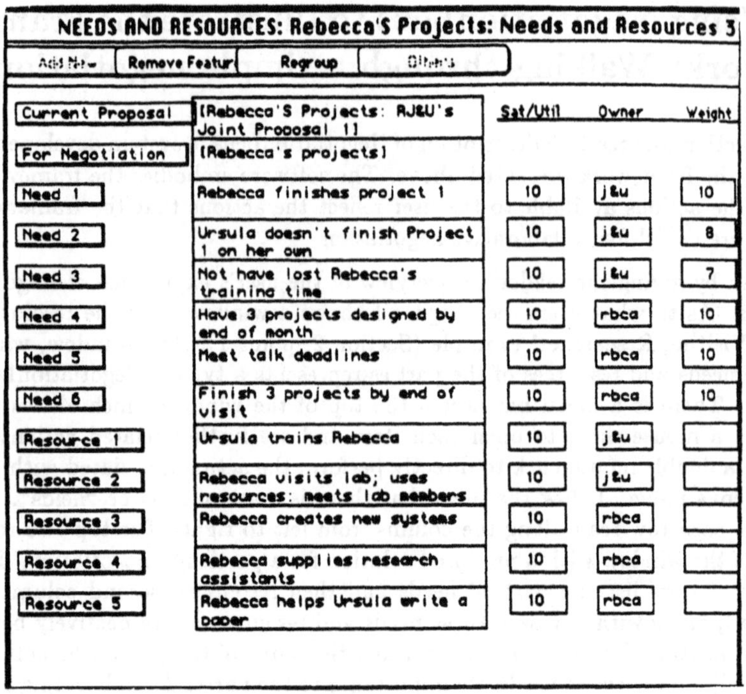

| NEEDS AND RESOURCES: Rebecca'S Projects: Needs and Resources 3 | | | | |
|---|---|---|---|---|
| Add New | Remove Featur | Regroup | Items | |

| | | Sat/Util | Owner | Weight |
|---|---|---|---|---|
| Current Proposal | [Rebecca'S Projects: RJ&U's Joint Proposal 1] | | | |
| For Negotiation | [Rebecca's projects] | | | |
| Need 1 | Rebecca finishes project 1 | 10 | j&u | 10 |
| Need 2 | Ursula doesn't finish Project 1 on her own | 10 | j&u | 8 |
| Need 3 | Not have lost Rebecca's training time | 10 | j&u | 7 |
| Need 4 | Have 3 projects designed by end of month | 10 | rbca | 10 |
| Need 5 | Meet talk deadlines | 10 | rbca | 10 |
| Need 6 | Finish 3 projects by end of visit | 10 | rbca | 10 |
| Resource 1 | Ursula trains Rebecca | 10 | j&u | |
| Resource 2 | Rebecca visits lab; uses resources; meets lab members | 10 | j&u | |
| Resource 3 | Rebecca creates new systems | 10 | rbca | |
| Resource 4 | Rebecca supplies research assistants | 10 | rbca | |
| Resource 5 | Rebecca helps Ursula write a paper | 10 | rbca | |

## The Visiting Researcher Case Study

Figure 1: Needs and Resources with Decision-Making Information Shown

training her to use the lab equipment) decided to negotiate a solution to their dispute.

In steps 1 and 2 the parties work separately, after that the effort is collaborative.

1. *Developing a Problem Statement:*
   Using NegotiationLens to create a problem statement, Rebecca was given the opportunity to express her concern over meeting her deadlines and to state her desire to use her and her assistants' time most efficiently in order to have three projects completed during her visit. Jose and Ursula, in a second problem statement, also had a chance to express their fear that either Rebecca would not finish the project and so the time Ursula had already put in would turn out to have been wasted or alternatively Ursula would be left to finish the project on her own thereby adding to her already considerable workload.

2. *Developing an Initial Solution:*
   Both parties then separately proposed an initial solution which was satisfying to their side.

   It has been found that this step ultimately allows the parties to move out of inflexible starting positions. A party strongly committed to an initial position frequently needs to be able to state a solution that accommodates that position in order to feel it has been heard and considered[6, 22].

3. *Deriving Underlying Needs and Resources:*
   By backing off from their 'Initial Solutions' and instead reviewing their 'Problem Statements', the parties then jointly turned their attention to their original problem statements, using the explanations contained there to develop a list of needs and resources. The two parties also entered a weight for each need.

4. *Matching Needs to Resources:*
   At this point, using the needs and resource list, the parties were able to create a joint solution in a newly created Problem Solution window. This solution contained a schedule and work assignments which allowed for the immediate design and eventual implementation of three systems which Rebecca wanted to create for the lab.

   The joint solution was constructed by matching each need against the listed resources. As mentioned above, systematic matching is critical both in discovering solutions based on non-obvious ways in which parties can help each other[3] and in increasing a sense of collaboration between the parties. The systematic matching process is facilitated by the system's grouping of needs separately from the resources. (In Figure 1, we see needs grouped above resources. But see point 5 for a discussion of the 'Regroup' or sorting feature on the menu bar.)

---

[3] See example in Section 5.1.

5. *Iterating on the Initial Solution:*

In the final stage the parties considered the goodness of the solution by entering a value indicating the extent to which each need was satisfied and each resource was utilized (Figure 1, third column from left).

This example turned out to be one which had a simple solution in which there was clearly a mutual gain and so it may not seem surprising that the satisfaction values were high and that both parties felt the initial joint solution was satisfactory. However, it must be stressed that the situation did *not* appear that way at the outset of the negotiation. It started out in a charged atmosphere which followed a period of stalemate and frustration. Because of the explosive atmosphere, it did not have the feeling of a problem which was going to be solved easily. It was only when the parties extracted their needs and resources from their problem statement that the solution presented itself as simple.

Another result of the negotiation was one which is highly desirable to those interested in group work. Each party reached a better understanding of the needs, strengths and concerns of the other, this resulted in a more relaxed group dynamic and allowed them to avoid future conflicts around these sorts of issues. Additionally, it strengthened the relationship between Rebecca and Ursula in that they agreed to (and did) jointly write a paper on the first project upon its completion.

In the case of more complex negotiations, if the parties feel dissatisfied with a newly developed solution, the system provides them with facilities for establishing the source(s) of their dissatisfaction. The parties can turn to the Needs and Resources window for the new solution and look at who put forth each need and resource; how important each need was; how well each need is being satisfied by the solution currently under consideration and how well each resource is being utilized. Additionally, selecting the regroup option on the menu bar in Figure 1 allows the parties to request that the needs and resources list be re-sorted by weight; by weight for each owner; by satisfaction/utilization; or by satisfaction/utilization for each owner.

Several situations can call for sorting and inspecting weights and satisfaction values. For example, if one or both of the parties are not satisfied with a solution, but are not sure why, they can first sort the needs by weight and then inspect the satisfaction values, allowing them to see whether important needs are both listed and being met. A new solution then be developed by revising the needs and/or resources or by making better use of the existing resources.

As a second example, if one party feels that the current solution is more favorable to the other side it can sort the list by owner and then within that by satisfaction values. The parties can then see if the solution is satisfying the needs of both sides equally. If not, a new solution can then be developed. This can be done by looking at the utilization values for the resources and either revising or making better use of them.

# 5 A Second Case Study, The Sufficiency of the Taxonomy and Future work

In this section we begin by presenting a second example of using the framework. We then analyze the features of the situations in the taxonomy set forth in Section 2. We use this analysis to discuss expansion to our taxonomy along interpersonal dimensions and the impact of those expansions on theoretical frameworks and support tools for negotiation.

## 5.1 Case Study: The New Faculty Member

In this example the negotiation began with a goal conflict and resulted in a mutual gain once one party reconsidered the legitimacy of part of his initial solution and as a result reformulated his goals. In this negotiation a young researcher (Dennis) was trying to negotiate the terms of a first faculty appointment with the help of a more senior colleague (Karen). In this example NegotiationLens was used only by the two colleagues to help the junior colleague define an optimal solution. The second party, Dennis' new department head, Isaac, was not directly involved in the use of the tool, although he was affected by the rethinking that resulted from its use. The implications of his direct participation are discussed in Section 5.2 below.

Initially Dennis wanted Isaac to allow him to buy out of teaching with some research funding he had been offered. More specifically, he wanted Isaac to use the buy out money to bring in one of Dennis' friends to teach his courses. He was particularly eager to have this friend as an intellectual companion in his new job.

Dennis and Karen used the tool to create a problem statement, an initial solution and a needs and resource list both for Dennis and, to the extent possible, for Isaac. Dennis and Karen then reviewed the needs and resources list in an effort to construct a proposal which would be acceptable to Isaac, since he had initially exhibited resistance to the idea of Dennis' buying out of teaching. Isaac believed that having the faculty teach the students provided the students with the best education.

In reviewing the list of needs it came out that Dennis' reason for wanting to buy out was that he wanted to do well at his new job and that underlying his thinking was the criterion of doing as much research (and therefore as little teaching) as possible. However, it also became clear in considering the department head's position that doing well included being willing (or better still eager) to teach. This suggested that Dennis should change his criterion as to what constituted doing well at the new job. As a result, he reformulated his goals with respect to the buy out. Having done this, Dennis and Karen then reviewed the extent to which the resources in the situation were being utilized. They noticed that if Dennis did not buy out he could use his research money to bring in his friend as a visiting professor (and possibly in the long term change the department head's attitude concerning the potential teaching contribution of visiting faculty.) Again Dennis established a new goal.

This process, in which Dennis reviewed the legitimacy of the criteria underlying his initial position and then reformulated his goals, led to a solution which benefited both parties.

## 5.2   Concluding Analysis and Future Work

Here we analyze the underlying motivational/interpersonal dynamics in the cases where we applied our framework and in the cases presented in Section 2. We do so in order to see how our framework holds up in situations which include these dynamics. That is, we ask what are the implication of these dynamics for a theoretical framework which seeks to prescribe actions for a range of negotiation situations? How does the framework need to expand and change? We also suggest research which would result in theory-based negotiation tools which would be effective in these situations.

As to dynamics, in the 'New Faculty' example (Section 5.1) the parties had unequal power. Being more powerful may, definitionally, mean having an inclination to withdraw from the negotiation because of the existence of other easily obtainable alternatives. It also may lead to a disinclination towards putting resources on the table. Had Isaac actually been present and had Dennis still made his needs explicit might Isaac have withdrawn the job offer? Might Dennis have sensed this and avoided revealing his ambitions/goals, which were different from Isaac's?

In addition to the issue of power, the 'Curriculum Development' and 'Matching Grant' cases bring up the issue of freedom to withdraw from a collaboration. In the curriculum development example the parties had been assigned to work together and there may have been a cost to withdrawing from the collaboration. As a result, they may not have wanted to enter into a negotiation which would have revealed their irreconcilable goal conflicts. In the matching grant example the parties did not have the alternative of withdrawing from the collaboration despite their mutual antipathy. Given this frame of mind, they too had no apriori motivation to enter into negotiations designed to improve the situation.

Our existing framework was based upon the presupposition that groups working together are predisposed because of their cooperative relationships to enter into collaborative negotiations. This assumption came from the successes that have been achieved when collaborative styles of negotiation have been used[25, 6, 22, 23, 10, 11, 16, 1, 2, 3]. However, the above discussion suggests that this assumption holds some, but not all of the time. This suggests a line of future research. First we need to generate an expanded framework by analyzing existing accounts of a range of negotiations. This framework would handle a dimension of conflicts orthogonal to those in our initial taxonomy. It would include conflicts stemming from the dynamics which are relevant to the interpersonal complexities of negotiation: Issues of power, freedom, situational histories and situational constraints. We would then systematically develop and test a set of tools based on the expanded framework.

The examples presented here suggest what some of these tools designed to bring initially disinclined parties into negotiating distance might look like.

For example, in situations where it is known that groups need to work together but are feeling animosity it might be helpful to have the parties refocus their view of things in order to include cooperation as a desirable higher level goal. In the matching grant example, had computer services and computer science been encouraged to cooperate they might have been able to look at the long term implications of cancelling the grant. Further, they might have been able to create more productive alternatives. For example, they could have settled on a solution in which they either shared the initial grant, or took turns benefitting from future grants offered by the computer company.

In situations where it is known that the parties have unequal power it might be useful to have a tool which helps the weaker party decide on the nature and strength of the stronger's commitment in order to assess what needs should be revealed. Further this tool could help the weaker party to look for hidden strengths of its own. On the other side, the tool could help the stronger party to accurately assess its perceived strength, thereby helping it to decide when a negotiation is actually worthwhile. For example, an employer might, to its own disadvantage, dismiss a demanding candidate before looking at the true desirability of the remaining candidates in the pool.

Concerning the issue of when there is a benefit from investing in a time-consuming negotiation, in the curriculum development example, had the parties had an advisory tool motivating them to assess the losses they were incurring from their stalemate they might have entered into the negotiation more quickly.

In closing we mention a potential broader implication of this line of research. As mentioned at the beginning of this paper, decision support has been a focus for those interested in group work. QOC, gIBIS, and Sibyl[5, 8, 19] provide a few examples of systems which provide support in the context of design rationale (also see Moran and Carroll's forthcoming book and HCI's 1991 double issue on design rationale). CYRUS and PERSUADER are examples of systems which support the negotiation process[17, 24]. All of these systems have strong implicit or explicit assumptions about supporting group work. Often this includes having users state goals and then asking the users to build supporting arguments for them. The users of these systems may be subject to the same pressures as users of negotiation software. If this is the case, then any results obtained here may also be of use to researchers in other areas of group work.

# References

[1] Adelson, B. Educational tools for what you wanted to do anyway. *Proceedings of the Fourteenth Annual Meeting of the Cognitive Science Society*, 1991.

[2] Adelson, B. A collaborative negotiation tool. *SIGCHI Bulletin.* October, 1991a.

[3] Adelson, B. and Jordan, T. Uncovering design rationale through the negotiation process. *Research in Engineering Design.* In press.

[4] Adelson B. and Jordan, T. The act of negotiating during design. Submitted.

[5] Bellotti, V. MacLean, A and Moran, T. Structuring the Design Space by Formulating Appropriate Design Rationale Questions. *SIGCHI Bulletin.* 1991. Vol. 23,(4), 85-86.

[6] Brockner, J. and Rubin, J. Entrapment in Escalating Conflicts NY: Springer-Verlag. 1985.

[7] Carroll, J. *The Nurnberg funnel: Designing Minimalist instruction for practical computer skill.* MIT Press: Cambridge, MA. 1990.

[8] Conklin, J. and Begeman, M. gIBIS: A hypertext tool for exploratory policy discussion. In Tatar, D. (ed.) *Proceedings of the Second Conference on Computer-Supported Cooperative Work.* ACM press. 1988.

[9] Crowston, K. *Towards a Coordination Cookbook: Recipes for Multi-Agent Action* Doctoral Dissertation, MIT Slaon School. 1990.

[10] Fisher, R. and Uri, W. Getting to Yes. NY: Penguin. 1981.

[11] Fisher, R. and Brown, S. Getting Together. NY: Penguin. 1988.

[12] Greif, I. Computer supported cooperative work. I. Greif (ed.). Morgan Kaufmann: San Mateo, CA. 1988.

[13] Groenbaek, K. Grudin, J. Bodker, S. and Bannon, L. Cooperative System Design. In *Participatory Design.* Schuler & Namioka (eds.) Erlbaum: Hillsdale, NJ. 1991.

[14] Grudin, J. Why CSCW applications fail. In Tatar, D. (ed.) *Proceedings of the Second Conference on Computer-Supported Cooperative Work.* ACM press. 1988.

[15] Grudin, J. Systematic sources of suboptimal interface design in large product development organization. HCI. June, 1991.

[16] Kolb, D. *The Mediators.* MIT Press: Cambridge, MA. 1983.

[17] Kolodner, Simpson and Sycara. A process model of case-based reasoning in problem-solving. IJCAI 85.in problem-solving. IJCAI 85.

[18] Lai, K., Malone, T., Yu, K. "Object Lens: A 'Spreadsheet' for Cooperative Work" ACM Transaction on Office Information Systems, 6(4) pp. 332-353. 1989.

[19] Lee, J. Sibyl: A qualitative decision management system. In P. Winston (ed.). *AI at MIT* Vol. 1, MIT Press: Cambridge, MA.

[20] Lee, J. and Malone, T. How can groups communicate when they use different languages? In R. Allen (ed.) *Proceedings of the ACM Conference on Office Information Systems.* Palo Alto, CA. 1988.

[21] Malone, T. and Crowston, K. *Toward an Interdisciplinary Theory of Coordination.* MIT Center for Coordination Science Tech. Report CCS TR 120. 1991.

[22] Pruitt, D. and Rubin, J. *Social Conflict: Escalation, stalement and settlement.* Random House: NY. 1986.

[23] Raiffa, H. *The art and science of negotiation.* Harvard University Press: Cambridge, MA. 1982.

[24] Simpson, R. A Computer Model of CBR in Problem-Solving. GA Tech PhD thesis, 1985.

[25] Susskind, L. and Cruikshank, J. *Breaking the Impasse: Consensual Approaches to Resolving Public Disputes.* Basic Books: NY. 1987

# From Undo to Multi-User Applications

Thomas Berlage and Andreas Genau

GMD (German National Research Center for Computer Science)
P.O. Box 1316
53731 Sankt Augustin 1
Germany
E-mail: berlage@gmd.de, genau@gmd.de

**Abstract.** The interaction history of a document can be modelled as a tree of command objects. This model does not only support recovery (undo/redo), but is also suitable for cooperation between distributed users working on a common document. Various coupling modes can be supported. Switching between modes is supported by regarding different versions of a document as different branches of the history. Branches can later be merged using a selective redo mechanism. Synchronous cooperation is supported by replicating the document state and exchanging command objects. Optimistic concurrency control can be applied because conflicting actions can later be undone automatically.

## 1 Introduction

In the context of the GINA [14] project at GMD we have developed a model for the generic implementation of mechanisms for multi-user applications for both synchronous and asynchronous cooperation. GINA is an object-oriented application framework to support graphical user interfaces.

Our model for the interaction history of arbitrary direct-manipulative applications is based on a tree of command objects. A single command object translates between two states. The meta-operations "undo" and "redo" can be used to get from one state to the other, so that each state in the tree can be reached.

Selective redo and undo enable the user to redo or undo arbitrary commands from the history tree in any state of the document. They work by creating an equivalent or reverse copy of the command in question, so existing parts of the history are never modified.

The history tree can be stored in a file as a persistent history, so there is simple support for asynchronous cooperation. If a document is being changed by two or more users in non-overlapping time intervals, a user can understand the changes of all other users not only by looking at the document itself, but also by replaying the operations performed by others.

If users work in overlapping time intervals on separate copies of a document, they create versions of the document that can be regarded as different branches in an abstract history tree. The crucial point in such a situation of decoupled cooperation is supporting the process of creating a single document state reflecting the different versions. In our approach, the histories can be recombined into a common tree and the selective redo mechanism can be used to merge the branches into a common state. The merging process can partly be performed automatically.

Synchronous cooperation is possible by replicating document state and history, and broadcasting command objects between the participants. An optimistic concurrency control mechanism can be applied because changes at one site that are later identified as conflicting can simply be undone. The model has the following advantages:

- Applications that already use command objects (as most object-oriented application frameworks do) can be extended to cooperative applications with a modest amount of work.

- Synchronous, asynchronous and decoupled cooperation are handled in the same way. Smooth transitions between the modes are possible.

- Multi-user applications using this model may exhibit flexible coupling, because the applications are coupled at a higher level than the device layer.

- Synchronous applications are highly interactive because the data are replicated and instead of locking, optimistic concurrency control mechanisms can be applied.

## 2 Related Work

One approach to implement collaboration is a shared window system, which intercepts and broadcasts events at the basic window system level [8]. Applications for a certain window system do not need to be modified. Most problems with this approach result from window systems not being designed for such a purpose.

A number of toolkits to implement multi-user applications have been described. DistEdit [7] implements a minimal set of operations for text editors. These operations are distributed by the kernel to replicated editors. MMConf [3] also uses a replicated architecture, but broadcasts low-level events. Both toolkits require minor changes to existing applications.

LIZA [6] and Rendezvous [11] support writing new collaborative applications from scratch. They use a centralized architecture with explicit user interface components for each participant.

Our model generalizes the DistEdit approach to arbitrary primitive operations (the commands). The commands are distributed to replicated applications. This model can be implemented with moderate effort in applications that use an object-oriented application framework like MacApp, InterViews/UniDraw [15], ET++ or GINA [14], because all these frameworks support command classes.

GroupDesign [1] implements a replicated architecture similar to ours, but for a specific application.

Quilt [9] and GroupWriter [10], usually have special features to maintain different versions as well as annotations. Our model handles versions independent of the application and offers automatic integration if possible. Annotations are not covered by our approach, they are application-specific.

The WeMet toolkit [13] implements a persistent history tree to support collaborative work. Our system generalizes the approach and also provides for resolving conflicts, flexible coupling and merging versions.

Most shared applications provide a floor control or locking to prevent concurrent updates by different users. Ellis and Gibbs [5] describe an optimistic algorithm for concurrency control in groupware systems used in the GROVE system. We use the same virtual time algorithm to detect parallel operations. They use a transformation to ensure that pairs of operations produce the same effect in either order. In contrast, we really reorder the operations so that no transformation is necessary.

Prakash and Knister [12] describe another selective undo mechanism based on transposing pairs of operations. Our mechanism uses similar ideas, but does not need to check every possible pair of operations (the number of cases increases quadratically with the number of different operations). Furthermore, whether selective undo is possible in our mechanism does not depend on the history in between but only on the current state.

## 3 The History Tree

A linear history mechanism can be realized using command objects (Fig. 1). A command object encapsulates a state transition. The command objects are stored in the sequence of their submission. There are two operations defined on command objects: *doit* and *undoit*. Undo is implemented by calling *undoit* on the previous command and redo is implemented by calling *doit* on the next command. Of course, *doit* is also called when a command is submitted. *Doit* and *undoit* can be implemented by remembering the state difference inside the command object, e.g. the old and new location of a graphical object that has been moved by a command.

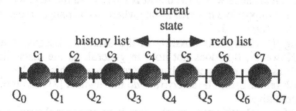

**Fig. 1.** A linear history of command objects representing state transitions.

What happens when the user submits a new command while there are commands in the redo list (see commands $c_5$ to $c_7$ in Fig. 1)? One cannot simply insert a new command in the history and keep the redo list, because the newly submitted command creates a new state. The first command in the redo list would be executed in this state instead of the original state, which might not be possible.

The following is an example for this situation. Suppose the user has moved an object and then undone this operation. The redo list now consists of the move command. If the user then deletes the object, redoing the move is impossible because the object no longer exists.

There are two possibilities to escape this dilemma. One is to discard the redo list and add the new command at the end of the history list. The old states in the redo list become unreachable, but the history remains linear. This model is used in the original GINA implementation because it is simple and easy to understand.

The other possibility is to create a branch in the history starting with the new command, leading to a history tree (Fig. 2). The consequence is that no states are ever lost.

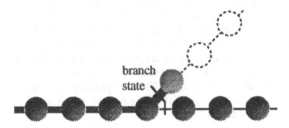

**Fig. 2.** Creating a branch in the history.

It is easy to see that one can reach every state in the history tree using a sequence of *undoit* and *doit* operations. When in a branch state, one can call *doit* on the first command in each branch and thus enter a particular branch. There is a current path starting from the root that leads to the current state.

## 4 Selective Redo

Suppose the user moves an object, undoes the move, and then changes some attribute of the object (such as colour). By navigation in the history tree, the user can only alternate between the state where the object is moved and the state where the object is recoloured. It is not possible to reach a state where both changes are in effect without submitting a new command

Combining the changes is possible in the example, because they are clearly orthogonal. However, this does not hold in general, as the discussion above has shown. Previous recovery mechanisms have allowed this kind of combination, placing the risk on the user. The *selective redo* mechanism [2] is a more user-friendly and secure alternative.

The idea of the selective redo mechanism is to preserve the tree structure of the history and never modify existing parts of the history. Instead, when a command from a different branch is redone, a copy is created that has an equivalent effect in the current state (Fig. 3).

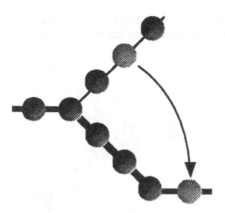

**Fig 3.** Selective redo by copying a command from a branch.

In the command model, there is an operation *selective_redo* defined for all commands that submits a new command in the current state. However, the new command should be in some sense equivalent to the old one (that is what the user expects).

The application programmer is responsible for choosing the interpretation of the new command. In practice it turns out that the new command object can be created as a physical copy of the original one if the *doit* and *undoit* operations are coded properly. Therefore, it is not too much additional work for a programmer to implement selective redo.

As the example above demonstrates, it might be impossible to find such a command. Therefore, there exists an operation *selective_redo_possible* for every command that determines whether such a copy can be found in the current state. Usually this operation is a very simple test.

Now the user may merge commands from other paths into the current path by selectively redoing them if possible.

## 5 Decoupled Cooperation

When used mainly as a recovery operation, the history branches other than the current one will usually be quite short. However, the history tree can also be used to represent alternative versions of a document.

For example, a user may make a number of changes to a document and then decide that the wrong approach was taken. After undoing all the changes, a new branch is started that leads to an alternative version. Selective redo can then be used to integrate changes from one version into the other one.

This approach becomes interesting when used in a collaborative environment. The document can be stored on disk together with the complete history. Copies of a certain version of a document can be distributed to a number of people, which subsequently make changes. All the changes can be reintegrated into a single history tree and the branches can be merged using the selective redo mechanism.

Combining two different versions into a single history tree is easy. One can mark the current history of a document when saving it with a unique identifier composed of the current time and the user id. If two modified copies of the document have to be integrated, all the commands in the history of one document except for the common parts are added as branches to the other document (Fig. 4).

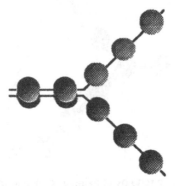

**Fig 4.** Reintegrating two different modifications of the same document into one history.

If the changes do not conflict, it is possible to integrate the changes automatically by selectively redoing all the changes of one version in the current state of the other version (Fig. 5). Automatic merging can be used if it is definitely known that the different users have modified orthogonal aspects, for example different sections.

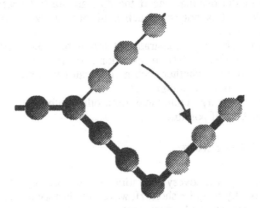

**Fig 5.** Merging two different branches in the history.

Unfortunately, in many cases conflicts arise, for example if one person has removed a paragraph where another person has made some changes. In such a case, merging has to be performed interactively, because someone has to decide which of the conflicting changes to perform and possibly add a different change manually.

There are semantic conflicts that the selective redo mechanism cannot detect and which must be resolved manually. For example, one user may have moved a circle to a location where another user has created a new object. Overlapping objects are usually not forbidden in a graphical editor, but the result may nevertheless be undesirable for the user's purpose.

Merging is performed by selectively redoing a complete history branch step by step, observing the effect of each command. The effect can be corrected manually, if desired, by submitting additional commands. If selective redo of a command is impossible, the command may be ignored or manual changes can make it redoable. To observe the effects of a non-redoable command, the user may "jump" to the state in the other branch (internally implemented by a number of undo and redo operations).

The merging process can even be performed in synchronous cooperation of all participants, as described in the section below.

The combination of the selective redo mechanism with the history tree to merge different versions of a document is an important difference to the WeMet toolkit [13].

## 6 Synchronous Cooperation

Command objects can be used to implement synchronous cooperation. In a shared application, multiple users work simultaneously on the same document. Changes by one participant are immediately visible for all other partners.

This can be implemented by running a separate copy of the document at each user's site and exchanging command objects. Whenever one user submits a command, the command is broadcast on a common communication medium and executed by all other participants as if they had submitted it themselves.

If a user never submits a command until the previous command is distributed to and executed by all instances, no problems arise. All instances will have the same history and the same state of the document. But a user at one site may submit a command before all commands from other sites are executed, so a system has to deal with concurrency control.

There are several possibilities how to implement concurrency control when broadcasting commands. *Floor control* ensures that only one user at a time may submit commands. A central instance can be used to maintain a global ordering among commands. Both approaches make an application less interactive.

It is desirable that each user can always submit commands and immediately observe their effects, without waiting for communication delays. However, to achieve a common state in such a situation, it is sometimes necessary to modify the effects of already executed commands.

A collision can be detected by broadcasting a state vector as a *virtual time* with each command, as has been described by Ellis and Gibbs [5]. To resolve the conflict they define a transformation matrix that for every parallel commands p and q gives variants p´ and q´ so that qp´=pq´, i.e. they define a transformation of the late-coming command so that the resulting effect on the application state is the same on both sides. However, the history is not the same on both sides.

In our approach, undo in combination with selective redo can be used to resolve collisions. Our approach is more manageable for the programmer, because all undo and redo is implemented individually for each command and there is no need to consider every possible combination of two commands.

Because the history is part of a document, it is not sufficient that all the participants have the same state, they must also have the same history. Therefore, all participants must agree on a common ordering among commands.

For this purpose, an arbitrary priority scheme is imposed on the participants. One is the master whose actions will always have priority and the others will always lose on collisions. Notice, that the priority scheme is only used to order commands, that are not conflicting, so only the history and not the state of the document is affected. For that reason an arbitrary priority scheme can be choosen automatically.

When a site detects that it has executed a command colliding with the one arriving, and the newly arrived command comes from a site with higher priority, the previous command must be undone and the new command will be executed. The previous command now resides in a branch.

Only the originating site tries to selectively redo this command (i.e. submit it and broadcast it with a new virtual time). If that is possible, the collision is resolved.

Although multiple operations are performed when resolving a collision, it is possible to blend them into a single operation from the user´s point of view by deferring screen updates until all operations are completed.

If selective redo is not possible, the collision must be resolved manually. The users will be notified that a conflict arose and what the nature of the conflict is, so they can negotiate what operations they can perform to achieve their intended effects.

## 7 Flexible Coupling

The command-based communication allows gradual changes from asynchronous or even separated work to full synchronous interaction. A user that temporarily wants to leave a session can be decoupled from the broadcast mechanism to pursue a personal history branch. This branch can then be reintegrated into a running session the way described in the previous section

Joining sessions in the middle requires exchanging the current state. Individual commands can be broadcasted to participants that do not yet have that part of the history. If a user wants to join a session with a long history, it is not necessary to replay the history, but the current document state can be saved as if written to a file and be sent to the new participant.

It is sometimes desired that not only the effects of other participants should be visible everywhere, but also the low-level actions and feedback when submitting a command (strict WYSIWIS—What You See Is What I See). This is accomplished by broadcasting commands when the interactive process starts, such as when the user starts pressing a mouse button. While the mouse button is pressed, the motion events are broadcast to all the duplicated commands, which then handle the feedback locally.

Users can also request to be able to keep a different local state, such as the selection or the scrolling position. This can be achieved by executing selection and scrolling commands only at the originating site. Because the state consistency of the applications regarding other commands in the history must not be violated, selection and scrolling commands must always be orthogonal to other commands. For example, this requires that commands operating on the current selection remember the set of selected objects, because the selection may be different when the command is executed at another site.

These different levels of coupling are similar to the ones discussed in [4]. It should be noted that replication and coupling modes are implemented generically in our framework.

# 8 Undo in Multi-User Applications

As described in [11], undo in a multi-user application is more difficult than in a single-user system. In particular, the user probably wants to undo the last local action and not the last global one. However, this may collide with other operations and the command to undo might not be the last one in the history.

In GINA, there is a *selective undo* that works similar to the selective redo described above and that can be used to undo arbitrary commands from the history (when sensible). It works by appending a reverse copy of the command to undo to the history [2]. We will use the selective undo mechanism to implement a generic user command *undo my last command* that is present in all applications

The transformation algorithm discussed in [12] is useful in the context of a text editor, where references (such as character positions) move when other commands are executed. In most other applications, there are stable references to objects mentioned in the history. In this case, it is not necessary to take the intermediate history into account in our mechanism.

# 9 Storage Requirements

The implementation of the history tree requires additional storage space for mainly three reasons:

- All information in the document is contained in the history as well. The information is stored differently and requires roughly the same storage space as in the document itself. Differences in the size of the two representations may occur due to time-space-tradeoffs not directly related to the history tree.

- When a user makes a lot of modifications to a document, the storage space required for the history will grow linearly with the number of commands required to record the changes.

- Every command requires a constant overhead for management, e.g. identification of the user and the command itself. As has been pointed out in [13], this factor can be reduced by the application programmer by choosing the right granularity for the commands, thereby reducing the number of commands to be stored.

Tests made with the WeMet-Toolkit [13] resulted in a 150KB history transscript for a session with three participants and a duration of half an hour. The authors state that this could be reduced by a factor of six using a better encoding for the commands and general compression techniques.

# 10 Current Status and Future Work

The model has been implemented as an extension to the GINA class library. Several existing single-user demo applications were turned into multi-user applications with modest amount of application specific work, e.g. a simple graphic-editor and a simple spreadsheet (Fig. 6). We will integrate these features into the GINA library and transfer them to even larger applications, such as the GINA interface builder.

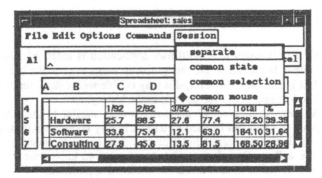

**Fig 6.** The multi-user spreadsheet showing the session menu where different degrees of coupling can be selected.

Future research will concentrate on how the basic mechanism can be presented most effectively at the user interface.

## 11 Conclusions

When using a command history, surprising similarities show up between single-user and multi-user applications. Storing the history for later use by the same user also provides a mechanism to communicate commands to other users. The history tree not only remembers mistakes of a single user, but can also represent alternative versions for multiple users. Selective redo and undo allows the final result to be combined from different sources. Only the virtual time algorithm is specific to synchronous multi-user applications.

We believe that our model can easily be used as the basis for an implementation of various multi-user applications that are mainly identical to their single-user counterparts. This is demonstrated by the integration into our GINA application framework.

## Acknowledgements

The model has evolved during discussions with the members of the GINA project team: Michael Spenke, Christian Beilken and Markus Sohlenkamp.

## References

1.  Beaudouin-Lafon, M. and Karsenty, A., Transparency and Awareness in a Real-Time Groupware System. In *Proceedings of the ACM Symposium on User Interface Software and Technology* (Monterey, CA, Nov 15-18, 1992), pp.171-180.

2.  Berlage, T., Spenke, M., The GINA Interaction Recorder. In *Proceedings of the IFIP WG2.7 Working Conference on Engineering for Human-Computer Interaction* (Ellivuori, Finland, Aug 10–14, 1992).

3.  Crowley, T., Baker, E., Forsdick, H., Milazzo, P. and Tomlinson, R., MMConf: An infrastructure for building shared multimedia applications. In *Proceedings of the Conference on Computer Supported Cooperative Work (CSCW '90)* ACM Press, Los Angeles, California, 1990, pp. 329-342.

4.  Dewan, P. and Choudhary, R.,  Flexible User Interface Coupling in a Collaborative System. In *Proceedings of the CHI Conference on Human Factors in Computing Systems* (New Orleans, Apr 28–May 2, 1991), pp. 41–48.

5.  Ellis, C.A. and Gibbs, S.J.,  Concurrency Control in Groupware Systems. In *Proceedings of the ACM SIGMOD International Conference on the Management of Data* (Portland, OR, May 31–Jun 2, 1989), pp. 399–407.

6.  Gibbs, S.J., LIZA: An extensible groupware toolkit. In *Proceedings of the SIGCHI Conference on Human Factors in Computing Systems (CHI '89)* ACM Press, Austin, Texas, 1989, pp. 29-35.

7.  Knister, M.J. and Prakash, A., DistEdit: A distributed toolkit for supporting multiple group editors. In *Proceedings of the Conference on Computer Supported Cooperative Work (CSCW '90)* ACM Press, Los Angeles, California, 1990, pp. 343-355.

8.  Lauwers, J.C. and Lantz, K.A.,  Collaboration Awareness in Support of Collaboration Transparency: Requirements for the Next Generation of Shared Window Systems. In *Proceedings of the CHI Conference on Human Factors in Computing Systems* (Seattle, WA, Apr 1–5, 1990), pp. 303–311.

9.  Leland, M.D.P., Fish, R.S. and Kraut, R.E.,  Collaborative Document Production Using Quilt. In *Proceedings of the ACM CSCW´88 Conference on Computer-Supported Cooperative Work* (Portland, Oregon, Sep 26–28, 1988), pp. 206–215.

10. Malcolm, N. and Gaines, B.R.,  A Minimalist Approach to the Development of a Word Processor Supporting Group Writing Activities. In *Proceedings of the Conference on Organizational Computing Systems* (Atlanta, GA, Nov 5–8, 1991), pp. 147–152.

11. Patterson, J.F., Hill, R.D., Rohall, S.L. and Meeks, W.S.,  Rendezvous: An Architecture for Synchronous Multi-User Applications. In *Proceedings of the Conference on Computer-Supported Cooperative Work* (Los Angeles, CA, Oct 7-10, 1990), pp. 317–328.

12. Prakash, A. and Knister, M.J.,  Undoing Actions in Collaborative Work. In *Proceedings of the Conference on Computer Supported Cooperative Work* (Toronto, Canada, Oct 31–Nov 4, 1992).

13. Rhyne, J. R. and Wolf, C. G., Tools for Supporting the Collaborative Process. In *Proceedings of the ACM Symposium on User Interface Software and Technology* (Monterey, CA, Nov 15-18, 1992), pp.161-170.

14. Spenke, M., Beilken, C.  An Overview of GINA – the Generic Interactive Application. In *User Interface Management and Design,* Proceedings of the Workshop on User Interface Management Systems and Environments (Lisbon,

Portugal, June 4–6, 1990), D.A. Duce et al., Eds., Springer Verlag, Berlin, pp. 273–293.

15. Vlissides, J.M., Linton, M.A., Unidraw: A Framework for Building Domain-Specific Graphical Editors. *ACM Trans. Inf. Syst. 8*, 3 (July 1990), 237–268.

# Software Cooperation with the Share-Kit:
# Influences of Semantic Levels on the Working Efficiency

Stefan Edlich

Technical University of Berlin
Communication and Operating Systems Research Group
Sekr. FR 6-3, Franklinstr. 28-29
D-10587 Berlin, Germany
edlich@cs.tu-berlin.de

**Abstract.** The Share-Kit is a toolkit that allows upgrading single-user software to groupware. It creates data structures and primitives that can be used by various applications to export data to share with other applications. This results in a high degree of independence from the underlying system-environment. During the development of this toolkit we had to face the question of what specific semantic levels would be supported for the cooperation: The data of an operation (e.g. the construction of a simple graphic) can either be sent after the operation is finished or each input/transaction can be sent immediately. This issue influences every semantic level down to that of the exchanged data. Software developers will be able to structure the semantic levels of their existing and future software application releases to achieve flexible cooperation.

## 1 Introduction

The aim of our research was to develop a software-toolkit that would permit the generation of cooperative applications, i.e. groupware in particular on the basis of existing single-user applications. While using basic function and communication primitives, the cooperative applications initiate the export of data desired to be shared with other applications. Examples of applications are text or graphics editors, however a wide range of applications can be supported.

Our study is not limited to supporting the collaboration of identical applications; it also supports the collaboration of different software applications of the same generic variety (e.g. different text editors), cooperative by means of different applications that work on the same types of generic information. This was motivated by the desire that a given user should be free to employ his own application of choice, because groupware has to be accepted from each participating user.

During the development and the use of such a toolkit, the question arises on what semantic level the cooperation should proceed. The data of a distinct operation (e.g. the construction of simple graphics objects) can either be exported upon completion of the operation or each input/transaction can be exported immediately. The definition of application parameters can be valid only locally or they can affect all cooperative applications. Imagine a *Popup-Box* in which to enter parameters for the behaviour of the application. The box can be made visible to each user or only to the originating user. In every case, the general aim is to let the user configure his applications in a way that is most suitable for him.

A further question is, how to handle user-preferences e.g. pre-defined settings for the application. Another important question involves differing (software/hardware) environments which can create different views of objects or even of the data of the application. These problem areas require suitable solutions. The question is how the different semantic levels can be handled and where the limits of the toolkits' supporting groupware are.

When taking a close look at existing toolkits to support cooperative work such as „SharedX" (shX [1]), one realizes that it is popular to provide shared windows or working areas. This is interesting but doesn't satisfy the requirements stated above to support different semantic levels or the cooperation of unequal applications. Of course this was not the intention of these toolkits.

Given the needs for a more suitable toolkit, it was an interesting task to examine whether this appropriate high-level support of the user and his applications-preferences can be achieved. This is the reason why we developed the *Share-Kit*. The *Share-Kit* is a toolkit consisting of various primitives that enable programmers to generate groupware from various existing and future application packages. The basic concept is to enhance the application by inserting primitives so that the desired data for cooperation can be exported by the application itself. This gains a high grade of independence from the underlying system-environment. The open definition of function and communication primitives by software-developers allows the development of standards for existing and future applications which support users directly.

Certainly there are some groupware systems that use precisely one application, and they transmit the visible output pixel- or blockwise to other participants of the session. In some settings (e.g. *Remote-Viewing*) this might be of interest, but for the purposes of the present study this should be disregarded. This paper examines primarily applications that cooperate synchronously and provide so called *joint-work*. Target applications are conference-like environments that provide video and audio transmission as well as additional applications such as text or graphics editors [7]. This corresponds to a well-known category of cooperation environments [19, 3, 16]. This paper will concentrate on applications where multiple users work on a common object of interest, such as text editors and graphics (e.g. drawing/sketching).

The second part of the paper describes issues about the question of semantic levels. The following sections describe the internals of the *Share-Kit* and practical experiences that have been made with the *Share-Kit*.

## 2  Semantic Levels

Users are often exposed to restricted applications and environments when working in a conference-like environment. Though some recent groupware applications have diverse possibilities, and can configure for group-communication, such as adjustments for *Floor-Control* (e.g. [6]), the level of operation is commonly not configurable. Most systems allow the disconnection of cooperative applications during a session to be subsequently employed as stand-alone applications. During cooperative work, almost every user-input is transmitted right away which results in a WYSIWIS (What You See Is What I See) [13] coupling of applications.

The various possibilities in between these extremes cannot be dealt with by the users of these applications. In the discussion follows, we will illustrate how it is possible for users to deal with the various degrees of cooperation desired. Imagine a simple graphics application that is used for cooperative work. Normally a graphics operation consists of several coordinate definitions, which leads to the question: At what time/phase of the operation does the user wish to transmit the corresponding data?

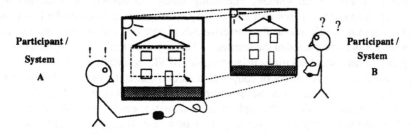

**Fig. 1.** Semantic levels in a graphics operation

During the simple definition of a rectangle, the user has to define one start-point first. Following this, a "rubberband" that indicates the size of the rectangle appears. After this, the second and final point will be defined, creating the rectangle. Either every single action or, alternately the operation as a complete whole can be visualized within cooperating graphics applications (figure 1).

This problem is just a simple example for a number of similar problems: (1) The definition of a polyline with various points. When will the polyline be visualized? (2) The deletion of an object. This can be achieved in two phases: a) The selection of the object, and b) the deletion of the object. (3) Inserting text in graphics applications. Is the distribution done character by character or after pressing 'Enter' by the user? (4) How does the handling of 'undoing'-operations work? Who has control of this operation? (5) How do users select parameters such as line-thickness? Does the same *Popup-Box* for the insertion of data appear for everyone in our cooperative environment? (6) How is a picture saved? Can one person save it for all participants?
Similar problems occur in text editors as well; especially in the following operations: undo, search/replace, spelling correction, the deletion of blocks, adjusting parameters, etc.

Beside the questions that occur on the higher – user – levels (e.g. the way objects, actions or visible areas are shared), the choice of a specific semantic level exists in almost every software level – even at the lowest levels of the application, i.e. the communication layers. These deep levels do not directly influence the end-user, but they do determine the architecture of groupware and the communication model.

In the case of cooperative graphics software, they lead to the decision whether to transmit whole operations or single pixels or mouse movement events for instance. These low-level problems are well-known within the design of cooperative editors. In some cases there is the need to transmit every single character, and in other cases one has also to transmit the actual position. Other cooperative applications transmit every single keypress or the result of a whole textual operation.

Some authors have reported the need for looser coupling than WYSIWIS [4, 13]. To relax the constraints that a WYSIWIS cooperation imposes, system designers often provide a private and a public window. The private window should fulfill the needs for autonomy in a collaborative session as users themselves might determine the time when to make the content publicly available. Our experiences with the *Share-Kit* show that changing the semantic level of the cooperation mode is sometimes more suitable than providing a whole private window. Interesting research in this area has been done by Dewan and Choudary [4] (see chapter 5). They investigated applications built with an interface toolkit that allows the flexible definition of coupling parameters. We coupled the entire application instead of the interfaces. This approach has some main advantages compared to traditional solutions using pure WYSIWIS applications with an optional private window: (A) A variety of cooperation models can be supported. Applications can either operate on equivalent data structures, e.g. the logical structure of a document [2], leaving the presentation to the application; or shared-screen facilities can be provided regardless of the underlying data-structures. In both cases the application programmer decides the granularity of the transmitted data when using toolkits like *Share-Kit*. (B) A better handling of the input devices might be possible. It is up to the application programmer to decide whether a telepointer appears on the screen or to determine the number and the control of cursor/mouse-pointers. (C) Different applications of the same generic variety can cooperate and different hard- or software-environments (e.g. window-systems) can be supported when having low level access to the application (where the primitives might reside).

The general questions for the cooperative interaction are: what parts of the application should be shared, and when are user actions/operations "correct" enough to become public. We feel that these problems can be solved better when using toolkits like ours. Of course it is impossible to achieve the high goal of a cooperation with all existing applications while having all semantic levels present at once. But an appropriate support of semantic levels is often much more efficient than WYSIWIS collaboration with an additional private window.

## 3 A Closer Look on the Share-Kit

To support cooperation of different applications from the same generic type, new possibilities must be explored. The availability of new communication services such as the *Multipoint Communication Service* (MCS) (CCITT T.122) [11] act as a catalyst, spurring our analysis of existing groupware architectures. Because *MCS* provides more than pure multicasting, and is especially designed for conference-like environments, it appears to be a suitable tool for CSCW. A prototype of the *MCS* was available during the development of the *Share-Kit* [14]. Besides the communication primitives which effect the data-transmission, the higher-layered functional primitives represent the more interesting part of the *Share-Kit*. This is because they reflect the semantics and function of the application. An example was described above regarding our modified graphics application. These operations transmitted predefined graphic operations as a whole by using their primitives. The operations precise creation is local; other cooperating participants obtain only the result not the original process. This example points to the need for toolkits that can generate data-structures and predefined operations for use by cooperative applications for their information exchange. Some existing tools like *rpc-gen* [17] generate *C*-code and use *Remote Procedure Calls* (RPC) for data transmission. Tools like these are used in the *Share-Kit*, but, to define more powerful primitives, one has to go one step further.

The following describes the generic architectural concepts behind higher primitives, rather than simply listing those of the *Share-Kit*.

One view of the real location of *Share-Kit* primitives within applications shows them as lying sandwich-like between the *User-Interface* and the generic program functionality. The former handles the data visualization; the latter provides the basic services (figure 2). That layer labeled "glue" represents the *Share-Kit* primitives.

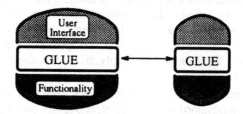

**Fig. 2.** Interfacing the *Share-Kit* to the application

The concrete behavior/definition of the primitives defines the level at which they reside in the application. This may be explained using two examples (figure 3): Case (I) indicates the location of the primitives –the glue– if the primitives know about the operations defined in the application and use them for cooperation. The primitives have knowledge of the operations required. We mentioned above the modified graphics application in this connection.

(I)      (II)

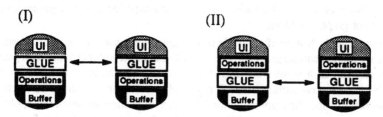

**Fig. 3.** Interfacing the Glue-Code to different levels in the application

On the other hand, primitives can for example watch internal buffers and inform other applications (also modified by the *Share-Kit*) of changes. In this case (II) *Share-Kit* primitives are adjoined to the buffers and do not therefore have any knowledge of higher level operations. These primitives watch for example the text buffer only and transmit all insertions and deletions of text to each cooperative application. These examples show that various distinct levels exist in applications and that some of these levels can be attached by primitives.

The main choice in the selection of such a powerful set of primitive as (I) is then the degree of knowledge they possess about the application to be upgraded. Whether primitives have internal state/knowledge, and whether they have the capacity to know each other or even exchange data among themselves strongly influences their ability to support distinct semantic levels. The qualitative difference between low-level primitives and the more powerful primitives is great.

## 4    Experiences with the Share-Kit

The following two sections avoid the implementation details as much as possible in order to present an overview of the potential of an evolving toolkit like the *Share-Kit*.

We want to explore the influence that the *Share-Kit* has on existing and future applications. We linked several applications to evaluate the use of *Share-Kit*. In the area of text editors, we linked different editors (GNU-Emacs, Epoch, MicroEmacs, Motif-TextWidget) as well as linking similar systems. Applications that are not text editors are of greater comparative interest. The first applications examined were those using raster graphics. The aim was not simply to transmit single pixels, but to use a higher semantic level.

Two graphics applications called *xped* and *sketch* developed at the Technical University of Berlin were examined and the equivalent graphics operations were identified. These operations are passed over to two primitives (named *InsertObject*, *DeleteArea*) and finally were transmitted by *Share-Kit* communication modules. Other better known graphics editors were investigated as well. Integrating the code and locating the points where graphic elements are processed or visualized was not very difficult, but we encountered some difficulty reconverting some graphics editors (such as xfig [18]) because it was difficult to locate a single input blocking routine [1].

Developers in our research group had no problem integrating predefined primitives while building new applications. It was no great effort to organize the I/O structure to permit the use of our primitives. The benefit for future applications is great, and the effort is not prohibitive. Only now are we gaining experience with applications other than text or graphics editors.

To evaluate the benefit of a flexible cooperation by the support of different semantic levels, we implemented a graphics editor (xmge) and a text editor (xmte). Each graphics editor can run as a stand-alone application or in a synchronous cooperation mode distributed to several workstations. Figure 4 shows the menu items to connecting or disconnecting a specific graphics editor. The most interesting feature of this application is that users can select among different levels of cooperation. Figure 5 shows the menu-items to select the desired semantic level. When selecting the *Event* item, all events generated by the Window-System are exchanged. The item *Operation* forces the transmission of completed graphics operations (including parameter settings). The item *Workspace* forces the sharing of the drawing-area; parameter-settings and therefore the whole rest of the application-areas are private properties. Enabling the user to change

---

[1] Applications running under some window-systems often have local input routines (installed with *XtAdd-EventHandler* in the X-Window System) embedded in many places throughout the program. This prevents us from using our primitives for the uniform data processing and distribution. Similar experiences had been made using *Dist-Edit*-toolkit ([9] see below) for connecting text editors.

levels dynamically was most helpful in studying the interactions between tasks and levels.

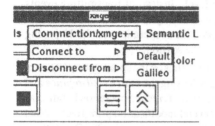

**Fig. 4.** Connecting the application

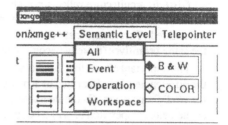

**Fig. 5.** Selecting Semantic Levels

The first trial runs with these applications showed some interesting results: (1) It was possible to combine some of these modes without encountering deep synchronization problems. For example, one user can view the detailed remote creation of a graphics object whereas the other sees the result of the operation. (2) Collaborative groups that started from scratch while using our tools felt uncomfortable using tightly coupled modes. The fact that their immediate actions in WYSIWIS mode could be observed, and therefore judged by others made them feel uneasy. When using collaborative editors they selected looser coupling modes to validate text blocks/sentences by themselves before broadcasting them. Groups that collaborated in editing existing objects, on the other hand, preferred close coupling modes for being more time efficient. The action of improving or just modifying a graphics or text object does not seem to require as high a grade of autonomy as the previous scenario.

In the future we will use different semantic levels to investigate and to compile statistics. We expect to confirm that some levels are more suitable for certain problems, applications, or users.

## 5 Related Work

Environments supporting the creation of groupware are well known (*Rendezvous* [15], *MMConf* [3], *ConversationBuilder* [8]). *LIZA* [5] and *GroupKit* [12] are pure toolkits for rapid construction of objects, ideas or protocols. These toolkits can be used to support different semantic levels, although they were not so designed; they were designed to be mere powerful building blocks.

The existing system that comes closest to meeting the requirements laid out earlier is the *DistEdit-Toolkit* [9], because it has demonstrated that the cooperative connection of different applications is feasible. This toolkit has a number of similarities to our *Share-Kit*. The *DistEdit-Toolkit* was built to upgrade interactive editors for the purpose of cooperative work. Therefore Knister and Prakash developed a kind of 'library' that includes various primitives. Some of them look like a base set of text-operations, and some primitives provide simple possibilities for group-coordination (*Update Primitives, Cursor Positioning Notification Primitive, Control Primitives*). Using *DistEdit* it has become possible to use existing but different text editors for cooperation by inserting these primitives. Knister and Prakash have demonstrated this by connecting two different editors (GNU-Emacs and MicroEmacs). Future editors can be enabled for cooperative work in the same way.

*DistEdit* architecture reflects a high semantic level. Instead of transmitting events immediately from the keyboard or the mouse, complete operations/modifications are transmitted. This means that new editors can support this cooperation standard by using the same primitives (thereby becoming able to join the session).

The important effects that the choice of the primitives has on the coordination between the different levels is described by Knister and Prakash using the *search-and-replace* and the *UNDO* operation. (Is the interactive *global search and replace* operation handled as an elementary operation or will it be split up into several modification primitives? What is the result of an *UNDO* operation after a non elementary operation?) The authors have done further research on this area in the CSCW-Proceedings of 1992 [10]. In addition to the question whether actions are elementary, one has to determine who has the interactive control over operations or indeed should have them.

*DistEdit* is designed only for text editors. *Share-Kit*, on the other hand, shows that primitives can be used to connect other applications than editors, e.g. graphics applications. This has lead us to examine whether the creation (or even generation) of classes of primitives for a flexible communication is possible. We demonstrate in this paper that it is indeed possible.

Theoretical approaches concerning different semantic levels are outlined by P.Dewan and R.Choudhary [4]. Their investigations focused on flexible user-interface coupling. They agree with other researchers [13] that coupling that is limited to *WYSIWIS* might be inefficient in some situations. The authors discuss several issues related to semantic levels using a coupled user-interface build with *Suite*, which is a toolkit supporting the construction of user-interfaces of both single-user and multi-user programs. Some of their issues are: Which interaction model should be supported (teletype- / editing-model)? Which changes shall be transmitted and received at what time? Which aspects of the coupling among shared window should the user be able to control? These issues are strong related to the issues discussed in chapter two.

## 6 Summary and Conclusions

Our investigations point out several issues related to semantic levels. Individual developers will use the guidelines laid out in this study as they design their own systematic methods/approaches to the resolution of the issues raised here. A very real risk exists in the commercial *joint-work* environments that are beginning to dominate the market. Some of these systems might have the effect of actually paralyzing *joint-work* research, because end-users tend to become increasingly dependent on them. In our opinion window-sharing systems are not enough. The real need is for a flexible accomodation to real roles and to the desires of the users themselves. We feel this can in fact be achieved by using more powerful toolkits.

Our experience with the use of *Share-Kit* communication modules using the *MCS*-service prototype was positive. Rapid development of such tools and especially wide dissemination among CSCW would seem to be very worthwhile.

Although we encountered some difficulty supporting certain particular semantic levels and in breaking up some applications, we did succeed in connecting distinct applications that are not editors. When the primitives are defined and they are widely-disseminated, then they take on the appearance of a 'quasi-standard', to be used in existing and future groupware. In most cases it would be no more difficulty to define and integrate primitives than it would to develop online-help or documentation. For minimal effort, the gain, as the result of the ability to cooperate, would be immense.

Finally I would like to propose some areas in which working-efficiency would be increased through the use of toolkits like the *Share-Kit*:

1. Greater user-efficiency, because users now would be able to retain their application of choice for cooperation (even though the cooperative use of all features might not be possible).

2. More efficient groupware development, because developers would be able to integrate well-known primitives supportable by other groupware. A fertile field for further research is the methodology for breaking up existing applications.

3. Higher user-acceptance of groupware, because users now would be able to choose the particular qualities that are appropriate to their needs of autonomy.

Of course, further studies in this area are needed to prove ultimately whether the distinction between semantic levels really has an influence on user-acceptance. The *Share-Kit* is, after all, a toolkit, and as such it is a continually evolving mechanism designed to investigate the cooperation of a wide range of applications. It will continue to improve and to offer ever better insights to cooperative groupware applications.

## Acknowledgements

Thanks to Jörg Ott, Peter Jahn, Indra G. Harijono for their implementations and to the referees for their useful suggestions. I wish to extend my thanks to Drs. Ute and Carsten Bormann of the Technische Universität Berlin for many helpful discussions. Prof. Dr. Sigram Schindler is to be credited for creating the research environment from which this work resulted.

## References

1. Michael P. Altenhofen. Shared X – a modified library to give dynamic multi-display support. Available on the Internet, 1992.

2. Ute Bormann and Carsten Bormann. ISOTEXT – A WYSIWYG editing and formatting system for ODA and SGML documents. In *Proceedings of the GI/ITG-Workshop „Offene Multifunktionale Arbeitsplätze" – von Btx bis B-ISDN*, Berlin, 1988.

3. T. Crowley, E. Baker, H.Forsdick, P. Milazzo, and R. Tomlinson. MMConf: An infrastructure for building shared multimedia applications. In *Proceedings of the Conference on Computer-Supported Cooperative Work, CSCW 90*, page 329, Los Angeles, CA, 1990. ACM.

4. Prasun Dewan and Rajiv Choudhary. Flexible user interface coupling in a collaborative system. In *Proceedings of the Conference on Human Factors in Computing Systems CHI'91*, pages 41–48. ACM, 1991.

5.  Simon Gibbs. LIZA: An extensible groupware toolkit. In *CHI'89 – Conference Proceedings on Human Factors in Computing Systems*, page 29, Austin, Texas, 1989. ACM.

6.  Saul Greenberg. Personalizable groupware: Accomodating individual roles and group differences. In *European Conference on Computer Supported Cooperative Work, ECSCW 91*, page 17, Amsterdam, 1991. North-Holland.

7.  Hiroshi Ishii. TeamWorkStation: Towards a seamless shared workspace. In *Proceedings of the Conference on Computer-Supported Cooperative Work, CSCW 90*, page 13, Los Angeles, CA, 1990. ACM.

8.  S.M. Kaplan, W.J. Tolone, D.P. Bogia, and C. Bignoli. Flexible, active support for collaborative work with ConversationBuilder. In *Proceedings of the Conference on Computer Supported Cooperative Work, CSCW'92:*, pages 378–385, Toronto, Ontario, 1992. ACM.

9.  Michael J. Knister and Atul Prakash. DistEdit: A distributed toolkit for supporting multiple group editors. In *Proceedings of the Conference on Computer-Supported Cooperative Work, CSCW'90*, pages 343–355, Los Angeles, CA, 1990. ACM.

10. Michael J. Knister and Atul Prakash. Undoing actions in collaborative work. In *Proceedings of the Conference on Computer-Supported Cooperative Work, CSCW'92*, pages 273–280, Toronto, Ontario, 1992. ACM.

11. Multipoint Communication Service: Draft T.122 (T.MCS). Standard, CCITT, Question 23, Study Group VIII, 1992.

12. M.Roseman and S.Greenberg. Building real-time groupware. In *Proceedings of the Conference on Computer-Supported Cooperative Work, CSCW'92*, pages 43–50, Toronto, Ontario, 1992. ACM.

13. M.Stefik, D.G.Brobow, G.Foster, S.Lanning, and D.Tatar. WYSIWIS Revised: Early experiences with multiuser interfaces. *ACM Transactions on Office Information Systems 5:2*, pages 147–167, April 1987.

14. Jörg Ott. CCITT T.122 Multipoint Communication Service - Implementation, Experiences and Extensions. Internal Paper. Technical University of Berlin., 1992.

15. John F. Patterson, Ralph D. Hill, Steven L. Rohall, and W. Scott Meeks. Rendezvous: An architecture for synchronous multi-user applications. In *Proceedings of the Conference on Computer-Supported Cooperative Work, CSCW 90*, page 317, Los Angeles, CA, 1990. ACM.

16. Sigram Schindler. Broadband Technology within the DIDAMES project (Race R1060). *International Conference on Integrated Broadband Services and Networks*, 329:148/52, 1990.

17. SUN. *rpcgen - RPC protocol compiler*, 1992. 'rpcgen' Programming Guide in the Network Programming Manual.

18. Supoj Sutanthavibul. A part of the M.I.T. X-Window System distribution., 1985. Facility for interactive generation of figures under the X-Window System.

19. Kazuo Watabe, Shiro Sakata, Kazutoshi Maeno, Hideyuki Fukuora, and Toyoko Ohmori. Distributed multiparty desktop conferencing system: MERMAID. In *Proceedings of the Conference on Computer-Supported Cooperative Work, CSCW 90*, page 27, Los Angeles, CA, 1990. ACM.

# MAP&ROOM:A Concept of Spatial User Interface for Accessing Network Services

Jun MIZUNASHI, Kumiko NAKAGAWA, Kazuhito KOJIMA
and Yutaka MATSUSHITA
Department of Instrumentation Engineering
Faculty of Science and Technology
Keio University
3-14-1 Hiyoshi, Kohoku-ku, Yokohama 223 JAPAN
Tel: +81-45-563-1141 Fax: +81-45-562-7625
E-mail: jun@myo.inst.keio.ac.jp

### Abstract

The demands from the user community of user interfaces better adapted to novice and casual users led to the development of interfaces based on a simple, easy and uniform method.

On the other hand, the rapid growth of computer networks will soon make it possible that novice users will use various kinds of services provided through a network.

Thus, it can be said that such novice users will soon come to need a communicating environment that will be both simpler, more direct and more transparent or intuitive for accessing services in a network.

We then propose an user interface concept named "MAP&ROOM" for easy and friendly communication in a network environment. In an application based on MAP&ROOM, a part of the network is expressed as a map metaphor in which a lot of buildings, shops, offices, etc. are located as objects for services provided by various parties, and the users can manipulate puppets as the other selves of himself or herself to walk around the map and access various services.

## 1   INTRODUCTION

Today, computers have been getting lower in price and higher in performance so that they are much closer and very popular to people. In addition, computer networks have been widespread among the world. So we can share many resources (informations, files and services) through the networks.

Consider the following common problems about computer networks: It is difficult for users to remember where to access the services which he or she had used. Though many users access to a computer network, only a few person knows the existence of useful resources on the network. There is no separation between the resources which should be kept by each user and which should be shared. No mattar what such networks have spread, the users may not use it effectively as a communication tool for personal use. (For example, we make the most of a computer network as E-mail, but we do not have the other practical direction.) Many users have the risk of disorientation while navigating the resources on such networks. Users get waste effort when they can not find the specific information he or she needs.

Why do they have such problems in using a computer network? There are several reasons to these problems. In the first place, it is very difficult for them to understand a computer network spatially, although an actual network has a spacial structure. In the second place, we think that it is because there is no environment in which we can move freely around spatially. In other words, there is no useful *Network User Interface*, the interface between users and services on a computer network.

Computers are much closer and very popular to ordinary people. But, at present, the most part of computer network users are persons familiar to computers. Thus novice users who have never touched a key boards will increase in number.

On the other hand, the rapid growth of computer networks will soon make it possible that novice users will use various kinds of services provided through networks. Can they start using a computer network and accessing services provided though it? We believe that a computer network will become a familiar communication tool like a telephone network. It seems that the current network interfaces for computer networks are not to be satisfactory for the future.

Ideally, the meaning of a user interface should be obvious to experienced users of a system, and also be evocative and self-evident to novice users. Novice users need a communication environment that is both simpler, more direct and more transparent or intuitive for accessing services provided through a network. Ordinary network interfaces are pretty difficult for novice users, so only experienced users can use them. One of the skemes of solving problems is a visual animated expression. A visual animated expression might help users express his interaction and interpret the reactions from the system. A visual animated representation is clearly a fruitful way for novice users to overcome the difficulties for accessing network services. The behavior such as *Walking on a road* is very common to people, and then the interface can help novice users start using a computer network easily and quickly by taking such behavior into consideration.

We propose an user interface concept named "MAP&ROOM" for easy and friendly communication in a network environment. MAP&ROOM, our interface concept for Network User Interface, helps network users to solve those problems by using the visual effect of such as *walking on a road in a map*. Using a map as a metaphor of a part of computer networks, users can easily recognize the network spatially. We begin by describing the three metaphors of MAP&ROOM interface and the several concepts. Then we present a more detailed *tour* of the system and describe its implementation.

# 2  WHAT IS MAP&ROOM?

In MAP&ROOM interface, there are three metaphors as follows:

- *maps* as a network

- *rooms and buildings* as a service

- *puppets* as a user

Further explanation is as following.

## 2.1  Maps as a network

Till now, a network has been expressed as a line which links one point to another. In this way, users can not feel the structure of a network spatially. However, using *Map* as a metaphor of a computer network, it is easy for the user to see the whole view of the computer network spatially. So a network is better by replacing a *point and line* with a *space and road in a map*.

We unconsciously memorize information by managing it spatially. For example, shopping at an unfamiliar supermarket, we can not get quickly the items which we want easily. It probably takes a long time to find out them because we do not know the locations of them. But on the other hand, shopping at a familiar supermarket, we can find out them quite easily. This is because these informations about the locations of the items are managed very spatially in the memory of human beings. What we mean by this is that we have a spatial map of the familiar supermarket in our mind. As this example, people are good at memorizing objects spatially. So the display like a map is very effective for network user interfaces.

## 2.2 Rooms and buildings as a service

In MAP&ROOM, a user can walk around and access a lot of services. A lot of buildings, shops, offices and the others are located on the map as services provided by various information providers. When a user enters a building, the service corresponding to the building will be invoked.

An example of the maps which includes many services is shown in Figure 1.

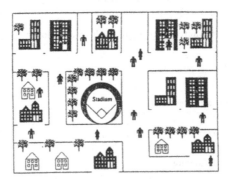

Figure 1: An image of MAP&ROOM

## 2.3 Puppets as a user

A user can manipulate a puppet as the other self of the user to walk about a map and access a lot of services. In using such a interface there are a couple of remarkable problems as follows:

- Since the user must walk on a map to access the service which he or she wants, the user spend long time to reach the service.

- Constantly making a communication between the users and the services (about location data of the puppets), there is always a load on the network.

But there are good features in MAP&ROOM interface. We believe that those good features compensate for these prblems mentioned above.

## 2.3.1 Encouters with the services

When a user accesses to services provided through a network, there are three cases:(see Table.1)

**CASE1:** The user knows both the existence and the address of the service.

**CASE2:** The user knows the existence but he or she does not know the address of the service.

Table 1: Three cases about users and services

| | EXISTANCE | ADDRESS | USABILITY | |
|---|---|---|---|---|
| | | | ORDINARY | MAP&ROOM |
| CASE.1 | O | O | O | O |
| CASE.2 | O | X | △ | O |
| CASE.3 | X | X | X | △ |

**CASE3:** The user do not know neither the existence nor the address of the service.

In the case of the first pattern, the user can access the service directly by ordinary interfaces for a computer network or can access by MAP&ROOM interface.

In the case of the second pattern, the user do not know the exact address of the service. Using ordinary interface to access the service, a user can not access to it directly. For example, when you want to use the FTP(File Trancepher Protcol) service, you have to know the exact address of the host providing the FTP service and have to access directly to the host. But using MAP&ROOM interface, a user does not have a need to know the address of the service. He or she needs only to know the existence of it.

In the case of the third pattern, a user do not know neither the existence nor the address of the service. sing ordinary interface(see Figure 2), a user can never know the existence of the service B and service D. He or she can only use the service A and service C. So, in this case, a user will never use the service B, furthermore he or she can not come to know that easily. But in MAP&ROOM interface, a user manipulates a puppet to access the service C, and on the way to access it he or she can find the other services(for example service A...). (Shown in Figure 2)

By this process, a user can use the service when he or she knows only the existence of it, and also will encounter several services unintentionally in the computer network, the existance of which is not known. So the user can use them effectively?

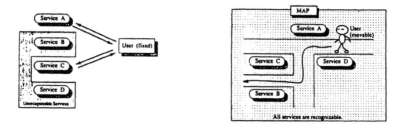

Figure 2: Ordinary interface and MAP&ROOM

### 2.3.2 Encounters with the other people

In addition to the encounter with the unknown services, there is another benefit, an unintentional encounter with the other people.

Many information technologies, such as virtual office, electronic libraries and databases, reduce the need to move about in order to get work done and therefore reduce the opportunities for casual interaction. Similarly, locating users in a distributed environment reduces the probability that they will occupy a common physical space, thereby it reduces the probability of informal interactions as well. The establishment and maintenance of a personal relationship is a creation of the glue that holds together the pieces of a collaborative research effort. So it's very important to support interactions with both acquaintances and strangers in a distributed environment.

In a physical environment, people often encounter with acquaintances in common spaces and make conversations with them. Therefore. physical proximity can be important in establishing and maintaining the personal relationships. As in a physical environment, virtual proximity is also needed in a virtual environment. In MAP&ROOM interface, the all users are represented as the puppets on the maps, then he or she can recognize the other people and feel them closely.

As mentioned above, till now, a network has been expressed as a line which links one point to another. On the other hand, in MAP&ROOM, a network is not expressed as "point and line" but as "space and road". Using MAP&ROOM, while accessing the service on the network, a user can encounter with other people using the same service. It also will be possible for a user to encounter with the others during walking on a road (while approaching to the service) by this interface. In such common spaces, users in a building can encounter others, and by moving around in a map can make opportunities for spontaneous and informal interactions. Furthermore, a user also has a possibility to get useful informations or knowledges through discussions with them. It seems that MAP&ROOM increases the use of computer networks as a communication tool.

# 3 HOW TO CONSTRUCT MAP&ROOM

We think that MAP&ROOM is useful for communication environment on a wide area network in which a lot of novice users can access many services. But we have no appliciate data network, this time we unwillingly implemented the prototype MAP&ROOM environment on the Ethernet in our campus.

## 3.1 Map server and MRclient

The basic architecture of MAP&ROOM is comprised of a lot of independent map servers. Each map server has particular responsibility for users connecting it and walking around in its own map. Each map server is also responsible for distributing services registered in its map, and ensuring those services required by users. The map server knows how to access services in its map, and when a user requires to access a service, the map server shows the way to access. A user then accesses the service through the network, and information is passed directly between the service server and the local client for user interface named MRclient. Thus a user can access a lot of services even if he or she has not known the existence of the services since the services are located on the map offered by the map server and the user can find them. The relationship between users and service servers is illustrated in Figure 3 & Figure 4.

MRclient, a local user interface client, is responsible for expressing information sent

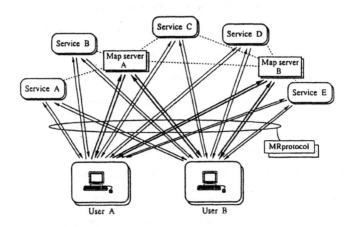

Figure 3: A protocol of MAP&ROOM

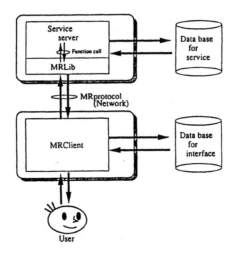

Figure 4: The relationship between users and service servers

from service servers. All information passed between servers and MRclients has to be sent by using a uniform protocol named MRprotocol which is something similar to Xprotocol. MRprotocol contains a lot of formats of information.

## 3.2 Typical use of MAP&ROOM

When a user connects a map server, at first it sends map information enough for MRclient to make map image for displaying the map

MRclient then sends user information such as his or her login name, his or her mail address and the style of the user's puppet. The services provided by the service server are described as objects occupying the map space (e.g. buildings, structures, rooms, parks and so on). When the user makes action to his or her puppet in the map, MRclient sends the information of actions to the server, and the server processes the information and sends back the location information. If the user's action indicates a particular service (e.g. the user's puppet is close to the shop), the map server sends MRclient enough information of the service to access. Then the MRclient makes a connection with the service server, and gets services from the service server directly. When the user finds another user's puppet, the user can move the puppet close to another's and can start talking to/with another user. In this case, it can be said that the user uses the talk service (We use the textbase talk service in this version.) Since the connection between the map server and the MRclient is kept even while the client is connecting the service, the user can walk around in the map and enter the services any time he or she wants.

# 4   A PROTOTYPE SYSTEM

Let us show two examples of services and utilities on the MAP&ROOM environment.

## 4.1   Visual shell

A visual shell on the MAP&ROOM environment is named MRShell. The main difference of the MRShell environment compared to other visual shell environments is the skeme for selecting and executing commands. A user might, in a fairly traditional fashion, start an application by selecting its icon and opening it. However, since MRShell is one of map servers, it has a map in it. In the map, objects occupying the map space(e.g. a room)

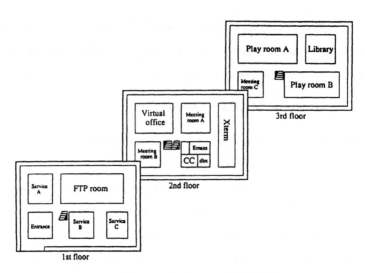

Figure 5: An image of MRShell

represent commands or applications(e.g. an editor). So a user can execute commands and applications by walking about in the map and putting puppet upon the objects Figure 5 shows a sample image of MRShell. Another remarkable difference of the MRShell environment is that MRShell supplies the chances for users to meet other users walking near by. Thus the users come to talk and do various activities with many network users in MRShell. When we an ordinary shell program, we are alone. We hope that MRShell might change our shell image into the more communicative application image.

## 4.2    Distributed meeting

Computer Supported Cooperative Work(CSCW) has been paid attention to a lot of research projects. MAP&ROOM, which manages a lot of persons accessing to a network with puppets and maps, is naturally suited for applications which have to control a cooperative work group consisting of a lot of persons. Therefore we can easily apply MAP&ROOM to electronic meeting systems which are one kind of CSCW applications. In MAP&ROOM, for example. an electronic meeting system is realized as a service, (probably expressed as a room) located on a map provided by a map server. (e.g. Meeting Room A or B in Figure 5) All participants joining the meeting are expressed as puppets, and all puppets are located and displayed in the same room at the same time. Then it is expected that the participants will feel a very close atmosphere as if they were really in a same room together.

## 4.3   Utilities

A map server based on MAP&ROOM offers some useful functions which free users from several restrictions and allow them to move in more various ways. We have two examples for the functions below.

**Wherever door** Basically, not to lose the spatial feature of a map, a user must walk to go anywhere and never jump to a goal. But sometimes walking is time consuming job. To avoid the waste of time *Wherever door* allows the user to jump to wherever he or she wants to go.

**Copy** A user can manage more than one puppets in a map. Only one of them is called *Original*, and every other puppets are called *Copy*. A Copy helps the user to do some jobs simultaneouslly. The user can make Copys invisible if necessary.

This concept can be applied to other services such as a used car shop, a video shop, a museum, a TV station, a database supplier, a library, a discount shop, etc. The key issue of realizing those services on a computer network is such a security problem as how to identify each user.

We believe that MAP&ROOM would be greatly assisted by the addition of sound effects such as footstep expressing "comming close" or "going further". Multiple media such as animation ,sound, etc. can be combined to produce compelling help and assistance systems.

## 5   CONCLUSION

We propose an user interface named "MAP&ROOM" to make a communication in a network environment easy to do and friendly to do. In an application based on MAP&ROOM, a network is expressed as a map metaphor in which a lot of buildings, shops, offices and the others are located as services offered by various parties, and the user manipulates a puppet as the other self of himself or herself to walk around the map and access various services.

Since the computer power is progressing rapidly, the chance for users to use and access the network. The age that we can share many resources(services) through the network will come. It has a big potential.

Therefore, we are sure that the need of *Network User Interface* (the interface between users and services on a computer network) which makes network easy-to-use will grow in the near future.

# References

[1] M. Ito, K. Jayanthi, G. Mansfield, H. Nunokawa and S. Noguchi, "A Metaphor Network-based Postal Service On The Heterogenesic Distributed System", *Proc. 43rd IPSJ conf.*, 2J-8, 1991[in Japanese].

[2] T. Winograd, et al, "Groupware", *BYTE*, December 1988.

[3] C. A. Ellis, et al, "GROUPWARE SOME ISSUES AND EXPERIENCES", *Communications of the ACM*, Vol.34, No.1, Jan. 1991.

[4] H. Ishii, "TeamWorkStation: Towards a Seamless Shared Workspace", Proc. CSCW'90, 1990.

[5] S.A. Bly and S.L. Minneman, "Commune: A Shared Drawing Surface", *Proc. COIS'90*, 1990.

[6] R.S. Fish, el al, "The VideoWindow System in Informal Communications", *Proc. CSCW'90*, 1990.

[7] C. Heath and P. Luff, "Disembodied Conduct: Communication Through Video in a Multi-Media Office Environment",*Proc. ACM SIGCHI'91*, 1991.

[8] N. Matsuura, S. Ichimura, S. Hiraiwa, K. Okada, Y. Matsushita, "A Teamware Workbench for Multimedia Information Management", *Proc. International Computer Symposium '90*, Dec. 1990.

[9] S. Ichimura, N. Matsuura, S. Hiraiwa, K. Okada, Y. Matsushita, "A Teamware Workbench for Information Management and Associative Retrieval in the Distributed Environment", *Proc. 1st International Workshop on Interoperability in Multidatabase Systems*, Apr. 1991.

[10] K. Okada, N. Matsuura, S. Ichimura, Y. Matsushita, "A Teamware Workbench for Concurrent Collaborative Work", *Parallel and Distributed Processing '91*, Apr. 1991.

[11] S. Hiraiwa, N. Matsuura and Y. Matsushita, "I-CEM: an Intelligent Communication System for Collaborative Work", *Proc. 1st International Conference on Parallel and Distributed Information Systems*, Dec. 1991.

[12] K.Y. Lai and T.W. Malone, "Object Lens: A Spreadsheet for Cooperative Work", *Proc. CSCW'88*, 1988.

[13] R. Beacker, I. Small and R. Mander, "Blinging Icons To Life", *Proc. ACM SIGCHI'91*, pp. 1-6, 1991.

[14] S.K. Card, G.G. Robertson and J.D. Mackinlay, "The Information Visualizer An Information Workspace", *Proc. ACM SIGCHI'92*, pp.181-188, 1992.

[15] W.W. Gaver, "Sound Support For Collaboration", *Proc. ECSCW'91*, pp.293-308, 1991.

# EVALUATING THE USE

# TestIt: An Automated Evaluation Tool for Human-Computer Interaction Projects.

Clark N. Quinn

Richard Preston

School of Computer Science & Engineering
The University of New South Wales
Kensington, NSW 2033
AUSTRALIA
cnquinn@cse.unsw.edu.au

This project is aimed at addressing the need for improvement in practice opportunities for students. The interface design process includes steps of analysis, specification, implementation, and evaluation, but student projects typically make only a single pass through the cycle and receive only a final evaluation. A more appropriate procedure that provides a idealistic and realistic practice experience is to include an evaluation component that students can incorporate into their design. A practical approach that not only provides the evaluation but also illustrates formal methods is to develop a computerized test program. We address how this tool fits into the curriculum and contributes to the practice of interface design instruction.

The trend in interaction studies has been to a focus on the user as the starting point of design (e.g. Norman & Draper, 1986). In particular, what is known about how people think, cognitive science, must be applied to the process of design, a "cognitive engineering" (Norman, 1986). Just as the principles derived from interaction research have relevance beyond computer applications (e.g. Norman, 1988), the process of designing for the user can apply to instruction as well as to systems. Thus, the process of designing instruction *on* user-centered system design is an exercise *in* user-centered system design (Quinn, 1992).

Teaching a complex process like the design of user-system interfaces requires both learning relevant knowledge and acquiring appropriate procedural skills. While the domain knowledge is fairly well understood and adequately treated in the texts, the process of interface design *practice*, the actual implementation of student projects, depends on the activities designed by the instructor, and may not include all components in the process (e.g. SIGCHI, 1992). An important aspect of skill acquisition, as identified in cognitive skill training frameworks like "cognitive apprenticeship" (Collins, Brown, & Newman, 1989), is the release of the activity to the student with a chance to practice on a realistic task in a supportive environment. "Problem-based learning" (Boud & Faletti, 1991) also supports the importance of a project for the application and integration of topic knowledge. Interface design courses typically present a large quantity of information about the user, the system, and models of the interaction as prerequisite knowledge while assigning small design projects to develop implementation skills in a particular development environment. For example, students may be acquiring knowledge about human visual processing characteristics at the same time they are learning a prototyping environment. Small assignments should be given which gradually exercise more extensive capabilities of the language and address more complex interaction problems. The process culminates in the assignment of a final project which is submitted to the instructor.

However, the process of interface design includes not only an accumulation of knowledge about the task, leading to a specification of the design and an actual implementation, but also an evaluation of the project. Ideally, this process is cyclical, with individual questions that arise from the specification being addressed by prototyped implementations and results from an evaluation being reincorporated into the specification. Two types of evaluation, formative and summative, are important. Formative evaluation is feedback that guides the design of the system while summative evaluation is used to determine the overall effectiveness of the design. Further, good interface design proposes that the user be involved in the formative evaluation. In practice, however, students receive only a final, summative evaluation of the project. A major improvement would be to provide some mechanism whereby students could receive and respond to a formative evaluation.

Several potential solutions arise. One solution would be to require the students to arrange for an evaluation on their own. This, however, is unsystematic and does not meet the ideal of a formal evaluation. A second solution would be to arrange for subjects and a testing schedule for each project. The logistics of such an endeavor are prohibitive, as suggested by Perlman (1989) who reported both time and knowledge difficulties in student testing. A third alternative is to have a program that systematically tests each student project, a program that acts like a user. This program can automatically create a log of the test (a second problem with human subjects is acquiring and coding the data) that can be provided to the students as feedback for their project which can be incorporated into their final design. Such a log would report situations where the commands did not perform as indicated, and would keep track of the number of steps required for each task. The idea of a programmed user has been explored but has remained in research and has not moved into practice (Booth, 1989).

To address this need, we are designing *TestIt*, an automated program evaluation tool. Several considerations exist for such a program: what language it will be implemented in, what strategies will be used for testing, and how it will be integrated into the subject. Currently, the students are taught HyperCard, a popular programming environment on the Apple Macintosh. This language has several advantages including that it is widely available, illustrates several interface issues, is easily learned, and is a popular prototyping environment. Students use this language to develop their projects. The structure of the language, being event-driven and incorporating message-passing, makes the creation of another program that can access and execute the projects a straightforward exercise. Such a program will require knowledge about the proper execution of the project, but it is an important exercise for students to specify how their project is to be used. For the purposes of TestIt, they can provide a script of interface actions for each task. Developing such a script again emphasizes the importance of rigor in interface development. TestIt will send the messages in the script and record the resulting state of the student project (see Figure 1).

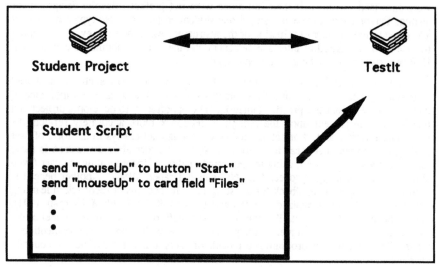

**Fig. 1.** TestIt interactions.

While the initial development will be in HyperCard, which is probably the most common environment for interface design instruction, portability of this work is possible. First, Toolbook, a development environment for IBM PC and compatibles is similar enough to HyperCard that transfer should be straightforward. Other tools such as Garnet (Myers, 1990) and SUIT (1992) are likely to support quick re-implementation.

Two additional mechanisms for testing projects are possible. To more accurately model a real user, errors typically performed, such as mode, description, and loss-of-activation errors (Norman, 1988), should be made by the program. Second, the heuristics used by an instructor to test student projects would be an additional benefit. These additions are are proposed as a second stage of development.

TestIt is designed to be used in conjunction with an early deadline for the final project to provide feedback and a revision opportunity for student projects. Students will submit their projects two weeks earlier than previously (also receiving the assignment earlier), and receive feedback from the program. The requirements for their reports on the project design, also submitted, will be expanded to include a report on the results of the test and the subsequent redesign. Student summative evaluation will be revised to incorporate both the results of the formative evaluation, and the subsequent redesign. As the response to the formative evaluation is more important than the initial design, both theoretically and practically, the initial design will be de-emphasized in summative evaluation.

It might be thought that students in such a situation might prepare projects that would make no errors, but experience suggests that, even with the knowledge that they are designing for a programmed evaluation, students will not design projects that will pass evaluation without problems. In the previously mentioned study on formative evaluation in a user interface project (Perlman, 1989) the results indicated that "students were surprised to find that their intuitions were not perfect", despite designing for testing. Personal experience also shows that student projects are also typically not well addressed to the summary evaluation of the instructor. Also, the strategy of developing for use is to be desired in interface designers and the practice should be encouraged. However, more concrete benefits are envisaged.

TestIt has several potential benefits. For one, frameworks such as "anchored instruction" (The Cognition and Technology Group, 1990) suggest the importance of including a more realistic practice situation. The opportunity to develop a project and then revise the project upon the receipt of feedback more accurately reflects the workplace environment. Formative feedback, although not always in the form of user testing, is a common process in interface design. The formative evaluation is more idealistically sound as well, using the preferred method of incorporating the user (even simulated) in the design process (e.g. Norman & Draper, 1986). Another benefit is both more and specific feedback for the students. The benefits of feedback in learning outcomes are widely recognized (e.g. Bangert-Drowns, Kulik, Kulik, & Morgan, 1991). A final benefit is the concrete illustration of the benefit of a programmed model of the user as an evaluation technique. In the presentation of evaluation in lecture, mention is made of the potential of programmed models of users, but TestIt provides a concrete example.

Evaluation of TestIt will be collected in several forms, and will depend on converging evidence to ascertain any pedagogical gain. In one sense, the evaluation methods are not yet known and will depend on creative interpretation, for this endeavor crosses the boundaries of human-computer interaction and education. On the other hand, two well-recognized methods for data collection and interpretation are proposed, machine traces or logs of user actions (Monk, 1986) and expert protocols (Ericsson & Simon, 1980), and the interpretation will be grounded in concrete outcomes for students. As a first level of evaluation, if TestIt can identify weaknesses in student projects that are verified by inspection, the program will have succeeded. A second form of evaluation comes from the difference between student projects before and after the feedback from the program. Finally, evaluation comes from the perception of the students as to the benefit of the addition and from their comprehension of the theoretical role of TestIt. Each of these will be assessed.

The first version of TestIt will be applied to the student projects and the resulting log, or trace, of results will be assessed to see if the program discovers any project weaknesses. The detection of such weaknesses means that the tool can substitute for the instructor in this respect. The results of this log will be compared to a protocol of an expert evaluation of the projects both to assess the utility of the program and to infer rules that can added to increase the utility.

The log will be returned to the students with an opportunity to incorporate the changes. Improvement in student projects will be carefully examined by comparing changes in the projects after re-submission, as well as the section of the accompanying report. The methodology currently used to perform summative evaluation, expert assessment, will be expanded to include this component. In particular, notice will be taken of revisions targeted to address problems identified in the formative evaluation, both to repair the problem and to not create any further problems. The expert assessment will also be evaluated for techniques that may be incorporated into TestIt.

The subject already has an evaluation component where students fill out a questionnaire directed towards improving instruction, so this form will be expanded to incorporate feedback about the utility of TestIt from the student perspective. Quantitative questions will assess student perception of the benefit of the addition, while qualitative responses will be analyzed to ascertain student perceptions of potential improvements to the process.

In addition, a two-part final examination process question will be added to assess the subject content benefit of TestIt. This question will ask the students to report the conceptual benefits of TestIt, which will be stressed in lecture, to determine the extent to which students comprehend the theoretical role that formative and automated evaluation plays in the interface design process.

During the evaluation of TestIt, ongoing development will target adding typical human errors into the testing routines. As data becomes available on expert heuristics, these too will be incorporated. Any information resulting from the first evaluation that impacts program design will also be incorporated. The second version of TestIt will be validated on the first version of the student projects again for comparison to the expert training.

This project is currently under implementation for the first stage, and the major hurdles of addressing the target project and assessing the state after execution of a script command have been overcome. One remaining obstacle to implementation is the inability of HyperCard to handle error messages. We are currently pursuing a solution through XCMD's (code packages that are implement external to HyperCard but can be called through a protocol). We intend to use the first stage of TestIt in the undergraduate Human-Computer Interaction subject offered in the first half of next year.

## References

Bangert-Drowns, R. L., Kulik, C. C., Kulik, J. A., & Morgan, M. (1991). The instructional effect of feedback in test-like events. *Review of Educational Research*. 61, 2, pp 213-238.

Booth, P. A. (1989). *An Introduction to Human-Computer Interaction*. Hillsdale, NJ: Lawrence Erlbaum.

Boud, B. & Faletti, G. (1991). *The Challenge of Problem-Based Learning*. London: Cogan Page.

Collins, A., Brown, J. S., & Newman, S. (1989). Cognitive apprenticeship: Teaching the craft of reading, writing, and mathematics. In L. B. Resnick (Ed.) *Knowing, learning and instruction: Essays in honor of Robert Glaser*. Hillsdale, NJ: Lawrence Erlbaum Associates.

Cognition and Technology Group at Vanderbilt, The (1990). Anchored instruction and its relationship to situated cognition. *Educational Researcher* 19(6), 2-10.

Ericsson, K. A., & Simon, H. A. (1980). Verbal report as data. *Psychological Review*, 87, 3, pp 215-251.

Mealor, T. (1992). Man/machine interface shaping the future. *PACE*, January, pp 10.

Monk, A. (1986). How and when to collect behavioural data. In A. Monk (Ed.) *Fundamentals of Human-Computer Interaction*. London: Academic Press.

Myers, B. (1990). Garnet. *IEEE Computer*, November, 71-85.

Norman, D. A. (1986). Cognitive engineering. In D. A. Norman & S. W. Draper (Eds.) *User-Centered System Design*. Hillsdale, NJ: Lawrence Erlbaum Associates.

Norman, D. A. (1988). *The Psychology of Everyday Things*. New York: Basic Books.

Norman, D. A., & Draper, S. W. (1986). *User-Centered System Design*. Hillsdale, NJ: Lawrence Erlbaum Associates.

Quinn, C. N. (1992, November). Teaching user-centred system design: a recursive exercise. *Proceedings of the Conference on the Impact of Computers on Design*. Sydney, NSW.

Perlman, G. (1989). *User Interface Development*. Software Engineering Institute Curriculum Module SEI-CM-18-1.1 Pittsburgh: Carnegie Mellon University.

(SUIT) Simple User Interface Toolkit Team (1992). The Simple User Interface Toolkit. *Internet, comp.human-factors*.

(SIGCHI) Special Interest Group in Computer-Human Interaction. (1992). *Curriculae for Human-Computer Interaction*. Association for Computing Machinery.

# Software-Evaluation based upon ISO 9241 Part 10[*]

Jochen Prümper

DATA TRAIN GmbH
Ibsenstraße 13, 10439 Berlin, Germany
☎ 030 - 47 24 130, Fax 030 - 47 24 129

**Abstract.** In this article the software evaluation instrument ISONORM 9241/10 is presented. This instrument was developed from `ISO 9241: Ergonomic requirements for office work with visual display terminals (VDTs), Part 10: Dialogue Principles`. The capabilities of this instrument are shown through two methods. First, two different kinds of computer-systems (with and without graphical user interface) are evaluated for their conformity to ISO 9241/10. Second, a procedure is shown in which ISONORM 9241/10 is used as a basis for moderation with user-groups, when in the beginning of a design-process, through the forum of a participative system-development, first demands are formulated. It is shown that the user-friendliness of systems with GUI is judged to be significantly superior in all seven principles of ISO 9241/10, to those systems without GUI. In the user-group meeting, through ISONORM 9241/10, many concrete recommendations for a new software to be developed could be generated.

## 1 Introduction

After many years of preparation (e.g. DIN 66 234/8, 1988 [3]; Dzida & Itzfeldt, 1978 [4]) in february 1993 the `International Organisation for Standardisation (ISO) presented the first `Draft International Standard` of `ISO 9241: Ergonomic requirements for office work with visual display terminals (VDTs), Part 10: Dialogue Principles` (ISO 9241/10, 1993 [10]).

ISO 9241/10 deals with software aspects and describes seven general ergonomic principles, which are independent of any specific dialogue technique; i.e. they are presented without reference to situations of use, applications, environments or technology.

The following table gives an overview of the seven principles of ISO 9241/10 and its corresponding descriptions.

---

[*] This article was produced as part of the software-development project "Verlag 2000" ("Publication 2000"). "Verlag 2000" is supported by a grant from the Work & Technical Fund of the Ministry of Research and Technology of the Federal Republic of Germany (No.: 01 HK 601 8). Thanks are due to Michael Anft and Mark Farah.

**Tab. 1.** The seven principles of ISO 9241/10 and corresponding descriptions

| Principle | Description |
|---|---|
| • suitability for the task | A dialogue is suitable for a task to the extent that it supports the user in the effective and efficient completion of the task. |
| • self-descriptiveness | A dialogue is self-descriptive to the extent that each dialogue step is immediately comprehensible through feedback from the system, or is explained to the user when requesting the relevant information. |
| • controllability | A dialogue is controllable to the extent that the user is able to maintain direction over the whole course of the interaction until the point at which the goal has been met. |
| • conformity with user expectations | A dialogue conforms with user expectations to the extent that it corresponds to the user's task knowledge, education, experience, and to commonly accepted conventions. |
| • error tolerance | A dialogue is error tolerant to the extent, if despite evident errors in input, the intended result may be achieved with either no or minimal corrective action having to be taken. |
| • suitability for individualization | A dialogue is suitable for individualization to the extent that the dialogue system is constructed to allow for modification to the user's individual needs and skills for a given task. |
| • suitability for learning | A dialogue is suitable for learning to the extent that it provides support and guidance to the user during the learning phases. |

Although the type of information in ISO 9241/10 is more a general guidance (and thus has a more informative than normative character), the principles are intended to be used in the design as well as in the evaluation of dialogue systems (see Prümper, 1993b [16]; see also Nielsen, 1992 [13]; Nielsen & Molich, 1990 [14]).

## 2  The Software-Evaluation Instrument ISONORM 9241/10

In order to analyse whether a software-system meets the seven principles of ISO 9241/10, those principles must be characterized through an evaluation instrument.

In this article an evaluation instrument based on ISO 9241/10 will be presented. Going forward, the name of this instrument will be ISONORM 9241/10 (see Prümper & Anft, 1993b [19]; 1993c [20]).

The intention in developing ISONORM 9241/10 was to create a competent, practical and compact instrument which can be efficiently used to evaluate software and to support software development.

For this purpose the questionnaire method is the most pragmatic because of its inherent advantages of little effort and easy use. In order to meet the claim of an economically usable instrument, the extent of the questionnaire was limited to five items for each of the seven principles of ISO 9241/10.

For the construction of the questionnaire, we decided upon a seven tier, bi-polar question format with an answer schema from "- - -" to "+++" (coded: 1 - 7). Through the opposite positioning of the positive and negative poles we believe that the subjects are motivated to reflect upon the statements in more detail and are not influenced to answer towards a particular side.

Figure 1 shows an example item from the questionnaire regarding the principle "conformity with user expectations".

**The software ...**

| | - - - | - - | - | - / + | + | ++ | +++ | |
|---|---|---|---|---|---|---|---|---|
| makes more difficult the orientation because of a non-conforming design. | | | | | | | | simplifies the orientation because of a conforming design. |

**Fig. 1.**  Example item from the questionnaire regarding the principle "conformity with user expectations"

According to action theory (Frese & Sabini, 1985 [7]; Frese & Zapf, 1994 [9]; Hacker, Volpert & von Cranach, 1982 [10]), we tried to formulate the items as close as possible to operation and activity.

The language itself was chosen so that the specific properties of different interfaces are sufficiently differentiated, but at the same time is appropiate for many software applications. With this "medium level of granulation" (see Rauterberg, 1992a [22]) ISONORM 9241/10 offers the evaluation of a wide range of software systems. Table 2 shows an example item for each of the seven principles.

**Tab. 2.** The seven principles of ISO 9241/10 and respective item examples

| Principle | Item |
|---|---|
| • suitability for the task | The software inappropriately meets the demands of the tasks. |
| • self-descriptiveness | The software offers insufficient information regarding the inputs which are allowed or necessary. |
| • controllability | The software forces an unnecessary inflexible sequence of commands. |
| • conformity with user expectations | The software makes more difficult the orientation because of a non-conforming design. |
| • error tolerance | The software gives unspecific information regarding error correction and management. |
| • suitability for individualization | The software is difficult for the user to expand if new tasks arise. |
| • suitability for learning | The software is difficult to learn without outside direction or handbooks. |

However, an evaluation instrument which judges user-friendliness of software is, among other things, only useful if it is able to differentiate significantly between different software programs (this rises the question of the validation of an instrument). Furthermore, from its use practible implications should arise.

This is proved by the following: First, two different kinds of software interfaces are tested for norm-conformity through the use of ISONORM 9241/10. Second, a procedure will be demonstrated in which ISONORM 9241/10 was used during the beginning of a design-process as a basis for the moderation of user-groups.

## 3 Comparison of Software With and Without Graphical User Interface Using ISONORM 9241/10

A graphical user interface (GUI) can be defined as an interface that allows users to choose commands and other options by pointing to a graphical icon and then activating the choice by either the keyboard or a mouse.

In the literature there is evidence that systems with graphical user interface which are characterized by direct manipulation of objects are superior to conventional systems.

For example, following a description of the most important characteristics of direct manipulation (model action world, direct information and direct action) Altmann (1987) [1] and Frese, Schulte-Göcking and Altmann (1987) [8] showed that *learning progress* was higher with a direct manipulation system than with a conventional system, and Téeni (1990) [26] demonstrated that direct manipulation enhanced *cognitive control* in a judgement task (the feedback generated by direct manipulation was more effective compared to distinct feedback in traditional human-computer dialogue). Ulich, Rauterberg, Moll, Greutmann & Strohm (1991) [27] conducted a comparison of a desktop interface (high transparency) and a conventional menu selection interface (low transparency) to prove the criterion of *transparency*, and demonstrated the superiority of the user interface with direct manipulation over the conventional user interface with menu selection, and Rauterberg (1992b) [23] showed in an comparison of menu-selection and desktop computer programs the superiority of the desktop user interface for beginners as well as for experts. Furthermore, Shneiderman (1988) [25] encouraged greater attention to direct manipulation in which the objects and actions are visible, the actions are invoked by selection or pointing, and the impact is immediately visible and reversible. Rosson & Alpert (1990) [24] - considering the potential of the object-oriented paradigm in easing the design process of interactive software design and improving the usability of the resulting system - came to the conclusion that object orientation allows a designer to generate an initial design model in the context of the problem itself, rather than requiring a mapping onto traditional computer science constructs.

Thus, because of theoretical reasons and empirical results it can be hypothized that software with graphical user interface is more user-friendly, i.e. meets better the principles of ISO 9241/10, than software with no graphical user interface.

## 3.1 Procedure

Until now 350 users from 20 different companies in the Federal Republic of Germany participated in the evaluation of software using ISONORM 9241/10. They were selected through different methods, such as articles in magazines and journals, contacts to companies or participation in software-development projects. The average age of the subjects was 35 years old, 64,2 % were female, 35,8% male. Those 350 users evaluated 66 different software programs (without differentiating versions). 106 users evaluated 22 different software-programs with a graphical user interface (mainly diverse Microsoft-Windows and Apple-Macintosh Programs) and 244 users evaluated 44 different software-programs with no graphical user interface (mainly software running MS-DOS, IBM AS/400, IBM /36 or Siemens BS 2000).

## 3.2 Results

The following graphic shows a comparison of programs with graphical user interface to those without graphical user interface using the seven principles of ISO 9241/10 (see Figure 2).

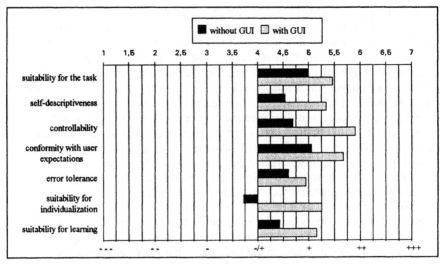

*Note:* All differences between systems with graphical user interface and without graphical user interface are significantly at p< .001 (t-test, one-tailed probability); N=350

**Fig. 2.** Comparison of programs with graphical user interface to those without graphical user interface using the seven principles of ISO 9241/10

As can be seen from Figure 2, the user-friendliness of the programs with graphical user interface is significantly superior in all seven principles of ISONORM 9241/10 to the user friendliness of programs with no graphical user interface. This can be interpreted as first proof of a successful realization of `ISO 9241: Ergonomic requirements for office work with visual display terminals, Part 10: Dialogue Principles`.

Moreover, the above results demonstrate that the user-friendliness of software in general is not yet to be judged as satisfactory. With a total-average for all programs of x=4,95 the user-friendliness of both the software with graphical user interface (x=5,38), and definitly the software without graphical user interface (x=4,52), are not very impressive. Only regarding the two principles "suitability for the task" (x=5,00) and "conformity with user expectations" (x=5,06) did the software without graphical user interface reach the "+" - mark; "suitability for individualization" (x=3,72) is even in the negative zone.

But even the user-friendliness of the software with graphical user interface still leaves much to be desired. In addition, none of these programs reached the "++" - mark at one principle ("controllability" with x=5,91 is rated the highest) and "error tolerance" didn't even reach the "+" - mark (x=4,61).

In conclusion, one can say that ISONORM 9241/10 is able to significantly distinguish between different types of software, and that the instrument can even point out areas for improvements of modern GUI software.

# 4 ISONORM 9241/10 in User-Oriented Software-Development

In the following, a procedure will be shown in which ISONORM 9241/10 was used as a basis for the moderation of user-groups, when in the beginning of a design-process first demands needed to be generated. This procedure took place in a soft-ware-development project for publishing-houses (see Prümper, 1993a [15]; 1993c [17]). In this project the software-development is managed in close participation with potential end-users. At the forefront, active participation is practiced where the users have the possibility to influence the design-process at its early stages. For this purpose end-users and software-developers come together from time to time under the guidance of industrial psychologists, in order to define the individual design-phases. At these meetings the later users are introduced to developing versions of the publishing software.

However, in most cases only a selected circle of end-users have the opportunity to take part in these meetings. Therefore, the rest of the future users will at the least get the status of passive participation. Although these users have no direct influence on the development of the software, their demands can also be taken into account. Here, ISONORM 9241/10 will be of usefull service.

## 4.1 Procedure

In order to realize active as well as passive participation, 42 users from three German publishing-houses evaluated their old "address"-module with ISONORM 9241/10 (passive participation). The average age of the subjects was 35 years old, 92,9 % were female, 7,1% male. From these publishers seven users participated in the first meeting of the user-group (active participation) to determine the existing weak points of the old "address"-module in order to generate suggestions for the new publishing-software.

At the beginning of the meeting item by item results of the inquiry were presented to the user-group and for every item examples were requested (with use of a flip-chart). Those examples were worked on in the form of group discussion and then fine-tuned. Hereby, the users had access to the software they had evaluated, to further demonstrate their examples. This procedure was repeated seven times according to the seven principles of ISO 9241/10. The time spent was seven hours (for details see Prümper & Anft, 1993a [18]).

## 4.2 Results

It wasn't always easy for the users to spontaneously generate an example for each item. In these cases, the moderator explained the items according to the "critical incident technique" (Flanagan, 1954 [6]) with positive and negative examples of other programs or asked the users to explore the system with smaller tasks. However, the fact that the users could not always precisely differentiate between the individual principles of ISO 9241/10 proved to be a difficulty. For example, some conceptual cases for "controllability" or "conformity with user expectations" should have been taken into account by the principle "suitability for the task". The reason for this overlapping does not only lie on the user side, but rather are inherent in the principles of ISO 9241/10 themselves: "The dialog principles are not independent, and it may be neceessary to trade off the benifits of one priniple against another" (ISO 9241/10, 1993, iv) [11]. The consequences were that the users were able to create more example from the principles which were presented at the beginning of the moderation than those in the end. However, the final conclusion of this procedure was that the user-group supplemented the results of the ISONORM 9241/10 inquiry with a number of concrete suggestions. As an illustration of the procedure, the principles and respective results are presented in Table 3.

**Tab. 3.** The seven principles of ISO 9241/10 and exemplary results from the user-
group

| Principle | Fault of the Principle |
|---|---|
| • suitability for the task | The address-screen contains unnecessary fields, which are rarely if ever used. |
| • self-descriptiveness | The address-screen does not distinguish between fields which are definitely necessary or just optional. |
| • controllability | When defining a new address the user is forced to enter an unnecessary screen, even though under the circumstances it is not required. |
| • conformity with user expectations | In the address-module the function-keys perform differently as in the book-module. |
| • error tolerance | If an address is incompletely entered, the cursor moves to the first field in the screen and the user receives the error-message: "Entry false or incomplete". It is not obvious which field is intended. |
| • suitability for individualization | If new codes are necessary (i.e. hobbies or subject-groups), the user can not supplement the codes by him- or herself. |
| • suitability for learning | Learning the computer is strenuous because no on-line help exists. |

Concerning "suitability for the task" one could say that the address-module does not offer all functions to fulfill the demands, and that unnecessary entries are required. Regarding "self-descriptiveness", it was criticised that no context-specific explanations are available. Negative comments were also noted concerning "controllability". It was especially mentioned that the software doesn't offer the possibility to interrupt the work without loss. Moreover, the user can hardly influence which type of information is offered to him. Concerning "conformity with user expectations", it was criticised that the software is not uniformly designed so that it is difficult to transfer knowledge from one module to another. In the context of "error tolerance", it was noted that the software did not give concrete information for error correction and management, and that it didn't always give direct feedback regarding false entries. In the rating of "suitability for individualization" it was noted that the address-module is hardly expandable if new tasks arise, and that it is difficult to mould the software to the individuals' working preferences. Finally, the software is critically judged concerning "suitability for learning" because it doesn't easily adapt when trying out new functions. Moreover, there is no on-line help available, so the software is very difficult to learn without outside aid.

Clearly by all principles, the users of the address-module in consideration asked for many improvements.

# 5 Discussion

In this article an instrument for software evaluation based on the ISO 9241/10 was introduced, and its capabilities were proven by two methods.

First, a comparison between systems with- and without graphical user interface was carried out. It was shown that the user-friendliness of systems with graphical user interface was judged to be significantly superior in all seven principles of ISO 9241 Part 10, to those systems without graphical user interface. The fact that the questionnaire ISONORM 9241/10 was able to clearly differentiate between software-systems is seen as first proof of the successful characterization of ISO 9241 Part 10. Moreover, it was shown that through ISONORM 9241/10 the user-friendliness of systems with graphical user interface as well as systems without graphical user interface is not quite satisfactory.

Second, in the forum of participative software-development the instrument ISONORM 9241/10 was used as a first analysis of weaknesses. In the case of the user-group meeting, the extraordinary quality was that ISO 9241/10 delivered an accepted criterion through which users and software-developers could discuss the product under consideration. The final result consisted of many concrete recommendations for the new software to be developed.

The questionnaire ISONORM 9241/10 does not claim to be an alternative to deeper analysis, such as error analysis through observation (Brodbeck, Zapf, Prümper & Frese, 1993 [2]; Prümper, Zapf, Brodbeck & Frese, 1992 [21]; Zapf, Brodbeck, Frese, Peters & Prümper, 1992 [28]; for an overview of evaluation methods see Dzida, Wiethoff & Arnold, 1993 [5]). Nevertheless, ISONORM 9241/10 can be a helpful alternative if a robust, economical software-evaluation instrument is sought, which is closely oriented towards international standards.

However, before its worth as a software evaluation instrument can truly be accepted, additional validity- and reliabilty-tests should be performed (see Kirakowski

& Corbett, 1990 [12]). These tests are currently being conducted and the preliminary results are quite promising.

The questionnaire ISONORM 9241/10 is available in both German (Prümper & Anft, 1993b) [19] and English (Prümper & Anft, 1993c) [20].

# References

1.  Altmann, A.: Direkte Manipulation: Empirische Befunde zum Einfluß der Be-nutzeroberfläche auf die Erlernbarkeit von Textsystemen. Zeitschrift für Ar-beits- und Organisationspsychologie 31, 108-114 (1987)

2.  Brodbeck, F.C., Zapf, D., Prümper, J., Frese, M.: Error handling in office work with computers: A field study. Journal of Occupational and Organiza-tional Psychology (1993, in press)

3.  DIN 66 234/8 Bildschirmarbeitsplätze: Grundsätze ergonomischer Dialogge-staltung. Berlin: Beuth 1988

4.  Dzida, W., Itzfeldt, W.D.: User-perceived quality of interactive systems. IEEE Transactions on Software Engineering SE-4, 270-276 (1978)

5.  Dzida, W., Wiethoff, M, Arnold, A.G.: ERGOguide - The quality assurance guide to ergonomic software. Delft University of Technology/German National Center of Computer Science 1993

6.  Flanagan, J.G.: The critical incident technique. Psychological Bulletin 51, 327-358 (1954)

7.  Frese, M., Sabini, J. (eds.): Goal-directed behavior: The concept of action in psychology. Hillsdale: Erlbaum 1985

8.  Frese, M., Schulte-Göcking, H., Altmann, A.: Lernprozesse in Abhängigkeit von der Trainingsmethode, von Personenmerkmalen und von der Benutzer-oberfläche (direkte Manipulation vs. konventionelle Interaktion). In: W. Schönpflug, M. Wittstock (eds.): Software-Ergonomie '87. Nützen Informa-tionssysteme dem Benutzer? Stuttgart: Teubner 1987, pp. 377-386

9.  Frese, M., Zapf, D.: Action as the core of work psychology: A German ap-proach. In: M.D. Dunnette, L.M. Hough, H. Triandis (eds.): Handbook of in-dustrial and organizational psychology (Vol. 4). Palo Alto, CA: Consulting Psychologists Press 1994, in press

10. Hacker, W., Volpert, W., von Cranach, M.: Cognitive and motivational as-pects of action. Berlin: Deutscher Verlag der Wissenschaften 1982

11. ISO 9241/10: ISO 9241 - Ergonomic requirements for office work with visual display terminals (VDTs), Part 10 - Dialogue principles - First Draft Interna-tional Standard, February 2, 1993

12. Kirakowski, J., Corbett, M.: Effective methodology for the study of HCI. Am-sterdam: North Holland 1990

13. Nielsen, J.: Finding usability problems through heuristic evaluation. In: P. Bauersfeld, J. Bennett, G. Lynch (eds.): CHI'92 Conference Proceedings. New York: ACM press 1992, pp. 373-380

14. Nielsen, J., Molich, R.: Heuristic evaluation of user interfaces. In: J.C. Chow, J. Whiteside (eds.): CHI'90 Conference Proceedings. New York: ACM press 1990, pp. 249-256

15. Prümper, J.: Benutzerorientierte, iterative Software-Entwicklung in der Praxis. In: W. Coy, P. Gorny, I. Kopp, C. Skarpelis (eds.): Menschengerechte Software als Wettbewerbsfaktor. Stuttgart: Teubner 1993a, pp. 630-647

16. Prümper, J.: GUIs sind noch weit entfernt von einer optimalen Beurteilung - ISO 9241 Teil 10 als Leitlinie für SW-Entwicklung und -Bewertung. Computerwoche 25, 46 (1993b)

17. Prümper, J.: Wie benutzerfreundlich ist Ihre Software? Börsenblatt 20, 24-26 (1993c)

18. Prümper, J., Anft, M.: Die Evaluation von Software auf Grundlage des Entwurfs zur internationalen Ergonomie-Norm ISO 9241 Teil 10 als Beitrag zur partizipativen Systemgestaltung - ein Fallbeispiel. In: K.H. Rödiger (ed.): Software-Ergonomie '93 - Von der Benutzungsoberfläche zur Arbeitsgestaltung. Stuttgart: Teubner 1993a, pp. 145-156

19. Prümper, J., Anft, M.: ISONORM 9241/10 - Beurteilung von Software auf Grundlage der Internationalen Ergonomie-Norm ISO 9241/10 (Questionnaire) 1993b

20. Prümper, J., Anft, M.: ISONORM 9241/10 - Software Evaluation based upon the Principles of Ergonomic Requirements ISO 9241/10 (Questionnaire) 1993c

21. Prümper, J., Zapf, D., Brodbeck, F.C., Frese, M.: Some surprising differences between novice and expert errors in computerized office work. Behaviour & Information Technology 11, 319-328 (1992)

22. Rauterberg, M.: Läßt sich die Gebrauchstauglichkeit interaktiver Software messen? Und wenn ja, wie? Ergonomie & Informatik 16, 3-18 (1992a)

23. Rauterberg, M.: An empirical comparison of menu-selection (CUI) and desktop (GUI) computer programs carried out by beginners and experts. Behaviour & Information Technology 11, 227-236 (1992b)

24. Rosson, M.B., Alpert, S.R.: The cognitive consequences of object-oriented design. Human-Computer Interaction 5, 345-379 (1990)

25. Shneiderman, B.: We can design better user interfaces: A review of human-computer interaction styles. Ergonomics 31, 699-710 (1988)

26. Téeni, D.: Direct manipulation as a source of cognitive feedback: A human-computer experiment with a judgement task. International Journal of Man-Machine Studies 33, 453-466 (1990)

27. Ulich, E., Rauterberg, M., Moll, T., Greutmann, T., Strohm, O.: Task orientation and user-oriented dialog design. International Journal of Human-Computer Interaction 3, 117-144 (1991)

28. Zapf, D., Brodbeck, F.C., Frese, M., Peters, M., Prümper, J.: Errors in working with office computers. A first validation of a taxonomy for observed errors in a field setting. International Journal of Human-Computer Interaction 4, 311-339 (1992)

# Diagnosing Quality of Life in Working Environments

*D. Cordelle, D. Bronisz*

**Cap Gemini Innovation**
7 Chemin du Vieux Chêne,
ZIRST 38240 Meylan (France)
Tel (+33) 76 76 47 47
Fax (+33) 76 76 47 48
Email : cordelle@capsogeti.fr

**ABSTRACT:**

The Esprit Project 5374 QLIS (Quality of Life in the Information Society) aims to develop a Software Scenario Support Tool (3ST) for the assessment and forecasting of the implications of IT applications for Quality of Life. In order to reach this goal, a consortium of partners with complementary knowledge was set up comprising sociologists with knowledge about quality of life issues; computer scientists who model their knowledge and build systems based on it; and industrial partners who supply case studies to assess the models and the 3ST. In this paper we discuss the sociologists' approach in assessing quality of Life in the Work Environment, and we present the prototype system which aims to reproduce this behaviour, with illustrations taken from a real situation in one of our industrial organizations.

**KEYWORDS:** Expert Systems, Knowledge Acquisition, KADS, Prototype, Diagnosis Quality of Life, Socio-Technical Model, Information Technology

Changes in information and telecommunications technologies are reaching further, faster and have increasing influence on daily life and society at large. These ongoing changes are associated with equally profound transformations in working life and have caused renewed concern with quality of life issues in general and especially questions regarding the Quality of Working Life.

This concern is manifested in several positions within organizations. A manager may be worried about the quality of working life in the organization and may desire a diagnosis with recommendations for improvement. Or he/she may be considering the assessment of the information technology in relation with the level of well-being of his/her employees.

Esprit Project 5374 QLIS (Quality of Life in the Information Society)[1] aims to answer such

---

[1]Funded in part by the Commission of the European Communities

preoccupations by developing a Software Scenario Support Tool (3ST) for the assessment and simulation of the implications of IT applications for Quality of Life.

In order to reach these goals, we have brought together a number of organizations with complementary knowledge and experience:

*Sociologists* (Istituto RSO) with knowledge about quality of life issues. Their knowledge is often used to solve problems or perform audits for clients.

*Industrial organization* (FIAT) with organizational problems they would like to solve.

*Computer scientists* (Cap Gemini Innovation) with experience in modelling complex domains and building expert systems that operate on these models.

Working together, the sociologists and computer scientists are developing a system (the 3ST mentioned above) that will be able to solve the industrial organizations' problems.

In this paper we will discuss the work being carried out on the 3ST as it applies to assessing quality of life in the work environment. The first part presents an Istituto RSO consultancy as a model of a reasoning process we want to follow. The second part shows a typical session with the 3ST, illustrated by a FIAT case study. Finally, the last part describes how we went about building knowledge models and implementing them in a prototype.

# 1. The Sociologists and their Approach

Most of the theoretical underpinnings of our work were developed prior to the QLISproject by Istituto RSO and a part of them is discussed here because it is necessary for an understanding of the prototype which we present in the following section. In the interest of brevity, we will give definitions of terms used only when strictly necessary, and we will give no (theoretical) justification of the model other than to point out that it is supported by over ten years of empirical study from Istituto RSO covering more than 100 case studies.

A first part presents the models of representation used, a second the typical reasoning process used in Istituto RSO's consultancy which is developed in the last part.

## 1.1. The Models

One of the most striking aspects of Istituto RSO's approach is that it does not try to find immediate causes for an observed problem, but considers a consistent group of population (unit or department) of the organization as a whole before finding a solution. This analysis process depends on two related models: a Socio-Technical Model (STM) which describes the organization [Butera 90], and a Quality of Working Life (QWL) Model describing the different aspects of the quality of life of people in the work environment [Bellini 90]. The STM comprises six dimensions: *professional profiles, processes, organization, personnel rules, social system,* and *technology in use.* The QWL model is also (coincidentally) composed of six dimensions: *body, mind, psyche, self, professional role* and *social role.*

The same type of representation is used in both models: Each dimension is represented by a tree which shows its decomposition into more detailed components. The leaves of the trees are specific enough to be characterized by simple values. Figure 1 shows a partial view of one of the dimensions of the *Professional Profiles* tree. (To save space, we abbreviate this as just *profession* in the diagram.) In this example, the node *Role* is defined by its components (*Main activities, Relationships, Goal*: a *Role* is what someone does in *Relation* with other people to reach a certain *Goal*) and by a set of possible values (*operative, operation-ccoordinative, technician, professional, managerial,entrepreneurial*)

These representations are not static and can be adapted in accordance with the organization studied, in order to adapt possible values and symplify or develop part of the different representation trees. For example the study of an R&D department requires to develop the *technology in use* dimension, whereas the study of a marketing department requires to focus on the *organization* dimension

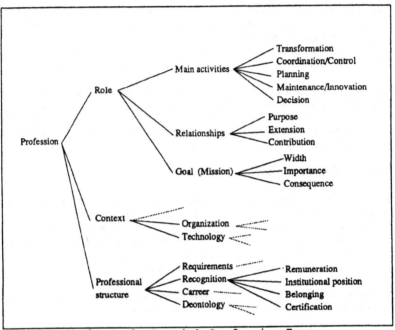

**Figure 1**: Partial *Profession* Tree
Source: Istituto RSO

| | | Role | | | | | |
|---|---|---|---|---|---|---|---|
| | | *1* | *2* | *3* | *4* | *5* | *6* |
| **Main** | *Executory* | X | X | | | | |
| **Activities** | *Skilled* | | X | X | | | |
| | *Specialistic* | | | X | X | | |
| | *Government* | | | | | X | X |
| **Relationships** | *Norm based* | X | X | | | | |
| | *Service oriented* | X | | X | X | | |
| | *Coordinative* | | X | | X | X | |
| | *Decision oriented* | | | | | X | X |
| **Goals** | *Local* | X | X | X | | | |
| | *General* | | | X | X | X | |
| | *Strategic* | | | | | | X |

*Values of Role:*     *1 Operative*     *2 Operation-coordinative*     *3 Technician*
*4 Professional*     *5 Managerial*     *6 Entrepreneurial*

**Table 1:  Role coherency table (Istituto RSO)**

## 1.2.  The Reasoning Process

The reasoning process is based on the propagation of values in the different representation trees of the STM and QWL models and the study of the deduced values with respect to the expected values.

The entry data for the propagation of values are the values of the leaf nodes in the dimensions (like *Transformation* or *Planning* in figure 1). These values are gathered via questionnaires which are distributed to a representative sampling of the group which is experiencing the problems. Then these values are propagated from leaves of the tree to the root of the tree, with the help of the **coherency tables**. For each node (except the leaves), there exists a **coherency table** describing which values of its subcomponents can be combined to form a coherent situation. The coherency table for *Role* (see Table 1) shows that an activity with the value *executory* accomplished in a *norm-based* relationship, for a goal with the value *local*, is a coherent set of values which describes a Role with the value *operative*. Furthermore, if we know that a *Role*'s components have these values, we can deduce that the value of *role* is *operative* or *operation-coordinative*. In fact, the coherency tables are not exhaustive and a great deal of heuristic knowledge is used in case of ambiguity or lack of information on the coherency tables. For example, in the previous case, the final choice (after application of the heuristic rules) would be an *operative* role.

There also exists a master coherency table which shows how the values for the different dimensions can be combined. Indeed this reasoning process is not only used to give values to the different dimensions but to characterize the population and the organization studied by the deduction of the type of population and the type of the organization. Then, according to these deduced types, and in comparison with the values of a ideal situation we should have in similar context, a diagnosis and the possible recommendations are generated.

## 1.3. The Consultancy

When Istituto RSO is engaged by a company, their approach for solving the client's problem consists of the following steps:

### Configuration and problem setting
The identification of the problem involves (i) the identification of the suspected *at risk* groups of individuals or segments of population on which apply the QWL analysis, (ii) the adaptation of the 3ST models and especially the structure of the different dimensions and the questionnaires needed to gather all the information.

### QWL analysis
For the QWL analysis, the questionnaires are given to each person of the selected population. The gathered information allows to define the type of each person (*delegant, indifferent, participating, or protagonist*) and to define the value of each of the QWL dimensions. According to the type of person, the values of QWL dimensions may reveal a potential problem in the environment of the person studied. So, for each person studied, and for each QWL dimension, the quality of life may appear to be good, not particularly relevant, or bad, depending on the comparison of the obtained results with the expected results coming from a reference population.

### QWL diagnosis
This diagnosis is made at the level of a segment of population. For each dimension, the results concerning the segment are summarised in a distribution of well-being/discomfort. The average of this distribution gives the level of potential problems attached to each QWL dimension.

### STM analysis
This step studies the coherence for each socio-technical dimension. This study of coherence is made on information deduced from data gathered for each STM dimension. In case of detected incoherencies (incompatibilities in the data) some recommendations are generated in order to solve this incoherence problem for each dimension.

### STM Diagnosis
This diagnosis is a cooperative STM inter-dimension coherence analysis. Indeed the deduced values for each STM dimension have to be coherent with the deduced type of organization. If the results obtained for one or several dimensions do not lead to this deduced type, recommendations are generated.

### Global diagnosis
This global diagnosis aims to explain a potential problem in the Quality of Working Life of the organization by a QWL/STM cross analysis, i.e. to relate the STM incoherencies to the QWL diagnoses. Indeed quality discomforts are assumed to come from the STM incoherencies.

## 2. The 3ST -- a System which Assists the Sociologists

All the previously described process of consultancy is supported by the 3ST we developed. In this section we will give an illustration of our prototype with data taken from an actual situation found at one of our industrial organizations' sites. The Italian car manufacturer FIAT wants to know *"if increased productivity and quality programs had until now generated problems in the quality of working life of their personnel"*, especially for the new engine product line in the Termoli plant.

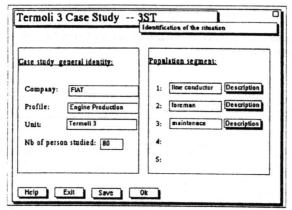

**Figure 2**: 3ST ; Identification of a Case Study.

Three critical roles or segments of population (*line conductor, foreman, maintenance worker*) were extracted for our study. Data gathering (80 questionnaires were filled in) was performed for a self consistent subset of the QLIS models (3 STM dimensions: technology, process and profession ; 2 QWL dimensions: cognitive life and professional integrity). This section gives the results obtained for the segment corresponding to the line conductors which is the only one which presents an incoherent situation.

Note that this paper will not illustrate the deduction process used for propagation of values in the different dimensions (detailed information is available in [Bronisz & al. 92]) and uses directly the deduced values for dimensions for the presented diagnosis.

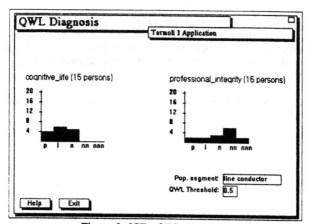

**Figure 3**: 3ST ; QWL diagnosis.

The QWL results seem to be acceptable for the quality of *cognitive life* which appears to be good (p) for 4 persons, not relevant (i) for 6 persons, and unsatisfactory (n) for 5 persons out of the 15 persons studied. The *professional integrity* dimension presents some problems in the quality of working life: out of the 15 persons studied, the QWL appears to be unsatisfactory (n) for 3 persons, bad (nn) for 6 persons, and very bad (nnn) for 2 persons.

This **QWL diagnosis** shows a suffering situation for line conductors for whom a higher level of professional integrity is required.

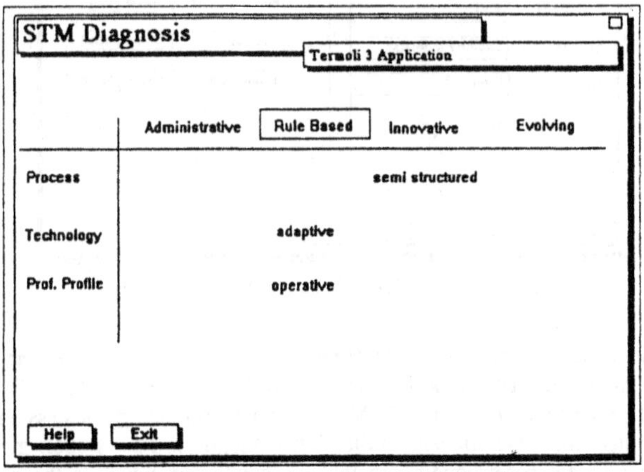

**Figure 4**: 3ST ; STM diagnosis.

The results for the **STM diagnosis** characterize the organisation as a *rule based* organization with a *semi-structured* process dimension, an *adaptive* technology in use and *operative* professional dimension. Note that the *process* dimension is not in direct accordance with the *rule based* type of the organization.

For the **global diagnosis** (see figure 5), the detected problem in the quality of working life of the line conductors is explained by the contradiction emerging in the socio-technical model. The *process* dimension should be corrected in order to be more *structured* instead of *semi-structured*. This correction would procure a job enrichment for the line conductors and increase their quality working life significantly.

Our colleagues in Istituto RSO were used as experts to corroborate the system's findings.

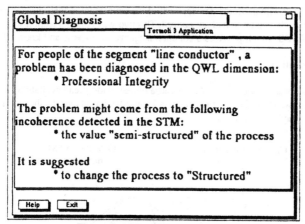

**Figure 5**: 3ST ; Global diagnosis.

## 3. How we proceeded to realize the 3ST

### 3.1. Specification

In Istituto RSO's approach to solving organizational problems, a great deal of heuristic knowledge is used in interpreting the models, in deciding which apparent incoherencies are insignificant and which must be acted upon, and in coming up with specific recommendations to solve the problems (especially since the client may have constraints on the actions that can be taken). The entire process is quite time-consuming (and thus expensive), and so Istituto RSO is very interested in obtaining a system which automates it to the greatest possible extent.

We therefore decided to use a software development methodology tailored to Knowledge Based Systems: KADS (Knowledge based system Analysis and Design Support). The methodology is the result of a European research effort (Esprit Project P1098), carried out between 1983 and 1989, in which Cap Gemini Innovation participated (note that the Commission of the European Communities has decided to start a KADS 2 project). Its goal is to develop an analysis and design a methodology for Knowledge Based System development that could be understandable, comprehensive, customizable and commercially viable [Hestek & al. 89][Hickman & al. 89].

The KADS development cycle [Brunet 92] describes the main phases of Knowledge Based System development process, the tasks to be carried out in each phase, the results to be obtained (with the associated decision points and control steps). Especially, KADS offers a modelling language [Wielinga & al. 86] which allows the expression of the domain knowledge and its reasoning at an appropriate layer to build the conceptual model.

The conceptual model [Qlis 1] was built from the reports of the 17 expertise meetings which were held between the experts in Istituto RSO and the knowledge engineers in Cap Gemini Innovation [Qlis 2]. The results obtained served as a basis for the design of the final system [Bronisz & al. 92].

The experts, in spite of the excellent work they carried out in formalizing their knowledge, took a keen interest in following the results of the application of KADS, and were even able to profit from it. Their work with us in the development of the conceptual model revealed several aspects of the domain that they hitherto had not noticed. This two-way communication was made possible by the use of KADS, which provides a common language for experts and knowledge engineers.

## 3.2. Implementation

For our project it was decided to use PCs because of their widespread availability and portability. On this platform we chose Nexpert Object as a knowledge-based system shell, and ToolBook as a user-friendly graphic interface.

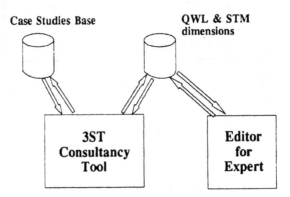

**Figure 6**: The 3ST architecture.

There are two types of tools realized:
- The **3ST consultancy** to conduct a consultancy. This tool involves the following functionalities:
  - general management and guide for a consultancy
  - access to the Case Studies base
  - access to the reasoning functions (propagation of information for each dimension, deduction of type of population, QWL and STM analysis and diagnosis).
- The **Editor for Expert**[2] to update, if needed, the models of theoretical dimensions.

## 3.3. Use of the 3ST

Before presenting the use of the 3ST, we want to stress the potential help that such a tool gives to the experts. They do not think that the 3ST has taken their place in a consultancy. On the contrary they say that it has improved the quality of their working life in the sense that they have a tool at their disposition, able to do time-consuming and repetitive tasks for them (deduction of value for each dimension, distribution analysis). Now they have more time to well define the frame of the study (definition of the population segments), to well adapt their models to the organization studied (with the use of the Editor for Expert) and especially to deal with the recommendations in order to introduce them adaptively in the organization. 3ST is now a tool which helps the experts in their consultancy to support their models and to give a good illustration of the reasoning process for their clients. The experts use the 3ST following the steps described in section 1.3

---

[2] The Editor for Expert was realized by Datamont.

After the industrial partners of the consortium have validated the 3ST, it will be used by the people responsible for the management of the Quality of Life in an organization, and for the impact of Information Technology on it. By default, the Human Resource Manger has this function, but it is likely that a specific role might be created in big organizations. The 3ST, as a decision support tool, will give support for the study of the advantages and drawbacks of several solutions, assessing organizational and managerial transformations.

We have already initiated some other case studies. FIAT plans to use the results of the QLIS project in several other plants in Italy. Our own company, Cap Gemini Innovation, is setting up an experiment to test different configurations of an important new software engineering tool, and will use the QLIS tool to evaluate the impact of this tool on the software development process.

## REFERENCES

.[Bellini 90] Roberto Bellini *Internal QLIS workshop for Quality of Life in Working environment* Milano January 1991.

.[Bronisz & al. 92] Didier Bronisz, Denis Cordelle, Thomas Grossi. *Knowledge Engineering for the improvement of Work Environments* The 2nd Pacific Rim International Conference on Artificial Intelligence. Seoul, Korea, september 92.

.[Brunet 92] Eric Brunet. *Tutorial KADS* The 12th International Conference on Artificial Intelligence, Avignon, June 92.

.[Butera 90] Federico Butera. *Il castello e la rete. Saggi tecnologia, organizzazione e persone* RSO (Franco Angelli 1990) Istituto RSO (Milano).

.[Hestek & al. 89] Philip Hestek and Toby Barett. *An introduction to the KADS methodology.* Final deliverable M1 of Esprit Project 1098.

.[Hicman & al. 89] Frank Hickman, Jonathan Killin and Lise Land. *Analysis for Knowledge-based systems. A practical guide to the Kads methodology.* Ellis Horwood 1989.

.[Qlis 1] Cap Gemini Innovation *Conceptual Model* Deliverables 5.1 and 5.4 of Esprit project 5374 Qlis.

.[Qlis 2] Cap Gemini Innovation *Expertise Elicitation* Deliverables 5.5 and 5.7 of Esprit project 5374 Qlis.

.[Wielinga & al. 86] B. Wielinga and J. Breuker. *Models of Expertise* Proceedings of ECAI. Brighton (UK), 1986.

# TOOLS FOR THE DEVELOPER

# Dialogue Independence Based on a Structured UIMS Interface

**Søren Lauesen, Morten Borup Harning**
**Hans Frederik Bøving**

Copenhagen Business School
Howitzvej 60, DK-2000 Frederiksberg
E-mail: {sl.iio,mbh.iio}@cbs.dk

**Abstract.** A User Interface Management System (UIMS) handles the dialogue between an application program and the end-user, and it provides tools for construction of the dialogue. Ideally, it should be possible to develop the dialogue part concurrently with the application part. This would speed up development and allow a user-centered dialogue design to be combined with a more formal application development. To what extent this is actually possible, depends on the interface between the UIMS and the application program.

This paper discusses interface problems between UIMS and application. We show a solution of the problems based on exchange of complex data structures and high-level (abstract) commands. We show how it allows concurrent development of the dialogue and the application, and how it can support various kinds of application programs like traditional programs, multi-tasked or distributed programs, and object-oriented programs.

## 1. Introduction

From a logical point of view, a software system consists of two parts: The *dialogue part* and the *application part*. The dialogue part shows data, menus, icons, etc. and receives user actions like input data and menu choices. The application part does the "real" work: It computes the results and retrieves, files, and updates data. In many cases the two parts are just "logical" parts, which do not correspond to physically separate program parts.

A User Interface Management System (UIMS) is a set of tools that makes it easy to design and implement the dialogue part. It should also make it easy to physically separate the dialogue part from the application part. Ideally, the two parts should be separated in such a way that they are independent of each other. The application part, for instance, should not assume a specific user dialogue.

If a sufficient degree of dialogue independence is achieved, it should be possible to develop dialogue part and application part concurrently. This would also allow a user-centered approach (based on prototyping) to be combined with a more formal development of the application. Since the dialogue part is typically half of the entire system, the development time span would also be reduced significantly.

Dialogue independence has mostly been discussed rather abstractly, and few examples of actual independence have been published. (One good example is found in [Rudolf & Waite, 1992]). Further, it is believed that the goal of dialogue independence is difficult to obtain fully [Cockton, 1987] [Coutaz, 1990].

Most publications about UIMSes focus on the dialogue part: how the user interface can be composed from simpler parts, how the dialogue parts interact, etc. Very little attention is paid to how the application part can be constructed and how it actually interfaces to the dialogue part. This paper focuses on the **application**

**interface,** i.e. the interface between dialogue part and the application part. This, we believe, is the critical issue in obtaining dialogue independence.

Below we will discuss the typical application interfaces in UIMSes. We will then present a UIMS called **Dian** which interfaces to the application by means of virtual, complex data structures and high-level commands. We will show how this interface allows a high degree of dialogue independence, so that the dialogue and application part can be developed rather independently.

The Dian interface can also give a good integration with traditional languages like C, Pascal, Cobol, and Fortran. This is possible because it directly supports the complex data structures found in these languages.

## 2. Interface Principles

In existing UIMSes we see two main principles for information flow between dialogue part and application part:

- Calls (messages) between objects.
- Exchange of data.

### Calls Between Objects

By far the most common principle is calls between objects. The simplest case is a **call-back** solution where the UIMS calls various functions in the application as a result of user actions.

In general, the application and the UIMS consist of several objects. The UIMS objects (dialogue objects) send messages to the application objects as a result of user actions; and the application objects send messages to the dialogue objects to show data, etc. Two wellknown examples are SmallTalk-80 MVC [Goldberg, 1984] and Garnet [Myers, 1990, 1992]. There are several problems with this approach:

(1) The developers need a lot of discipline to separate application objects from dialogue objects. Often the application ends up being embedded in several dialogue objects.

(2) If message passing is done synchronously (like subroutine calls), the receiving object must respond fast to let the dialogue proceed. If message passing is done asynchronously, the receiving object is a separate process (also called "task" or "agent"). This causes synchronization problems because messages are passed in both directions across the interface. [Trefz & Ziegler, 1990] [Coutaz, 1990].

(3) The approach does not work well with traditional programming languages like Pascal or Fortran. Garnet, for instance, is Lisp-based.

(4) Because the state of the application objects is not directly available to the dialogue objects, it becomes difficult to give fast semantic feedback to the user [Dance et al., 1987].

It might be possible to solve these problems in a general way, but solutions do not seem simple and have not been published. Currently the job is left to the developers using the UIMS.

It seems to us that the call-back approach itself is a key root of the problems: It gives no rules for distribution of information between dialogue and application, it does not provide help for synchronization, and it makes semantic feedback difficult. So it is worth looking at other approaches.

**Exchange of Data**

If we do not exchange information between objects, it seems that the dialogue and application part have to agree on some data structures to be exchanged. The actual structures will vary from one application to another, but they must have a common meta-form.

What are our choices? In the world of programming we find two dominant ways of organizing complex data: The database approach, e.g. the relational data model, and the record/array approach as we find it in data declarations within Cobol, Pascal, C, etc.

Some UIMSes use the database approach, e.g. Serpent [Serpent, 1991] [Bass et al., 1990] or the Smalltalk-based system described in [Bentley, 1992]. The dialogue part consists of objects internally, but it interfaces to the application through a database.

With this approach, the dialogue and application part agree on a database structure for the exchange. The application part writes into the database to show data, and the dialogue part writes into it to reflect user input. Some problems with the database approach are:

(1) Databases are not well integrated into the programming languages in spite of SQL, etc. Actually, the application programs have to extract data from the database and operate on them in the form of records, arrays, or records linked by pointers. There is a performance penalty here, particularly because database addressing is done through keys that have to be looked up for each access.

(2) There are synchronization problems because the two parts share the same data.

(3) The database approach is useful for output because it is equivalent to updating the database. But in case of input, it is necessary to invent a way to tell the application what data has been changed. (This has been done in UIMSes based on the database approach.)

(4) The exchange of commands have to be handled by additional mechanisms or disguised as data.

A few UIMSes use the record/array approach [Trefz & Ziegler, 1990] [Dewan & Vasilik, 1990]. Here, the two parts agree on a (complex) data structure to exchange. This approach integrates better with the programming languages, but the other problems remain. A new problem tends to turn up:

(5) If the two parts actually share the data structure, they cannot choose a convenient representation of it for their own purpose. For instance, the dialogue part may want to attach some dialogue-related data, and the application part may want to attach some data to improve computations.

In spite of the problems, the data structure approach seems the most promising for fast semantic feedback and for a smooth integration with traditional programming languages. So we decided to base the Dian project on it and repair the weaknesses. It turned out later that the approach gave other advantages, for instance the ability to specify the application interface early and then develop the application and dialogue concurrently.


# 3. The Dian Interface

The principle in Dian's interface to the application can be explained as follows (details in [Lauésen et al., 1992]):

Dian and the application agree on a set of (complex) data structures. These **interface structures** can for instance be specified as a set of C declarations. They also agree on a set of commands. Each command is associated with a part of the interface structure, and it can be regarded as a high-level operation on that part. Examples of commands are: *Complete* (a part of the data structure is completed by the operator and can be finally checked and filed). *Insert* (a new entry in an array is to be inserted). *Quit* (end the application).

Finally, they agree on a set of error message identifiers. Commands and error message identifiers can for instance be specified as special comments in the C declarations.

This interface specification does not mention the agents (concurrent tasks) involved in the application. Actually, this decision can be made later as part of the application design. It is also a matter of later application design whether the application is to be structured as objects or ordinary tasks using a read/write style.

Based on the interface specification, the following information can flow between Dian and the application:

(1)     Data changes (flow in both directions)
(2)     Commands (from Dian to application)
(3)     Enable/disable of commands (from application to Dian)
(4)     Error messages (from application to Dian)

A crucial point is how to identify the field or fields changed, or the fields associated with a command. We have developed a mechanism for sending a "reference" to fields or sub-structures in the interface structures. These "references" tell the other party the field or sub-structure involved and the necessary indexes (we show an example under Step 4 below). This **Path** mechanism is highly efficient and does not add any significant overhead. In fact we consider it a key factor in the interface.

Both Dian and the application keep their own copy of the interface structures. There is no need for them to keep this copy in exactly the same form as specified in the interface. Arrays can for instance be replaced by linked lists or files. Auxiliary data can be added, etc.

Dian maps its own copy into presentation objects, determined by the dialogue designer, but unknown to the application. An array can for instance be shown as a scrollable table of records or as a graph. An integer can be shown in digital form, or reflected as an object position on the screen, as a color, etc. The mapping is specified by means of attribute formulas in a manner well-known from other UIMSes (often called "constraints").

Similarly, Dian maps certain user events into commands and sends them to the application. User events could be a selection from a menu, a drag-and-drop operation, a changed field, etc. The application does not know whether the resulting command came from a menu, a drag-and-drop, etc.

The dialogue designer can provide quite a lot of **semantic feedback** based on the state of the interface information. For instance, the cursor shape can change to reflect data values in the interface data. As another example, the enable/disable state of the commands is part of the interface data, so menus, etc. can immediately reflect the proper choices. What happens here is that the application updates the enable/disable state as a result of semantic actions. This means that the information is available to the dialogue when needed.

The application communicates with Dian by means of a set of interface functions (subroutine calls). There are functions to write data (i.e. ask Dian to update part of its copy), get data (from Dian's copy), insert or delete array elements, enable/disable commands, wait for commands relating to all or part of the interface structure, etc. A total of 24 functions are used for such purposes.

In addition to these functions, Dian supplies a set of interface functions for "configuration". Some configuration functions modify the interface structures, for instance adding a new field. Others create or modify presentation objects, for instance adding a table object, or inserting and compiling an attribute formula.

The configuration functions work also while the application program is using the ordinary functions that show data, get input, etc. Dian ensures a consistent updating of cross-references between formulas and data structures, etc.

In practice, the configuration functions are not used by ordinary application programs as this would violate the dialogue independence. But they are used by special programs like the Dian **Configurator** program, which sets up the interface structures based on a C declaration. They are also used by the Dian **Painter** program, which constructs the user dialogue and the presentation objects based on a paint-and-drag interface. But basically, these configuration programs are ordinary applications that might be developed or modified by application programmers.

Since the Painter runs as a separate task (agent), the dialogue designer can construct or modify the dialogue on-line - while the application is running. (Smalltalk-80 and Garnet have also some degree of on-line painting).

## 4. A Development Scenario

We will now show how the interface could be used in a typical development project. Let us assume that we have a project group that is going to develop an order entry application. (This example is chosen because it should be familiar to the reader - not because Dian is intended mainly for business applications.)

When the design phase starts, the group has a vague idea about how an order should appear on the screen and how the application should handle the order. In a traditional approach, they would first develop the program and the detailed screen pictures - and later check the system with the users. In a user-centered approach, they would start develop prototypes of the screen pictures and later implement the real program.

With Dian they can to a large extent do the prototyping and the real development in parallel. What is needed is an initial specification of the data of potential interest to the user and the commands of interest to the application program. We will show the steps involved in the process:

### Step 1: Interface Specification

The project group specifies the interface data and commands in a file. A C-based version of this **interface file** is shown in Figure 1.

The file specifies that in the *Order* picture, the user should be able to see and edit a customer number, a customer name, the current balance on the customer account, and a maximum of 100 item lines. Each item line should comprise an item number, an item name, etc. In the full application, several pictures will be specified in the same manner.

The interface file contains also some special comments /* cmd ... */. They specify the commands expected by the application. For instance, the user can *Insert* and *Delete* order lines or *Ask* for further information about items.

As default, the user can edit all fields, but we can specify a field as read-only. The *Balance* field has such a specification, saying that the *Data* command is off for that field. At run-time, the program can enable and disable the edit status and other commands.

Error message identifiers, etc. are also specified as "comments".

```
/* Order handling, interface file */

#define NameSize 63

typedef struct {
   long       ItemNo;
   String     ItemName[NameSize];
   float      UnitPrice /* cmd Data off */;
   int Quantity;
} ItemLine;

picture Order {
   long       CustNo;
   String     CustName[NameSize];
   float      Balance /* cmd Data off */;
   ItemLine   Lines[100] /* cmd Insert, Delete, Ask */
} /* cmd Complete, Quit, Cancel */

/* message NoCustomer, NoItem */
```

Figure 1. An interface file describing the necessary interface data and commands for order entry.

Our experience is that it is much easier to agree on such an interface specification than on screen pictures or program behavior. (For business applications, much of the information is available from datamodels or database descriptions.)

We have learned from practice, that it is useful to include from the beginning all data that might be of interest to the user. The dialogue designer does not have to show all of it at once, but if user experiments show a need for it, he can redesign the presentation or create buttons or menu points that make the data appear.

### Step 2: Creating an Initial Dialogue

The interface file is now passed through the Dian *Configurator*. It creates a standard presentation and dialogue and describes it in a Dian *Format File*. The Configurator makes one more file: A *Definition file* which defines constants that identify the fields and commands in the interface file. These constants may be used by the application program to refer to fields, etc.

### Step 3: Designing the Dialogue

The dialogue designers can now start their work. They use the Dian *Painter*. Based on the Format File, the Painter can show the screen pictures and allow the designer to modify the presentation, specify the dialogue, etc. The result is a modified Format File.

Essentially, they compose a screen picture from predefined window classes. They map some window attributes to interface data so that the window reflects the data or sends input to a field. The same data can be shown or reflected in many windows at the same time. Through other window attributes they specify the result of user events (clicks, keyboard actions, etc.). A result could be that a command is sent to the application program.

They can try out the dialogue, refine it, etc. However, the system is not very responsive at this stage as no application program is available initially.

The details of this design process are not interesting here since they correspond to well-known tools in other UIMSes.

## Step 4: Making the Application Program

The application programmer can make the first version of the program and run it as soon as the standard dialogue has been created (step 2).

A very simple first program version is shown in Figure 2. It responds to only some of the commands and treats the entire order structure as a single form. This first version looks somewhat like programs working with a traditional forms generator, but later (step 5) we will see how it can become a fully interactive version, which still uses the same interface specification.

The program includes a Dian header file (specification of the 24 interface functions, etc.), the interface file from step 1, and the definition file from step 2.

It may be a bit surprising that the C compiler accepts the interface file. However, it just skips all the command specifications since they are comments, and it interprets *picture* as *struct* due to a macro in the Dian header file.

The main program has a loop which writes an empty order form, reads the completed form, and processes the order. The program calls several Dian interface functions, and we will explain the more interesting ones briefly.

### WritePict(1, AllPath, Buffer(order))

This call writes order data to an open picture (active picture 1) so that the operator can see it. *AllPath* is a "reference" to the full interface structure, specifying that in this case all the interface data in the picture are to be written. The values written are in the structured variable *order*, i.e. the entire contents of the order form. *Buffer* is a macro which corresponds to two function parameters: the address of *order* and the size of *order*.

Dian updates its copy of the interface data, so that it can redraw picture parts at any time without asking the program for data values. The dialogue designer can also provide much semantic feedback based on the available interface data and enable/disable status.

### ReadPict(1, AllPath, &changePath)

This call waits for the operator to edit picture 1. *AllPath* specifies that in this case the operator may edit all editable fields in picture 1. ReadPict returns when the operator activates one of the commands *Complete, Quit*, etc. The function value is the command identifier, and *changePath* refers to the interface field related to the command.

If the operator activates the *Quit* command, our simple program breaks the loop and terminates. Any other command causes the program to get the new order data and process the order.

In contrast to most UIMSes, Dian works concurrently with the application. This means that the user can perform dialogue actions while the application acts on the command or the new data values. The response time requirements to the application are thus significantly reduced.

Note that ReadPict initiates reading, but does not transfer data to the program. That is done by the next call:

### GetData(1, AllPath, Buffer(order))

This call transfers interface data from Dian's copy to a variable in the program. In this example the entire updated order form is transferred to the variable *order*. For *GetData* and *WritePict* we could choose to transfer the data in smaller pieces by replacing *AllPath* with a reference to a - possibly composite - field.

```
/* Lazy order handling*/

#include <dian.h>      /* Dian interface functions */
#include <order.h>     /* Interface file from Figure 1 */
#include <order.def> /* Constants identifying fields and commands */

struct Order order, initOrder={0};
struct Path changePath; /* Returned reference to fields */

void main(void) {
OpenPict(1, "orderappl.ff", _Order);
/* Creates and shows active picture 1 as an order form.
   The dialogue specification is in the file "orderappl.ff" */

do { /* For each order */
  order=initOrder;
  WritePict(1, AllPath, Buffer(order)); /* Initializes fields */
  if (ReadPict(1, AllPath, &changePath) ==_Quit) break;
  /* Waits for operator to edit picture and issue a command */
  GetData(1, AllPath, Buffer(order)); /* Transfer picture data */
  /* Process the order . . . */
} while (TRUE);

ClosePict(1); /* Deletes the active picture */ }
```

Figure 2. A simple C program which uses Dian for order entry. The program shows an empty order form, allows the operator to edit it, and reads the completed form.

In general, we refer to an interface field by means of a **Path**, i.e. a data structure which serves as a reference to a field. If we want to write item line *Lines[j]*, we would make this call:

```
WritePict(1, Path(_Lines,j), Buffer(aLine))
```

Here, _Lines is a constant denoting the field name. We can also use multiple indexes. For instance we could write the character *Lines[j].ItemName[k+1]*, like this:

```
WritePict(1, Path(_ItemName,j,k+1), Buffer(c))
```

The entire mechanism provides much the same effect as a language-based approach, e.g. [Dewan & Vasilik, 1990], but without modifications to the language.

The program need not store the order as one big variable. It could choose another representation, for instance a linked list to hold the item lines. In that case it transfers the order in smaller pieces, but it still uses the same Path-values to identify the pieces.

## Step 5: Integrating Dialogue and Application Part

When the programmer has a reasonable program version, he should let the dialogue designer use it for further user tests and dialogue modifications. During the tests, the interface designer can use the Painter to modify the dialogue while the program is running. He does not have to compile or link anything.

Similarly, when the dialogue designer has a better dialogue, he lets the programmer use the corresponding format file.

A reasonable next program version would be more interactive. Instead of acting only on the entire order form, it should act whenever the user has edited a field. For instance, when the user has edited the customer number, the program should get the customer name from the database and write it to the interface data.

Such a program is quite similar to the simple version. It only needs to use the function *ReadInside* instead of *ReadPict*. *ReadInside* returns whenever the customer has edited a field or issued a command. Dian returns a Path to the field, and the program can efficiently switch on the field number in the Path and retrieve the new value. The full program is about 60 lines and handles also all the commands in the interface file.

### Step 6: Modifying the Interface Specification

The dialogue and the application match each other as long as they both use the same interface description. Sooner or later it will of course be necessary to modify the interface specification. That is done as follows:

- The project group revises the interface file.
- The new interface file is passed through the Configurator, telling it to combine the new interface file with the old format file. This recasts the dialogue into a form consistent with the new interface file.
- The programmer recompiles his program with the new interface file and definition file (produced by the Configurator).

After this synchronization of efforts, the development can continue as before.


# 5. Multi-tasking and Distributed Processing

The program above was very traditional. It consisted of only one task (agent). It communicated complex data in a read/write style, although the user had a free dialogue where he could edit the fields and issue commands in any sequence.

Let us now look at an application with multi-tasking: A process control system. Typically, such a system has an *operator task* which handles the dialogue with the user, plus a number of *sensor tasks* that continuously scan the physical environment through sensors and update an internal database (normally consisting of complex data structures). These tasks might be on the same computer or distributed among several.

With Dian, this works as follows: The interface specifies a view of the internal database, and the dialogue allows the user to see the data as diagrams, control it through buttons and gliders, etc.

The operator task uses *ReadInside* where it responds whenever an interface field is changed. The sensor tasks update the internal database and write the changes into the interface structure. Dian will then reflect these changes in the presentation.

A major issue in multi-tasking is the synchronization. Several tasks try to update the screen at the same time. Dian solves that problem by handling only one call at a time - and all calls are brief. Whenever a task calls Dian, Dian locks all access to its internal data structures. This makes other calls wait until the first call is complete.

The locking mechanism is needed already for simple applications, because the user dialogue proceeds concurrently with the application program. So when a presentation object responds to a user event, it will lock access to the internal data structures. As a result, it will always see a consistent data structure.

It is also possible to have several tasks reading at the same time. Each task specifies its "field of interest" in the call of the read function, and Dian distributes commands and data changes accordingly. In this way the processing is distributed so that one task handles one part of the interface, while another task handles another part.

## 6. Supporting Object-oriented Programs

If the application program is object-oriented, we need some mechanism to pass messages to the application objects. Dian cannot do that directly, since it has no information about the application objects.

However, it is easy to structure the application program as a high-level dispatcher which receives the commands and data changes and calls the appropriate application objects (sends them a message). The object is determined from the field and the message from the command. In practice, we structure most of our applications this way.

We have also made a standard high-level dispatcher, which - when included in the application - makes the program appear to be written in the call-back fashion.

The necessary interface function is once again *ReadInside*, but compared to traditional call-back, the synchronization problems have been solved, the application can still take its time to respond, and interface data is available for fast semantic feedback.

An interesting question in this case is what the interface data represent. In an ordinary object-oriented solution, the presentation objects would have to call application objects to get values for presentation to the user. Strictly, the object states should not be stored outside the object itself, but that is exactly what the Dian interface data do.

The idea is that the interface data should correspond to part of the object states: Those parts that should be visible to the user in some form. The advantage of this approach is that the presentation objects have fast access to this state information, for instance for semantic feedback.

## 7. Performance

A major goal has been to give a performance sufficient for large projects. It turns out that the handling of complex data structures, mapping to presentation objects, etc. do not take much time.

Under the OS/2 Presentation Manager, the bottleneck is somewhere else: In the locking necessary for the synchronization, and in handling of output to the screen.

As an example, assume that we want to write a number in text form in a Presentation Manager edit window. Done directly, it takes about 10 ms on a slow computer. If we write it through Dian's WritePict, it takes about 13 ms composed as follows:

| | |
|---|---|
| OS/2 locking and unlocking: | 2 ms |
| Dian administration: | 1 ms |
| Presentation Manager: | 10 ms |

Out of this, the field addressing by means of the Path concept accounts for only 0.1 ms. If we write several fields at the same time with WritePict, the overhead for locking will count only once.

There are of course many other performance aspects, but the one explained above is a key issue.

## 8. Current Experience and Problems

Danish software developers have shown much interest in Dian, but at present Dian is not sufficiently complete for industrial use.

We have completed smaller applications, the largest one being about 1500 lines of C application plus a corresponding amount of dialogue specification. One example is a process control application with a very precise simulation of an existing, complex heat control unit. It uses three concurrent tasks in addition to the on-line Painter task.

In these cases, the concurrent development of dialogue and application has proved to be easy, and we have been surprised at the degree of freedom allowed in implementing the two parts. In particular we have found that we could construct many more dialogues than we imagined from the beginning - and without changing the interface specification.

We have used Dian from C, Modula-2, and Fortran. That was easy because all calls of Dian interface functions use only simple parameters (no real pointers or functions appear as parameters).

Another positive observation is that the application interface is very robust: Many programming errors are caught by Dian and no "surprising" events are returned to the program. This is in contrast to the huge problems one experience when using a window system directly.

We have, of course, also found weaknesses in the current system, but the essential weaknesses are not related to the application interface, but to the dialogue part:

(1)     We need more window classes and simpler means for adding new ones.
(2)     We need a more powerful dialogue specification language. For instance, we need dialogue variables and support for more general function calls. Otherwise, the application would have to provide these things, and that violates the dialogue independence.

Fortunately, other UIMSes have shown how to provide a more powerful dialogue specification language, and we are currently working to provide similar mechanisms.

## 9. Conclusion

We believe that more attention is needed to the interface between dialogue part and application. An interface based on exchange of complex data structures and high-level commands is promising, because it solves many of the problems inherent in traditional call-back solutions:

It allows an early specification of the interface, and it can provide a high degree of dialogue independence. Furthermore, it can solve the synchronization problems, it integrates well with traditional languages, it can support many styles of application programs, and it gives a good performance.

Our experience also shows that a high degree of dialogue independence requires a strong language for specifying the dialogue.

## Acknowledgements

The project was initiated by Jan C. Clausen in 1986, where he proposed some of the basic ideas. Tage Henriksen helped with a crucial point, the Path concept. The project was supported financially by the Danish Scientific-Technical Research Council.

## References

Bass, L., Hardy, E., Little, R. & Seacord, R. (1990): Incremental development of user interfaces. Proceedings of IFIP WG 2.7 Working Conference. North-Holland, 1990.

Bentley, R. et al. (1992): Prototyping environment for dynamic data visualisation. Engineering for Human-Computer Interaction. Proceedings of IFIP Wg 2.7. Finland, 1992.

Cockton, G. (1987): A new model for separable interactive systems. Proceedings of second IFIP Conference on Human-Computer Interaction - Interact 87, North-Holland, 1987.

Coutaz, J. (1990): Architecture models for interactive software: Failures and trends. Proceedings of IFIP WG 2.7 Working Conference. North-Holland, 1990.

Dance, J.R. et al. (1987): The run-time structure of UIMS-supported applications. Computer Graphics. Vol 21,2. April 1987, pp 97-101.

Dewan, P. & Vasilik, E. (1990): An approach to integrating user interface management systems with programming languages. Proceedings of IFIP WG 2.7 Working Conference. North-Holland, 1990.

Goldberg, A. (1984): Smalltalk-80: The interactive programming environment. Addison-Wesley, Reading, MA, 1984.

Lauesen, S., Borup, M. & Bøving, H.F. (1992): Dian: A programmer-friendly UIMS with on-line dialogue design. ISSN 0903-6571 92/1. Copenhagen Business School, Copenhagen.

Myers, B.A. et al. (1990): Garnet: Comprehensive support for graphical, highly-interactive user interfaces. IEEE Computer 23(11), pp 71-85, November, 1990.

Myers, B.A. et al. (1992): The Garnet reference manuals. Carnegie Mellon University, Pittsburg. CMU-CS-90-117-R2.

Rudolf, J. & Waite, C. (1992): Completing the job of interface design. IEEE Software, November 1992, pp11-22.

Serpent (1991): Serpent overview - User interface project. Carnegie Mellon University, Software Engineering Institute, Pittsburg, Pensylvania 15213, CMU/SEI-91-UG-1, May 1991.

Trefz, B. & Ziegler, J. (1990): The user interface management system DIAMANT. Proceedings of IFIP WG 2.7 Working Conference. North-Holland, 1990.

# A Human Factors Based User Interface Design

Harald Reiterer

German National Research Center for Computer Science (GMD), Institute for
Applied Information Technology , Human-Computer Interaction Research
Division, PO. Box 1316 D-53731 St. Augustin

Phone: +49 2241 14-2729 Fax: +49 2241 14-2618 Mail: reiterer@gmd.de

and

University of Vienna, Institute for Applied Computer Science and Information
Systems, Liebiggasse 4/3-4, A-1010 Vienna

**Abstract:** This paper reports first results of the GMD project "User Interface
Design Assistance (IDA)". The objective of this project is to develop computer
based design aid tools for a human factor based user interface design. The reasons for concentrating on human factors are their increasing importance in the
new European Economic Area and the lack of knowledge of the designers in
the area of human factors. The design aid tools are integrated in a user interface
management system (UIMS) to support the designers during the development
process. The aim is to impart human factors knowledge for innovative user interfaces (e.g. object-oriented graphical interfaces; 3-D user interfaces; hypermedia user interfaces) to the designers. This will be done with the help of design aid tools, like a composition tool, a tutoring tool and a quality assurance
tool. They are presented in some detail. First results have shown, that it is principally possible to realise such design aid tools.

## 1 The Increasing Importance of Human Factors Based User Interface Design

One reason for the increasing importance of human factors based user interface design is the new European Economic Area (EEA, consisting of EC and EFTA). To establish common working conditions for visual display terminal (VDT) users, the
European Community published a "directive concerning the minimum safety and
health requirements for VDT workers" [13]. The national governments of the EC
members have to transform this directive into national law. In this process the
European standardisation activities of the CEN (Comité Européen de Normalisation)
and the international standardisation activities of the ISO (International Organisation
for Standardisation) concerning ergonomic requirements for VDTs will have great
influence. Especially the ISO standard 9241 "Ergonomic requirements for office
work with VDTs" [22] (CEN 29241) plays an important role [8]. In the future this
standard will often be an integral part of software requirements specification.

Therefore software designer will have to take the requirements and principles of this standard into consideration.

Does the software designer know how to apply standards like the ISO 9241 in the design process? Empirical results have shown that most of the software designers have no or only very limited knowledge about human factors [2, 3, 31]. Therefore most of them were not able to apply standards from the area of human factors in the design process. In Beimel et al. [3] designers were asked what kind of support to they prefer to overcome their lack of human factors expert knowledge. A great amount of them said that they would prefer computer based design aids which should be integrated in their design tools (e.g. interface builder, UIMS). What they won't like is "paperware", e.g. manuals or technical reports with a great amount of written style guides or guidelines. Some other authors come to very similar results. They defined some "success factors" for the efficient use of standards and style guides like:

- "... having development tools that support implementation of interfaces that follow the standard including concrete examples of correctly designed interfaces" [46],

- "... the interface style needs to be carried in the examples, facilitated by tool kits, illustrated by interactive demos or well-formed applications, and supported by iterative usability testing." [45],

- "Our most valuable weapons in the arena of fast-paced design and development are our skills and tools for turning design ideas into prototypes of the user interface ..." [32].

So software designers need excellent tools for user interface design, especially for graphical and hypermedia user interfaces. These tools allow the designer to concentrate on the design process and on the quality of the design results, e.g. usability. Tools as for example User Interface Management Systems (UIMS) help the designer to specify, design, prototype, implement, execute, evaluate, modify, and maintain user interfaces. UIMSs are to interface development what CASE tools are to development of application components [19]. The big difference from UIMS to other tools like user interface tool kits and interface builders is that they support the designer during the construction of the presentation layer (static component) as well as during the definition of the dialogue scripts (dynamic component). Therefore they consist of a WYSIWYG-Editor for the presentation layout and a script editor for the dialogue flow. Normally they have the availability to simulate the results (user interface prototype without any application code), so that the designer can use a prototyping approach during the design of the user interface. The handling of UIMSs is easy in comparison with other user interface design tools (e.g. tool kits) or conventional programming language, so that also non programmers like graphic designers or human factors experts could use them during the user interface design. This fact opens the opportunity to carry out user interface design activities with a team of different specialists.

# 2 How can We Reach a Human Factors Based User Interface Design?

The increasing importance of human factors based user interface design, the lack of human factors knowledge of the designers and the availability of new user interface design tools were starting points for a new GMD project called "User Interface Design Assistance (IDA)". The objective of this project is to develop design aid tools for a human factor based user interface design. These design aid tools are integrated in a UIMS to support the designers of innovative user interfaces (e.g. object-oriented graphical interfaces; 3-D user interfaces; hypermedia user interfaces) during the development process. The aim is to impart human factors knowledge for innovative user interfaces to the designers. Therefore the designers should have direct access to the human factors knowledge from their development tool. The presentation of the design knowledge is based on object-oriented, multimedia and knowledge-based techniques. There are multifarious reasons for developing design aid tools for the user interface designers using a UIMS:

- to overcome the lack of human factors knowledge of the designers ("training on the job"),

- to overcome the resistance of the designers reading and using written guide lines, standards, etc. ("new design aids"),

- to reduce the costs developing user interfaces using predefined models ("reusability of software"),

- to assure easy of use of user interfaces ("usability"),

- to guarantee the conformity of the user interface with standards and style guides ("quality assurance").

### 2.1 Design Aid Tools for a Human Factors Based User Interface Design

An important pre-condition for developing computer based design aid tools is to formalise human factors knowledge to allow a computer based presentation. Especially in the area of object-oriented graphical user interfaces the GMD Human-Computer Interaction Research Division has a deep understanding of the necessary design principles and design guidelines, the relevant international standards, the available style guides and the construction and use of evaluation methods for usability testing, e.g. EVADIS [36, 37]. In the area of 3-D and hypermedia user interfaces the Human-Computer Interaction Research Division is doing much R&D activities. The results of these R&D activities and the available experiences in the field of Human-Computer Interaction are the basis for constructing new design principles and guidelines for innovative user interfaces. The human factors knowledge is summarised in a "Human Factors Style Guide", which is the foundation for the computer supported design aid tools. The content of this "Human Factors Style Guide" isn't restricted to commercial available user interface style guide requirements, e.g. OSF/MOTIF Style Guide [34], OPEN LOOK Style Guide [44], IBM Common User Access [20, 21], Microsoft Windows Style Guide [29], SIEMENS/NIXDORF Style Guide [41], APPLE Style Guide [1], NeXT Style

Guide[33]. The content of our style guide is based on a broader approach and also includes user interface design requirements from the relevant international standards, e.g. ISO 9241 [22], DIN 66234 [11] and literature [e.g. 5, 6, 12, 28, 35, 42]. The focus of the first version of our "Human Factors Style Guide" is on state of the art user interfaces (GUIs). Our research activities during the IDA project we will be the basis to include new design principles and requirements for innovative user interfaces (e.g. 3-D, hypermedia).

Figure 1 shows three design aid tools that assist the designers during the user interface design using a UIMS ("new design aids"). These design aid tools are under development in the IDA project:

- A *composition tool* to construct innovative user interfaces; based on a library of interaction objects and dialogue scripts [e.g. 24].

- An *advice tool* to present the human factors knowledge; based on hypermedia documents [e.g. 7, 30], a library of interaction objects and an expert system.

- A *quality assurance tool* to evaluate the conformance of the user interface with the human factors knowledge; based on an expert system [e.g. 14, 15, 16, 17, 23, 27, .39]

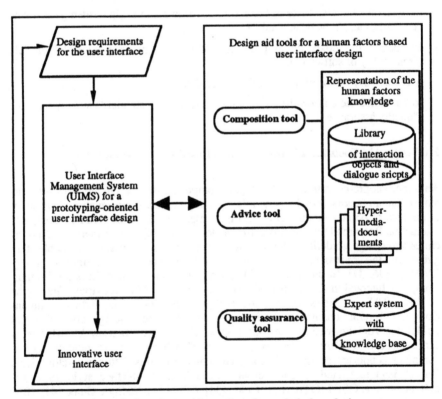

Fig. 1. Design aid tools for a human factor based user interface design

The GMD is starting cooperations with some companies to construct the design aid tools for specific application domains. For this purpose some workshops with members of companies, which are developing software applications and members of companies, which are developing UIMS were arranged. In the realistic context of such application domains the usefulness and usability of the design aid tools will be evaluated.

### 2.1.1 Composition Tool

The *composition tool* supports the process of constructing the user interface and is based on a library. The content of the library is a collection of predefined generic and domain specific interaction objects and dialogue scripts. The generic interaction objects and dialogue scripts are application independent. Their "look" and "feel" is based on the principles of the "Human Factors Style Guide". The "look" and "feel" of the domain specific interaction objects and dialogue scripts is determined by the application domain, e.g. office system, telecooperation system, CSCW under consideration of the principles of the "Human Factors Style Guide". With the help of an information retrieval component (e.g. structural browser) the designers could search for a relevant generic or domain specific interaction object or dialogue script and use it as a part of the user interface. On the basis of predefined interaction objects and scripts the designers will be able to build the final interface ("reusability of software"). To construct the library an object-oriented mechanism is used. The interaction objects and scripts are designed as models or templates with the UIMS. Each model (object class) can transmit its "look" and "feel" to a specific interaction object (instance of this object class). If the designers chance the "look" and "feel" of a model, each "child" will also chance its "look" and "feel".

In the lead time of this project we have designed a small library with the UIMSs "ISA/Dialog Manager" and "XFaceMaker2" on SUN Workstations and on PCs. The library consists of a small set of interaction objects and scripts based on the Common User Access (CUA) of IBM. It was shown, that it is principally possible to design such a library as a basis for a composition tool.

### 2.1.2 Advice and Explanation Tool

The *advice and explanation tool* presents the designers the human factors knowledge of the "Human Factors Style Guide" with the help of hypermedia documents and an expert system ("training on the job"). The knowledge is presented in a textual, graphical and animated form in the hypermedia documents. If the designers need support in the area of human factors design, they could get object-sensitive advise. After pressing a push button, they get advise when and how to use a specific interaction object and what should be the "look" and "feel" of this interaction object (*advice level* of the tutoring tool). If the designers wants deeper information, for example why the "look" and "feel" should be so, they get them in a hypertextual form, e.g. by double clicking the relevant advise information (*explanation level* of the tutoring tool). So there are two levels of tutoring available: the advise level with short information and the explanation level with deeper information.

If there exists a relevant model for an interaction object or a script in the library, the designers have the possibility to retrieve it from the library directly in the hypermedia document (link to the library).

A more active form of design support is based on the expert system. If the inference mechanism of the expert system detects some design deficits, a commentary is generated automatically. It shows the designers the analysed deficit and presents them the relevant human factors knowledge in form of a hypermedia document or shows them a relevant interaction object of the library. With the help of these instructions the designers could improve the user interface.

In the lead time of this project we have designed some hypermedia documents with the hypermedia system "DIDOT" (from ISA GmbH, Stuttgart) on SUN Workstations. The content of the hypermedia documents is based on the Common User Access (CUA) of IBM. It was shown, that it is principally possible to design such a tutoring tool .

### 2.1.3 Quality Assurance Tool

The *quality assurance tool* evaluates the conformance of the user interface with human factors knowledge. The knowledge is also based on the "Human Factors Style Guide" and is represented in a knowledge base of an expert system with the help of rules, frames and constraints [25, 40, 47]. The expert system uses the results of the user interface design process as an input and analysis - with the help of the knowledge base and an inference mechanism - the conformance of the user interface with the human factors knowledge ("quality assurance"). The results of the evaluation are comments that show existing deficits and give the designers some advise and explanations to improve the user interface. For this purpose the expert system activates the relevant topics in the tutoring tool or a relevant interaction object in the library. The use of the quality assurance tool is based on the assumption that the designers will use a prototyping approach [18]. After each design cycle the user interface prototype will be evaluated by the quality assurance tool. In the next design cycle all detected deficits can be removed.

In the lead time of this project we have evaluated some expert system shells for the purposes of this project [43]. We use a C/C++ based expert system shell (ProKappa from Intellicorp), because we have strong performance and portability requirements. We have built a small knowledge base - based on the Common User Access (CUA) - to demonstrate the possibility to analyse user interfaces with the help of an expert system. We use an analytic critic approach [15], which checks products with respect to predefined features and effects. In analytical approaches, critics do not need a complete understanding of the product. The quality assurance tool uses a set of rules to identify undesirable features among user interface units, but it does not identify all possible problems within user interface design. Its rule base allows it to criticise user interfaces without exactly knowing the requirements and preferences of the user interface designer.

## 2.1.4 Integration, Tool Independence and Maintenance of the Design Aid Tools

An important requirement for the project is to present the different design aid tools to the designer in an integrated fashion. For this purpose we have realised a control program called Interface Design Assistant (IDA). The designer could communicate with IDA by the help of a little window, which is permanent placed on the screen (see Figure 2). If the designer wants some help, he or she presses one of the push buttons in the IDA window and gets the support of the selected design aid tool.

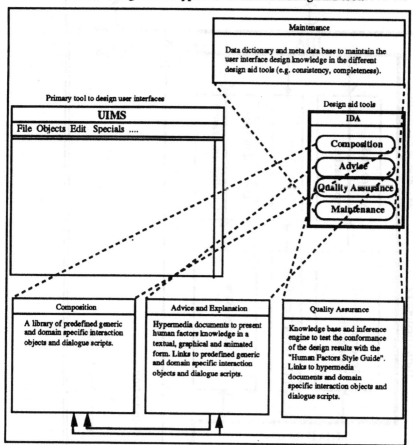

Fig. 2. Integration of the design aid tools

Another important requirement for the project is to realise tool independent design aid tools. In principle it should be possible to integrate the design aid tools in each C-based UIMS. Therefore different UIMSs will be used as platforms for the integration of the design aid tools, e.g. the "XFaceMaker2" (from Concept asa, Frankfurt and NSL, Paris), the "ISA/Dialog Manager" (form ISA GmbH, Stuttgart). The control program IDA controls the communication and the data flow between the UIMS and all the design aid tools (see Figure 3). So there is a clear interface between different

UIMSs and the design aid tools. IDA is also responsible for the co-ordination of the different design aid tools. If for example the quality assurance tool detects a deficit IDA got a message to activate a relevant hypermedia document of the tutoring tool at the advise or explanation level. Therefore IDA acts also as an interface between the designer and the different design aid tools.

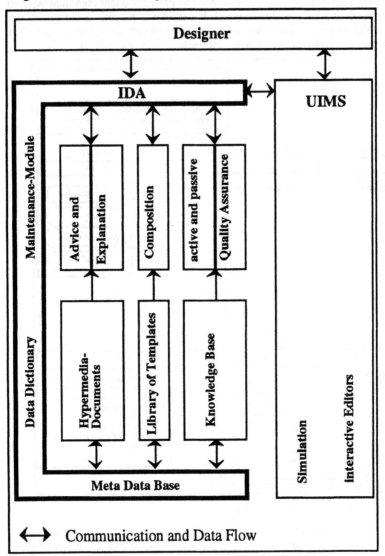

Fig. 3. Tool independence and maintenance of the design aid tools

Another important feature from IDA is the support of the maintenance of the human factors knowledge in the different design aid tools. For this purpose a maintenance module (e.g. a structural browser based on a data dictionary and a meta data base) shows the designer where the knowledge is situated. If chances are necessary or new knowledge should be included the designer could see where the knowledge is located or should be included. In the data dictionary and the meta data base all necessary maintenance information is saved.

## 2.2 Integration of the Design Aid Tools in the Software Life-cycle

It's clear that the user interface design has to be embedded in the software development life-cycle. Today a lot of methods and tools for the application development (e.g. Structured Analysis, Entity-Relationship Model, Structured Analysis and Design Technique, Object-Oriented Method) are available. There are also some special methods for the user interface development (e.g. State Transition Networks, Grammars, Rules and Constraints, Multiagent Techniques). Till now little work has been done to integrate methods of application development and user interface development. We think that the new object-oriented paradigm offers a good chance for such an integration. This assumption is based on the fact, that modern graphical user interfaces (GUIs) also use the object-oriented paradigm (e.g. X-Toolkit). The aim should be to come to one general method for the whole development process. Therefore we are planning to integrate the use of the design aid tools in an object-oriented development life-cycle [e.g. 4, 9, 10, 38].

# 3 Summary

In the future a software development environment (e.g. CASE Tool) should contain both, a user interface development environment (UIDE) and an application development environment (ADE). Both environments will contain common tools including programming language compilers, linkers, loaders, debuggers, code analysers, configuration version control managers, and documentation tools. Each development environment will also contain special tools. This paper concentrates on tools and facilities that are unique to the UIDE. In an ideal UIDE the following tools and facilities should be included [26]:

• Tools for specifying user interfaces

• Libraries of reusable software

• Guidelines and advisers

• Tools for evaluating user interfaces

Today commercial UIDE normally includes only tools for specifying user interfaces and in some innovative UIDE you can also find libraries with limited use. In this paper we present some ideas how we can reach a real UIDE including sophisticated libraries of reusable software (composition tool), guidelines and advisers (advice and explanation tool) and tools for evaluating user interfaces (quality assurance tool). We called our tools design aid tools, because their primary focus is not to support the design process (like editors) but to give the designers some advice and evaluation during the design process. We are sure that with the help of such design aid tools the aim "to construct more usable innovative user interfaces" could be reached.

# References

1. Apple: Macintosh Human Interface Guidelines, Menlo Park, California: Addison Wesley, 1992.

2. Aschersleben G., Zang-Scheucher B.: Der Prozeß der Software-Gestaltung - Eine Bestandsaufnahme in Wissenschaft und Industrie, in: Maaß S., Oberquelle H. (Hrsg.): Software-Ergonomie '89, Stuttgart: Teubner, 1989, S.244-253.

3. Beimel J., Hüttner J., Wandke H.: Kenntnisse von Programmierern auf dem Gebiet der Software-Ergonomie: Stand und Möglichkeiten zur Verbesserung, schriftliche Fassung eines Vortrages, gehalten auf der Fachtagung der Sektion Arbeits-, Betriebs und Organisationspsychologie des Berufsverbandes Deutscher Psychologen "Arbeits- Betriebs- und Organisationspsychologie vor Ort" (25.-27.5.1992 in Bad Lauterbach).

4. Booch E.: Object-Orientied Design, Redwood City, California: Benjam Cummings, 1991.

5. Brown C. M. L.: Human-Computer Interface Design Guidelines, Norwood Ablex Publishing, 1988.

6. Brown J.R., Cunningham S.: Programming the User Interface, Principles and Examples, New York: John Wiley & Sons, 1989.

7. BRUIT-SAM: An Interface for User Interface Guidelines (HyperCard stack), School of Information & Computing Sciences, Gold Coast, QLD, 4229, Australia: Bond University, 1992.

8. Cakir A.: EG-Richlinie für Bildschirmarbeitsplätze, Office Managment, 1-2/1991, S.46-53.

9. Coad P., Yourdan E.: Object Oriented Analysis, Englewood Cliffs: Prentice-Hall, 1991.

10. Coad P., Yourdan E.: Object Oriented Design, Englewood Cliffs: Prentice-Hall, 1991a.

11. DIN 66234 Teil 8: Bildschirmarbeitsplätze, Grundsätze der Dialoggestaltung, Februar 1988.

12. Dumas J.S.: Designing User Interfaces for Software, London: Prentice-Hall, 1988.

13. EEC: European Directive Concerning "The minimum safety and health requirements for work with display sreen equipment", 90/270/EEC.

14. Fischer G., Nakakoji K., Ostwald J., Stahl G. Sumner T.: Embedding Computer-Based Critics in the Contexts of Design, INTERCHI '93 Proceedings, April 1993, pp.157-164.

15. Fischer G., Lemke A., Mastaglio T., Morch A.: The Role of Critiquing in Cooperative Problem Solving, in: ACM Transactions on Information Systems, Vol. 9, No. 3, April 1991, p.123-151.

16. Foley J., Kim W., Kovacevic S., Murray K.: UISW - An Intelligent User Interface Design Environment, in: Sullivan J., Tyler S. (eds.): Intelligent User Interfaces, ACM Press, New York, 1991, pp.339-384.

17. Gorny P., Viereck A.: EXPOSE, Ein Software-Ergonomie-Expertensystem, in: Rauterberg M., Ulich E. (Hrsg.): Posterband zur Software-Ergonomie '91, Zürich: IfAP-ETH Zürich, 1991, S.152-161.

18. Hartson H., Smith E.: Rapid prototyping in human-computer interface development, in: Interacting with Computers, vol. 3, no 1, 1991, pp.51-91.

19. Hix D.: Generations of User-Interface Management Systems, in: IEEE Software, September 1990, pp.77-87.

20. IBM: Systems Application Architecture, Common User Access, Guide to User Interface Design, 1991.

21. IBM: Systems Application Architecture, Common User Access, Advanced Interface Design Reference, 1991.

22. ISO 9241: Ergonomic Requirements for Office Work with Visual Display Terminals.

23. Jansen C., Weisbecker A., Ziegler J.: Generation User Interfaces form Data Models and Dialogue Net Specifications, in: INTERCHI'93 Proceedings, pp.418-423.

24. Johnson J., Nardi B., Zarmer C., Miller J.: ACE: Building Interactive Graphical Applications, in: Communications of the ACM, April 1993, Vol. 36, No. 4, pp.41-55.

25. Klahr P., Waterman D.: Expert Systems, Techniques, Tools and Applications, Menlo Park, California: Addison-Wesley, 1986.

26. Larson J.: Interactive Software, Tools for Building Interactive User Interfaces, Yourdon Press Computing Series, Englewood Cliffs: Prentice Hall Building, 1992.

27. Löwgren J., Nordquist T.: Knowledge-Based Evaluation as Design Support for Graphical User Interfaces, in: CHI'92 Porceddings, pp.181-188.

28. Mayhew D. J.: Principles and Guidelines in Software User Interface Design, Englewood Cliffs: Prentice Hall, 1992.

29. Microsoft: The Windows Interface, An Application Design Guide, Microsoft Press, 1992.

30. MITRE: Dynamic Rules for User Interface Design, DRUID 2.0 (HyperCard stack), Bedford: MITRE Corporation, 1991.

31. Molich R., Nielsen J.: Improving a human-computer dialogue, in: Communications of the ACM, vol. 33, no. 3, 1990, pp.338-348.

32. Mulligan R., Altom M., Simkin D.: User Interface Design in the Trenches: Some Tips on Shooting form the HIP, in: CHI '91 Proceedings, pp.232-236.

33. NeXT: Interface Builder Styleguide, Release 2.0, 1991.

34. Open Software Foundation: OSF/MOTIF Style Guide, Revision 1.2, London: Prentice-Hall, 1993.

35. Reiterer H.: Ergonomische Kriterien für die menschengerechte Gestaltung von Bürosystemen - Anwendung und Bewertung, Dissertation, Universität Wien, 1990.

36. Reiterer H.: EVADIS II: A new Method to Evaluate User Interfaces, in: Monk A., Diaper D., Harrison M.D. (eds.): People and Computers VII, Cambridge: University Press, 1992, pp.103-115.

37. Reiterer H., Oppermann R.: Evaluation of User Interfaces, EVADIS II - A comprehensive Evaluation Approach, in: Behaviour & Information Technology, 1993, in press.

38. Rumbaugh J., Blaha M., Premerlani W., Eddy F., Lorensen W.: Object-Oriented Modeling and Design, Englewood Cliffs: Prentice-Hall, 1991.

39. Rusell F., Pettit Ph., Elder S.: INTUIT: A Computer Assisted Software Engineering Support For User-Centred Design, in: Galer M., Harker S, Ziegler J. (Eds.): Methods and Tools in User-Centred Design for Information Technology, Amsterdam: North-Holland, 1992, pp.345-370.

40. Schildt H.: Artificial Intelligence using C, McGraw Hill, 1987.

41. Siemens/Nixdorf: Style Guide Richtlinien zur Gestaltung von Benutzer-oberflächen, München: Siemens/Nixdorf, 1990.

42. Smith L.S., Moiser J. 1986: Guidelines for Designing User Interface Software, Bedford: MITRE Corporation, 1986.

43. Stylianou A.C., Madey G.R., Smith R.D.: Selection Criteria for Expert System Shells: A Socio Technical Framework, Communikations of the ACM, Oct. 1992, Vol. 35, No.10, pp.30-48.

44. Sun Microsystems: Open Look Style Guide, 1989.

45. Tetzlaff L., Schwartz D.: The Use of Guidelines in Interface Design, in: CHI '91 Proceedings, pp.329-333.

46. Thovtrup H., Nielsen J.: Assessing the Usability of a User Interface Standard, in: CHI '91 Proceedings, pp.335-341.

47. Wenger E.: Artificial Intelligence an Tutoring Systems, Los Altos: Morgan Kaufmann, 1987.

# ActorStudio: An Interactive User Interface Editor

Marja-Riitta Koivunen, Ora Lassila[1],
Juha Ahvo, Minna Rankinen, Sirpa Riihiaho, Bodil Riihinen

Helsinki University of Technology
Department of Computer Science
Otakaari 1, SF-02150 Espoo, Finland
`mrk@cs.hut.fi`

**Abstract.** ActorStudio is a graphical, interactive user interface editor. It is targeted for designing application specific interaction techniques referred to as actors. Actors can be combined to actor hierarchies describing complicated user interfaces. An actor, in turn, can be built from components that define the basic and the reactive appearances, and the behavior of the actor.

ActorStudio provides the designer components that are easy to comprehend. They can be combined to form a user interface by using direct manipulation edit actions. To help the designer in making better design decisions ActorStudio offers several different views to the user interface under development. For instance, the views examine the typography, logical structure, behavior and the simulation of the user interface.

As a result of edit actions, ActorStudio produces a description of a user interface under development in a language called Screenplay. This description can be stored or used to create a simulation of the user interface. Furthermore, the description can be used to analyze the user interface against a set of user interface guidelines, which are written as rules. A separate tool called Critic has been developed for that purpose.

ActorStudio has been implemented for Macintoshes using Common Lisp and CLOS. It also uses an object oriented toolkit called WimperActors developed in Helsinki University of Technology.

**Keywords:** user interface editing tool, direct manipulation, interactor model, user interface description language.

## 1. Introduction

User interface design tools have developed enormously during the last couple of years. Standard toolkits, such as OSF/Motif, are widely available. These toolkits typically provide a library of established interaction techniques, such as menus, scrollbars, and windows. Also graphical editors for placing the techniques to a user interface have been developed from experimental systems, such as vu [Singh88], to a commercial necessity. Even standard guidelines exist that explain how these techniques should be used to form the user interface. Unfortunately, these tools don't usually give much support for the development of novel interaction techniques.

Some tools, such as extendible object oriented toolkits, have been developed to support the design of novel, application specific user interfaces. However, the support offered by these toolkits remains on a relative low abstraction level. Programming-by-example editors, such as Peridot [Myers88], are very inventive and suit well certain

---

[1]Presently at Carnegie-Mellon University

purposes. Unfortunately, they always restrict the possible user interfaces by using a preprogrammed model of what the user might be doing. A novel design is at least very tedious to create, because these kinds of tools present the more common alternatives first.

A plain WYSIWYG layout editor does not usually give enough information of the user interface to the designer. Additional graphical views are needed, for instance, to visualize the structure and the modes of the user interface. Lapidary [VanderZanden91] uses graphics, constraints and direct manipulation successfully in the design of novel, application specific user interfaces but it overlooks the need to see different overall presentations of the user interface. In addition, it does not support user interface critiquing.

Critiquing of the created user interface is an important area of support for the user interface designer. This is because the user interface designer is often a programmer who does not have enough time to read the general user interface guidelines not to mention the ability to apply them. Even specific style guides are often overlooked. Some critiquing tools, such as [Fischer90, Löwgren92] have been developed. However, they are very system specific and do not offer general means to support critiquing of novel, application specific user interfaces.

ActorStudio is a graphical user interface editor integrating several of the above mentioned features. ActorStudio gives support to the user interface designer on different abstraction levels with concrete easily manipulated objects. The editor's main target is to support the creation of application specific interaction techniques referred to as *actors*. For that purpose it offers components that define the basic appearance, the reactive appearance and the behavior of the user interface. These components are called correspondingly as *image*, *feedback object*, and *interactor*. They can form sophisticated actor hierarchies that enable modular building of complicated user interfaces. In fact, the whole user interface is often one big actor consisting of several hierarchical *subactors*. The carefully selected concepts encapsulate unnecessary details on higher design levels but provide access to them when needed.

To support the designer ActorStudio offers several different views to the user interface under development. For instance, *image-view* is used for editing the graphical appearance of an individual actor, *interactor-view* is used to edit the behavior scripts of actors, and *structure-view* is used for attaching images, interactors, and subactors to already existing actors. In addition, several *attribute-views* are offered for setting values to user interface objects. The structural editing uses components that are based on the selected concepts. The behavior editing utilizes interactors, as well as the concepts of *selection-set* and *mode*.

As a result of editing a user interface, ActorStudio produces a description of the user interface in a very flexible language called Screenplay. This description can be stored or used to create an immediate simulation of the look and feel of the user interface in a *simulation-view*. Furthermore, the Screenplay description can be used to analyze the user interface it describes against a set of user interface guidelines, which are written as rules. A separate tool called Critic [Janhunen93] has been developed for that purpose.

The paper is organized as follows. The architecture of ActorStudio is described in section 2. Section 3 presents the usage of ActorStudio. Section 4 describes the Screenplay language and section 5 gives a short introduction to Critic. Finally, we discuss ideas for future work and present the conclusions.

## 2. The Architecture of the System

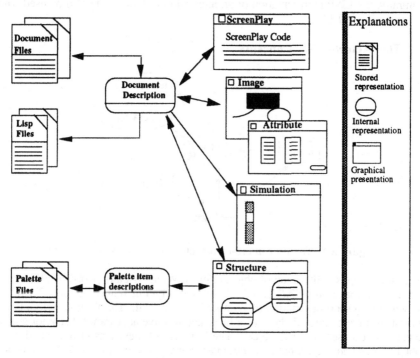

**Figure 2.1:** Components of ActorStudio.

ActorStudio consists of a collection of views and palettes, which are used for editing actors. The *structure-view* is used for creating actors and attaching user interface objects, such as images, interactors and subactors to them. The *structure-palette* is used for selecting the object that is to be attached to the actor. The structure-palette is divided in two parts: icons for system defined objects and pop-up menus for user defined objects. System defined objects include an actor template, interactors and feedback-objects. The user can easily add new interactors, images and actors to the pop-up menus when needed. The graphical outlook of a selected actor can be drawn by using the *image-view*.

The *attribute-view* is actually a set of views; one for each class of objects. These editors are implemented as fill-in-forms. An attribute-view is most often used for naming the created objects, such as actor and image instances, but it is possible to define almost any object attribute by using these editors. For instance, it is possible to change the key activating the interactor, or to change the mode in which the interactor can be activated. Because the concepts used by ActorStudio are carefully selected, the attribute-views provide rich possibilities for customizing the objects.

The operations performed in ActorStudio can be stored by using a user interface description language Screenplay. This language resembles an object based definition of a user interface. If the developer wants to, the language can be observed in a *Screenplay-view*. In this view it is also possible to make changes to the code. The Screenplay description can be interpreted to LISP and the result can be shown in a

*Simulation-view.* In this view the actor can be tried out with its proper look and feel. Naturally, the LISP representation of an interaction technique can also be used while programming in LISP.

## 2.1 The ActorStudio Concepts

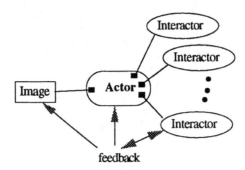

**Figure 2.2:** The user interface object structure of WimperActors.

ActorStudio is built on top of object oriented WimperActors [Koivunen91] toolkit, and the concepts used by ActorStudio have their origin in WimperActors. Therefore, we will give a short description of WimperActors as well. The WimperActors toolkit consists of object oriented classes for basic and reactive appearance, behavior and the semantics of a user interface object. The instances of these classes are called correspondingly as *images, feedback objects, interactors,* and *actors* (figure 2.2). A feedback object or a feedback function performs as a mediator between the other objects modifying the image as feedback to user actions.

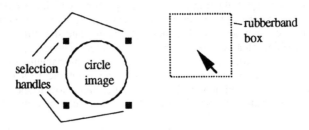

**Figure 2.3:** Default feedback in moving a circle.

Interactors define the behavior of the actor they are attached to. For instance, a move-interactor can move the actor and use a rubberband box as feedback while a selection interactor uses selection handles (figure 2.3). These handles in turn are actors that are attached with a grow interactor. The interactor concept used in WimperActors toolkit is further developed from the concept used in Garnet [Myers90].

The interactors can be seen as encapsulations of short-term modes, which are usually presented as a tool palette. In WimperActors the long-term or task modes are defined by a special *mode* property. With this property the activation of the interactors can be restricted because the interactors can be made active only in certain modes. For instance, a drawing application might have a selection mode for selecting, moving and resizing objects; a rectangle mode for creating rectangles, a text mode for creating text, and a text edit mode for editing text actors. The usage of interactors and modes makes it possible up to a certain extent to define rules for analyzing the behavior of the user interface.

In the WimperActors tool, *selection-sets* are used for the factoring of commands [Foley88]. The selectable actors in the user interface may be divided into these sets. The activation style of the selection can be defined when the selection set is created. Also the selection-sets can be defined to be active only in certain task modes.

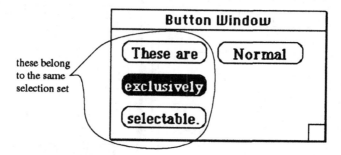

**Figure 2.4:** Three exclusively selectable buttons and one normal button.

A default selection-set is used for turning actors on and off independently of the other actors. For instance, check boxes and clickable buttons use the default selection set. Radio-buttons can be easily defined from normal clickable buttons, just by adding the button actors to the same selection-set. In figure 2.4 the three buttons in the first column belong to the same selection-set but the button named "Normal" doesn't.

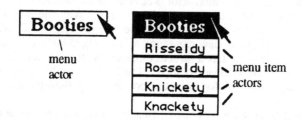

**Figure 2.5:** A pop-up menu before and after selection.

The actors in WimperActors can be attached to each other to define aggregate actors. For instance, a window actor can contain a button actor or a scrollbar actor can contain a thumb actor. An aggregate can contain at times invisible components, for instance, a pop-up menu consists of menu-item actors that are visible only when a selection is made (figure 2.5).

# 3. Usage of ActorStudio

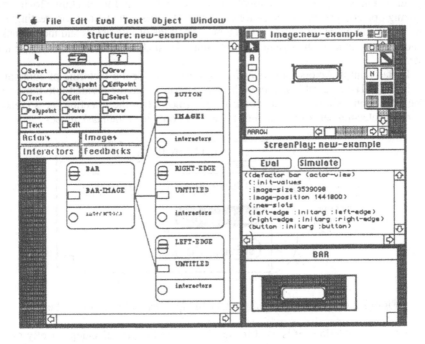

**Figure 3.1:** An overview of ActorStudio user interface.

ActorStudio provides the user interface designer multiple views to the user interface under development. Figure 3.1 is a screendump presenting an overview of the ActorStudio interface. The button actor is selected in the structure-view, which automatically shows the button image in the image-view. Also the Screenplay-view is updated whenever changes are made to the other views. The "BAR" window on the bottom right is a simulation-view presenting a full-fledged instance of the developed actor. The structure-view has a structure-palette on the left for selecting actors, images, interactors, and feedback-objects. The image-view has several palettes for selecting drawing attributes, for instance, tool-palette, pattern-palette and pen-size-palette.

The editing process starts by creating an actor in the structure-view (figure 3.2a). This actor is presented as a block consisting of an actor part, an image part, and an interactor part. The actor part shows the name of the actor. The image part shows the name of the used image and the interactor part shows the attached interactors in rectangular boxes under itself. Each interactor shows its class name and the name of the used feedback object (figure 3.2b). The actors, images, interactors, and feedback-objects can be opened up into attribute-views. These are fill-in forms for further modifying the relevant slots of each object.

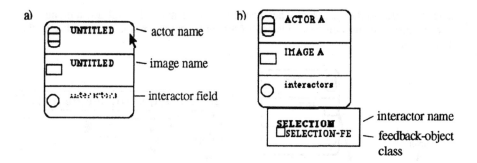

**Figure 3.2:** An empty actor (a) and an actor with a selection interactor (b).

After an actor is created an image can be attached to it. An already existing image can be selected from the structure palette or a totally new image can be drawn by using the image-view (figure 3.3). The image-view has a set of graphical tools for drawing and writing text. After the editing is finished the resulting image is automatically attached to the selected actor.

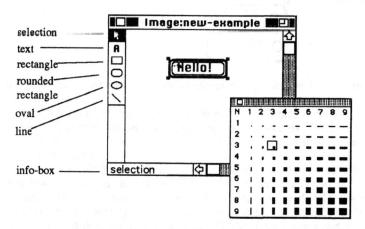

**Figure 3.3:** The image-view and the pen-size-palette.

Encapsulated behavior can be attached to an existing actor by selecting a suitable interactor from the structure palette and then by clicking the actor. The selected interactors cover basic interaction tasks, such as select, move, grow, gesture, polypoint, text, and edit-text. Usually no changes or only minor changes are needed to the interactor default values. For instance, the designer may want to use a different feedback object.

New actors can be attached under an already existing actor to form a hierarchical aggregate structure. This structure is logical and shouldn't be confused with the underlying window system structure. For instance, a pull-down menu may consist of a button actor with the menu title having several menu-items as subactors to the button. All these actors are laid out parallel. Attribute-view can be used to create new slot-names to refer to the subactors when needed. For instance, the pull-down menu may have a special menu-items slot instead of a generic subactor slot for referring to the menu-items.

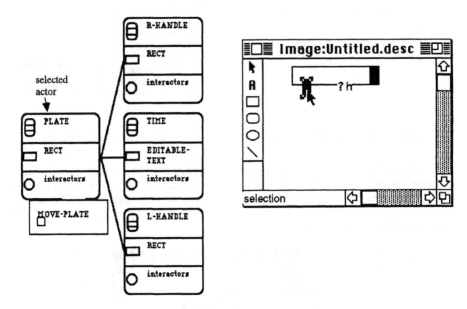

**Figure 3.4:** A sample aggregate object shown in structure- and image-views.

A sample aggregate is shown in the structure-view in figure 3.4. It describes a metal plate in an interaction technique timing the use of roller mill resources (figure 3.5). The length of the middle bar describes the time required to roll one plate. When the plate is selected it is shown in the image-view. The subactors to the plate are shown also to be able to adjust the relational placing of the actor's and subactor's images. The two black handles on both ends of the plate are used to change the length of the plate. They have grow interactors attached to them. These interactors define the object of the resizing in customizing an actor-to-change slot to refer to the plate. The plate itself has a move interactor that can be used to move it to a different roller or schedule it to a different time.

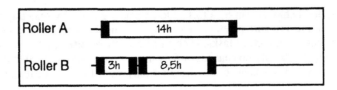

**Figure 3.5:** Interaction technique for timing roller mill resources.

Constraints in the grow-interactors are defined at the moment by an appropriate constraint function. This function can be selected from a predefined set covering the constraints in left, right, up and down directions and inside another actor. Alternatively the constraint function can be specified in Lisp. Our plan in the future is to integrate a graphical constraint system, such as [Cardelli88], to allow flexible constraining without low level references to functions.

Semantic functions can be attached to the interactors to provide information to desired actors or to the application. Normally, they cover such situations as starting, stopping, and continuously running an interactor action. For instance, every time a grow interactor calls a stopping action a message can be sent to the underlying application informing that the timing of a metal plate has been changed on roller A.

## 4. The Screenplay language

While a user interface is being defined by ActorStudio a Screenplay description of the user interface is formed automatically. This description follows the tree like structure of the user interface actors. In addition to subactors, each actor in the tree contains attributes, such as interactor and image attributes. In the Screenplay language a tree like structure of nodes and arcs is mapped correspondingly to actor instances and actor properties. For instance, to describe the user interface shown in figure 4.1 we first define a window with name win1 and a button with name button1 and attach the button to the window. Also the button's attributes :text and :font can be defined. The main structure of the Screenplay description presenting the user interface in figure 4.1 looks as follows:

```
(defactor win1
    (:is-a actor-window)
    (:init-values (:image-size (60   20)))
    (:subactors button1)
    (:image window-image))


(defactor button1
    (:is-a button)
    (:init-values (:text  "Push me!")
                  (:font  "Times"))
    (:parent win1)))
```

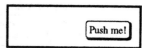

**Figure 4.1:** A simple window.

The behavior of the actors can be expressed by using interactors. For instance, a movable button has a move-interactor and can be defined as follows:

```
(defactor button1
    (:is-a button)
    (:parent win1)
    (:interactors
       (move-interactor
                :mode edit-mode)))))
```

Usually the Screenplay language is compiled into an internal form, where different programs can use accessors for getting the information they need. However, it is also possible to see the Screenplay description of the developed actors in a special Screenplay-view.

## 5. A Critiquing Tool

The Screenplay language is designed not only for storing the description of the user interface. It can be also used for user interface critiquing purposes. A critiquing tool has a special description language describing rules that the user interface should obey. These rules can be unified with the Screenplay description of the user interface. When the unification succeeds an explanation is given.

Figure 5.1 presents the components of a Critic rule. A rule consists of a *condition* and an *action*. A condition consists of a *gluing-tree* which is unified with a selected user interface tree. This tree may contain special types of arcs or trees that control the unification. For instance, the gluing-tree may contain *predicates* that filter the results of the unification process on certain level of the gluing-tree. The action part of a rule consists of an optional *modifier* for describing the modifications to the user interface and an *explanation* to the user of what went wrong. All of these components can have variables. These are given values based on the unification of the gluing-tree with the user interface tree.

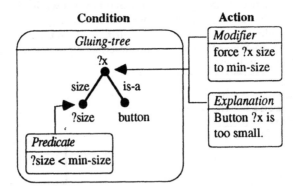

**Figure 5.1:** Components of a rule

## 6. Future Work

The designer usually defines constraints, such as moving the cursor only vertically, from a wide selection of predefined alternatives. If more possibilities are needed they can be coded as a lisp function. In the future our main goal is to integrate a constraint system with the WimperActors tool and provide a graphical view to the constraints from ActorStudio.

Sometimes the designer operates on one window; sometimes she has many associated windows to develop. We have mainly concentrated on the contents of one window but in the future we also want to provide the designer a view for hierarchical window strategies [Koivunen89] and several possible predefined strategies to select from. This would help the designer in developing main outlines of the user interface.

## 7. Conclusions

Many useful tools have been developed to support the development of a user interface. ActorStudio has successfully integrated three beneficial features that stand out in those tools. First, it uses concepts that allow the separation of an interaction technique into concrete components presenting the basic appearance, reactive appearance, behavior and semantics. These components have been successful in supporting easy combination of complicated application specific interaction techniques.

Second beneficial feature provided by ActorStudio is the selection of different views to the user interface under development. These views are very helpful in giving several types of information to the designer so that she can make better design decisions. A plain WYSIWYG layout editor would be much less informative.

The third beneficial feature is the use of a description language. The Screenplay language is not used to write the user interface (although it could) as the earlier description languages. It is used as an intermediate language for storing, and simulating the user interface. From the point of the designer its main benefit is, however, that this language can be used by other tools, especially for critiquing purposes. The description is very powerful and flexible because it can easily be extended to cover new user interface objects and attributes.

## Acknowledgments

We want to give our special thanks to Seppo Törmä who has given us invaluable help while implementing the system. We also want to thank Prof. Martti Mäntylä for his useful comments while writing this paper.

## References

[Cardelli88]
Cardelli, L. (1988)
Building User Interfaces by Direct Manipulation. In *Proc. of ACM SIGGRAPH Symposium on User Interface Software 1988*(Banff, Alberta, Canada, October 17-19, 1988), pp. 152-166.

[Fischer90]
Fischer, G. et.al. (1990)
Using Critics to Empower Users. In *Proc. of CHI, 1990* (Seattle, Washington, April 1-5, 1990), ACM, New York, pp. 337-347.

[Foley88]
Foley, J. (1988)
Earnshaw, R.A. (Ed.)
Models and Tools for the Designers of User-Computer Interfaces. In *Proc.Theorical Foundations of Computer Graphics and CAD* (Italy, July, 1987), NATO ASI Series, Vol. F40. Springer-Verlag, pp. 1122-1151.

[Janhunen93]
Janhunen, T. and Koivunen, M. (1993)
Critic: A User Interface Analysis and Modification Tool Using an Interactor Based User Interface Model. Helsinki University of Technology, Technical Report TKO B-88, p. 16. A revised version available.

[Koivunen90]
> Koivunen, M. (1990)
> WSE: An Environment for Exploring Window Strategies. In *Proc. of Eurographics'90, 1990* (Montreux, Geneve, September 3-7, 1990), North-Holland, Amsterdam, pp. 495-506 .

[Koivunen91]
> Koivunen, M. and Lassila, O. (1991)
> WimperActors: An Improved Interactor Model.  Helsinki University of Technology, Technical Report TKO B-70, p. 16.  A revised version available.

[Löwgren92]
> Löwgren, J. and Nordqvist, T.  (1992)
> Knowledge Based Evaluation as Design Support for Graphical User Interfaces. In *Proc. of CHI, 1992* (Monterey, California, May 3-7, 1992), ACM, New York, pp. 181-188.

[Myers88]
> Myers, B.A.  (1988)
> *Creating User Interfaces by Demonstration.*  Academic Press, p. 276.

[Myers90]
> Myers, B.A.  (Jul 1990)
> A New Model for Handling Input.  *ACM Transactions on Information Systems*, Vol. 8, No. 3, pp. 289-320.

[Singh88]
> Singh, G. and Green, M.  (1988)
> Designing the Interface Designer's Interface.  In *Proc. of ACM SIGGRAPH Symposium on User Interface Software 1988*(Banff, Alberta, Canada, October 17-19, 1988), pp. 109-116.

[VanderZanden91]
> Vander Zanden, B. and Myers, B.A.  (1991)
> The Lapidary Graphical Interface Design Tool. In *Proc. of CHI, 1991* (New Orleans, Louisiana, April 27 - May 2, 1991), ACM, New York, pp. 465-466.

NEW AND OLD METAPHORS

# Natural Training Wheels: Learning and Transfer Between Two Versions of a Computer Application

Marita Franzke and John Rieman

Institute of Cognitive Science
University of Colorado
Boulder, CO 80309-0345
(303) 492-7299
mfranzke@clipr.colorado.edu

**Abstract.** Users of personal computers must deal with frequent major upgrades of software packages. Major upgrades typically provide increased functionality without changing the conceptual framework of the program, but they may force the user to learn how to use new menus, dialog boxes, and other controls. We suggest that early versions of a program provide a natural training wheels environment, in which novice users can learn a program's basic operation while avoiding potential confusion caused by advanced features. Experiments with two versions of a graphing program confirm this hypothesis, with some restrictions.

## 1. The Upgrade Problem

As regular users of personal computers, it sometimes seems that we spend as much time installing and learning upgrades to our software as we spend actually using the applications. To give some idea of the magnitude of the problem, we are writing this paper in version 5.1 of a word-processing program, running under version 7.1 of an operating system, on a computer (an Apple Macintosh) that was introduced in January 1984. By convention, a "major" upgrade is indicated by a change in the units place of the version number, so we have gone through a total of ten major upgrades of the word processor and operating system in less than ten years.

Using these numbers as a basis, consider the plight of an office worker who relies primarily on three basic applications, such as a word processor, a spreadsheet, and a graphics package. Keeping these three programs up-to-date, along with the operating system, will require the user to learn an upgraded version on the average of every six months. Each major upgrade will include many new features, some that may allow the user to do new things with the software, others that may force the user to learn new techniques for things the old software could already do. The new features will show up in reorganized menus, added controls in dialog boxes, and other changes to the application's appearance.

How do users handle these changes? Can they simply refuse to upgrade and continue to work with the older system? Will they enroll in classes for formal training? Or will they learn the upgrade on their own, possibly using tutorials, or the manual, or unstructured exploration? Research in human-computer interaction has been relatively silent on these questions, concentrating instead on the issues of learning entirely new applications and transferring to different programs (e.g., [9, 7]). In this paper, we suggest some general answers, then focus on data we have collected concerning learning and transfer of specific skills from one version of an application to the next.

## 1.1 The User's Response to Upgrades

Faced with the opportunity to upgrade a piece of software that is already doing its job, a user may consider simply staying with the old version. This is at best a short-term solution. For most users today, the desktop computer is part of a shared computing environment, and sharing files with colleagues or supervisors requires compatible versions of software. The reluctant user of the older version will soon be pulled along with the many users who need (or think they need) the new version's increased functionality. In larger companies, central systems-support staff may even force the upgrade of all machines to the same version, since a consistent software base is easier to maintain.

Formal training is seldom an option. In situations where personal computers are used today, basic computer skills are listed as part of the job requirement. Newly hired employees may be sent to classes to learn specific software, but our experience in offices suggests that both managers and users view upgrades as trivial changes that do not justify the time and cost of further training.

Users, then, are faced with learning the upgraded software on their own. In one sense, they are surprisingly successful at this. An entire culture of users has evolved in sophistication along with the software they use. As an example, compare the simple interface of the early Macintosh and its associated basic software to the complexity of the Macintosh Multifinder and the powerful programs it runs today. It seems likely that today's Macintosh (or today's PC with Windows), introduced in 1984, would not have been received as an intuitive, easily learned, computer for everyone. We believe that the simple systems of the mid 1980s provided what Carroll has called a "training wheels" environment [2], an environment in which individuals and the culture of users as a whole could learn basic computer skills. Successive upgrades then gave users the opportunity to build on those skills.

## 1.2 Exploratory Learning of an Upgrade

The broad view of how users deal with upgrades, then, is that they learn to work with the revised software on their own, without any formal training. We now narrow our attention to the question of how users structure their learning activities.

Studies reported by Carroll [2] and Carroll and Rosson [3] have shown that users prefer to learn software by exploration, that is, by trying out actions to discover their effect. Carroll's work [2] suggests ways to design software and training environments that support this activity. The focus of Carroll's work is primarily on users' early interactions with a new application, often with the assumption that they will take time to engage in a dedicated training session.

To investigate the learning activities of users during their ordinary daily activities, Rieman [8] performed a series of diary studies. The studies showed that many users would only make an effort to learn new features of their software when the need arose. A few users would create small tasks for the purpose of investigating a new or revised program. In either case, users would be faced with a task-oriented need to use a new feature of a program, and they would employ a variety of investigatory techniques, including exploration, looking in manuals, and asking other users or system support personnel for help. The preferred method varied with the user and the situation. More experienced users relied more heavily on manuals, while novices were more likely to ask for help. Novices would sometimes start with a manual, but were often frustrated by not knowing the appropriate term for the interaction they wanted to learn about.

The diary studies describe the situation in which learning about upgrades typically occurs, and we used those results, in part, to define the experiments reported in the next sections. The experiments narrow our focus even further, to concentrate on the details of learning and transfer for identical or similar tasks with two versions of a software package.

## 2. Experiment 1

Experiment 1 was designed primarily to collect data in support of ongoing work with cognitive models of display-based interfaces [5]. Although the question of transfer between two software packages was not the principle focus of the investigation, the experiment's design and results provide an essential foundation for understanding the further experimental work reported later in this paper.

The experiment investigated users' interactions with versions 1 and 3 of the Cricket Graph software, which we will refer to as CG-1 and CG-3.[1] Cricket Graph is a program that generates graphs from spreadsheets of data and allows the graphs to be edited. Some of the editing operations that can be performed on a graph after it is created are changing the style of the plot lines and data-point symbols, changing the font and size of labels and titles, and changing the range information on each axis. Following the pattern we have described for upgrades, the early version is a fairly simple but effective program, with some notable limitations. The later version is a much more powerful system, providing additional functionality at the cost of a more complicated interface.

Because of questions that arose in our cognitive modeling efforts, we were especially interested in observing how people would manage the selection of data for the X and Y axes from a dialog box provided by the program. We expected a relatively successful interaction driven by a label-following strategy [7] for CG-1, where the dialog box provides only relevant choices (see Figure 1). In CG-3 the dialog box provides additional choices that might mislead novice users and make the selection of X and Y axes less obvious.

Additionally, we were interested in seeing if skills learned during an interaction in one interface would transfer to a similar interaction with the other version. To this end, subjects in the first experiment started with a task on either CG-1 or CG-3 and were transferred to the same task on the other version immediately thereafter.

### 2.1 Subjects

Twelve undergraduates from the University of Colorado subject pool participated in this experiment for class credit. Six of these subjects were randomly selected to serve in the 1-3 (CG-1 followed by CG-3) condition, and six subjects served in the 3-1 (CG-3 followed by CG-1) condition. The subjects had an average of 2 years of experience with Macintosh systems but no experience with Cricket Graph.

---

[1]   Cricket Graph™ is produced by  Computer Associates, Inc., One Computer Associates Plaza, Islandia, NY 11788-2000, USA. The original version was designed by Jim Rafferty and Rich Norling. The program we refer to as "CG-1" is CA-Cricket Graph, version 1.3.2, released in 1989. The newer version, which we call "CG-3," is CA-Cricket Graph III, v. 1.01, released in 1992. As far as we know there was no Cricket Graph II.

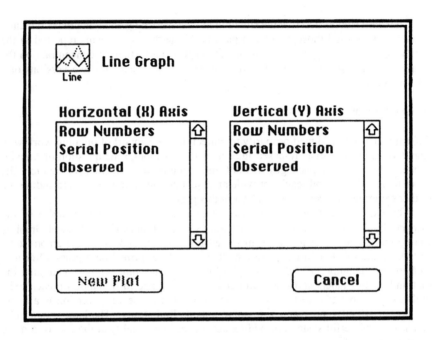

**Figure 1.** Axis selection dialog boxes from CG-1 (top) and CG-3 (bottom).

## 2.2 Tasks and Procedure

**Cricket Graph Tasks.** The experimental task given to subjects consisted of two main phases: (a) creating a new graph from a data file provided to the subjects, and (b) editing the default graph to match it to a given sample graph. The data was provided in a Cricket Graph data file that the subjects could use without further modifications. Subjects also received a sample graph that differed from the default created by Cricket Graph in a number of dimensions. To create a near-perfect duplication of the sample format, subjects would have to change the style of the graph title and axes labels, the Y-axis label, the data-point symbol and plot-line style, the style of the legend label, the location of the legend, the style of tick marks, and the range of the axes.

Subjects had to decide on the types and the order of modifications they wanted to attempt. A perfectly duplicated format was impossible, since the sample graph had been created with a different program than Cricket Graph. The freedom of subjects to choose their own goals, combined with the imperfect sample, gave us the opportunity to observe goal instantiation and management in a relatively natural task environment, without enforcing a particular grain size or order of subgoals.

The instructions were written in a small HyperCard stack, which included general instructions, a sample graph, and details about the data, graph type, and data-axis mappings. Subjects could page through the three instruction cards by clicking on labeled buttons, and the stack was designed to ensure that the subject looked at each card at least once before beginning the task. An opened folder in the Macintosh finder contained the appropriated Cricket Graph version and the data file. The folder window was partially covered by the stack and could be activated and brought to the front by clicking on it. The HyperCard stack was accessible during the whole task. This setup enabled us to record precisely when subjects consulted the sample graph or the written instructions for further directions.

**Warm-Up Tasks.** Before subjects were presented with the main graphing tasks, they had to be warmed up to two procedures: thinking aloud and using Macintosh Multifinder. Initial screenings of the tasks warned us that our subject population might not be accustomed to moving back and forth between different application windows. To give them some practice in toggling between the HyperCard instructions and the task window, subjects first had to perform a brief word-processing task using Microsoft Word, in which they were asked to format document to match a sample text given on HyperCard. This task and the instructions had a similar format to the Cricket Graph task and familiarized subjects with the Multifinder environment.

While subjects were doing these tasks they were encouraged to think aloud [4]. With this method we were able to collect additional information on what goals subjects were pursuing throughout the task, as well as which interface object they were attending to. Prior to any tasks involving the computer, subjects were warmed up to thinking aloud with a brief verbal problem-solving task. All computer tasks were performed on a Macintosh IIcx computer with a 13-inch color monitor.

**Procedure.** Upon arrival subjects were instructed in the thinking aloud procedure and did the verbal problem-solving task. After this the experimenter directed their attention to the Macintosh display and asked them to read through the instructions aloud and follow the instructions on their own. Subjects were informed that the experimenter would remind them to verbalize their thoughts but would not answer any questions or provide any hints about the task. Subjects were given ten minutes to complete the word-processing task.

After the word-processing task was completed, the experimenter brought up the instructions for the graphing task as well as the folder containing the data and the respective Cricket Graph version. At this point, half of the subjects were given CG-1 and the other half CG-3. Subjects were not allowed to use the Cricket Graph manual. The lack of a manual reflected the finding in diary studies that novice users were often unable to find what they needed in documentation, even if it was available. Similarly, telling the subjects that the experimenter would not answer questions forced the user to perform some exploration, simulating a natural situation in which asking questions requires more initial effort than searching for a command in the interface. If subjects persistently failed to discover critical interaction techniques and continued to explore the same parts of the interface, the experimenter would volunteer brief hints, such as "try working directly on the graph" (intended to divert attention from the menus).

Subjects were allowed ten minutes to complete the first Cricket Graph task. If they had been unable to accomplish any of the editing subtasks, because they did not discover the methods that would lead to their completion, they were given a brief demonstration by the experimenter. Essentially, the experimenter showed the subject how to accomplish the immediate goal(s) that the subject had been working on. This manipulation ensured that all subjects entered the transfer task with some knowledge about successful interface techniques in one Cricket Graph version.

After the experimenter's demonstration, subjects were transferred to the other version of the software, where they performed a second task. In this experiment, the second task was identical to the first, using the same HyperCard instructions and data file. Procedure and allowed task time were the same as for the first Cricket Graph version. The complete experimental procedure lasted approximately 45 minutes and was videotaped by a camera that recorded the interactions visible on the monitor, along with the thinking-aloud protocols.

## 2.3 Results

We recorded the time that it took subjects from first clicking on the folder containing the application and data file to clicking the OK button in the dialog box for selection of X and Y axes. There is essentially one correct sequence of actions that leads to the creation of the default graph: Opening the data file, choosing *Graph* from the menubar, selecting *Line Graph* from the palette of iconic graph types (the palette drops from the menubar in CG-1, but it doesn't appear until the *New Graph* item is selected from the pulldown menu in CG-3), selecting a column label for the X axis and another for the Y axis from two scrolling lists, then clicking *New Graph* (CG-1) or *OK* (CG-3). Hereafter we refer to this button in both versions as the "OK button."

To measure the time that it takes to create a new graph, we time stamped the moment when subjects first clicked on the folder containing the application to the moment where they clicked OK after having selected the appropriate axes for the graph. From this total time we subtracted task-encoding times, that is, the times that subjects spent looking at the instructions for more details about the data or the task. It could be expected that subjects would have learned this information by the time that they were transferred to the second task (recall that the instructions and data files for the two tasks were identical), and the additional task encoding time would have unduly inflated our measurement of interface learning time in the first task. We did not

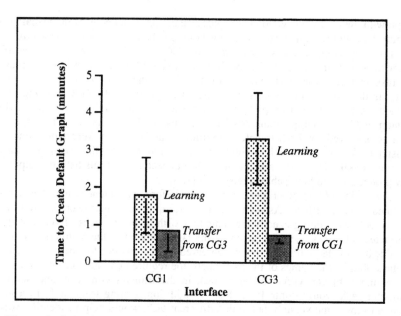

**Figure 2.** Learning and transfer times for graph creation in CG-1 and CG-3 (Experiment 1). Subjects who learned CG-1 transferred to CG-3, and vice versa.

subtract thinking aloud times, because thinking aloud happened in parallel to the interface actions, and we expected the same rate of thinking aloud in all conditions.

The results for the learning time (time to OK button if the version was used for the first task) and transfer time (time to OK button if the version was used for the second task) for CG-1 and CG-3 are represented in Figure 2. The two key points of interest in these results were the large difference in original learning times between the two versions and the considerable amount of reduction in time in using both Cricket Graph versions in the transfer condition. Three independent sample t-tests were performed on these differences.

First, we found a significant difference between the learning times for CG-1 and CG-3, $t(10) = 2.34$, $p < .05$. It was generally easier to learn to create a default graph in CG-1 than in CG-3. Second, there was a significant difference between learning and transfer times for CG-3, $t(10) = 5.07$, $p < .001$, showing that learning of CG-3 after previous exposure to CG-1 (the transfer condition) was easier than learning without previous exposure to any version of Cricket Graph. Finally, the difference between learning and transfer times for CG-1 was marginally significant, $t(10) = 2.08$, $p < .07$. Subjects who transferred to CG-1 after previous learning of CG-3 were faster creating a graph than subjects who learned CG-1 without any previous experience with Cricket Graph.

## 2.4 Discussion

These results piqued our interest in the upgrade problem for several reasons. Most importantly, it was easier to learn to create a default graph in the older version of Cricket Graph. The added functionality in CG-3 comes at the cost of lower explorability. We believe that the primary source of the difficulty in creating a default graph with the upgraded version is the presence of additional choices in the dialog box (Figure 1), coupled with an additional level of menu hierarchy leading to the box.

But, surprisingly, users transferred from CG-1 to CG-3 were about three times faster than first-time users of CG-3. In fact, the total time to learn in CG-1 plus do the task in CG-3 was less than the time to learn the task in CG-3. This result suggests that users can ignore the additional complexity of CG-3 after they have learned the correct solution path in the simpler version. Training on the previous version of Cricket Graph transferred to learning the later version. The large time savings observed for both transfer conditions was somewhat surprising, since the transfer took place after only a single, brief session with another version. Current theories of skill acquisition assume that subjects need many trials before compiling a new production and being able to retrieve it [1, 6].

The design of this experiment, as we noted before, was intended in part to support a related research effort. As such, it left several questions unanswered. First of all, our subjects were doing exactly the same task with both interfaces. Even though we subtracted the times spent on encoding the task (looking at the instructions), it was possible that the large transfer that we observed was simply due to a better encoding of the task, that is, the names of the axis labels, the required editing changes, and so on. Presenting subjects with a different task in the transfer condition and adding a distractor task would control for this. In addition, testing transfer from a given version to the same version, but with a different task, would help us identify exactly what had been learned in the training condition.

A second question that we wanted to investigate was the extent to which subjects had actually encoded the procedures discovered in the training condition into long-term memory. Would the single-trial presentation of a version leave traces that were still retrievable and useful after a delay of several days? Finally, we were interested in how much reduction in performance time would be associated with practice on the same version as compared to transfer to another version.

## 3. Experiment 2

Experiment 2 was designed to address these questions. In this experiment, all subjects were introduced to CG-1 first, doing the same graphing task as in Experiment 1. After this, half of the subjects were transferred to CG-3, and the other half to CG-1. Both of these groups would do a second, different task, involving the same actions for creating a graph, but with different data and a different sample format to match in the editing phase. Half of both transfer groups would do their second task after a brief (approximately 10 minutes) delay, whereas the other half of the subjects came back for the second task after a 1-week delay.

### 3.1 Subjects

Twenty-two undergraduates from the University of Colorado subject pool participated in this experiment for class credit. Subjects had an average of 2.4 years of experience with Macintoshes but not with Cricket Graph. Five subjects were randomly selected to serve in the 1-3/short (CG-1, CG-3; 10 minutes delay) condition, Five served in the 1-3/long (CG-1, CG-3; 1 week delay) condition, six served in the 1-1/short (CG-1, CG-1; 10 minutes delay) condition, and six served in the 1-1/long (CG-1, CG-1; 1-week delay) condition.

## 3.2 Tasks and Procedure

The procedure closely followed the procedure described for Experiment 1. Upon arrival, subjects were warmed up to thinking aloud. Then they performed the word-processing warm-up task, and then went on to perform the first graphing task with CG-1. After completing the first graphing task, further treatment depended on the assigned condition. Subjects in the short delay condition were briefly distracted with a second word-processing task for ten minutes, and then did the second graphing task in either CG-1 or CG-3. Subjects in the long delay condition came back after one week, were briefly warmed up with the second word-processing task, and finally did the second graphing task with the respective version of Cricket Graph.

## 3.3 Results

For this experiment, we analyzed both sections of the task: (a) the time to create the default task, and (b) the time for each editing subgoal from the graph modification part of the task.

**(A) Time to Create the Default Graph.** Graph creation times were extracted from the video protocols as discussed for experiment 1. The times to create a graph are represented in Figure 3. The learning times for CG-3 are taken from the first experiment.

First, comparing the learning times for CG-3 from the first experiment with the learning for CG-1 in the second experiment, there is no statistically significant difference. An independent samples t-test showed that $t(26) = .51$, p > .1. Learning

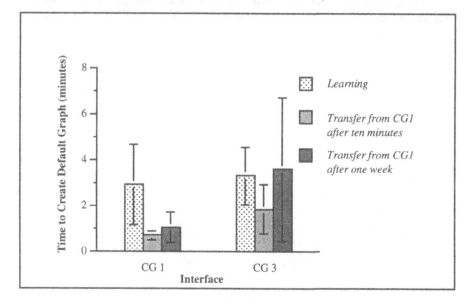

**Figure 3.** Learning and transfer times for graph creation for CG-1 and CG-3 after ten minutes and a week delay (Experiment 2).

times might have been generally slower in the second experiment; however, a comparison of CG-1 learning times from Experiment 1 (mean = 1.73 minutes) with CG-1 learning times from Experiment 2 (mean = 2.93 minutes) was not reliably different, $t(26) = 1.71$, p > .09.

There is improvement in using CG1-1 due to practice with CG-1. Two t-tests for paired samples were performed. Subjects creating a second task with this same version are significantly faster, $t(5) = 5.22$, p < .01. The practice times after one week delay are not significantly different, $t(5) = 1.6$, p > .1, due to large variance in subjects' performance.

Two t-tests for independent samples were performed on the graph creation times for CG-3. The improvement in using CG-3 due to practice with CG-1 is marginally significant if the transfer happens after the short delay, $t(9) = 2.05$, p < .08. Practice on CG-1 looses its beneficial effect after a week delay, however, $t(9) = 0.42$, p >.5.

## (B)   Editing Times per Subgoal.

For the editing part of the task, many orders, methods, and subgoals were possible. Therefore, we merely recorded the time from the clicking of the OK button through the completion of the task, as well as the number of subgoals completed. Each of the major changes to the graph that we enumerated above, such as changing the style of the axis labels or the line style, was counted as a completed subgoal. Multiple adjustments to a single item in the graph, such as repeated changes in font size in an attempt to match the sample graph, were merged into a single subgoal. The results for this section of the task will be reported in terms of time per completed editing subgoal.

The editing times per completed subgoal in modifying the default graph are represented in Figure 4. The learning times for CG-3 are again taken from the first

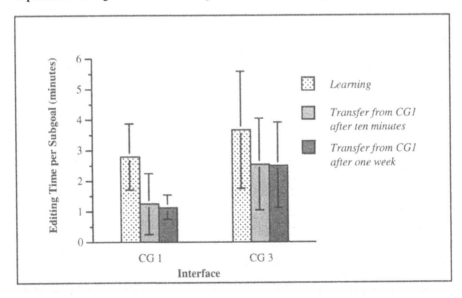

**Figure 4.** Learning and transfer times for completing each editing subgoal in CG-1 and CG-3 after ten minutes and a week delay (Experiment 2).

experiment. Even though the graphical representation suggests that the learning times for CG-1 are shorter than for CG-3, this difference is not statistically significant; an independent sample t-test showed that $t(24) = 1.61$, $p > .1$. However, there is improvement in using CG-1 due to practice on the same version. This difference is only marginally significant for the short delay condition: t-test for paired samples, $t(5) = 2.177$, $p < .1$. In this case, there is also improvement due to practice even after a week's delay, $t(5) = 4.18$, $p < .01$. For the subjects who were trained on CG-1 and then transferred to CG-3 there is a trend towards improving on the editing times of the subjects who learned CG-3 with no prior training in experiment 1, but the differences are significant neither for the short delay (independent sample t-tests, $t(8) = 1.32$, $p > .2$), nor for the long delay condition, ($t(8) = 1.45$, $p > .1$.)

## 3.4 Discussion

The results of this second experiment suggest that the differences in learning times for the two versions may not be as dramatic as we expected from the first experiment. For the graph creation part of the data there is evidence for learning and transfer after a short ten-minute delay. This finding supports our earlier result. Subjects show improvement even after they are transferred to a different task after being distracted with an unrelated interfering task. However, after one week delay, there was no significant improvement over original graph creation time, both for subjects using the same Cricket Graph version for the second time, as well as for subjects who transferred to a different version.

For graph editing times the results are slightly different. Here, we only find significant improvement for subjects who did their second task in CG-1, but not more than a numerical trend towards improvement for subjects who transferred to CG-3. Interestingly, performance does not seem to drop off for the one week delay condition. We believe that the particular interface action that CG-1 users must apply to modify all parts of the graph (double-clicking on the relevant graph objects), is difficult to discover, but easily recalled. For the transfer subjects, double-clicking is only one of several interface actions required to select to select relevant graph objects, therefore there is additional functionality that must be discovered by exploration, no matter how long the delay between training and practice is.

A methodological problem with this second experiment is that we are comparing learning times for CG-3 from experiment 1 with learning and transfer times from experiment 2. This may have been the cause for the statistically less clear results in this experiment. We are also still lacking a true learning baseline for CG-3, which would make transfer interpretations more meaningful [e.g., 9]. We are addressing these issues in our current experimental work.

## 4. Summary Discussion and Conclusions

Our conjecture when we began the experimental work was that earlier versions of a software package provide a natural training wheels environment for later, more complex upgrades. The experiments confirmed this hypothesis, at least for the software we tested. In the best case, Experiment 1, subjects actually spent less total time performing two tasks, one in CG-1 followed by one in CG-3, than they did performing a single task in CG-3 with no preparation. In the weaker case of Experiment 2, subjects showed a marginally significant improvement in performance times for certain subtasks when tested 10 minutes after training on an earlier version, although they showed no significant improvement after a full week.

Practically, these results suggest that earlier versions of software could be useful for training, either in a formal training program or as production software for novice users. The success of either approach would depend on both the users' tasks and the differences between versions of the software. With Cricket Graph, for example, users would clearly benefit from learning to create a graph in the earlier version, because the simple path to success in that package is still available in the later version, although with many more potentially distracting options. The earlier version's lack of distractions is exactly the source of its strength as a training environment. On the other hand, an earlier version of software will have little training benefit if it teaches techniques that are of limited use in the current version, as the results in the editing phase of the experiments demonstrated.

A more basic finding of the research was that different interaction styles (filling out dialog-boxes, clicking and dragging objects, or accessing menu items) may have different learning and retention functions. We are currently working on an analysis of the tasks on a smaller grain size, to identify specifically which interactions lead to the savings reported here. We have also broadened our data collection to interfaces that provide more different interaction styles, and to a more controlled retention design.

**Acknowledgements.** We thank Clayton Lewis and Peter Polson for many insightful discussions of the data and the experimental design presented in this paper. Special thanks to Troy Davig for his excellent assistance in collecting the data. Funding for this work was provided by the National Science Foundation, Grant IRI 9116640.

# References

1. Anderson, J.R. (1993) *Rules of the Mind.* Hillsdale, NJ: Lawrence Erlbaum.

2. Carroll, J.M. (1990). *The Nurnberg Funnel.* Cambridge, MA: MIT Press.

3. Carroll, J.M., and Rosson, M.B. (1987). The paradox of the active user. In J.M. Carroll (ed.), *Interfacing Thought: Cognitive Aspects of Human-Computer Interaction.* Cambridge: MIT Press/Bradford Books, pp. 80-111.

4. Ericsson, K.A., and Simon, H.A. (1984). Verbal reports as data. *Psychological Review,* 87, 215-251.

5. Kitajima, M., and Polson, P.G. (1992) A computational model of skilled use of a graphical user interface. *Proceedings of CHI'92 Conference on Human Factors in Computing Systems,*. New York: Association for Computing Machinery, 241-249.

6. Polson, P.G. (1987). A quantitative theory of human-computer interaction. In J.M. Carroll (Ed.), *Interfacing thought: Cognitive Aspects of Human-Computer Interaction.* Cambridge, MA: Bradford Books/MIT Press.

7. Polson, P.G. and Lewis, C.H. (1990). Theory-based design for easily learned interfaces. *Human-Computer Interaction, 6,* 191-220.

8. Rieman, John (1993). The diary study: A workplace-oriented research tool to guide laboratory efforts. Proceedings *of InterCHI'93 Conference on Human Factors in Computing Systems,*. New York: Association for Computing Machinery, 321–326.

9. Singley, M.K., and Anderson, J.R. (1989). *The Transfer of Cognitive Skill.* Cambridge, MA: Harvard University Press.

# Beyond Bars and Hour Glasses: Designing Performance and Progress Indicators

Sabine Musil

University of Vienna
Vienna User Interface Group
Lenaugasse 2/8, A-1080 Vienna
E-Mail: musil@ani.univie.ac.at

**Abstract.** Alternative design options for performance and progress indicators are introduced. Selected methods are then implemented on a HyperCard stack and tested against each other in an empirical user test. The design of the test and its results are presented.

**Keywords.** Performance Indicators, Progress Indicators, User Interface Design

## 1 Motivation

Although computers are becoming faster year by year it still takes them some time to perform certain operations. Human Computer Interaction (HCI) researchers have long realized that it is important to show the user that the user has not done something wrong, but that the machine is working. Accordingly two types of indicators have evolved. A performance indicator is a static piece of information that is permanently on the screen while the system is busy. A progress indicator however is a dynamic piece of information that informs the user not only that the system is working but also gives a hint of how long it is going to take or how much of the task already has been done.

Performance indicators are said to be more suitable for short routine tasks, progress indicators for tasks and actions that take longer than 2 seconds, otherwise it is very hard to perceive what is happening on the screen. But this still leaves the question of what to show during this time. Various existing systems use various methods but searching for alternatives seemed worth the effort. This paper tries to give an overview about possible alternatives for designing performance and progress indicators. An empirical test was regarded to be the most suitable method of testing on the one hand the thesis that performance indicators are better for short actions and progress indicators for long ones and on the other hand the acceptance of alternative indicator designs. So a test was elaborated and run with 21 people.

## 2 Related Work

Myers points out the importance of progress indicators in [9]. He also indicates the superiority of graphical solutions to textual ones. Shneiderman deals in [11] with the acceptability of waiting periods that could be altered by the usage of performance indicators. Baecker et al. talk in [1] about the possible use of animated icons, which gives a hint to the design of progress indicators. Muller deals in [8] with the possibility of loading functions into a cursor and showing them to the user, which also could be of some use for the design of performance indicators. Buxton et al. give an excellent overview over the uses of sound for human computer interaction in [2], which serves as a reference for designing indicators based on sound.

Existing systems most often use clocks, hour glasses and similar time measuring instruments as performance indicators [12, 7, 6, 4]. For some applications they also use progress indicators, most of the times some sort of bar that grows from left to right [4]. Computer games can also be a good source for alternative performance indicators [10, 5].

## 3 Indicator Design Possibilities

The existence of uncountable applications and millions of different kinds of users seems to open a much more wider field for performance and progress indicators than just clocks and bars. In order to adapt the computer to the user and not vice versa we have to search for more ideas to give a software designer the possibility to choose among a lot of alternatives the one he thinks best suits to his application. This section shall give an overview about some possible performance and progress indicator design opportunities. In order to do so it is necessary to group the alternatives according to the hardware facilities at the target workplace.

### 3.1 ASCII Monitors

Table 1 gives an overview over the possibilities for this kind of monitors.

| Method | Application area | Type |
|---|---|---|
| Blinking Cursor | Global | Performance |
| Status Line with static information | Global | Performance |
| Status Line with changing information | Global | Progress |
| Bars made of ASCII letters | Global | Progress |
| Count down of numbers | Global | Progress |

**Table 1.:** Alternatives for ASCII Monitors

### 3.2 Graphical Monitors

At least three differnt kinds of performance indicators can be distinguished according to their features: symbols that represent the passage of time (e.g. clocks), symbols that show that work is done (e.g. moving gear-wheels) and symbols that show the user what to do (e.g. drink a cup of coffe in the meantime). The following is a collection of symbols belonging to one of these categories, but is not ordered according to them.

Clocks are the most common alternative used as performance indicator, no matter if they are wrist watches, hour glasses or pocket watches. They can be applied globally as their usage has become very common.

Animations can also be used as a performance indicator. The movement of the object shows that the system is working. Possible objects are a bee, a sweeping apprentice and moving gear-wheels. All alternatives are globally applicable, the first two especially for beginners. The last is perfectly suitable for an application that runs in a factory.

Other possible symbols for performance indicators are a balloon with the word "THINK" in it, a sitting Buddha or the statue "The Thinker" [5], a coffee cup [10], a hand [10] or a shovel. The application area of the two statues is reduced to applications where the users know who or what these two mean. The shovel should be used for actions where there is something transported. All other symbols can be used everywhere.

A last means for producing a performance indicator is to change the colour of an object when it is busy. This method is especially suitable for multi-window systems and does not belong to one of the categories mentioned above, as it is an abstract representation.

As for progress indicators we can again distinguish at least three forms: indicators that move forward and so show how much has already been done (e.g. a bar), indicators that move backward and thus show how much remains to be done (e.g. a flower, that loses leaves), and indicators that show both the work already done and the remaining part (like an hourglass whose sand is flowing from one side to the other). The following paragraphs give examples from all categories, but again are not ordered after that.

Bars are the most common way of presenting a progress indicator. They always fill from left to right and the most striking difference between them is not their filling pattern, but the additional information that is given, e.g. whether this is a percent number or the name of the action. They can be used for any kind of application as they are very abstract.

Using the same idea of filling an object one can think of other "bars", too. For example a thermometer that fills, a blossom that gets its leaves while the action is in progress, a revolution counter that goes from zero to overdrive or a bottle that slowly fills, not to forget the hour glass whose sand flows from one side to the other [3]. All these alternatives are very good for real-life look applications[1] as they are not as abstract as a simple bar.

---

1     Real life look applications have user interfaces that show objects taken from the real life like a printer, a cupboard or a pencil, which can be used via direct manipulation for what they are normally used,.

Other alternatives for progress indicators could be a backwards running stop-watch (analog and digital), a person that moves a rock onto a hill (like the ancient Sisyphus, which carries the danger of the users expecting the work to fail and restart automatically), or a pile of sand that is moved to a new place bit by bit.

### 3.3 Sound

To use sound as a performance indicator one can implement a certain tone or a constant melody or text that can be heard when the system is busy. To use it as a progress indicator one could implement a tone scale. The task is subdivided into eight parts, to each of which corresponds a note. Another possibility would be a sound that is indicating the changing amount of "time space" to be filled in such as a changing echo or the sound of a bottle being emptied [2].

The application area of sound is limited to areas where it can be heard and to a loudness that isn't a nuisance for other people.

## 4 Test Design

Six alternatives have been chosen for the test, which are shown in Fig. 1. The first three (pocket watch, balloon and sweeping apprentice) are performance indicators, the other two (thermometer and blossom) are progress indicators. The last one can't be seen as it is a tone scale and therefore can only be heard.

One goal is to take as different methods as possible. The pocket-watch and the thermometer have been chosen as the "well-known" alternatives in their group. The apprentice and the blossom have been chosen as the alternatives "especially for the beginner" and the balloon and the tone scale as the "new and unconventional" ones. The choices are of course rather random, but for a first tryout this type of choice was regarded suitable.

These alternatives are implemented with HyperCard. For every alternative there are four actions with different lengths, which are started by pressing a button. Fig. 2 shows the screen of the thermometer. The lengths of the actions vary between 3 and 30 seconds and have their order changed after the third method in order not to let the user build up a certain expectation

The first three alternatives are performance indicators the other ones progress indicators. This grouping is done to be able to compare the different performance and progress indicators first within their group and only in the end within the types of indicators.

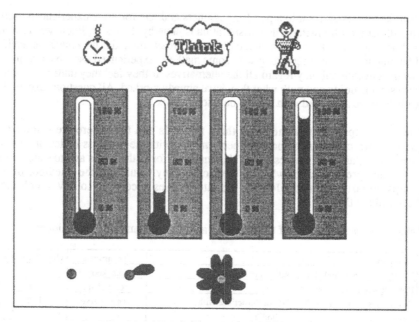

Fig. 1.: Implemented Methods

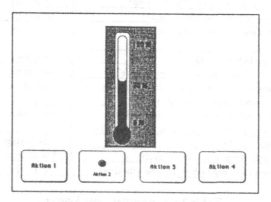

Fig. 2.: Screen for thermometer

The test itself is split into 12 blocks of questions, each of which has to be answered after performing two actions. Users have to estimate the length of the action by choosing one duration out of four possible and to state on a scale of six how impatient they have become during waiting. After the first three methods the users also have to compare their impression of the durations for every method and to state how much they liked each method, if they would like to work with each individual alternative and for what kind of action they would use it.

Then the test separates into a part for beginners and one for more experienced users, but without their knowing. The classification is done by the tester. Beginners have to say how much they know each method from everyday-life and if they have the feeling of having done something wrong with some method. Experienced users have to judge how unconventional they regard all the alternatives, if they feel they understand what the system is doing and with what they have already worked. All questions except the last have to be answered with a mark on a scale of six.

The same happens after the other three methods and then there are some final questions which try to compare the performance with the progress indicators. Users have to compare their impression of the durations for both groups and to state which group they prefer and for what kind of action they would use the methods of the groups. Finally users should rank the alternatives according to how much they shortened the time.

Table 2 shows a summary of the questions and the used answering techniques.

| Question | Technique | User Category |
|---|---|---|
| How long do you think did the action last? | 4 checkboxes | both |
| How impatient were you? | scale of six | both |
| How do you consider the durations of the actions with method X in comparison with method Y? | scale of five | both |
| How much did you like the method? | scale of six | both |
| Would you like to work with a system that uses this method? | scale of seven | both |
| Would you use this method for short or long actions? | scale of six | both |
| How unconventional do you regard the method? | scale of six | experienced |
| Was the information about the progress of the actions sufficient for you? | scale of six | experienced |
| With what have you already worked? | fill-in form | experienced |
| How well do you know this method from everyday life? | scale of six | beginner |
| How strong was your impression of having done something wrong because no success information was given? | scale of six | beginner |
| How do you consider the durations of the actions with the methods of group one in comparison with the ones of group two? | scale of five | both |
| Which of the groups would you prefer? | 2 checkboxes | both |
| For what kind of actions would you use group X? | 4 checkboxes | both |
| Rank the alternatives according to their shortening the time? | fill-in form | both |

**Table 2.:** Summary of questionnaire

The whole test takes about 20 minutes. The tester is sitting beside the tested person, who may not wear any watch and fills out the forms by himself. The HyperCard stack and the forms have to be used simultanously.

## 5 Results

21 persons were tested, thirteen were more experienced users, eight were beginners. The tested persons proved the thesis that progress indicators are better suitable for longer actions as they seem to shorten the waiting period. Table 3 gives the results of

the direct comparison and for the various methods. The users also became less impatient when having to wait for a long time, they felt better informed and had less feeling of having made a mistake.

| Method \ Action | only short | shorter | both | longer | only long |
|---|---|---|---|---|---|
| clock | 6 | 7 | 5 | 3 | 0 |
| apprentice | 8 | 0 | 7 | 0 | 6 |
| balloon | 5 | 5 | 8 | 1 | 2 |
| thermometer | 1 | 1 | 13 | 3 | 3 |
| tone scale | 8 | 8 | 4 | 0 | 1 |
| blossom | 3 | 2 | 14 | 0 | 2 |
| Group \ Action | short | long | both | none | |
| performance | 14 | 0 | 5 | 2 | |
| progress | 0 | 4 | 15 | 2 | |

**Table 3.:** Results on what kind of actions users regarded a certain method or group of method suitable

Within the group of performance indicators the balloon was liked most, but people were rather undecided if they wanted to work with it. They also liked the sweeping apprentice, but nearly no one actually wanted to work with. As for the balloon no clear statement can be made. People liked it, but were rather undecided whether they wanted to work with it. In my opinion not many people want to work with this progress indicator, as they became rather impatient during the long action and they also ranked the balloon rather badly in connection with time shortening. Table 4 gives the statistic information about the performance indicators.

| Method \ how much liked? | very much | much | rather | not much | little | not |
|---|---|---|---|---|---|---|
| clock | 2 | 0 | 2 | 8 | 3 | 6 |
| apprentice | 0 | 3 | 7 | 6 | 2 | 3 |
| balloon | 2 | 5 | 6 | 1 | 4 | 3 |
| thermometer | 2 | 10 | 5 | 2 | 1 | 1 |
| tone scale | 3 | 4 | 2 | 5 | 3 | 4 |
| blossom | 8 | 2 | 3 | 2 | 3 | 3 |
| Method \ want to work with? | very much | much | rather | not much | little | not |
| clock | 1 | 4 | 6 | 3 | 4 | 3 |
| apprentice | 0 | 1 | 4 | 5 | 6 | 5 |
| balloon | 2 | 4 | 6 | 3 | 4 | 2 |
| thermometer | 0 | 11 | 5 | 3 | 0 | 2 |
| tone scale | 5 | 2 | 0 | 3 | 5 | 6 |
| blossom | 5 | 4 | 0 | 4 | 6 | 2 |

**Table 4.:** Results on how much people liked the various methods and how much the wanted to work with it.

Concerning the progress indicators the thermometer was liked most. Not only that people liked its design, they actually wanted to work with it. The blossom was also liked very much, but not many people wanted to work with it, too. The tone scale wasn't a very big success as the users, though they felt it shortened the time, had the feeling of not being informed or having made a mistake and therefore didn't want to work with it. This shows that the use of sound for such purposes is not a trivial thing to do. Probably the example was not well chosen. Used as is it can only be an assistance to some visual information, but it would be interesting to try out other examples of sound progress indicators in the future. Table 4 shows the results on how much people like each method and how much they want to work with them.

The results on the whole were not very significant, on the one hand due to the small number of people tested and on the other hand caused by some not totally clearly formulated questions, but one could see trends and for some aspects even draw conclusions. If the test were run again with improved questions and a bigger number of people, one could make clearer statements.

## 6 Conclusions

The test has shown that it makes sense to think about the design of performance and progress indicators although they seem so small and unimportant. But they are the carriers of a certain piece of information, namely that the system is busy. Therefore using the most common methods is a poor solution as users possibly prefer other methods more and feel better informed by them. It also seems reasonable to use both types of indicators in an application, one for the short actions and the other for actions that take longer.

The search for more alternatives has shown that there certainly exists more than just clocks and bars. One just has to think and search a little while. Of course not every solution is suitable for every application, but it is the duty of a responsible user interface designer to think about the best solution for his purpose and not just to adopt the most widely used ones.

## 7 References

1.  Baecker R., Small I., Mander R.: Bringing Icons To Life in: Robertson S.P., Olson G., Olson J.S. (Editors): Reaching Through Technology, CHI '91 Conference Proceedings, ACM, Addison Wesley Publishing Company, 1991, p. 1-6

2.  Buxton B., Gaver B., Bly S.: The Use of Non-Speech Audio ar the Interface, CHI '90 Tutorial Notes, Seattle, 1990

3.  CorelDRAW! 2.0, Corel Systems Corporation, 1990

4.  Systems Application Architecture, Common User Access, Advanced Interface Design Guide, IBM, 1989

5.  Battlechess, Interplay, 1988

6.  Inside Macintosh, Volume 1-5, Apple Computer, 1985

7.    Microsoft Windows Software Development Kit, Version 2.0., Application
      Style Guide, Microsoft, 1987

8.    Muller M.J.: Multifunctional Cursor for Direct Manipulation User Interfaces
      in: Soloway E., Faye D., Sheppard S.B. (Editors): Human Factors in Computer
      Systems, CHI '88 Proceedings, ACM, Addison Wesley Publishing Company,
      1988, p. 89-94

9.    Myers B.A.: The Importance of Percent Done Progress Indicators for
      Computer Human Interfaces in: CHI '85 Conference Proceedings, 1985, p.
      11-17

10.   Leisure Suit Larry 3, Sierra On-Line Inc., 1989

11.   Shneiderman B.: Designing the User Interface, Strategies for Effective
      Human-Computer Interaction, 2nd Edition, Addison Wesley Publishing
      Company, 1992

12.   OPEN LOOK Graphical User Interface, Functional Specification, Sun
      Microsystems, 1989

# The Problems of Untrained Authors Creating Hypertext Documents

Margit Pohl        Peter Purgathofer

University of Technology Vienna
Dep. Design and Assessment of Technology
A-1040    Möllwaldplatz 4/187    Vienna, Austria
email: pohl@iguwnext.tuwien.ac.at        purg@iguwnext.tuwien.ac.at
Fax: +43 1 5041188

**Abstract.** One of the main arguments for the introduction of hypertext is that developing hypertext documents is more natural than writing linear text because information is stored in human memory in the form of semantic nets. There is still little practical evidence for this hypothesis. At our institute we asked the students to create hypertext documents instead of writing traditional seminar papers. Our experience indicates that the transition from text to hypertext is very complicated, and that especially untrained authors have difficulties creating hypertext documents. A possible solution for this problem is the use of an authoring tool with restricted functions.

**Keywords.** hypertext, hypermedia, authoring systems, learning   models, evaluation methods and tools, user models.

## 1. Introduction

One of the main arguments for the introduction of hypertext concepts is that developing hypertext documents is more natural than writing linear text because information is stored in human memory in the form of semantic nets. Practical evidence for this hypothesis could be the fact that authors usually do not just start to write linear text but rather make notes or write a concept at first. The idea is that information is stored in chunks in human memory, and that these chunks are connected more or less strongly. The process of authoring consists in bringing these chunks of information into a rational and comprehensible order. But there is so far little empirical evidence for this process (For a critical discussion of this hypothesis see [5]).

Moreover, the process of authoring, especially when inexperienced authors are concerned, was not studied as intensively as for example learning from already existing hypermedia systems [6]. Nielsen also points out that it is more plausible to assume that linear texts are written more easily because it has been learned since childhood "through writing endless numbers of essays in school". Furthermore, there are studies which indicate that the process of developing a hypertext document is a very complicated one. Rada et al in a study on collaborative writing [7] found that building a semantic net is as sophisticated an activity as developing an index for a book. One of the main problems of the students was how to create and use links.

The following text describes our experience at the Institute for Design and Technology Assessment at the Technical University of Vienna with the introduction of a hypertext system as a means of writing seminar papers. The system used was Hypercard for the Macintosh. This experiment is part of the development of a comprehensive information system for our institute that is meant for research as well as for instructional purposes. One of the main advantages of this project directed by Prof. Peter Fleissner is its ecological validity. The whole project is part of the day to day work of the institute. The entire work on this system - the development as well as the evaluation of the usability of the system - is financed by the "Fonds zur Förderung der wissenschaftlichen Forschung".

In the following we will discuss the reason for the transition from linear text to hypertext, the main problems that arise, the reaction from the students and possible means to overcome the difficulties.

## 2. Institutional Setting

The original aim of the use of a hypertext system was to store every (more or less) scientific work performed at our institute in an easily accessible way. The hypertext concept was chosen because of its interactive quality and its advantages for learning, especially for more advanced students. It can be shown [4] that linear text is more efficient for reproductive memory tests. On the other hand hypertext structures lead to superior performance in more complex tasks when students were asked to write an essay and develop their own ideas. Originally the usability study which accompanies the implementation of the system was planned to test these assumed advantages. In the course of the research process we realised that there was another serious problem we had not anticipated - the writing of hypertext documents by inexperienced authors.

Most of the students who attend our seminars study computer science. On the other hand only a few have experience with Macintosh (Only 3.3% had experience with Macintosh computers to a high degree, 9.7% to a medium degree and 87% to a low degree or no experience at all). The numbers for the variable "Experience with Hypercard" are even worse. About half of them had never heard of Hypertext or Hypermedia. As a consequence, most of them had serious difficulties in writing hypertext documents. Basically there were two groups of problems. The first one was the use of Macintosh and Hypercard as such. And the second one was the concept of hypertext. Apparently, the idea of hypertext is not self-evident and has to be explained in great detail. Roulet [9] points out that the use of hypertext systems requires a lot of cognitive monitoring, a term that is meant to describe the subjects' awareness over their own cognitive processes. This awareness varies according to individual or situational factors and might therefore be the reason for the fact that usability studies concerning hypertext often yield insignificant results. One of the main difficulties was the transformation of linear text, the form in which the students had presented their papers, into hypertext. This process is a very complicate one as Rada describes it in his article [8] and comprises at least two stages. The first stage leads from linear text to first-order hypertext and includes links that are explicitly present in the text as for example headings or footnotes. Second order hypertext also includes links that are not explicit in the text as for example links that may be derived from word pattern. Our experience indicates that inexperienced users very often do not even take into account elements of first-order hypertext.

## 3. Three Generations of Authoring Tools

Since students at our institute had to write hypertext-documents from the very beginning of the project, we decided to support them in their task with an authoring tool. As mentioned above, one of the main problems of the students was the use of the Macintosh and Hypercard as such. The authoring tool was meant to overcome this problem and to enable us to concentrate on the difficulties in the creation of hypertext documents in the research process The development of an appropriate authoring tool is part of the project itself, so we simultaneously used the students as testers and evaluators for our implementation of an authoring tool. The three generations of the program that were used are described in the following passage.

### 3.1. First Generation

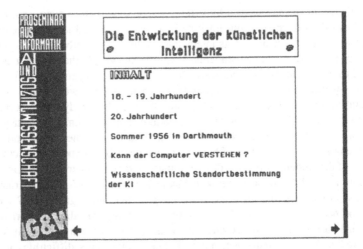

**Fig. 1.** Typical screenshot of a first generation document. Note that the authors had total freedom in the placement of text on the card.

In the very beginning of the project, the first students had to cope with the situation of having almost no authoring support. The project had not even started regularly, and the institute was new, thus having no structures to build upon. When we decided to initiate the project we had almost no resources and only small personpower to invest into the development of an appropriate tool. But it was our belief that students of computer science would be able to master the situation of being left unassisted with a few technical tools for the nontechnical task of writing their seminar papers.

As a consequence the first generation authoring tool fulfilled only the most basic needs of the authors. It consisted of a Hypercard stack with only one background and a single card. Adding nodes to the document was achieved by adding new cards to the stack. Two background buttons were available on every card to jump to the next resp.

previous card. There were no fields, neither in the background nor on the card.

On the creation of a new card the user was asked for the name of this card which was entirely internal and used only for linking cards. To enter text on a card the user had to create a new field which was equipped with a script that enabled her/him to fill in link anchor words and destinations for links they wanted to appear in the text. Text fields were allowed to have scroll bars and to contain up to 30.000 characters.

Apart from handing a copy of this stack to each group of (two) students, we gave them a lecture on how to create links in Hypercard stacks (appr. 35 minutes) and general hypertext issues (appr. 20 minutes). With these prerequisites students implemented fifteen stacks which we call the first generation stacks.

As we will see in detail later, first generation stacks have the smallest number of cards and links, and least complexity.

## 3.2. Second Generation

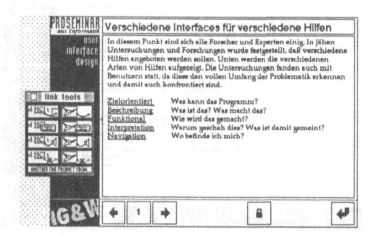

**Fig. 2.** Typical generation two screenshot. The Symbol that looks like a small bag in the lower part of the picture is supposed to be a padlock, switching between unlocked (authors) and locked (readers) mode.

Until the next seminar six months later we had enough time to implement a first prototype of a real authoring tool (which we named „link tools") based upon the experiences with the first generation. "Link tools" was a palette that was available in copies of a special Hypercard stack, still giving the full Hypercard functionality to the author. It offered tools to create button links or text links, tools to integrate sounds and to show hidden fields where the authors could enter special information (annotations, comments, bibliographical information).

In addition we decided to stop the freedom of text positioning. We restricted text entry to two predefined, fixed fields, one for the headline, and one for floating text. The first field allowed only one line of text in large letters, the second field was designed to hold 18 lines of text.

For the sake of easy navigation during the process of authoring we added three buttons that were available on every card: "go to the next card", "go to the previous card" and "go to the first card" (which served as a table of contents) respectively. Our intention was to disable the first two buttons for readers, so that navigation was only possible by using the hypertext links. This led to the necessity of distinguishing two modes: authoring and browsing. One could switch between these two modes by clicking the symbol of an open/locked padlock.

After giving a short (appr. 15 min.) demonstration of the tool and a brief talk about hypertext in general (same as above) we again handed a copy of the tool to the students. This resulted in nine stacks of the second generation.

Stacks authored using this tool are generally more complex than first generation stacks.

### 3.3. Third Generation

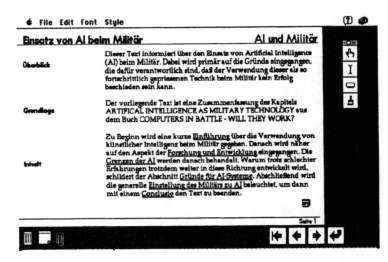

**Fig. 3.** A third generation document. Note the annotational tools in the bottom left of the picture, as well as the little annotation icon in the lower right corner of the text area.

The first two generations gave us enough material to redefine our concept of the authoring tool. One of our main problems seemed to be the limitation to two modes (authoring and browsing). In the new tool there are four modes. Authors can choose between browsing, text mode, button mode and paint mode.

Browsing is used to follow links and test the system. It is the only mode that is permitted to the readers. The text tool enables the user to type text into fields and create text links. In a similar way it is possible to create buttons and links from buttons with the button tool. Finally, the paint tool simply made the Hypercard paint tools available to the author.

The most obvious change from the previous system was that we removed all unnecessary menu options from the menubar. In this way, we enforced the authors' impression of using a separate hypertext writing tool instead of messing around with Hypercard (as with the first generation). We added some new tool-dependent menus to activate certain functions specific to that program. By enhancing the existing navigational buttons (next/previous/first card) by a button to go back in trail of visited cards we added another element to the interface. Furthermore, we started to implement a function for the reader to interactively express his/her opinion in the document. The interface elements for this function resemble a bunch of post-it notes (annotations), paper clips (bookmarks) and a trash to remove existing post-it notes/paper clips. Since these elements are meant as a support for the reader, we prohibited the authors from using them while writing their documents.

As in the second generation the tool was demonstrated to the students. This was followed by a talk about general hypertext issues. Because this tool was meant to have a more or less final character we also wrote a short user manual and gave this to the students. Since our deadline for the submission of this year's documents is still not over we only had six stacks of the third generation available for this study.

These stacks are, compared to generation one and two stacks, more elaborated and consits of more nodes and links. The following part of this paper deals with the comparison of each generations stacks and our interpretation of this information for the development of a new generation of the authoring tool.

## 4. Three Generations of Students' Documents

The process of evolution of the authoring tool had massive impact on the documents that were written by students. Generally we observed an improvement in document quality and a decrease in diversity hand in hand with „persistent" errors we have not been able to eliminate yet . This process will be discussed further in the following passage.

While we have two documents from the first generation that do not contain any links at all  no such failure occurs in later stacks. A similar phenomenon is that there are some stacks with isolated subtrees in the first two generations, but no such stack in the third generation. While there are several stacks from generation one that contain dead end cards (cards with no link anchors), this mistake was eliminated in the following generations by adding general navigational buttons (jump to the first card, go back). Generally the number of links (but not necessarily the quality of links) increased from an average 1.2 links/card in generation one to 1.8 links/card in the third generation. The increase in the average number of cards that was 13.4 in first generation stacks and 18.2 in third generation documents shows a similar development. It is important to remember that the number of nodes and/or links in a hypertext system is generally no measurement of quality; what we may conclude is that with the increase of author's support by the software there is also an increase in the number of nodes and links created by an author. It is somewhat obvious that when it is easy to create links, one will create links. Nevertheless, the best stack created during the project is one from the third generation.

# 5. Reactions of the Students

To get a first and quick overview on the reactions of the students we developed a short questionnaire. Its most important aim is to find out the subjective views of the students on their work with a hypertext system and to get hints about the most serious problems. Generally one gets the impression that the students are moderately content to work with hypertext and would be interested to work with the system that is being created. Apparently for many of them working with a hypertext system was not an annoying duty but a creative task as can be seen from the additional comments they made on the questionnaire.

In the following we will present a few of the most important results of the questionnaire:

**Question**: To get a clear overview of a text would you prefer linear text or hypertext?

| | |
|---|---|
| Hypertext | 74.1% |
| No preferences | 6.5% |
| Linear text | 9.7% |
| I do not know | 9.7% |

**Table 1**: Preference for linear text/hypertext

There is a clear preference for hypertext as regards comprehensible structures.

**Question**: Is it useful to develop seminar papers in the form of hypertext rather than in the form of linear text?.

| | |
|---|---|
| Hypertext | 41.9% |
| No preferences | 45.2% |
| Linear Text | 9.7% |
| I do not know | 3.2% |

**Table 2**: Usability of hypertext for seminar papers

The result of this question is not so clear. Although a relative majority prefers hypertext, there are also many students who have no preferences.

The most important disadvantage of the model "seminar papers as hypertext" lies in the fact that the documents are too short to think of really useful links (Most of the documents consist of seven to twelve nodes). At least, this is the subjective view of the students.

Another interesting result concerns the concepts the students use when they create nodes. They can be divided roughly into five categories:

1. Link from a word to an explanation or definition
2. Creation of a hierarchical link structure
3. Categories 1 and 2 together
4. Intuition
5. Links between topics that occur frequently

**Table 3**: Concepts used for links

If we only consider the subjective impression of the students links of category 1 were most frequently used in hypertext documents. Intuition on the other hand was only mentioned by one student as the concept for the creation of links.

In addition, the students made many positive and also many critical remarks. One student found that using hypertext was not advisable because it was impossible to develop a consistent structure from so many different documents. Many of them mentioned that a decision for or against hypertext always depended on the quality of the hypertext that would be created. One student wrote that in hypertext information cannot be really "comprehended" or "perceived". Some of the students remarked that hypertext was hard to learn but also an interesting and new alternative.

These first results of our questionnaire can be interpreted as a moderate support for our concept of writing seminar papers as hypertexts. On the other hand the criticism of the students must be taken seriously. They need more help in the form of software tools and structured lectures.

## 6. Main Problems of the Students

We observed some typical problems of the students writing hypertext which changed over the generations of our project. In the following we will describe some of these problems and possible/realised solutions for them.

**Structure of the document:** One of the main difficulties of the students was the transformation of linear text to hypertext. Usually, they stuck very much to the text of their seminar papers.

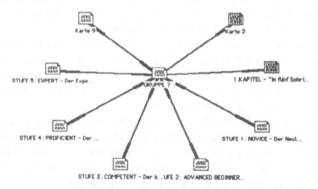

**Fig. 4.** Linear Structure in a hypertext document of generation one.
In this graph, the thick end of a link shows its direction.

Most of them only made links explicitly present in the text (first-order hypertext) as for example a table of contents leading to the separate chapters or links between two cards containing the same term. They very seldom restructured their linear text fundamentally to adapt the structure to the new medium. Looking at the documents of our students one would rather come to the conclusion that information is stored in the brain in the form of a stream of unstructured thoughts than in the form of semantic nets. As a consequence, in many stacks there is a contradiction between medium and organisation of the text, and the structure of the document is not clear. Furthermore, the students were apparently not able to anticipate the "lost-in-hyperspace" problem, and organised their cards rather arbitrarily, made no overview cards, and used no consistent principles for the cards or buttons. One possible solution for this problem could be the use of templates - "sets of pre-linked documents which can be duplicated". [2]

**Links:** Typed links are considered being a good method of structuring the hyperspace with only little additional cognitive load on the reader. Up to now link typing in our authoring tool was only possible by the distinction between text links and button links although it is possible to find out the type of link by looking at the node it is pointing at.

A qualitative look at the students' links showed that only a few different types of links were used. This is also enforced by the results of the evaluation of the questionnaire (See 5.). There are, for example, (almost) no links leading to nodes with opposing points of view, even if the material contains such information. Apparently, the students' use of links is rather restricted and not very creative. One reason for this might be that students generally have problems to express their thoughts in a concise manner and to perceive relations between different topics. But this ability, in our opinion, is a condition for developing a meaningful link structure. Another reason probably is that there is no hypertext literacy among the students. Nonetheless we believe that this problem can be solved (at least partly) by certain functions of the authoring tool.

[10] suggest that the usage of explicitly typed (and labelled) links helps authors to overcome such limitations. Since we consider this a fairly good idea, we are going to implement a similar solution with our new authoring tool.

The specific idea for our solution comes from one student who wanted to use explicitly typed links in her (third generation) document. To achieve this aim, she used the readers' annotation tool. Since these annotations look different from authors' button-links she had achieved two different anchors for different kinds of links, a feature she used for structuring the hyperspace.

This induced us to use the easily comprehensible interface objects for readers and conceptualised an object oriented interface for the next generation of our authoring tool. Within this solution we can represent different types of links (e.g. links to facts, to further elaboration, to details, to overviews) as different interface objects, thus encouraging the usage of different link types in the document.

**Linkfree hypertext, isolated nodes/subtrees:** In our first generation system authors had to create nodes (cards) before he/she connected them with links. This led to the existence of documents in which certain nodes could not be accessed by following links (except, of course, by using the next/previous buttons). One document did not even have one single link. This problem was solved in later systems. In these systems the creation of a card was only possible when a link pointing to this card was defined.

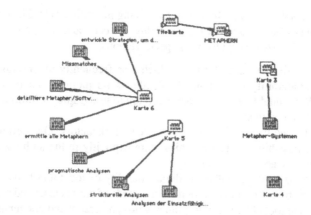

**Fig. 5.** Lost substructures in a generation two document. Again, the thick end of a line stands for the direction of the represented link.

This minor change drastically influenced the way hyperdocuments were written. While in generation one most students first created all nodes before interlinking them, in generation three this was impossible. Authors had to link while writing, thus being endangered of getting lost in hyperspace as much as the reader. Anyway, there are no lost substructures any more.

**Navigational problems of authors and readers:** To evaluate the students' documents we implemented a small graphical drawing tool that is capable of drawing a simple map of a document, thus revealing its link structure to us. We found this tool to be extremely useful, so we want to incorporate it in the future system. It is supposed to be used by the author to create a (manually) optimised map of his/her stack. This map will be integrated into the stack as an overview card for the browsers. Furthermore, authors can check their own documents for typical hypertext errors (which will be shown in written form).

Apart from that we noticed that quite a few errors result from the possibility to page through the document using the next/previous card buttons. These „hard" links, or rather their frequent usage by the authors, impose a linear structure upon the document that should not be there.

Our suggestion for a solution of this problem is to remove those buttons even for the authors. We will instead provide them with a popup-menu of all nodes which they can use to jump directly to a card.

**Text:** Another typical error was connected with the amount of information, that could be placed on a card. Since it was possible to put up to 30.000 chars in a scroll field onto a single card, some of the stacks had only a few cards, almost no links and an almost linear structure.

Combined with this problem is the ingenuity of the authors as regards the positioning of text on the cards. We have documents where the text is in different locations on every card. In this case, there is apparently a contradiction between user friendliness and flexibility of the instrument.

We tried to solve these problems by restraining the author [11]. She/he now has to use the given size and location of the text fields on a card, and is not allowed to change the typeface or its size (except for very special reasons).

**Graphics:** Unlike the use of sound which was frequently incorporated from the moment of availability (generation two), almost no pictures can be found in the documents. We would like to encourage authors to use graphical information as well as maybe video or animation.

In this case we have no solution that seems satisfactory. Our current idea is to point out the possibility to use graphics more explicitly to the authors; furthermore they will have free access to a scanner.

This leads us to the problem of the availability of tools and know-how for the students. In the past, we tried to anticipate the needs of our students and provided them with appropriate tools like paint programs, word processors and conversion software. In the future, we are going to collect the requirements by a questionnaire. This method enables us not only to provide tools, but also the know-how to perform all necessary steps to create multimedia hypertext.

Last, but not least, examples will play a central role in our future system. Since there is still no comprehensive theory about what constitutes good hypertext, the best way for students to learn this is browsing in other writers' hypertext [6]. Therefore, considerable effort will be necessary to create instructive examples.

## 7. Conclusion

When we started using hypertext for students' seminar papers we had two aims. One of these aims was to change students' attitudes to their seminar papers and to induce them to be more precise about what they want to say. The other aim was to gain a more efficient access to students' work ourselves. The experiment yielded interesting results and seems, at least in tendency, to be successful. Until now, we have about 30 documents from this project. The documents give us new insights into the process of authoring hypertext by untrained authors. They enabled us to refine our authoring tool by providing direct and indirect feedback about authoring support in the different systems to us.

Our future system will make extensive use of a straight, interface object oriented approach that, as we believe, will increase ease of use as well as the general document quality.

For future evaluation we plan to use system logging of authors as well as readers actions. Furthermore we currently try to implement other methods for the analysis of hyperdocuments as suggested by [1].

Our experiences do not support the hypothesis that hypertext is more natural than writing linear text. If the semantic net model of human memory is correct the relation between learning and storing information must be more complicated than previously assumed. Furthermore, our experiences indicate that the problems of untrained authors of hypertext documents are a topic that in the future should be studied more thoroughly.

# References

1. R.A. Botafogo, E. Rivlin, B. Shneiderman: Structural Analysis of Hypertexts: Identifying Hierarchies and Useful Metrics. In: ACM Transactions on Information Systems V10, N2, 142-180 (1992)

2. K.S. Catlin, L.N. Garrett, J.A. Launhardt: Hypermedia Templates: An Author's Tool. In: Hypertext 91. Third ACM Conference on Hypertext - Proceedings. San Anonio, Texas December 15-18 1991, pp. 147-160

3. R.E. Horn: Mapping Hypertext. Analysis, Linkage, and Display of Knowledge for the Next Generation of On-Line Text and Graphics() Lexington, MA, The Lexington Institute 1989

4. R.A. Jones, R. Spiro: Imagined Conversations: The Relevance of Hypertext, Pragmatism, and Cognitive Flexibility Theory to the Interpretation of "Classic Texts" in Intellectual History. In: D. Lucarella, J. Nanard, M. Nanard, P. Paolini (eds.): Proceeding of the ACM Conference on Hypertext. Milano 1992, pp. 141-148

5. R. Kuhlen: Hypertext. Ein nichtlieares Medium zwischen Buch und Wissensbank. Berlin, Heidelberg, New York: Springer 1991

6. J. Nielsen: Hypertext & Hypermedia. Boston: Academic Press 1990

7. R. Rada, B. Keith, M. Burgoine, St. George, D. Reid: Collaborative writing of text and hypertext. In: Hypermedia Vol. 1, No. 2 (1989), 93-110

8. R. Rada: Converting a Textbook to Hypertext. In: ACM Transactions on Information Systems, Vol. 10, No.3, July (1992), 294-315

9. J.-F. Rouet: Cognitive Processing of Hyperdocuments: When Does Nonlinearity Help? In: D. Lucarella, J. Nanard, M. Nanard, P. Paolini (eds.): Proceeding of the ACM Conference on Hypertext. Milano 1992, pp. 131-140

10. M. Thuring, J.M. Haake, J. Hannemann: What's Eliza Doing in the Chinese Room? Incoherent Hyperdocuments -- and How to Avoid Them. In: Hypertext 91. Third ACM Conference on Hypertext - Proceedings. San Anonio, Texas December 15-18, 1991, pp. 161-177

11. K. Andrews, F. Kappe: Straight-Jacketing the Authors: User Interface Consisitency in Large Scale Hypermedia Systems. In: H.P. Frei, P. Schäuble (eds.) HyperMedia Proceedings der Internationalen Hypermedia '93 Konferenz, Zürich, 2./3. März, Berlin: Springer 1993, pp.130-137

# STUDYING THE DEVELOPER

# What is so Special About Exceptional Software Professionals?

Sabine Sonnentag

Department of Psychology, University of Giessen
Otto-Behaghel-Str. 10/F, D-35394 Giessen, Germany
email: sabine.sonnentag@psychol.uni-giessen.d400.de

**Abstract.** This paper concerns differences in action styles and psychological well-being between exceptional and average software professionals. A field study with 33 exceptional and 80 average software professionals was done. The study shows that exceptional persons are neither more planful nor more goal oriented than their colleagues. But they experience a higher psychological well-being. Additionally, exceptional software professionals show less irritation/strain when their goal orientation is high, while there is no association between goal orientation and irritation/strain in average software professionals. Consequences for the selection and the work situation of exceptional software professionals are derived.

## 1 Introduction

### 1.1 Previous Research

The development of modern software systems requires highly skilled and competent people. Many authors emphasize the importance of 'good', 'great' or 'exceptional' designers for the success of a software development project [2, 3, 5]. Therefore the question raises what characterizes such exceptional software professionals. This question is essential for managers of software development projects selecting team members, for educational institutions thinking about adequate curricula, and for software professionals as well wishing to improve their competence. It is also of relevance to the research on human-computer interaction since it incorporates the investigation of individual differences into the growing body of knowledge about developmental and design processes.

Regarding the empirical literature on expertise in software design and programming there are mainly three different types of studies:

(1)    Comparisons between novices and experts, i.e. comparisons between beginners in computer science or programming and advanced students or professionals (e.g. [11, 15, 19])

(2)     Comparisons between high and low performance software professionals while performing an experimental task (e.g. [21, 22])

(3)     Case studies of persons who are assumed to be very good software designers (e.g. [1]).

The different kinds of studies show that experienced and high performance persons have more specific knowledge, show better problem solving strategies, and have a more abstract representation of programs. However, in these studies the subjects had to perform relatively simple tasks in experimental settings. Therefore there is only little knowledge how exceptional software professionals proceed in their everyday work situation where the tasks are more complex and high communication requirements occur.

Curtis et al. [5] conducted a field study in 17 software development projects. They reported that exceptional designers had an excellent knowledge about the application domain of the software, they showed very good communication skills, and did much of the design work while communicating with others. Additionally, they revealed a high identification with the project. While the focus of Curtis et al. was on aspects of communication and application domain knowledge little is known about other characteristics of exceptional designers. In this paper action styles such as planfulness and goal orientation, and disturbances of psychological well-being will be examined. Disturbances of psychological well-being are not only subjectively important for the individual, they may also have an impact on performance, absenteeism, and turnover rates.

## 1.2  Action Styles

Exceptional software professionals may differ in their action styles from the average software professional. Action styles can be described as propensities to act. Two important action styles are planfulness and goal orientation [10]. Planfulness refers to the way a person plans his or her actions, goal orientation refers to the way of setting goals. Studies with various samples showed substantial associations between a person's performance on the one hand and his or her planfulness and goal orientation on the other hand [9, 10].

Also for the domain of software development it can be assumed that planfulness and goal orientation are essential for high performance. Vitalari and Dickson [22] found that high performance system analysts showed more goal setting behavior than low performance persons. Vessey [21] reported that good programmers' approaches to debugging and problem solving were 'disciplined' without changing the reference point within a program too often. This can be seen as a sign of planfulness. These results were found in experimental studies with relatively simple tasks. Data from complex tasks in professional software development are needed to generalize these findings.

## 1.3 Disturbances of Psychological Well-Being

In many studies associations between the work situation, disturbances of psychological well-being, and other strain variables were found [7, 17]. This is also true for software professionals [18, 23]. But there is no research on the work-related psychological well-being of exceptional software professionals. Two contrary results are possible. On the one hand exceptional software professionals may have a reduced psychological well-being since they are intensively involved in the stressful development process. This assumption is shared by Curtis et al. [5]. On the other hand it is possible that very good software professionals show a better psychological well-being because that have more effective problem solving strategies that help them coping with stressors and difficulties [13].

# 2 Method

## 2.1 Sample

In this study data of 33 exceptional and 80 average software professionals were compared[1]. These 113 persons worked in 25 software development projects from 17 German and Swiss companies. In the various projects software was produced for a broad application domain (e.g., administration, applications in the domain of banks and insurances). The software was to be produced for end users who were usually not software professionals. The project size ranged between 3 and 17 members (mean=9,3). Among the 113 subjects were 79 system designers and programmers, 34 team and subteam leaders. The average age of the subjects was 33 years, the average experience in software development projects was 5,6 years. Eighty percent of the subjects were male, 20 % were female.

## 2.2 Measures

**Identification of exceptional software professionals.** In order to identify exceptional software professionals a 'peer nomination' method was used. In previous studies peer nomination methods revealed satisfying validity measures [6,

---

1   This sample is a subsample of 200 software professionals who were studied by the project IPAS (a German acronym of "Interdisciplinary Project about the Work Situation in Software Development"). The project IPAS consists of a computer science part (University of Marburg: U. Bittner, W. Hesse, J. Schnath), a social science part (SPG Sozialwissenschaftliche Projektgruppe, Munich: F. Weltz, R. Ortmann), and a work psychology part (University of Giessen: F.C. Brodbeck, M. Frese, T. Heinbokel, S. Sonnentag, W. Stolte). The project is supported by a grant from the Work and Technology Fund of the Ministry of Research and Technology of the Federal Republic of Germany (No. 01 HK 319). The author takes the responsibility for this publication.

16]. In the present study members from 29 software development projects were asked during an interview: "Which person of your team is a very good software professional"? For every person in the sample it was computed by how many persons he or she was described to be a very good software professional. Persons named at least by two different team colleagues were categorized as exceptional software professionals. Those who were not cited at all were categorized as average software professionals. Persons named only once were excluded from further analysis. In four teams less than 50 % of the questioned members regarded someone to be a very good software professional. All members of these teams and also user representatives were excluded from the analysis as well. Therefore the analysis was done with 113 persons from 25 projects. Because of missing data the degrees of freedom in the analyses are slightly differing.

**Action styles.** Planfulness and goal orientation were measured with two questionnaire scales developed by Frese et al. [10]. The scale planfulness comprises 8 items (e.g. "I think quite a while how I am going to do it"; 5-point Likert items), the scale goal orientation 6 items (e.g. "I take all my goals very seriously"; 5-point Likert items). The subjects related their answers to specific tasks (e.g. designing, programming, testing a module), but it can be assumed that these actions styles have a cross situational generality [10]. In the present study planfulness and goal orientation did not differ across the various tasks ($F(7,108)=.60$; n.s. for planfulness and $F(7,108)=1.26$; n.s. for goal orientation respectively). In this sample Cronbach's Alpha was .71 for goal orientation and .63 for planfulness. Frese et al. have shown that these self report measures of planfulness and goal orientation are correlated with ratings by peers and observers in a quasi experimental situation.

**Disturbances of Psychological Well-Being.** For assessing disturbances of psychological well-being a scale developed by Mohr [20] was used. This scale is called "irritation/strain". It comprises 8 items (7-point Likert items) and measures the exhaustion of psychic resources (Cronbach's Alpha=.85). Since disturbances of psychological well-being can be caused by a stressful work situation also stressors and overtime were assessed. Stressors were ascertained by a 20-item scale comprising items such as "I have too much work" and "Informations come too late or are too vague" [8]. Cronbach's Alpha was .88. Overtime was measured by a single questionnaire item.

## 2.3  Design

It can be assumed that action styles and disturbances of psychological well-being are not only associated with one's competence but also with his or her tasks in the project. For example planning is crucial for team and subteam leaders. Additionally, it is possible that team leaders experience more disturbances of well-being as a consequence of a more stressful work situation. Therefore a person's function in the project (system designer or programmer, team or subteam leader) was also taken into account. An anova design resulted with two factors: competence (exceptional vs. average software professional) and function in the project (system designer or programmer vs. team or subteam leader).

# 3 Results and Discussion

Compared with systems analysts and programmers leaders of teams and subteams were more often regarded to be exceptional software professionals by at least two team members (Chi$^2$=10.17; df=1; p<.01). This is not surprising since normally persons who show high performances are promoted and become team or subteam leaders.

## 3.1 Action Styles

Figure 1 shows that across both functions exceptional persons were not more planful than others (F(1,98)=.71; n.s.). There was also no effect of the function in the project (F(1,98)=2.34; n.s.). Concerning goal orientation there were no main effects neither for competence (F(1,96)=.00; n.s.) nor for the function in the project (F(1,96)=.02; n.s.; Figure 2).

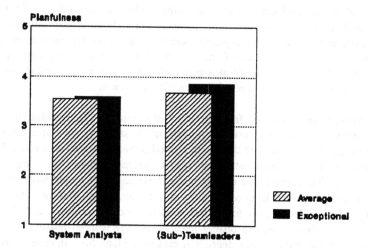

Fig. 1. Means of Planfulness

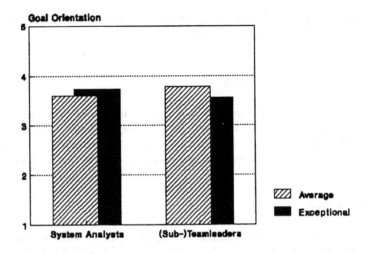

**Fig. 2.** Means of Goal Orientation

This means that - contrary to the assumptions - exceptional software professionals are not more planful and goal oriented than others. One reason for this could be that planful and goal oriented behavior is well trained in nearly all software professionals and forced by development methods (e.g. structured programming) so that there is no essential effect of the individual competence. Alternatively it is possible that because of the 'philosophy' of structured programming subjects reported to work top-down and planful, even if they did not.

Another reason can be derived from the work of Guindon [12]. She described that highly experienced designers used an opportunistic strategy and not a top-down decomposition. This means that they often shifted between various abstraction levels and began with low level activities before having finished the high level decomposition. Therefore in the questionnaire these designers would have probably reported a low or medium level of planfulness. Hornby, Clegg, Robson, MacLaren, Richardson, and O'Brien [14] found that relatively novice analysts tended to use methods 'by the book', what probably means that they worked relatively planful. Thus, it is possible that the same degrees of measured planfulness in exceptional and average software professionals are due to two different underlying planning processes.

Exceptional and other software professionals do not differ in the *way* they pursue goals. But it can not be excluded that the *content* of their goals differs and that exceptional software professionals orient their actions towards more important and promising goals. It is also possible that exceptional persons have more knowledge and more skills that allow them actually achieving their goals.

Additionally, it must be taken into account that possibly planfulness and goal orientation have other consequences for exceptional software professionals than for others. This aspect will be examined in the next subsection.

## 3.2 Disturbances of psychological well-being

The differences in disturbances of psychological well-being for the various groups are presented in Figure 3. Exceptional software professionals showed less irritation/strain than average persons $(F(1,97)=5.96; p<.05)$. Additionally system analysts and programmers had lower scores than team and subteam leaders $(F(1,97)=4.01; p<.05)$.

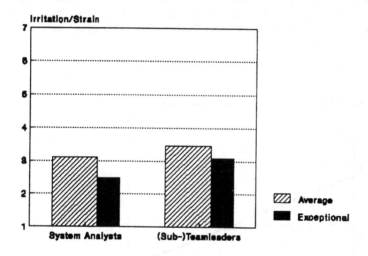

**Fig. 3.** Means of Irritation/Strain

The effect of competence remained stable when perceived stressors or overtime were introduced as covariates in the analysis of variance. This means that the lower scores on irritation/strain of exceptional software professionals were not due to less stressful work situations. In contrary the effect of the function in the project disappeared when perceived stressors or overtime were taken into account. Thus, the higher irritation/strain of team and subteam leaders reflected their more stressful work situation.

Since exceptional software professionals do not have a less stressful work situation but lower irritation/strain scores one can assume that they have better possibilities to cope with difficulties and stressors. Generally, planfulness and goal orientation might be helpful in order to avoid strain, but it was shown that exceptional persons are not more planful or more goal oriented than others. Additionally, it must be considered that action styles could have different effects for exceptional and average software professionals.

In order to test this last assumption a moderated regression analysis was done [4]. The dependent measure was irritation/strain. In a hierarchical procedure first perceived stressors, goal orientation and planfulness respectively, competence, and function were entered into the equation. In the second step the interaction term (competence with goal orientation and competence with planfulness respectively) was entered. The analysis revealed - besides the generally lower irritation/strain scores in exceptional persons and the effect of perceived stressors - a significant interaction effect of competence and goal orientation ($R=.45$; $R^2=.21$; Change of $R^2=.06$; Beta of interaction term=-1.38; $p<.05$). This effect held for system

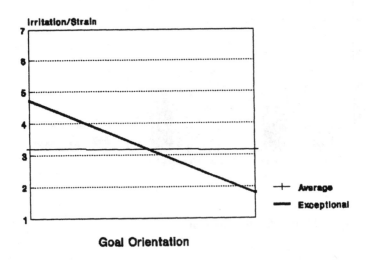

**Fig. 4.** Interaction Effect of Competence and Goal Orientation.

analysts and programmers and team and subteam leaders alike. For planfulness no interaction effect with competence was found. The interaction effect of competence and goal orientation means that in exceptional software professionals high goal orientation was associated with low irritation/strain - and vice versa - while there was not such an association in average software professionals (see Figure 4).

Thus, goal orientation is essential for exceptional software professionals in order to avoid psychological disturbances, but it does not help average persons. This fact could be due to different requirements in the work situation of high performance persons that make goal oriented behavior more necessary. Another reason for this result could be that exceptional software professionals need long range goals for their well-being and feel more strained when they loose their 'vision' or when they are hindered in pursuing their goals. That an exceptional software professional is actually 'keeper of the project vision' was found in another study [5]. It is also possible that other team members expect that the exceptional persons in the team are very goal oriented, that they have clear ideas of what they want to achieve, and that they are very persistent in realizing their goals. So it can be assumed that in the case exceptional software professionals can not fulfill these expectations their irritation/strain will rise.

# 4 Overall Discussion

The results of this study showed that exceptional software professionals were not more planful and goal oriented than others. But exceptional software professionals had lower irritation/strain scores without perceiving their work situation more stressful. The crucial finding was that goal orientation played a different role in exceptional and average persons. Although very good software professionals were not more goal oriented they showed less strain when their goal orientation was high. There was not such a relation for average software professionals. Thus, there is some evidence to the notions that competence in software development comprises also coping skills.

This study has some limitations. Planfulness and goal orientation were assessed with a self report measure. The subjects reported their perceptions of their action styles. Maybe they oriented their answers toward the image of how they wished to behave and not how they behaved in reality. Therefore it would be useful to study the action styles of exceptional and average software professionals with an observation method.

Another weakness of the study lies in its cross-sectional design. Thus no final answer can be given to the question of the causal relation of goal orientation and irritation/strain in exceptional software professionals. It can not be excluded that high irritation/strain causes low goal orientation in exceptional persons. However, this is not very plausible because one would expect the same effect for average persons, too.

Practical consequences of this study concern the high importance of goal orientation for the psychological well-being of exceptional software professionals. This is not only relevant for the individual persons but also for the software development project since low psychological well-being can be a precursor of illness, turnover, and low performance. As a first consequence goal orientation should be an important issue when selecting high performance personnel. It should be taken into consideration that the applicant is highly goal oriented. Furthermore exceptional software professionals should be given the possibility to act goal oriented while doing their jobs. This means to allow them to develop long range goals. They should be encouraged to take their goals seriously. It should be avoided to give them too much additional tasks that make it difficult for them to pursue their initial goals. Additionally goal orientation could be taught in a training.

# References

1. Adelson, B. & Soloway, E. (1985). The role of domain experience in software design. *IEEE Transactions on Software Engineering, 11,* 1351-1360.
2. Brooks, R. (1987). No silver bullet. *IEEE Computer, 20,* 10-19.
3. Christiansen, D. (1987). On good designers. *IEEE Spectrum, 24,* 851.
4. Cohen, J. & Cohen, P. (1975). *Applied multiple regression/correlation analysis for the behavioral sciences.* Hillsdale, NJ: Erlbaum.
5. Curtis, B., Krasner, H., & Iscoe, N. (1988). A field study of the software design process for large systems. *Communications of the ACM, 31,* 1268-1287.
6. Dobson, P. (1989). Self and peer assessment. In P. Herriot (Ed.), *Handbook of Assessment in Organizations* (pp. 421-432). Chichester: Wiley.
7. Frese, M. (1985). Stress at work and psychosomatic complaints: a causal interpretation. *Journal of Applied Psychology, 70,* 314-328.
8. Frese, M. (1988). *Besser führen. Streßmanagement.* München: Mensch und Arbeit.
9. Frese, M., Kreuscher, R., Pruemper, J., Schulte-Goecking, H., & Papstein, P.v. (in prep.). Action styles and performance: the role of planfulness and goal orientation in five ecologically valid performance studies. University of Munich.
10. Frese, M., Stewart, J., & Hannover, B. (1987). Goal orientation and planfulness: action styles as personality concepts. *Journal of Personality and Social Psychology, 52,* 1182-1194.
11. Guerin, B. & Matthews, A. (1990). The effects of semantic complexity on expert and novice computer program recall and comprehension. *The Journal of General Psychology, 117,* 379-389.

12. Guindon, R. (1990). Designing the design process: Exploiting opportunistic thoughts. *Human-Computer-Interaction, 5*, 305-344.
13. Hacker, W. (1986). *Arbeitspsychologie*. Bern: Huber.
14. Hornby, P., Clegg, C.W., Robson, J.I., MacLaren, C.R.R., Richardson, S.C.S., & O'Brien, P. (1992). Human and organizational issues in information systems development. *Behaviour & Information Technology, 11*, 160-174.
15. Jeffries, R., Turner, A.A., Polson, P.G., & Atwood, M.E. (1981). The processes involved in designing software. In J.R. Anderson (Ed.), *Cognitive skills and their acquisition* (pp. 255-283). Hillsdale, NJ: Erlbaum.
16. Kane, J.S. & Lawler, E.E. (1978). Methods of peer assessment. *Psychological Bulletin, 85*, 555-586.
17. Karasek, R.A. (1979). Job demands, job decision latitude, and mental strain: Implications for job redesign. *Administrative Science Quarterly, 24*, 285-308.
18. Kumashiro, M., Kamada, R., & Miyake, S. (1989). Mental stress with new technology at the workplace. In M.J. Smith & G. Salvendy (Eds.), *Work with Computers: Organizational, Management, Stress and Health Aspects* (pp. 270-277). Amsterdam: Elsevier.
19. McKeithen, K.B., Reitman, J.S., Rueter, H.H. & Hirtle, S.C. (1981). Knowledge organization and skill differences in computer programmers. *Cognitive Psychology, 13*, 307-325.
20. Mohr, G. (1986). *Die Erfassung psychologischer Befindensbeeinträchtigungen bei Arbeitern*. Frankfurt/M.: Lang.
21. Vessey, I. (1986). Expertise in debugging computer programs: An analysis of the content of verbal protocols. *IEEE Transactions on Systems, Man, and Cybernetics, 16*, 621-637.
22. Vitalari, N.P. & Dickson, G.W. (1983). Problem solving for effective system analysis: An experimental exploration. *Communications of the ACM, 26*, 948-956.
23. Weiss, M. (1983). Effects of work stress and social support on information systems managers. *MIS Quarterly, 7*, 29-43.

# System-Adaptation and Reality´s own Dynamism

Michael Paetau

GMD-Institut für Angewandte Informationstechnik
Schloß Birlinghoven, D-53757 Sankt Augustin
paetau@gmd.de

**Abstract:** In the course of discussions on designing a socially acceptable technology greater importance has recently been attached to criteria such as flexibility, adaptability and configurativity. The related idea of a "soft" technology that can be adapted and moulded to changing conditions "on the ground" (i.e. within the field of application) has gradually developed in computer science and led to several new concepts of varying breadth. As an issue of software-ergonomics it was first discussed in the 1980s under the concept of "individualization" and found its way into various guidelines and evaluative frameworks for the human-oriented design of application software [9]. Here, discussion first centred on the question of adapting application systems to personal characteristics of the user, such as this level of expertise in using the system, individual preferences for utilizing the system as a result of individual differences in style of acting, thinking and learning etc. In this discussion the research domain expanded step by step to problems of tasks and organizational contexts. Consequently, in software ergonomics we now speak of four mutually influencing factors (and thereby design factors): human, technology, tasks and organization. The following paper is based on research conducted as part of the SAGA project at the GMD (German National Research Center for Computer Science). This research drew on psychological and sociological investigations in order to examine the practical relevance and software-ergonomic quality of flexible systems. The point of departure for our investigations was a debate, which had already begun some time ago in computer Science, on suitable forms for the technical realization of system adaptation.

## Introduction

Unlike social systems, which have an evolutionary character that enables them to go through changes autonomously on the basis of their systemic processes of adjusting to changed environmental conditions, it has so far only been possible to transform technology through external intervention, i.e. on the part of software engineers. Technology is basically inflexible once it has been implemented in the social system. That goes for information technology just like any other technology. The problem is that only at the time of actual application do those interrelationships between the social and the technical systems become effective, making it at all possible to experience the consequences, to judge the appropriateness or inappropriateness of a particular technical solution and, in turn, to make this the starting point for practical and transforming intervention. Inflexible software cannot follow the dynamics of the social system. Rather, it blocks the process by which social systems adapt to changed environmental conditions. This problem has already been recognized in computer science for some years, and in two sub-disciplines it has spawned relevant research activities: first in the sphere of software engineering and second in the sphere of software ergonomics.

In *software engineering* the criticism of phase models led to process-oriented models of software development. Similarly to the approach taken in software ergonomics, the following aspects are now emphasized:

- it is impossible to provide correct, complete and fully consistent descriptions of complex organizational structures;

- organizations find themselves in an ongoing process of development and change and cannot therefore be described with lasting validity;

- due to the underlying disparity between technical and social systems, it is impossible to construct models of social reality in accordance with technical criteria;

- users and developers belong to different »linguistic worlds« so that attempts by software engineers to describe the world of work are always accompanied by misinterpretations, information losses and distortions;

- currently available survey and description methods have a very strong technical character and are thus unsuitable for grasping complex social and organizational relationships.[1]

Methodologically, modern software engineering concepts try to take account of this situation. But they, too, make a number assumptions which only apply in the case of a particular class of development situations; they, too, are based on the idea of a design process carried out in sequential stages and leading to some final result, which then has validity for a largely unspecified period of time. In this conception, necessary changes are only made through the initiation of a new »software development process« . There is no attempt to analyze the process of self-development (i.e. both organizational and technical) occurring in the subsystemic organizational units. Any intervention in the software is only understood in the framework of the software development process. That is why such concepts are - despite the emphasis placed on participative system design - primarily intended for software engineers.

In *software ergonomics* the key word under which this debate was taken up is »system adaptation« . One may well see this debate as an attempt to respond to an unsolved problem of software technology, i.e. by reducing the problem to the individual human-machine relationship. Whereas software technology focuses on the cyclic nature of the development process and tries to find suitable forms of renewed intervention by software engineers (e.g. through prototyping), software ergonomics starts at the point where the software engineers have already taken leave of the process. Whereas software engineers are asking how the activity of software experts can still be effective after the systems have gone into practical application, the ergonomists would prefer to keep these experts out of the application process as far as possible.

Although "Adaptation" of technology to "human beings" is a demand that was first raised long ago by engineers in relation to their development approaches, it is a demand which is still repeatedly expressed and continues to provoke fresh discussion in the light of changing technological possibilities. Generally system, adaptation can only be conceived as something that takes place through the intervention of engineers in the course of a cyclical development process. Since we are concerned with adaptation to the real dynamics of the world of work, the prerequisite is close coupling between technological development and work design. The close connection between application and technological development has long been a focus of interest in the field of computer science. The principle has been quite frequently advanced, for example, that the starting point for developing software systems should be work design. However, there are several obstacles realizing this idea; after all, even if technological development and work design are viewed as "inseparably" linked, they are still not one and the same. They are (generally) executed by various actors, at

---

[1] A summary presentation of this critique can be found in [13]

various times and in various places. And the greater the social, spatial and temporal distance between the two, the more difficult it becomes to find an adequate description and specification of the set of real-world problems to be addressed by the software. This is especially apparent in the case of software developed for an anonymous market (standard software) or software developed for specific basic research problems, where it is impossible to forecast the precise field of future application; in this case software engineers are too far removed from the application stage of their evolving software. Since in such cases the normal process of feedback (as found in, say, software development rooted in a particular field of application) is not available to software engineers or only occurs after great delay through the mediation of the market, they have no way of approaching the future application system other than to engage in anticipatory model-building. Such models are - and this has been no secret in computer science for some years now - in principle inadequate; indeed, they are inadequate in several respects: with respect to the individual task to be described, with respect to the activities in which that task is embedded, with respect to the persons who carry it out, and with respect to the structures of the organizations in which the activities are being done. .

Application development therefore finds itself caught between the construction of systems that correspond as closely as possible to desired applications and provide good support for concrete tasks, on the one hand, and the development of standard systems that have a broader scope, support a large number of possible types of task, but in so doing have to generalize from the concrete features of a task. Systems that closely fit their tasks are preferred in practice because they do not require the user to spend a great deal of time and effort adjusting and adapting the system. Their disadvantage is the limited ability of such systems to be used for different tasks or for changing tasks. This usually means that the user must - depending on how complex his activity is - work with various systems. He is often required to learn a number of different system functionalities and user interfaces. Where this is the case, the standardized systems have a great advantage; they put together a complex system which can, in principle, be used by the user for all his tasks. However, experience shows that most of these systems turn out to be suboptimal and still require appropriate adaptation, i.e. necessitate the presence of expert consultants or of user expertise in handling instruments for adaptation, which are generally very complex and, in our experience, can hardly be mastered by the average user [11].

From the software engineering perspective, system adaptation mainly serves to bridge the distance between system development and application. It is well known that one of the most basic problems in the development of application software is to anticipate the potential situation for using and applying the embryonic product accurately enough to meet the requirements of "task-appropriate" and "user-adequate" support for the target group. These requirements are more likely to be fulfilled the more closely software engineering is linked to the field of application, and the more narrowly work activities are circumscribed, and the more precisely the special work styles of the targeted users are known. However, a trend has been observed in recent years -at least in the clerical sphere - which tends to point in the opposite direction: as a result of the widespread use of PCs a growing proportion of software is standard software and there has been a decline in systems developed within the application context (e.g. by companies' own data-processing departments or by specialist software firms contracted to provided customized company solutions). The reasons are primarily economic; after all, although far-reaching specification of software in terms of a particular type of task and user can improve a product's usefulness, it also increases the production costs. Any software produced for an anonymous market, i.e. not in a definite application context, necessarily faces the basic dilemma of having to create a system which, on the one hand, is universal enough to be used by as many persons as possible in a particular class of application while, on the other hand, can be employed in response to very special user requirements and needs which are not even known to the software engineer and which, as a consequence, he cannot model, or at best can only model inadequately. System adaptivity is intended to meet this underlying problem of all software engineering.

## 1. Dimensions of Adaptation

Reasons for constructing flexible (adaptable or adaptive) systems may be advanced from three different perspectives: first from the viewpoint of the user, second from standpoint of the tasks to be processed by the user, and third from the perspective of the organizational context in which these tasks are carried out.

### 1.1 Users

The arguments in favour of the adaptability of technical systems from the users persepctive has emerged in the context of ergonomic studies. In particular, the findings of work psychology concerning the personality-advancing effect of greater degrees of freedom in the performance of work [8] and the basic doubts surrounding the development of work systems geared to the idea of "one-best-way" [22] have given rise to the demand that information-technology systems should not only prescribe a specific mode (conceptually anticipated by the systems engineer) of using and processing information, but should also enable users to develop individual problem-solving strategies, to support them in discovering or creating new possibilities for action, in influencing and transforming traditional forms of task-solving and in adapting dynamically to new situations (e.g. environment conditions). In this way, the usefulness of information-technology systems cannot be measured merely by the degree of efficiency with which given tasks are fulfilled, but by the potential for transforming intervention in the structures of the task-solving process.

The basic question of user-oriented system adaptation is which criteria should be used to specify the adaptation features. Discussion have centred on adaptation facilities geared to the level of experience of a user in handling a particular system (level of expertise), to the style in which the individual processes information ("verbalizer" versus "visualizer"), to the degree of flexibility in a person's actions ("flexible" or "rigid"), to the degree of self-reflection ("reflective" versus "impulsive"), to the extent of "field-dependence" or "field-independence" in cognitive recall, and to the individual's problem-solving style ("holistic" versus "sequential" forms of problem-solving).

One of the most important criteria for classifying and modelling users is the level of expertise. The Measurement is derived from various approaches in cognitive psychology. In particular, the works of Johnson-Laird (analogy models) [10], Anderson (production models) [1], Norman & Rumelhart (network concepts) [17] and Minsky (schema concepts) [16] have influenced the discussion. Various user-models can be designed on the basis of certain assumptions about the differences in the cognitive structuring of knowledge and different forms of access to this knowledge [cf. 6].

A study done by Karger [11] of the literature on the user models contained in various implementations of adaptive systems distinguishes between the following dimensions of modelling:

a) orientation on firmly defined user types or on individual users (stereotypes versus individual models);

b) specification of models through explicit stipulation (system designer, user) or through system-side derivation on the basis of user behaviour (explicit versus implicit models);

c) modelling on the basis of long-term or short-term characteristics, such as the user´s general field of interest, expertise or task field, or situation-specific user behaviour when solving a quite specific task (long-term versus short-term models).

To categorize users by criteria such as those listed above, the systems need variables to determine particular features. "AID"[2] for instance is utilizing the variables "error frequency", "help-referral frequency", "frequency of use of the system itself", and specific commands in particular. With Help of these variables the system categorizes the user in user-classes for which a specific type of support is then provided by the system and for which the appropriate depth and detail of help-information or feedback from performed actions[3] is regulated. The goal is to respond to the individual differences in user expertise in the handling of a system. In ascertaining individual differences other systems draw on particular user stereotypes which are made up of various features, such as learning strategies (e.g. "MONITOR" or "AKTIVIST").[4] These systems compare the actions actually performed by the user with previously defined action plans that are characterized as "efficient", with the object of identifying suboptimal operations and automatically supplying relevant help options.[5]

The assumptions that go into this kind of model construction do not all hold good from the standpoint of cognitive psychology. Karger [11] points out that knowledge cannot be treated as context-dependent and stable. Whether a command is easy or difficult for a user to remember depends on so many factors that it is difficult to create a uniform user-class on this basis. Moreover, there are considerable problems in transferring the learning situation - usually communication between a (human) teacher and a (human) learner - to a machine-mediated tutorial situation. With these objections in mind, one might conclude that ultimately the respective users themselves must be the ones who - on the basis of their often changing personal or work-organization situation - actually decide on the necessary adaptive measures.

## 1.2. Tasks

Alongside the concept of user adaptation, discussion has also centred on the concept of "adapting to work tasks", which is sometimes explicitly presented as an opposing position.[6] As in the case of user-oriented adaptation, the problem raised here is the choice of criteria by which such adaptation should be undertaken. The attempt to develop models of office-sector tasks (similar to the aforementioned user models) with which a system might control its adaptive behaviour or be controlled by the user does, however, seem to me be a very doubtful undertaking.

Efforts to produce a generalized description of office activities usually draw on classifications found in industrial sociology and business administration; these were compiled either to generalize empirical findings on particular trends in the evolution

---

[2] This refers to the adaptive user interface for an e-mail system based on UNIX. The development was carried out by STC Technology, Essex.
[3] Repeated complaints about poor feedback have been voiced by users of UNIX systems in particular
[4] Both prototypes are active and application-independent help-systems, MONITOR was developed by the National Physical Laboratory (NPL) Teddington, UK, [3,4], and AKTIVIST at the University of Stuttgart, Germany, by the INFORM project group [2].
[5] A detailed description is given in [11].
[6] This was one of the issues discussed at the workshop on "Possibilities and Use of individual System Adaptations" on 30.1.90 held in the GMD, Schlöss Birlinghoven.

of work and organizational structures, or to offer a rough orientational framework for companies to use in practice. One of the central criticisms made of this approach is that in a real work activity the dimensions of content, form and role-specification are intermingled and their meaningfulness as indicators is limited [18] In our view, a meaningful description of office activities should distinguish between the following three dimensions:

*a) an expert-domain-oriented dimension:* referring to the substantive purpose of work and the specialist skills and qualifications that are needed. Historically, specialized areas have evolved in the different occupational branches. The activities of clerical workers are segmented along these lines, e.g. the preparation of loans in banks, the administration of policies or processing of damage claims in insurance institutions, etc.);

*b) a functional role-oriented dimension:* that is, work activities geared to the smooth functioning of task-fulfillment procedures (e.g. coordination operations) but largely independent of the specialist-content objective of organizational assignments. Here, we can identify a broad spectrum of activities ranging from directing to pure implementation activities;

*c) a formal information-processing-oriented dimension:* that is, the pattern of information-processing activities through which the other dimensions are connected, i.e. activities that cope with expert-domain or role-oriented work. In performing these tasks, the people are processing knowledge (their own or external). Information is gathered, generated, stored, evaluated, transformed, modified etc.).

Computer-Systems which try to support all possible combinations of these three dimensions are almost bound to fail. Although the user facilities of such systems might cover all conceivable general cases, they are usually suboptimal for the individual activities. In many sectors the demand for systems suitable for specific tasks has led to the development of highly specialized applications tied to particular expert-domains. These systems can certainly be very broad-based in the range of object-classes to which they are applied (e.g. processing of texts, graphics, files etc.), but they only allow to manipulate objects within the narrow boundaries determined by particular expert-domains (e.g. acquisition support for insurance representatives, a warehouse management system etc.). In theses systems the use-complexity is reduced to those functions which are necessary to deal with the specialized expert-domain. The result is an increase in task-adequacy but a restriction in flexibility. Other products are more designed with respect to dimension c) (formal information-processing).[7] and leave both other dimensions, the expert-domain and the role-orientation largely unspecified. They concentrate on a few object types (e.g. text, graphics, data etc.) which can, however, be processed for a variety of specialist-content task-types. Since most tasks require different object types - e.g. in preparing a conference one needs structured data, continuous text, graphics etc. - the user is forced to employ several application systems (or highly complex multifunction packages) to do his job. The task-adequacy of such systems is limited by the object types that are available. On the one hand, this approach is flexible because the system's use is not restricted to pre-defined specialist-content task-types but, on the other hand, it increases the cognitive requirements with respect to finding and using system facilities.

The point of an adaptation concept oriented to tasks or task-types is to reduce the aforementioned pressures by enabling a user or user-group to make a task-adequate configuration of the system functions.

---

[7] E.g. general purpose database systems, word processing systems, spread sheets, etc.

### 1.3. Organizations

Models which go beyond the formal context of individual tasks structured by the division of labour and attempt to replicate cooperative work, i.e. the social action associated with task solving, have so far hardly proved useful in view of the real complexity of social systems [21]. Although the structural coherence of individual tasks may be described in the form of flowcharts, network diagrams, etc., but when it comes to the process of problem solving in the framework of a social network, such descriptions are not very useful. Yet it is precisely the "process character" of organizations that is at the centre of the latest research into organizations, especially in all those approaches which take up the new systems-theory paradigm, described above.

The character of organizations has long been idealized. Max Weber considered organizations as ideal-typical embodiments of rational action; seen as goal-oriented planned systems they were ascribed a (more or less permanent) objectified structure [24]. In the older conception of organizational theory, deviations from the ideal-type were understood as "informal phenomena", which then became the object of supplementary "hygiene" measures designed to guide the action of organization members (e.g. the human relations approach). New approaches in organization theory (from sociological, psychological and business administration perspectives) have since corrected this picture. The assumption today is generally that organizational structures and processes are contingent.[8] Attention focuses more on the following points:

- Organizations are conceived as action contexts with cultures and subcultures. People work in organizations, but they do not only work. They also live and love in them, dream and fight, and rules are laid down and broken in them. There is order and chaos, and yet (or perhaps for that reason?) they function.

- The mechanistic view of an organization expressed in organigrams and flowcharts, i.e. the image of hierarchical relations and formal structures, derives from an external standpoint and remains superficial. It tells us little about the real actions and operations through which an organization constantly reproduces itself and evolves.

- The structures relevant to the functioning of an organization can best be considered as being created by the interaction of subjectively interpreted ideas held by working individuals concerning the content of work, the distribution of competence, the ways and means of reciprocal interaction etc.

- Not only are organizational structures partly the result of goal-oriented, rational planning and action, they are for the most part the outcome of internal, situative action constellations [25] in which different interests reciprocally act on one another.

- "Rational system behaviour" cannot be explained by a relation between environmental dynamics and organizational structure. In the recent literature hardly any organizational theorists still maintain a determinism between particular environmental situations and system behaviour. Earlier attempts to identify ideal-typical relations between context variables (e.g. industrial branch, market situation, company size, forms of technology etc.) and internal organizational structure-variable (e.g. form of specialization, decision-making centralization etc.) have largely been dropped.

In view of the above characteristics of organizations, considerable doubt attaches to

---

[8] I use the term "contingent" here in the general sociological sense (as in Luhmann [15] or Parsons [19]). This should not be confused with the "contingency-theory approach" known from business organization theory e.g. [12].

the attempt to devise an anticipatory model description of organizational structures and processes on which technological design can be guided. First, what one can describe are the formal elements of an organization, such as the specialist-content definition of subsystemic units, the formal definition of areas of competence, the hierarchical structures, the tasks laid down in job plans and the flow of material and files needed for the work process, etc. However, this does not depict the actual social process of cooperative work. Central to the special quality of organizational action are, above all, aspects such as the forms of social integration that are expressed in group relationships, the formation of constellations of influence and power, the course taken by inter and intra-group conflicts, the development of action-guiding group norms, the modes of interaction, group solidarity and forms of consensus-seeking and conflict.

The major difficulty for software engineering here is the awkwardness of such - often called "informal" - elements of organizations,[9] in contrast to formal descriptions and specifications. Yet it seems to me there is growing recognition that despite the difficulties involved we should not lose sight of the fact that these elements exist and, indeed, have a constitutive function for the entire organizational process; for it is precisely these elements that increasingly offer a key to optimizing rapid and flexible reaction to changed situations (external market positions, sets of internal company actions etc.). The transgressing of rules, the breaking out of fixed role expectations by organization members and the situational taking of responsibility for a particular event (e.g. to prevent an accident) are processes that make it at all possible for organizations to react to unforeseen situations. Anything that limits this informal sphere and ties down the members' scope for individual discretion and independent action ultimately suppresses the potential for the flexible unfolding of organizations.[10]

Computer science faces a dilemma, for, in contrast to organizations (which as social systems are capable of self-referential evolution), technology - and the same applies to software - is only genuinely flexible during the development process. By the time it is implemented in the socio-organizational system technology has already become rigid and can only follow the given rules. Its application primarily strengthens the sphere of formal action in organizations by expanding the scope for action and behaviour in that sphere. At the same time, however, it tends to confine informal, spontaneous, rule-breaking and role-transforming actions [7]. In other words, the very area in organizations that facilitates autopoiesis is being impeded; namely the flexible potential for organizational action. The discussion on adaptive systems starts with this problem. What adaptive systems should look like, which system levels and system elements should be encompassed by adaptive features, how complex can adaptive tools and methods be while remaining controllable, and which actors should perform the adaptive measures - these are all questions for which a number of different ideas have been put forward.

## 2. System Adaptation as a Cooperative Problem

Adaptive facilities can operate on various levels of the technical system and have very different points of orientation. As a whole we can identity four different dimensions by asking the following questions:

1. To what should the adaptation be oriented? There are two or three possible foci:

---

[9] Recent works tend to speak of "organizational culture".
[10] These functions are behind the effectiveness of the "work to rule" tactic in conflicts of interest between employer and employee.

the user (action style, learning style, habits, etc.), the task (different types of task) and the position of the task embedded in its organizational context (e.g. changing organizational arrangements).

2. What range should the adaptive measures have? We would like to separate four different levels: the task level, function level, operation level and input/output level [23].

3. Who should undertake the adaptive measures? Conceivable modifications are those performed automatically by the system (auto-adaptivity),[11] by the end user or group of end users, by the user's own advisors (in large companies usually located in the user-service of the central data-processing department) or by the consulting experts of the software producer or systems engineer (especially for major alterations and servicing which cannot be carried out by the user's data processing department, as is the case with expert systems).

4. What means can be used for adaptation? In addition to the software-engineering tools in use, which of course can in principle also be used for adaptive measures (even though their use requires the availability of software-engineers), one can distinguish between "application-internal" adaptation tools (e.g. command configurations, batching operations into macros etc.) and "application-external" means (e.g. generic interface tools).

In terms of their scope, previous adaptation options have concentrated mainly on the low-level human-machine relationship, the operations level and the input/output level. This is particularly the case with auto-adaptive systems, which have therefore proved to be very partial as solutions. The initial expectations in the modelling and technical representation of user types or task-types as a means of producing adaptive options at the higher levels (task level and functional level) have proved too optimistic. The only aspect which can be given an adequate description is the formal and constant structure of definite tasks; and that is not sufficient for automatic adaptation to user work activities. However, the task and function levels are of great significance for those involved in social, human-oriented work design who want to go beyond molecular and merely routine actions. With other words, there is a need for dynamic adaptations whose concrete form can hardly be anticipated. And this requirement holds up the question for adaptation tools with easy access, without restricting the adaptation ranges.

The analyses carried out in the SAGA project have clearly shown that system adaptation constitutes a cooperative problem, not only in relation to the execution of adaptation measures but also with respect to the outcome.[12] These cooperative problems must be taken into account in a realistic concept. The adaptation tools must be developed in such a way that (in addition to the software-ergonomic requirements for transparency, cognitive intelligibility etc.) they contribute to initiating a step-by-step learning process in the group which gradually does away with the need for support from data-processing experts. This is achieved by broadening the existing qualification base (i.e. the various detailed know-how and special skills found among group members) to create an overall set of skills and expertise for the group as a whole. The aim must be to start a social group-process by supporting the distribution of the collective expertise onto the shoulders of all the group members and starting

---

[11] On the technological preconditions for the auto-adaptive version of a system adaptation cf. [14, 20].

[12] Cf. the operational problems discussed earlier concerning support and advice for users, substitution and replacement in the event of illness or other forms of absenteeism, networking with other workstations and power over and transparency of the work performance in a company.

the necessary synergetic process which releases this expertise when a concrete problem needs solving. To this end one must ensure that the old structures in the relationship between data-processing experts and work specialists do not reproduce themselves in the form of a sort of microcosm (e.g. by certain work specialists with special data-processing know-how developing into "mini-advisors" within the group).

The adaptive tools must have groupware character and support those areas of cooperative work which can break the rigidity of "collective thought-worlds" that exist in a group (i.e. the internalized division of tasks between data processing experts and work specialists) and change these thought-worlds. I am thinking here above all of forms of system support for explorative and communicable processes in which the results of configurations can be made transparent, and can be easily exchanged with other groups or individuals (this also applies to the question habitually arising in organizations of which system elements have to be standardized and which can be freely configured).

## 3. Methods for Configurativity

From the software engineering perspective, the approach described here is based on object-oriented thinking. It foresees a free configurability of objects or object-classes (the free structuring of text, language, object and pattern graphics, structured data), basic applications (object processing, managing, transportation and communication, organization aids) and functions (processing methods), that users would, however, to be able to control without programming skills. Through the configuration of special objects (including the necessary basis applications and functions) which are adequate for a particular set of concrete tasks it should be possible to perform system adaptation measures on a task-related basis. The users themselves shall decide just how adequate the adaptive options are. They then have the possibility of reviewing the configuration by bringing their own practical experience to bear and, if necessary, modifying it. By combining a chain of objects they also have the option of linking typical sequences used to solve problems. This means they "configure for themselves" not only ideal-typical objects but also ideal-typical (and always reversible) action processes.

The class formation of the various modules, as understood here, should not follow the traditional object-classes, such as text, graphics, data etc., but rather elementary task-types. In other words, a module brings together task units which in one sense are bigger than usual (i.e. they cover different object-classes) but in another sense are smaller (they only carry part of the tools and methods associated with traditional object-classes). The class formation of the modules must be empirically determined. It must not be too specific since the user would then find it too complicated to combine the modules. Yet it cannot be too universal either, because that would prevent it from offering efficient task support and ultimately lead to the same dilemma faced by today's standardized systems, which then have to be stuffed with a large number of adaptive facilities.

Since the configuration of basic applications, objects and functions should not require programming knowledge on the part of the user, standardization has to be set at a relatively high level. That can happen in the form of pre-constructed modules which the user only has to put together. The assembling of the functionality is achieved with the help of a tool-box giving the users access to the object-classes, basic applications and functions provided by the system; users can then make configurations and record them in special (task-oriented) system versions.

# 4. The Problem of Competence

The problem of demanding too much of users by expecting them to perform complex configurations is a central concern of all the concepts of system configuration, adaptation or individualization. I believe that user expertise is not activated by calling up knowledge that has been developed at some point and is then, in principle, available. In the case of highly complex systems, like an integrated office system, new learning processes are needed on a continuous basis above all where the system features in use are not routinized. Learning takes place intentionally during problem-solving, error discovery and correction, incidentally during casual observation of work processes, and, of course, via tutorials and exploration.. A high level of system complexity can prevent this learning effect because understanding and localization of a problem is made more difficult and navigation difficulties arise by exploring the system. If learning is to be supported as an interactive process, the totality of all the elements to be learnt must be limited to the immediate problem-solving procedure being tackled in a particular context. In this sense the fostering of competence cannot be understood as a kind of repair job on suboptimal work; rather, as a guidance towards the system-functionality relevant for the user's actual problem solving situation by enabling and supporting an active confrontation with the system, that also allows for coperation with others.

In contrast, the conveying of knowledge via tutorial learning takes place in the form of "canned" units and the user has to leave the ongoing work process. The transfer of the identified abstract problem-solutions into one's own working environment has to be performed by the users themselves. This type of learning (learning by knowing) requires other cognitive efforts as the above type of learning (learning by doing). Active learning for computer work has been increasingly emphasized in recent years. Empirical studies show that active learning leads to high efficiency in the correction of planning errors and is superior to tutorial instruction [cf. 11]. On the basis of these findings has arisen the concept of a gradual expansion of functionality made dependent on the user's know-how [5] and this can be seen in rudimentary form in the Macintosh environment where user's choose between "short" and "full" menus. However, such concepts have not been realized in task-specific form. We argue that real support is provided for the learning process when the functions appearing on the user interface are directly geared to the problem area connected with the immediate task at hand. Only then will the user (trying to remember what he has already learned or perhaps forgotten) venture along the path of exploration; whereas an interface offering the entire functionality will tend to scare the user off. For this reason task-specific reduction of complexity is a key element for system adaptation.

# 5. Conclusion

Whereas it was still possible for traditional machine-oriented ergonomics to, as it were, measure man and his work and to derive ideal-typical constructions and norms by which individual machine elements could be constructed, this is no longer the case in the design of computer systems. Computers are a means of mechanizing mental activities and socio-organizational structures. These elements are subject to substantially stronger dynamics of change than, say, the parameters of man's physical features such as the length of an average arm or sitting postures, etc. In the development of human mental work we are dealing with an evolutionary process whose range and speed cannot be compared to the evolution of the physical characteristics of human work.

One of the most important finding of general validity to come out of the SAGA project, is that *configurability* within the application field will be a central design criteria for information-technology-based systems built to match the contingent and complex character of organizations. Organizational arguments derive above all from new insights into the contingency and internal dynamics of organizational systems. In contrast to earlier (hierarchical) conceptions, it is now generally understood that organizations are social networks with complex and dynamic configurations so that their behaviour is not subject to a simple determinism. By grasping the character of organizations as self-referential systems which can autonomously generate constant structural changes, we reveal a key distinction vis-á-vis technical systems. Once technology has been implemented in the respective sphere of application and the development process has been brought to an end, the prospects of further modification to adapt the system to the dynamics of a living organization are generally very poor. Thus, the interest in adapting technical systems is basically concerned with the attempt to extend the development phase into the application process, to shorten the distance between development and application in a user-controllable form so that technical systems can still be shaped in the application field.

# References

1. Anderson, J.R.: The Architecture of Cognition. Cambridge, Mass. 1983: Harvard University Press

2. Bauer, J. et al.: Hilfesysteme. In: Fähnrich, K. P. (Hg.): Software-Ergonomie. State of the Art. München - Wien 1987: Oldenbourg. S. 118 - 128

3. Benyon, D. & Murray, D. (1988): Experience with adaptive interfaces. In: The Computer Journal, 31, S. 465-473.

4. Benyon, D., Innocent, P. & Murray, D. (1987): System adaptivity and the modelling of stereotypes. In: Bullinger, H.-J. & Shackel, B. (Eds): Human-Computer Interaction - INTERACT '87.

5. Carroll, J.M.; Carrithers, C.: Training Wheels in a User Interface. Communication of the ACM. Vol. 27. pp. 800 - 806

6. Eberleh, E.: Beschreibung, Klassifikation und mentale Repräsentation komplexer Mensch-Computer-Interaktion. Regensburg 1989

7. Falck, M.: Arbeit in der Organisation. Zur Rolle der Kommunikation als Arbeit in der Arbeit und als Gegenstand technischer Gestaltung. Arbeitspapier Berlin

8. Hacker, W.: Allgemeine Arbeits- und Ingebieurpsychologie. Psychische Struktur und Regulation von Arbeitstätigkeiten. Bern - Stuttgart - Wien 1978: Huber

9. ISO-9241: Ergonomic Requirements for Office Work with Visual Display Terminals (VDTs). Part 10: Dialogue Principles. First Commitee Draft. 1991:

10. Johnson-Laird, P. N.: Mental Models. Cambridge, Mass. 1983: Cambridge University Press

11. Karger, C.; Oppermann, R.: Empirische Nutzungsuntersuchung adaptierbarer Schnittstelleneigenschaften. In: Ackermann, D.; Ulich, E. (Ed.): Software-Ergonomie '91. Benutzerorientierte Software-Entwicklung. Stuttgart 1991: Teubner. pp. 272 - 280

12. Kieser, A.; Kubicek, H.: Organisationstheorien. Band I und II. Stuttgart 1978: Kohlhammer

13. Koslowski, K.: Unterstützung von partizipativer Systementwicklung durch Methoden des Software Engineering. Arbeitspapiere der GMD Nr. 242. Februar 1987. GMD

14. Krogsaeter, M. et al.: Flexel: adding flexibility to a comercially available software system. Engineering for Human-Computer-Interaction. Proceedings of

the 5th International IFIP-Working Conference on User Interfaces, 1992, August 10-14. Ellivuori, Finland 1992

15. Luhmann, N.: Soziale Systeme. Grundriß einer allgemeinen Theorie. Frankfurt am Main 1987: Suhrkamp
16. Minsky, M.: Framework for Representing Knowledge in Mind Design. In: Haugeland, J. (Hg.): Readings in Knowledge Representation. Cambridge, Mass.. 1981: MIT-Press. S. 95-128
17. Norman, D. A.; Rumelhart, D. E.: Explorations in Cognition. San Francisco 1975: Freeman & Co.
18. Paetau, M.: Mensch-Maschine-Kommunikation. Software, Gestaltungspotentiale, Sozialverträglichkeit. Frankfurt am Main - New York 1990: Campus
19. Parsons, T.; Shils, E. (Hg.): Toward a General Theory of Action. Cambridge (Mass.) 1951
20. Quast, K.-J.: PLANET. Planerkennung mit aktivierten Handlungsnetzen. GMD-Studie Nr. 195. Juli 1991. GMD
21. Türk, K.: Neuere Entwicklungen in der Organisationsforschung. Ein Trend Report. Stuttgart 1989: Enke
22. Ulich, E.: Über das Prinzip der differentiellen Arbeitsgestaltung. Industrielle Organisation. 47 (1978). pp. 566 - 568
23. VDI-5005: Richtlinie "Software-Ergonomie in der Bürokommunikation". Düsseldorf 1990: VDI
24. Weber, M.: Wirtschaft und Gesellschaft. Tübingen 1972: Mohr
25. Weltz, F.: Wer wird Herr der Systeme? Der Einsatz neuer Bürotechnologie und die innerbetriebliche Handlungskonstellation. In: Seltz, R.; Mill, R.; Hildebrandt, E. (Ed.): Organisation als soziales System. Berlin 1986: Sigma, pp. 151 - 161

# DEVELOPING FOR
# SPECIAL ENVIRONMENTS

# SOFTWARE ERGONOMICS FOR REAL-TIME SYSTEMS

Andreas M. Heinecke

Universität Hamburg, FB Informatik / ANT, Troplowitzstr. 7,
22529 Hamburg, Germany
Tel.: +49 40 4123-5308  Fax: +49 40 4123-6629
heinecke@rz.informatik.uni-hamburg.d400.de

**Abstract.** Software Ergonomics mostly deal with office applications. In order to determine whether results obtained by studies of office systems can be transferred to real-time systems the differences between these classes of applications have to be analysed. The crucial factor is timeliness: in process control it puts demands not only on the response time of the system, but also on that of the user. In order to avoid mental overload, an adequate amount of data has to be displayed at the right time. Combining an action-oriented model of the operator in process control with a model of user interfaces we obtain a framework for the design of ergonomical user interfaces in real-time man-machine systems.

**Keywords.** Software ergonomics; user interfaces; process control; real-time systems

## 1 Introduction

With computers becoming more powerful, especially with regard to graphical input/output devices, software ergonomics have aroused more and more interest since the first half of the 1980s. On the other hand, the number of real-time systems has grown, especially in applications like process control. However, only a few contributions to conferences on software ergonomics deal with real-time applications, and even less contributions to conferences on real-time systems deal with human-computer interaction.

### 1.1 Software Ergonomics

Early conferences on man-machine systems were held in the 1960s, and in 1969 the International Journal of Man-Machine Studies appeared for the first time (see Gaines, 1985). However, only when new computers with powerful graphics opened new ways of human-computer interaction in the 1980s, did interest in software ergonomics grow. Important series of national or international conferences have been established since then, like "Analysis, Design and Evaluation of Man-Machine Systems" in 1982, "INTERACT" in 1984 and "Human-Computer Interaction" in 1984, "CHI" (USA) in 1982 or "Software-Ergonomie" (Germany) in 1983.

Since then, software ergonomics have become an interdisciplinary area of research aiming at an ergonomic design of data processing systems. As this includes questions like task adequacy and functionality of an application we should prefer the term "software ergonomics" to "human-computer interaction", although the latter is mostly used in the same meaning.

A lot of theoretical and empirical work has been done which led to several national and international standards or draft standards (e.g., DIN 66234 "Bildschirmarbeitsplätze"; ISO 9241 "Ergonomic Requirements for Office Work With Visual Display Terminals"), company style guides (e.g., Apple, 1987; Open Software Foundation, 1990) and other recommendations (e.g., Smith and Mosier, 1986).

## 1.2 Real-Time Systems

According to Illingworth (1990) a real-time system is "any system in which the time at which output is produced is significant. This is usually because the input corresponds to some movement in the physical world, and the output has to relate to that same movement. The lag from input time to output time must be sufficiently small for acceptable timeliness. ... Real-time systems are usually considered to be those in which the response time is of order milliseconds; interactive systems are those with response times of order seconds ... . Examples of real-time systems include process control, embedded computer systems, point-of-sale-systems, and computer-aided testing."

Obviously this definition is based on the response time of the computer system only. Thus a lot of very different systems becomes subsumed under real-time systems. By far the most important application of real-time systems is process control. Many conferences on real-time systems deal more or less with process control only. Most series of conferences on real-time systems started earlier than those on software-ergonomics. The first German conference "Prozeßrechner" (Process Computers), now called "Prozeßrechensysteme" (Process Computing Systems), was held in 1974, whereas the first "Software-Ergonomie" (Software Ergonomics) was held in 1983, for example.

## 1.3 Research on Software Ergonomics for Real-Time Systems

As errors in operating real-time applications like process control may cause extensive damage in terms of money and even human lives, one should expect that user interfaces and operating procedures of real-time systems would have been a focus of conferences on software ergonomics, but in fact software ergonomics and real-time systems seem to be two areas which have rather little interest in each other. Less than 10 % of the contributions to conferences on software ergonomics deals with real-time applications, except the IFAC conferences on Man-Machine-Systems with about 30 %.

On the other hand, there are very few papers in typical conferences on real-time systems covering aspects of man-machine interaction. This seems to suggest that there are no problems in human-computer interaction with respect to real-time systems or, at least, that there are no problems that are different from those in any other application. In order to find out whether this is true it is necessary to examine how software ergonomics deal with time, as time makes the difference between interactive and real-time systems, if we follow the definition given above.

# 2 Time in Human-Computer Interaction

There are three aspects of time in human-computer interaction: In any given application the response time of the system to the user's input is crucial for acceptance, and the time required of a user to fulfil a certain task is a criterion of quality. In applications where data are time-dependant there must be means for the visualization of these dependencies. In real-time applications timeliness may be not only a demand on the system but also on the user.

## 2.1 Time as a Criterion for Usability

**Response time.** Interactive systems must respond to the user's input within a certain time. The length of the tolerable response time depends on the type of input. A complex database query may need several minutes for execution, whereas a movement of the mouse must be echoed on the screen immediately. Response time is an important factor for the acceptance of a system by the users.

**Task performance time.** The time a user needs to perform a certain task with an interactive system indicates the quality of the system with respect to this task. In many studies task performance time has been used in order to determine the best of several input devices, menu layouts, means of information presentation, or ways of interaction. In most cases results of such studies cannot be generalized as they refer to a single task or at best to a certain class of similar tasks.

## 2.2 Time as a Part of Information

**Data as a function of time.** Frequently data are a function of time. For example, in office systems we may have data like sales in certain months or years, in process control we may have measurements at certain moments. Such data can be presented by different diagrams like bar graphs or curves. Usually there is no difference between diagrams where data are a function of time and diagrams where data are a function of other values.

**Time dependant data.** In information systems which relate to the physical world data are mostly valid only for a certain period of time. Often it is necessary to hold such data for a period of time which is longer than that in which those data remain unchanged. In some databases this problem is dealt with by time stamps. In other applications we may have different versions. From the view of software ergonomics it is important that the user always knows whether data shown on the screen are valid for the given period or moment of time. For example, in many real-time systems it is possible to call a status report showing the current states of all processes in memory (running, dormant, waiting for a semaphore and so on). If such a listing remains unchanged on the screen until another output is produced, states of some processes may have changed meanwhile. Thus the user may get an incorrect view of the system.

**Data on temporal behaviour.** Whereas the previous two topics apply to real-time applications and other applications as well, information about temporal behaviour of processes appears only in real-time systems in the wider sense. Decortis and de Keyser (1988) have stated the problems of operators in perceiving such temporal data and in developing temporal strategies. Unfortunately, so far there has been hardly any research in ergonomical presentation of data related to temporal structures of processes, although similar problems occur in the visualization of project planning.

## 2.3 Timeliness

**Demands on the system.** As stated in the definition a real-time system has response times of order milliseconds. However, this does not refer to the user interface but to the process interface. From the user's point of view a real-time system appears as an interactive system. The response time to user inputs must be of order milliseconds only if these inputs are to influence processes. In other cases it may be longer.

**Demands on the user.** In real-time applications like process control timeliness requires not only small response times of the system but also small response times of the user acting as an operator of the process plant. Depending on the physical processes monitored by the system the operator has to react correctly within a certain time in order to avoid damage. From the view of software ergonomics this makes the difference between real-time systems and interactive systems.

# 3 Real-Time Man-Machine Systems

If there are demands of timeliness on the computer system and on the user as well, we shall speak of real-time man-machine systems. Unlike in office applications, where the user acts and the computer system reacts, in real-time man-machine systems the rolls of the acting and reacting part may change. Especially in process control the operator has to react to unpredictable events reported by the system. An action-oriented model of process control shows us crucial factors for correct and timely reaction of the operator.

## 3.1 An Action-oriented Model of Process Control

Besides phases like start-up or close-down process control is often a monitoring task (Fig. 1). The operator has to perceive data displayed by the control system, to decide what has to be done, and to carry out the necessary actions (perception - decision - manipulation). These are the basic tasks of the operator in process monitoring.

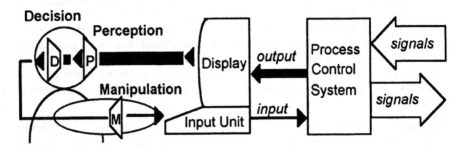

**Figure 1.** An action-oriented model of process control (Heinecke, 1985).

### 3. 2 Bottle-Necks in Operating Process Control Systems

When failures occur within processes which are controlled by the system, the operator may become over-stressed in each of the basic tasks mentioned above. If there are too many data to be perceived by the operator, we call it a perception bottle-neck. A decision bottle-neck occurs, if the operator perceives all the data and understands the situation but is not able to make up the necessary decisions quickly and correctly enough. If he has decided what to do, he may have problems in handling all necessary inputs. This will be a manipulation bottle-neck.

## 4 Concepts for an Ergonomical User Interface in Process Control

A model of the user interface describes all the subjects of design for an ergonomical real-time man-machine system. Regarding the three basic tasks of the action-oriented model of process control we may operationalize the principles of software ergonomics providing certain criteria for the design of the user interface. A prototype called ALCOSY tries to fulfil these criteria by four basic concepts.

### 4.1 A Framework for the Design of the Iser interface.

The goal of software ergonomics is often referred to as "user friendliness". This term can be interpreted in many different ways. Englisch (1992) cites more than 20 different approaches. For example, ISO 9241 as one of these approaches names as principles of ergonomic design Suitability for the task, Self-Descriptivness, Controllability, Conformity with user expectations, Error tolerance, Individualization, and Learnability. Most of these principles cannot be examined in terms of the whole user interface but have to be related to single aspects of it. Thus it is necessary to divide the user interface into single topics for design.

In order to provide a structuring frame for the design of real-time man-machine systems we use a model of the user interface which is based on the IFIP WG 6.5 user interface model (IFIP, 1981, and Dzida, 1987). According to this model there are four main parts (input/output part, dialogue part, tools part, and organization part) for which the subjects to be designed can be studied in detail (Fig. 2).

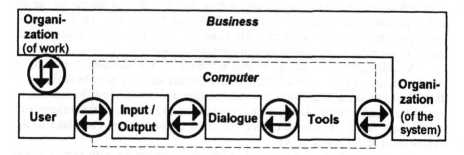

**Figure 2.** A model of the user interface

In order to describe all of the design subjects the four main parts can be organized in a hierarchy of components and sub-components. All structural and dynamical aspects of the user interface can be classified according to these components. Their actual design determines the properties of the user interface. This hierarchical scheme is an aid for discussion and doesn't require the software to be structured in the same way. Fig. 3 shows a part of the scheme. Similar schemes have been successfully used for discussion and evaluation of user interfaces of office systems (Oppermann et al., 1988) and CAD systems (Heinecke, 1991).

```
I Input/Output
    I.1 Input/Output Devices
        I.1.1 Input Devices
            I.1.1.1 Keyboard
            I.1.1.1 Trackball
            ...
        I.1.2 Output Devices
        ...
    I.2 Input/Output Syntax
    ...
    I.3 Semantics of Input/Output
    ...
    I.5 Organization of Input/Output
        I.5.1 Screen Layout
        ...
D Dialogue
    D.1 Elements of Dialogue Structure
    ...
```

**Figure 3.** Components of the user interface (partially).

### 4.2 Criteria for Ergonomical User Interfaces in Real-Time Man-Machine Systems

Research on user interfaces for process control has concentrated mainly on the input/output part and less on the dialogue part. Studies dealing with the tools part or the organization part are rather rare. There are very few attempts for integrated approaches covering all the interfaces with respect to the user's tasks.

A major goal of the design of user interfaces for process control must be to avoid over-stressing the operator. That means, the user interface must be designed so that it eases perception, decision and manipulation in order to allow the operator to react timely and correctly. Using the model of the user interface and the principles of ergonomical design we can determine how each component can contribute to the achievement of this goal (Fig. 4).

By operationalizing the principles of software ergonomics with respect to the three basic tasks we get criteria for the design of the components of the user interface. In order to fulfil these criteria we developed a prototype of a small process control system called ALCOSY (ALarm and Control SYstem). It aims at reducing the operator's workload by facilitating decisions in critical situations, by providing a consistent way of man-machine interaction, and by providing means for individualization with respect to the user's needs.

---

**Component: I.5.1 Screen Layout**
    Task: Perception
        Failure messages should appear within a message window always at the same defined location of the screen (principle: Conformity with user expectations). The user shall be able to move the message window (principle: Controllability) and store this new location as default (principle: Individualization).
        ...

    Task: Manipulation
        For interactions which have to be performed often and quickly labelled buttons should be used instead of menus (principles: Suitability for the task, self-descriptivness).
        ...

...

---

**Figure 4.** Development of criteria for ergonomical design (example).

## 4.3 The ALCOSY Prototype.

ALCOSY combines four basic concepts of a control system, namely messages with decision aids, emergency displays, multi-level process control, and adaptability, within a uniform handling surface based on a window system with direct manipulation by means of a trackball. As these concepts have already been discussed in detail (Heinecke, 1988) we shall give a short survey only.

A failure in the technical process activates a textual message indicating the technical sub-system where the message comes from, the priority of the message (alarm or warning), the nature of the failure, the possible effects of the failure, and the recommended actions (Fig. 5).

For some emergency situations which are to be expected but cannot be avoided there are pre-defined displays that serve to start emergency actions by remote-control. These displays contain additional information and a checklist for further actions (Fig. 6).

There are different views of a single technical sub-system on different levels of abstraction. These views correspond to different levels of automation ranging from full automation to a kind of manual operation (Fig. 7). The user may individualize the system according to his needs by changing parameters as, e.g., screen colour and language of texts, by editing message texts and status displays, and by editing the rules for message activation and process control.

A trackball or a mouse can be used as the positioning device for direct manipulation (Shneiderman, 1983). It must have one button to mark objects on the screen. By keeping the button pressed objects can be moved around. Thus windows can be positioned or, e.g., lines of a text can be printed by dragging them to the printer icon.

Process control can be performed by clicking at symbols in a status display and answering in the dialogue that will be executed.

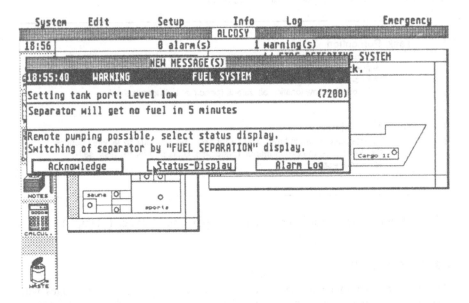

**Figure 5.** ALCOSY prototype: Message with decision aids.

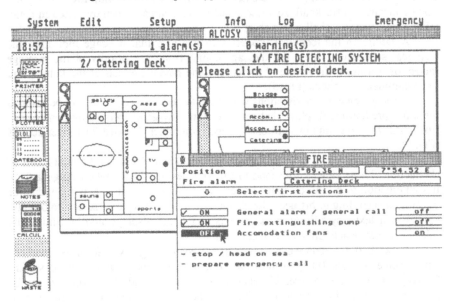

**Figure 6**. ALCOSY prototype: Emergency display covering two status displays

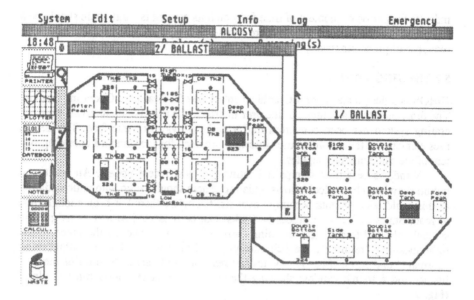

**Figure 7.** ALCOSY prototype: Status display with different views of a single system

The ALCOSY concepts have originally been developed for the application of monitoring a ship's technical systems from the ship's bridge (Heinecke, 1986). A first prototype based on a semi-graphic process control system has been tested in a ship handling simulator. From the results of these tests the window based prototype has been developed. Unfortunately, we have only been able to evaluate ALCOSY informally by presenting it to nautical and technical officers. Formal evaluation of process control systems is rather difficult as it requires a simulation of the process and the working environment. Test personnel must be experts in the domain of controlling the process whereas office systems can often be evaluated using untrained persons. Due to high costs for personnel and simulation facilities formal evaluation of the prototype has been beyond the scope of our project.

# 5 Other Aspects of Software Ergonomics in Real-Time Systems

Whereas the previous section discussed ergonomic support for timeliness of real-time man-machine systems, this chapter deals with time as a part of information. Programming and testing of real-time software can be supported by visualization of temporal data and temporal behaviour of software processes. Such visualization can be integrated in conventional graphical user interfaces, as a design study shows.

### 5. 1 Visualization of States and Processes

Window systems on micro-computers have been successful both as application environments and as operating system environments. In order to apply them to real-time systems we assume at least three additional features to be necessary: A window must indicate the period or moment of time for which its content is valid, there should be a representation for task states, and there should be a representation for the execution sequence of processes (tasks).

## 5.2 The GIROS Design

GIROS is a design study for a Graphical Interface of a Real-time Operating System. The functionality of a command line user interface of a micro-computer real-time operating system has been converted into a desktop-style user interface. The design uses elements of the graphical user interface provided for the standard operating system of the same micro-computer.

Windows bear time stamps indicating the most recent update. An additional button showing a little clock allows updating. There should be no automatic updating as this could result in data becoming over-written before there has been enough time to read. States of software processes (tasks) can be presented as text or as graphic symbols, the red traffic light meaning "waiting for a semaphore", the green traffic light meaning "running", the bell meaning "scheduled", the half moon meaning "dormant" and so on (Fig. 8). For testing real-time software a diagram of the task history and a source window showing the current line of execution can be helpful (Fig. 9).

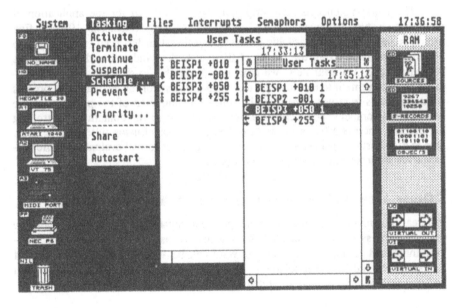

**Figure 8.** GIROS design study: Windows with time stamps showing task states

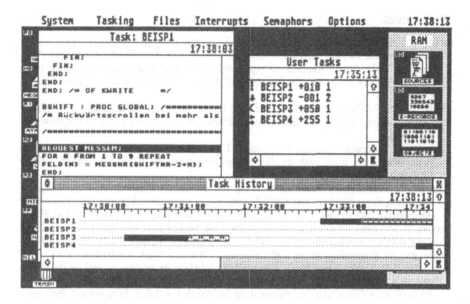

**Figure 9.** GIROS design study: Diagram of task execution history

## 6 Conclusions

On the one hand, we have shown that there are substantial differences between real-time man-machine systems and other applications: in process control the operator has to respond to the system, and he has to do that within a certain time. On the other hand, models and methods of software ergonomics that have been developed mainly for office systems can be used in real-time systems, too. By combining the model of the user interface with the action-oriented model of process control we have tried to establish a framework for an ergonomic design of user interfaces in process control. In a similar way we have tried to develop criteria for the visualization of states and processes in real-time operating systems.

In the past, the design of process control systems has often been carried out by control engineers and computer scientists. Software ergonomics have concentrated on office applications. Although there has been some interdisciplinary research, a lot remains to be done. There are many open questions of visualization and graphical interaction in real-time systems (Heinecke, 1990) which need the efforts of scientists from different fields like informatics, psychology, control engineering, and ergonomics. This demand results from another difference between real-time man-machine systems and other applications: Errors due to deficiencies in the design of user interfaces for process control may cause a lot more damage than those in office applications. The application of principles of software ergonomics is enforced by the European Communities' Council Directive on the Minimum Safety and Health requirements for Work with Display Screen Equipment (ECC, 1990) which demands binding national regulations on software ergonomics for all kinds of application software and hence for real-time systems, too.

# References

Apple Inc.; 1987: "Human-Interface Guidelines, The Apple Desktop Interface".

Decortis, F. and de Keyser, V.; 1988: "Time: the Cinderella of Man-Machine-Interaction", in: Ranta, J. (Ed.); 1989: "Analysis, Design and Evaluation of Man-Machine-Systems 1988, Selected Papers from the Third IFAC/IFIP/IEA/IFORS Conference". Pergamon Press, Oxford.

Dzida, W.; 1987: "On tools and interfaces". In: Freese, M., Ulich, E. and Dzida, W. (Eds.), "Psychological Issues of Human-Computer Interaction in the Work Place". North-Holland, Amsterdam.

ECC; 1990: "European Communities' Council Directive on the minimum safety and health requirements for work with display screen equipment (90/270/ECC). Bulletin of the European Communities No. L 156/14.

Englisch, J.; 1992: Systematische Entwicklung von Evaluationsverfahren zur Beurteilung der Benutzungsfreundlichkeit von CAD-Systemen. Forschungsberichte aus dem Institut für Arbeitswissenschaft und Betriebsorganisation der Universität Karlsruhe, Band 4 - 1992.

Gaines, B. R.; 1985: "From Ergonomics to the Fifth Generation: 30 Years of Human-Computer Interaction Studies". In: Shackel, B. (Hrsg.); 1985: "Human-Computer Interaction - Interact 84. Proceedings of the IFIP Conference". North Holland, Amsterdam.

Heinecke, A.M.; 1986: "Design of a man-machine interface for process control on the bridge of a ship", in: Haase, V.H. and Knuth, E. (Eds.); 1987: "Software for Computer Control 1986 (SOCOCO'86), Selected Papers from the Fourth IFAC/IFIP Symposium". Pergamon Press, Oxford.

Heinecke, A.M.; 1985: "Konzeption eines ergonomischen Prozeßleitsystems mit veränderlicher Mensch-Maschine-Schnittstelle", in: Bullinger, H.-J. (Hrsg.); 1985: "Software-Ergonomie'85, Mensch-Computer-Interaktion, Tagung III/1985 des German Chapter of the ACM". B. G. Teubner, Stuttgart.

Heinecke, A.M.; 1988: "A Desktop Style User Interface in Process Control", in: MacLeod, I.M. and Heher, A.D. (Eds.); 1989: "Software for Computer Control 1988 (SOCOCO'88), Selected Papers from the Fifth IFAC/IFIP Symposium". Pergamon Press, Oxford.

Heinecke, A.M.; 1990: "Visualisation and Graphical Interaction in Process Control Systems", in: Finkelstein, A., Tauber, M. and Traunmüller, R. (Eds.); 1990: "Human Factors in Analysis and Design of Information Systems". North-Holland, Amsterdam.

Heinecke, A.M., 1991: "Developing recommendations for CAD user interfaces". In: Bullinger, H.-J. (Ed.); 1991: "Human Aspects in Computing - Design and Use of Interactive Systems and Work with Terminals, Proceedings of the Fourth International Conference on Human-Computer Interaction, Stuttgart, F.R. Germany, September 1-6, 1989, Volume 1". Elsevier , Amsterdam.

IFIP (Ed.); 1981: "Report of the first meeting of the European User Environment Group of IFIP WG 6.5". GMD, St. Augustin.

Illingworth, V. (Ed.); 1990: "Dictionary of Computing, 3rd Edition". Oxford University Press, Oxford.

Open Software Foundation; 1990: "OSF/Motif Style Guide".

Oppermann et al., 1988: "Evaluation von Dialogsystemen - Der software-ergonomische Leitfaden EVADIS". De Gruyter, Berlin.

Shneiderman, B.; 1983: "Direct Manipulation: A Step Beyond Programming Languages". Computer, Vol. 16 (8).

Smith, S.L. and Mosier, J.N.; 1986: "Guidelines for Designing User Interface Software". Report ESD-TR-86-278, The MITRE Corporation.

# Interface Design
# for Clinical Information Systems:
# An Ecological Interface Design Approach

Kip Canfield, PhD

Kerry Petrucci, PhD CRNP

Laboratory for Healthcare Informatics
Department of Information Systems
University of Maryland, UMBC
Baltimore, MD 21228 USA
canfield@icarus.ifsm.umbc.edu

Department of Physiological Nursing
School of Nursing
University of Washington
Seattle, WA USA
petrucci@u.washington.edu

**Abstract.** This paper uses results from research in Clinical Information Systems (CIS) design, the psychology of clinical reasoning, and Ecological Interface Design (EID) to motivate general design concepts for the human-computer interface of CIS for ambulatory care. There are three primary contributions of this paper to the fields of HCI and Healthcare Informatics. (1) EID is generalized to the very different complex domain of healthcare decision making, (2) The previous work in clinical domain modeling informs the interface design principles of EID, (3) EID holds together a top-down theoretical approach to interface design and a bottom-up approach from specific domains. A specific design for an implemented ambulatory care CIS for geriatrics is used to illustrate the generality of EID.

## 1. Introduction

This paper uses results from research in Clinical Information Systems (CIS) design, the psychology of clinical reasoning, and Ecological Interface Design (EID) to motivate general design concepts for the human-computer interface of a CIS for ambulatory care. Each area is reviewed below and then their impacts on our specific CIS design project are discussed. EID is used as a framework to explore design issues that are domain-oriented and user-oriented. Other frameworks address some of the same issues and are equally valuable at this high level such as the domain-specific cooperative systems of Fischer [5] or Participatory Design [8].

### 1.1 Clinical Information Systems

Computer-based patient records (CPR) are now practical because of advances in computer technology and a steady decline in hardware prices. They are not very commonplace in current medical practice, where paper medical records are still the standard. This section discusses:

o       The need for CPR in ambulatory care.
o       The problems in acceptance and development of CPR.

The issues involved in designing and delivering CPR for health care organizations are at their most basic, clinical concerns. Clinical providers are the ones who must record and consume clinical information. Most direct productivity of such organizations is based on the actions of clinical providers. If those providers can better document and better use clinical information, the productivity of the organization can be significantly improved.

The major areas that drive the need for CPR are:

o    More emphasis on chronic disease.
o    Management benefits (Cost, QA).
o    Benefits to patient care.

As the population ages there are more chronic disease conditions for clinicians to manage. Chronic disease is usually managed in ambulatory care settings and requires continuity of care. This continuity is provided by the medical record. Healthcare costs are widely considered to be out of control. There is great pressure to increase the reporting requirements for governmental and insurance reimbursement. The great failure of many current computer-based reporting programs is that they are geared only for administrative purposes and are of no direct use to clinicians who are in the best position to document patient states.

Management benefits include: quality assurance, protocol standardization, practice management, resource management. These tasks can use the historical database from a CIS to track resource utilization for future planning and strategic management. For example, one could do a "problem-oriented" audit of resource utilization if there were links between medical orders and documented patient problems [1]. This means that one could track how much named resource was consumed per problem as defined for the analysis.

The major benefit to patient care is better communications for patients and interdisciplinary providers. Independence from the single physical paper record allows better access to patient information. Reporting flexibility reduces double data entry. Alerts, reminders, and decision support systems give providers and managers control over process in the clinical setting.

The following problems impede the development of CPR:

o    Data entry
o    Provider compliance

Data entry is one of the biggest obstacles for CPR. Data entry is usually done indirectly in current record systems. Providers fill out encounter sheets or dictate findings and then data entry personnel enter the data into the computer. This indirect entry system has major drawbacks such as the errors due to lack of provider control and the fact that no interactive applications are possible.

Provider compliance is a function of both clinical relevance and ease of data entry. Most current systems separate the documentation of clinical states for medical management and administrative reporting. Providers then see documentation as a chore that does not give them clinical advantages. With CPR, the information is used for clinical patient management and can feed all information needs for reimbursement because billable items are a subset of the clinically needed information. The CIS described below attempts to remedy the problems of use and compliance with an interface that presents a useful clinical information tool- not just a documentation task. The major impediments to CPR are not technological, but ones of organizational practice.

## 1.2 Clinical Reasoning

There has been a tremendous amount of research into the nature of clinical reasoning by healthcare providers, but that research has had little impact on interface design. Two major areas are briefly (and incompletely) reviewed below:

o        Clinical information.
o        Clinical expertise.

A major theoretical study of the nature of medical information is found in Blois [2]. He reviews the structure of medical descriptions and pays special attention to the nature of hierarchical levels in those descriptions. There are complex interactions between the levels of a hierarchical description that affect decision making.

> The distinction that I wish to draw here is between "simple" problems (dealing with low-level objects or processes or with abstractions of higher-level ones) and "complex" problems (which are associated with high-level processes that resist abstraction). The former types of problems typically have a "correct" answer. Answers are either true or false. [...] Problems arising at the high levels do not always have correct answers.. [Blois:62]

Blois notes that in the passage from low hierarchical levels to higher ones (such as descriptions of disease), ambiguity and fuzziness arise. This is because at the higher levels, the descriptions are conceptually too complex for simple and exact words. Our shared experiences in various human subworlds (such as medicine) allow these ambiguities to be resolved in most cases.

Groen and Patel [4] note that most work on the nature of expertise focuses on problem solving (process) rather than comprehension (structure). Since medical expertise is a verbally complex area, they suggest that the structural issues of comprehension are very important. Groen and Patel use a combination of the comprehension theory of van Dijk and Kintsch and the situation model of Kintsch and Greeno [6] to describe a propositional model of clinical reasoning. It is a text model of a clinical situation that assumes a microstructure for observations (such as symptoms), a macrostructure for higher-level propositions (such as diagnoses) that are entailed by the lower-level ones, and a superstructure that organizes the macropropositions. They show that the forward reasoning that providers typically exhibit follows from this model and the deductive (backward) model that is often held out as a goal in medical reasoning is counter-productive.

Patel, Evans, and Groen [10] show that it is easier and more natural to embed basic-science information in a clinically-oriented medical curriculum than vice-versa. This is due to the model of clinical reasoning outlined in the last paragraph. Successful clinicians rarely rely on causal models for diagnosis.

> There is little evidence that basic biomedical science plays a role in establishing a diagnosis; and only a minor role in establishing a fit between textual propositions and the situation model suggested by the diagnosis. If there is a role for basic science here, it may be to reduce uncertainty by suggesting preferred relations among the predicted, competing, alternative classifications of findings. [Patel:21]

This tendency to prefer surface control and the hierarchical nature of medical descriptions are important theoretical points for EID.

### 1.3 Ecological Interface Design (EID)

Vicente and Rasmussen [12] give the theoretical foundations of EID. Their goal is to extend the benefits of direct manipulation interfaces to complex work domains. They have done most of their work in the area of industrial process control, but many of the ideas are relevant to a complex but more verbal area- healthcare decision making.

A man-machine interface is a part of a control system. Since complex systems require complex controllers, for all but the simplest systems the controller will be the operator. The interface must not impede the operator's control in a complex and open environment. A better strategy is to make the constraints of the work domain a part of the man-machine system.

The authors use an abstraction hierarchy to represent the structure of complex systems. The abstraction hierarchy has the following five properties:

1. Each level of the hierarchy deals with the same system.
2. Each level has its own concepts.
3. The selection of level is operator determined.
4. The requirements for each level appear as constraints.
5. Understanding of the system increases as you move up levels.

This representation tool allows an operator to view information at various levels depending upon the task at hand and becomes a way of dealing with complexity. It also allows the operator to use goal-directed problem solving rather than a process-oriented strategy. The abstraction hierarchy provides the "foundation for interface design by specifying the information content and structure of the interface." [Vicente:594]

The authors describe multiple levels of cognitive control in three categories: skill-based behavior (SBB), rule-based behavior (RBB), and knowledge-based behavior (KBB). These behaviors can be recategorized into two groups by noting that KBB is concerned with analytical problem solving for symbolic representations while RBB and SBB are concerned with perception and action. Vicente notes several examples from the problem-solving literature to support the fact that people prefer perception and action to analytical problem solving. The results indicate that experts often rely on *recognitional modes* of decision making even when the information for analytical modes is available.

Vicente explains that "the problem with many existing interfaces is that they penalize, rather than support, operators' preference for lower levels of cognitive control." [Vicente:596] Since realistically complex tasks require all three levels of control, the interface should allow free movement between them. The authors suggest the following (paraphrased) design principles dealing with cognitive control:

1.      SBB- The display should be a direct manipulation one where the structure of the displayed information should be isomorphic to the conceptual model of the domain. Multiple levels should be visible at the same time.

2.      RBB- Provide a consistent one-to-one mapping between domain tasks and their representation or cues.

3.      KBB- Represent the work domain in the form of an abstraction hierarchy that reflects the domain mental model for problem solving.

Vicente and Rasmussen dealt with the domain of process control but speculated that their ideas would be useful in other domains. The following section applies EID to the domain of ambulatory clinical information systems.

## 2. GERI- An Ambulatory CIS for Geriatrics

Our group has developed a CIS named GERI for a geriatric research clinic at the Baltimore Veterans Affairs Medical Center. It is a part of a Geriatric Research, Education and Clinical Center project under the direction of Andy Goldberg, MD. The following design goals attempt to maximize the benefits of CPR and minimize the problems discussed above:

o      Clinical usefulness (domain model-based).

o      Ease of use (all levels of cognitive control).

o      Open systems, client/server, modular design (implementation issues).

Clinical usefulness is defined as making the basic design goal clinical patient management as opposed to administrative reporting although that is also supported. For ease of use, we chose a database development system that offers a Graphical User Interface (we used the client-server development environment from Gupta Technologies Inc.- SQLWindows and SQLBase) The GUI allows direct manipulation of the interface and does not require learning commands. For example, coded findings require a large and comprehensive data dictionary. If the entry of these coded findings is easy enough, provider compliance will allow much of the information that is traditionally free-text narrative in the progress note to be structured in a database. This allows the information to be manipulated by query and reporting programs.

We use an open system architecture based on relational database management systems (RDBMS) and client/server network connections. A client/server database system is one where the client workstation does local processing for the interface and query result manipulations. The server processor does the actual query processing. The RDBMS offers a standard data framework across vendors with a standard query language SQL (Structured Query Language). The database system runs as a process under the network operating system (Novell's Netware in this case) and the client interface builder allows connections to all major RDBMS vendors.

## 2.1 GERI Description

The core of the GERI CIS is the care planning module, which is the clinical interface to the system. Figure 1 shows this interface. It allows clinicians to see all patient information with a minimum of difficulty. Dynamic views, order entry, and reporting are supported. The remainder of this section describes this interface.

Figure 1 shows the entire screen of a PC running GERI under MSWindows. To the right of GERI is an icon bar that gives the user access to other applications. The top of the GERI window shows general patient and provider demographic information. The *Chief Complaint* and *Comment* fields are for free-text entry. All typical word processing functions (word-wrap etc.) are active in these and similar areas. The scrollable area under the *Comment* field is a table window that lists all encounters (by date) for the selected patient. When a user selects an encounter, the interface is updated to display information specific to that encounter. The separate table window *Interventions* at the bottom of the GERI window lists all patient events for the selected encounter. For example, the patient had a standard review of systems exam on 6/1/93. This window can be maximized and minimized.

**Fig. 1.** The Main GERI Window.

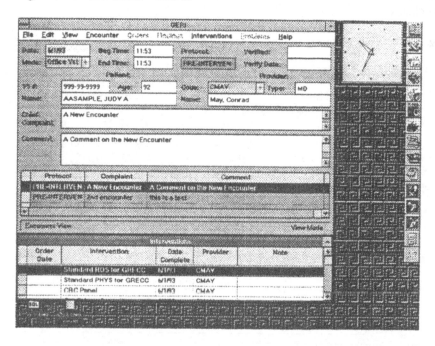

Most of the display function of GERI is controlled through the *View* menu item that is magnified in Figure 2. GERI offers three views of the patient data in the bottom-most window. The *Encounter View* is the default and shows *Interventions* restricted to a specific encounter. The *Plan View* shows all *Interventions* (or other category) for a specific problem regardless of the encounter. This allows the provider to see the history of findings and orders linked to a problem. The user is prompted with a list of current active problems to choose from when this view is selected. The *All View* shows all *Interventions* regardless of encounter or problem. Different categories of clinical information from the data dictionary can be displayed in the (currently selected) *Interventions* window and are listed in the middle section of the *View* menu.

An important feature of this care plan is the fact that all orders (or non-orders) are linked to problems in the record. This allows more detailed information for quality assurance, billing, and clinical research. Providers can link data to problems in one of two ways. They can order something using the *Orders* dialog box (not shown) that allows them to also choose a current active problem for a link. They can also use the *Protocol Orders* window shown in Figure 3. This window allows providers or administrators to store a protocol (set of orders) with a research code. This allows the clinician to double click an item in this window and automatically initiate an order linked to the current research protocol. The order is documented as usual in the system and the *Date Completed* field offers an easy way to track protocol compliance.

**Fig. 2.** The View Menu.

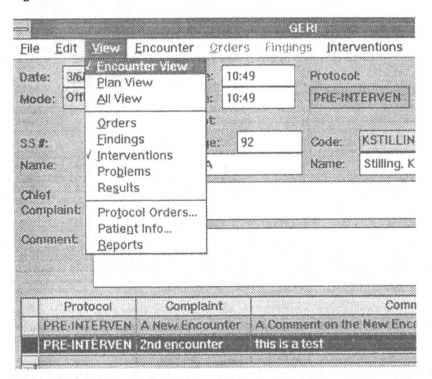

This clinical interface offers providers a flexible tool to browse patient information. It supports process aspects of clinics such as order entry and protocol documentation without compromising flexibility. The order entry process allows orders (events to be done-time 1), interventions (carried out orders-time 2), and results (e.g. lab values-time 3). The *Protocol Orders* facility documents the history of protocol entry and compliance for patients. Clinicians spend about 40% of their time browsing paper patient records and GERI has shown reductions in that time for users at our clinic.

### 2.2 Implications for EID

The design for GERI was guided by the principles of a cognitive model (abstraction hierarchy) and cognitive control (SBB, RBB, KBB). Important points of contact between GERI, EID, and domain models are emphasized below.

An abstraction hierarchy was important in the works of Blois and Groen and also for EID. This hierarchy is the domain model of most clinically relevant tasks and decisions. Most of the machinery of GERI is geared for providing documentation functions for patient states. This is a very important first step in designing a CIS. A major problem with most work in Healthcare Informatics and CIS is that designers and researchers (understandably) want to immediately tackle difficult problems in decision support (at the KBB level) before there is an appropriate information systems infrastructure to support such systems. GERI has been carefully designed at the architecturally low-level of infrastructure.

GERI supports relevant hierarchical views. Patient events have been modeled as hierarchically-coded propositions. The GERI data model makes the application driven by the data dictionary. If we change the structure or content of the hierarchy, the application adapts. Providers are not required to view the patient information constrained by any macrostructured view. They can get a low-level, global representation of the patient with a direct manipulation interface and then proceed up the abstraction hierarchy (by means of link types) if needed.

**Fig. 3.** Protocol Orders Window.

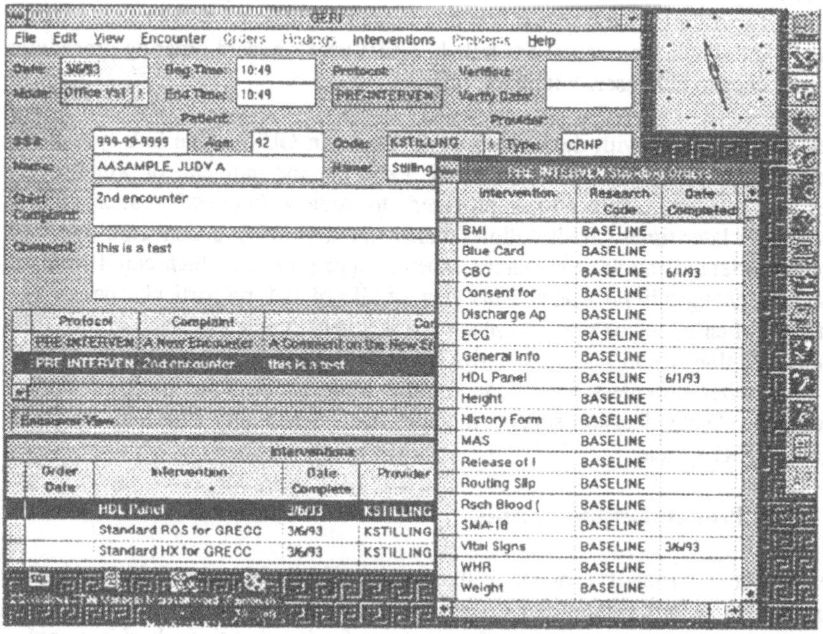

Cognitive control levels are also supported in the GERI interface. SBBs are somewhat different (but prevalent) in healthcare fields than in the process control ones that Vicente considered. Physical exam and graphical device output interpretation (X-ray films, etc.) are examples of important skills-based behaviors of healthcare providers. We have not focused on particular support for these yet although documentation of their findings is supported. The design of GERI as a modular, scalable, client/server system allows natural extensions for these SBBs. For example, direct manipulation of graphical representations of the human body could support physical exam analyses. The client/server architecture allows extensions to the system to supply high quality graphics and video. The ability to directly manipulate imagery in the context of the medical record should give the benefits of operating at the skills level to the CIS. Recent advances in compression (e.g. JPEG) allow almost diagnostic-grade imagery to be delivered on 486 SVGA PC clients on a network [9]. GERI is now being modified to support integration of full-motion video for patient simulation in a case-based clinical educational program.

RBBs in GERI are supported with a standard, event driven GUI and constraint-based process support. Most standard window-based operating systems (Macintosh, MSWindows, OS/2, XWindows) offer a (variably) consistent event driven interface that prevents users from becoming trapped in dead-end process lines. For example, one can cancel any event and return to a neutral state. This positive feature must be limited (in an unobtrusive way) by important domain constraints. For example, one cannot cancel a medical order in the middle and commit a partial order. This is analogous to rolling back a transaction in a financial database. Users must be aware of when and why a transaction has failed. GERI uses standard ordering procedures and state cues to help users with these rules.

KBBs are supported with the concept of link type in GERI. One link type is the problem/order link. Providers can easily document the problem for which every order was placed. This allows providers to review (indirectly) their clinical reasoning at later times. It also allows management views of patient care such as a "problem-oriented" audit of resources expended per problem which could result in behavioral changes in providers. This view of all orders for a particular patient is a plan view of care. A cross-patient plan view is a very simple extension in the GERI architecture that would give substantive decision support to providers. They could see what other providers have done for the same problem in the same patient population. Other decision support modules can be naturally added to the basic, scalable GERI system.

### 2.3 GERI Project: Lessons Learned

This project is basically a major reengineering effort. We started from a paper-based patient record system and designed not only an application interface, but a complete database system and set of procedures for its operation. In this complex development environment, it is difficult to see clearly what effect any particular aspect is having in isolation. Most serious problems that we are encountering in this project are related to organizational and database issues rather than the GERI interface.

The interface was designed iteratively and in close collaboration with clinicians. These clinicians use the system in a way that shows a reduction of time spent browsing for patient information. They also feel that GERI offers them a working environment that facilitates their clinical decision making. In general, clinicians that are motivated by a desire to improve the patient record and have computer experience, respond very positively to GERI, even if they were not involved in the development.

On the other hand, clinicians without a special interest in reengineering and without computer user experience tend to ignore or disparage the system. The learning curve of PC fundamentals, MSWindows basics, and the GERI model is evidently an overload for an uninterested user. The problem seems to be that GERI does not implement a user model similar to the one that clinicians use with the paper record. GERI presents a new (but simple) model that one must assimilate to use the system effectively. The uninterested users do not engage the system enough to learn this model and fail. We plan future studies to try to refine this subjective observation and attempt to address the problem.

## 3. Conclusion

We have described a CIS that was designed using principles from the literature of the domain modeling of clinical reasoning and Ecological Interface Design. There are three primary contributions of this paper to the fields of Human-Computer Interface and Healthcare Informatics.

1.      EID was developed in the area of industrial process control and assumed to be more general. The generality of the basic ideas to the very different complex domain of healthcare decision making has been explored.

2.      The previous work in clinical domain modeling has shown promise for informing the interface design principles of EID. This means that for any other complex domain it is probably true that designers should mine the literature for models. This seems trivially true but is not common in practice.

3.      EID seems to be the glue that holds together a top-down approach to interface design (theory about general design principles) and a bottom-up approach from specific domain contexts.

In the book *Designing Interaction* [3], numerous authors question HCI as a basic science and rightly complain that it has had little effect on real design. The following passages from that book give the flavor of the critique.

> The working context for an application can itself be so singular, so complex, and so potent that either the standard techniques cannot be employed at all or it is difficult to see how to modify them." [Carroll:3]

For the most part, useful theory is impossible, because the behavior of human-computer systems is chaotic or worse, highly complex, dependent on many unpredictable variables, or just too hard to understand [...] and will not necessarily generalize. [Landauer:60]

You cannot have a theory of practice, and what practical fields need are perceptive people with some sensitivity to the tasks at hand, the potential for new technologies to help or bypass them, an ability to ask the right questions, and some training on how to answer such questions empirically in particular cases. In other words, there is no substitute for wisdom in dealing with real life. [Pylyshyn:48]

EID recognizes that flight from real life is deadly for HCI and that HCI design needs a domain-orientation. The largest contribution of HCI is in the areas of methodology and evaluation. The rest of it is the actual process of design.

# References

1.      G. Beeler, P. Gibbons, C. Chute, Development of a Clinical Data Architecture (*16th SCAMC*, M. Frisse, McGraw-Hill, pp. 244-248, 1992).

2.      M. Blois, *Information and Medicine: the Nature of Medical Descriptions* (University of California Press, Berkeley, CA, 1984).

3.      J. Carroll, Introduction, Designing Interaction:  Psychology at the Human-Computer Interface in in    *Designing Interaction* J. Carroll, Eds. (Cambridge University Press, New York, NY, 1991),

4.      G. Groen, V. Patel, The Relationship Between Comprehension and Reasoning in Medical Expertise in *The Nature of Expertise* M. Chi, R. Glaser, M. Farr, Eds. (Lawrence Erlbaum Associates, Hillsdale, NJ, 1988),

5.      G. Fischer, Domain-oriented design environments. *Proceedings of the Seventh Knowledge-based Software Engineering Conference.* IEEE Computer Society Press, 1992, pp. 204-213.

6.      W. Kintsch, J. Greeno,Understanding and solving word arithmetic problems., *Psychological Review* 92, pp. 109-129 (1985).

7.      T. Landauer, Let's Get Real: A position paper on the role of cognitive psychology in the design of humanly useful and usable systems in *Designing Interaction* J. Carroll, Eds. (Cambridge University Press, New York, 1991),

8.      M. Muller, S. Kuhn, Participatory Design: Introduction (Special Issue Editors), *CACM* 36:4, 1993.

9.      C. McDonald, Delivering X-Ray Images on Hospital Computer Networks *MD Computing* (1992), pp. 348-350.

10.     V. Patel, D. Evans, G. Groen,Biomedical Knowledge and Clinical Reasoning, Manuscript (1989).

11.     Z. Pylyshyn, Some Remarks on the Theory-Practice Gap in *Designing Interaction* J. Carroll, Eds. (Cambridge University Press, New York, NY, 1991),

12.     K. Vicente, J. Rasmussen,Ecological Interface Design: Theoretical Foundations, *IEEE Transactions on Systems, Man, and Cybernetics* 22, pp. 589-606 (1992).

# POSTER PRESENTATION I

# On the Effects of Individual Differences with Reference to Spoken
# Language Dialogue Systems

Stephen Love, John C. Foster and Mervyn A. Jack

Centre for Speech Technology Research
University of Edinburgh
80 South Bridge, Edinburgh EH1 1HN
love@cstr.ed.ac.uk

This paper presents results from research into the effects of individual differences on subjects' performance when using an automated telephone service with a spoken language interface. In considering the relevance of individual differences for the design of interactive human-computer services using voice, it is important to identify the salient individual characteristics which effect user's performance. Once identified, these characteristics can then be accommodated in the system design.

The problem for the dialogue designer lies in the identification of individual characteristics which are stable across different dialogue tasks and different situations. Previous work in this area suggests that cognitive factors such as spatial ability and verbal reasoning, together with personality factors, can be indicators of the relationship between individual characteristics and performance on a human-computer interaction task. However, most of this work has been carried out in the context of graphical, command line and menu driven interfaces. One important feature of the research reported here is the evaluation of these findings with reference to spoken language interfaces.

The research explores the issue of individual differences in the use of a spoken dialogue using a new implementation of the Wizard of Oz (WoZ) experimental technique. The Wizard of Oz system used in the experiments reported here is distinguished from most previous versions of this technique by the degree of control the software provides over the experimental variables. One of the major new features of the WoZ technique is that it uses a realistic simulation of an available automatic speech recognition technology allowing experimentation with recognition performance levels extrapolated beyond those currently available.

The experimental set-up using this Wizard of Oz scheme requires users to select and order an item from a catalogue over the telephone using spoken m input. Subjects are also given a series of psychometric tests to obtain measurements on specific cognitive and personality characteristics which are considered to be good indicators of the relationship between individual differences and performance on a human-computer interaction task. The AH4 Group Test of General Intelligence is used for the cognitive measurements, testing both verbal and spatial ability. The test also gives a measure of general intelligence. For the personality test the NEO Personality Inventory (NEO PI-R™) is used. This particular test has been chosen since there is an emerging consensus in the study of personality that the basic structure of personality consists of five super ordinate factors: neuroticism, extroversion, openness, agreeableness and conscientiousness.

This paper describes the Wizard of Oz experimental method plus the results of the psychometric tests. It provides an analysis of the influence of individual differences on user performance while using an interactive speech system. It also offers the basis for an experimental paradigm which allows the successful identification of the relevant individual capabilities in a human-computer interaction task of this kind and suggests ways in which these attributes can be accommodated in an intelligent spoken language dialogue system.

# Understanding Natural Arabic Text

Al-Khonaizi M[1]; Al-A'ali M[2] and Al-Zobaidie A[1]

[1] School of CIT,Greenwich University
a.alzobaidie@greenwich.ac.uk
London SE18 6PF, U.K.

[2] Department of Computer Science,
University of Bahrain, Bahrain.
P.O. Box 32038; Fax (+973) 682582.

**Abstract:** Recent research indicate that achieved work in natural Arabic text understanding is still in its infancy. Related work in both Arabic and some other languages have been surveyed and a new approach to allow processing the natural Arabic text is proposed. In most natural languages, while classifying words according to their categories is the role of the Parsers, the rich semantic available in the Arabic language obviate the need of the parser. The proposed approach is based on classifying words into categories of Bases and represents them as a form of Semantic Network. New words can be deduced and used later to answer queries.

## 1 Introduction

Arabic is the official language of twenty-one countries, and spoken by around 200 millions [1]. There is a need for a sophisticated intelligent system to extract specific information from important literature through queries. The introduction of an Expert System (ES) as a tool to help understand the Natural Arabic Text (NAT) would be a significant achievement.

The use of ES for processing NAT is a relatively new field. Most of the recent research in NAT processing focuses on sentence parsing and relies on the linguist to enter the grammatical rules of the Arabic sentence directly into a Knowledge Base [2,3]. There are attempts in using techniques, other than parsing, for natural language processing [4,5].

The approach presented here is different from the above in capturing most of its rules directly from the rich semantics of the input Arabic text. This is achieved by introducing different classes and categories of the words and grouping them together into classified Bases.

## 2 The Classification Approach (CA)

The Classification Approach is based on the semantic network representation technique [6]. This representation approach proved to be very efficient in capturing the relationships between objects (in this case words). The rest of this poster briefs the proposed classification approach. Readers who are interested in more details could consult [7].

### 2.1 The Classified Bases القواعد المصنفة

The Arabic language is composed of *words*, and the word could be a *noun, verb,* or *letter.* However, *adjective, time, place,* and *number* could be derived. The *noun* itself is divided into a *human* and *nonhuman* nouns. So, if we take *human* noun اسم عاقل as a Base class, with the occurrences such as "Mohammed محمد", "Ali علي", etc. then we have formed one CB. Similarly, verb فعل could be another CB with occurrences such as "Eat أكل", "Write أكتب", etc. The CA assumes that each Arabic word belongs to a specified class.

## 2.2 The Question Tools ادوات الاستفهام

Certain words ask about specific type of information, those words are considered to be the QTs and the type of information is considered to be the Base. For example, "when متى" asks about the *time,* so *when* is the QT and *time* is the Base. Similarly , "where اين" asks about the *place,* "what ماذا" asks about *nonhuman,* and "who من" asks about the *human* noun.

## 2.3 Analyzed Sentences الجمل المحللة

A natural sentence like "Ali ate an apple اكل علي تفاحة", which consists of three words, is classified into Bases. The first word is "Ali علي" belongs to the Base *human,* the second is "ate اكل" belongs to *verb* and the third is "an apple تفاحة" belongs to *nonhuman.* A query containing the tool "who", would be answered with "Ali علي", since both "who" and "Ali علي" are linked to the Base *human.* Similarly, the answer for the QT "what ماذا " is "an apple تفاحة"and for "did فعل" is "ate اكل", see figure 1

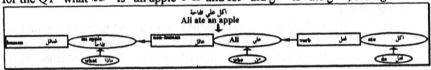

Figure 1, the analyzed sentence

## 3 Conclusion

The approach presented here demonstrated very encouraging results. It could convert natural Arabic sentences into a special format, and then processes natural Arabic queries in order to extract certain type of information embedded in the text. The efforts are continued to increase the efficiency of the approach.

## References

1 Alkhazin , Arab population at 2020, Al Hayat, No 10643, 29th March 1992, p 1.

2 El-Naggar A., *A finite state automata of the Arabic grammar,* The proceedings of IEEE international workshop on tools for Artificial Intelligence: Architectures, Languages and Algorithms, 1989, p. 693-9.

3 Mehdi S. A, *Arabic Language Parser,* International Journal for Man-Machine Studies, 1986, 25, pp 593-611.

4 Li-Li Chang; Juei-Chu Huang; et.al., *Classifications and cooccurrence restrictions in Chinese simple noun phrase,* The Proceedings of International conference on Chinese and oriented language computing, pp 107-110.

5 Frail, R.P.; Freedman, R.S., *Text classification in fragmented sublanguage domains,* Proceedings. Seventh IEEE Conference on Artificial Intelligence Applications, p. 33-6.

6 Winston P. H, *Artificial Intelligence,* Third Edition, Addison wesly, 1992.

7 Alkhonaizi, M.; Alaali, M.; Alzobaidie, A., *Al-Khabier Al-Arabie,* The proceeding of the Second National Expert Systems and Development Workshop ESADW-93, Cairo, 2-6 May, 1993, pages 193-200.

# Structure Browsers
# Enhancing the Interface Concept of Graphical Editors

R. Schleich

University of Zurich, Department of Computer Science, Multi-Media Lab
CH-8057 Zürich-Irchel, Switzerland, schleich@ifi.unizh.ch

**Abstract.** Modern graphical editors, like Computer Aided Design systems (CAD) are often complex and difficult to use. Usually they only display the resulting geometrical objects. However, there is much other, non-visualised information which is important for understanding how to work with graphical editors. This poster abstract briefly describes work in progress to visualise this additional information.

## 1 Introduction

CAD systems are the subclass of graphical editors with the highest development costs. The result of a comparison between ten high-level CAD systems and low-level graphical editors such as MacDraw™ shows that modern CAD systems are often complex and difficult to use, resulting in their potential not being fully exploited by the user. So the challenge is to design high-level systems with usable interfaces for a wide spectrum of end users.

In CAD systems various relations between graphical objects play a crucial role in the design process. In the existing systems they are not visible. Our "philosophy" is that everything in computer graphics should be visible on screen. Towards this end we are developping various kinds of structure browsers. A structure browser shows an iconic representation of the graphical primitives, of different hierarchies and relations between components. Structure browsers will also allow direct selection and manipulation. This will simplify understanding and reduce learning time.

## 2 Problems

Today, large CAD systems usually display graphical primitives only. However, there is a lot of other, *non-visualised* information which is important for understanding how to work with graphical editors. These are part hierarchies, constraints, styles for attribute assignment, parametric dependencies, information about functionality, etc. No visualisation also mean no possibility to use direct manipulation. In the following, different subproblems are mentioned:

1. A composite graphical object combines other graphical objects. A house, for example, is not a single object. A house consists of a roof, masonry, windows, etc. A user wants to have access to these parts at different levels. He wants to select or manipulate a special window, the window type or the whole house. In today's CAD systems the information about the *structure* of composite solids is not visible and there is no possibility for its direct manipulation.
2. CAD systems display a *large amount* of highly structured graphical objects. Normally a 2D or 3D wire-frame representation of a composite graphical object is too complex for an easy to use direct manipulation environment because of the enormous amount of primitives. The access to hidden objects or object parts in intersecting areas is impossible or ambiguous.

3. Today's CAD systems only display the *result* of a design process. The information about the objects and operations used during the design process, the constraints which influence the geometry or the relations between the objects, etc., cannot be displayed in an easily understandable way. The visualisation of this kind of information is a precondition for its direct manipulation.

## 3 Related Work

Various systems offer solutions to one of the subproblems mentioned above. The visualisation of the design process is useful to remember the own work or to understand the work of other persons. A simple solution is to display the solid tree, which represents the solid design process, in a text window.

To reduce the complexity of a drawing screen, the use of a layer technique is a frequent solution. But the mental model for the layer technique is poor because the user has to remember which parts belong to which layer or has to use different operations to find the parts on various layers.

Direct access to hidden objects or invisible composite objects is impossible. User Interface Builders have the same difficulties as CAD systems while placing or accessing structured objects like buttons, groups of buttons, etc. Simple hierarchy trees are helpful to select a specific element.

## 4 Structure Browsers

As a general solution to the problems mentioned above we propose to add structure browsers to graphical editors to visualise relations between objects or object groups iconically. Structure browsers enable the user to understand the solid design process and allow easy access to a large amount of highly structured graphical objects with direct manipulation techniques. Figure 1 shows a simple example.

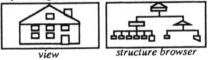

view      structure browser

**Fig. 1.** Composite graphical object "house" with corresponding structure browser.

The use of structure browsers for graphical editors has the following advantages:
1. An enormous number of primitives can be managed by a structure browser. Uninteresting parts of the hierarchy can be condensed and iconified.
2. Different types of structure browsers are useful. These are browsers for the part hierarchy, 'isa' hierarchy, design history, attribute manipulation, constraints, parametric dependencies, etc.
3. Structure browsers simplify the interaction with the graphical editors. The user can either select a part in a view or in a structure browser. Selections and modifications in one place are immediately updated by change propagation.
4. Graphical objects are characterised by attributes such as colour or line width. Each object manages its own attributes. Groups of objects also can be characterised by attributes. If all attributes of the same type are equal in a group of objects, then an imaginary group object can manage the attributes, for all its objects. A structure browser is an appropriate representation to visualise this kind of operations and make the attributes available for direct manipulation.

Currently, we are implementing a graphical editor with several structure browsers. A solution for part hierarchies has already proven to be of immense practical value.

# "RELIEF" - Herstellung von tastbaren Bildvorlagen für blinde oder sehbehinderte Personen:

Ruth Grünfelder

Institut für Allgemeine Elektrotechnik und Elektronik
Technische Universität Wien, Gußhausstraße 27/359/B, A-1040 Wien
Tel: 0222/58801/3887, FAX: 0222/5042477, e-mail: rg@fortec.tuwien.ac.at

Der Schulunterricht für blinde Schüler baut hauptsächlich auf der Verwendung tastbarer Vorlagen auf. Die Wiedergabe von Texten durch Blindenschrift stellt heute durch den Einsatz moderner Herstellungsverfahren kein besonderes Problem dar. Hingegen muß man sich bei der Darstellung von Zeichnungen als tastbares Relief entweder mit geringer Qualität zufrieden geben oder verhältnismäßig großen Aufwand in Kauf nehmen. Das Projekt "RELIEF" befaßt sich mit der Entwicklung eines computergestützten Herstellungsverfahrens für tastbare Bildvorlagen.

Dieses Programmpaket besteht aus einem Zeichenprogramm zur Erstellung von Grafiken als Fräsvorlagen für die Herstellung eines Modells für die Tiefziehanlage sowie einem Programm zur Umwandlung dieser Grafikdaten in eine Steuerdatei für eine NC-Fräse.

Das Zeichenprogramm berücksichtigt die speziellen Anforderungen an die Tastvorlagen (Auflösung: minimal tastbare Abstände und Höhenunterschiede, maximal unterscheidbare Anzahl von Höhenschichten).

## 1 Anforderungen

- PC mit grafischem Farbbildschirm für die Erstellung der Vorlagen.
- CAD-Software "RELIEF": Ein Zeichenprogramm, das die Einschränkungen bei der Herstellung taktiler Vorlagen automatisch berücksichtigt.
- NC-Fräse: Fräst eine dreidimensionale Vorlage.
- Vakuum-Tiefziehanlage: Fertigt die Tastvorlagen.

## 2 Beschreibung der Software für die Bildherstellung

Unter Benutzung von Tastatur und Maus wird die gewünschte Zeichnung am Bildschirm entworfen. Die spezielle Software - mit einem Online-Hilfesystem versehen - unterstützt den Anwender in vielfacher Hinsicht. Z.B.: Die Software verhindert, daß Zeichnungen überladen werden bzw. daß zu kleine Elemente oder zu geringe Abstände gewählt werden.

Das Zeichenprogramm stellt Funktionen wie Punkt, Kreis, Kreisbogen, Linie, Rechteck, Polygon, Streckenzug, Freihandkurve,... zur Verfügung. Als zusätzliches Hilfsmittel zum Erstellen der Zeichnungen kann ein Raster verwendet werden.

Die Geschwindigkeit der Maus, der Warnton und die Farbgebung können vom Benutzer individuell eingestellt werden.

Es besteht die Möglichkeit, Objekte mit verschiedenen Arten von Mustern zu füllen, auch die Linienart (strichliert, punktiert, strichpunktiert) und -dicke ist variabel. In einer Bibliothek ist eine Sammlung von Standardelementen enthalten, sodaß die wichtigsten grafischen Muster nur in gewünschter Weise zusammengesetzt werden müssen.

Das Programm unterstützt das Anfertigen von Reliefs mit mehreren Ebenen. Das heißt, auf erhabene Flächen können mehrmals wieder tastbare Elemente aufgesetzt werden. Wichtigster Anwendungsfall ist hier das Braille-Beschriften von Flächen.

Beschriftungen, die auf der tastbaren Bildvorlage später in Braille erscheinen sollen, werden am Bildschirm wahlweise in Braille- oder in Schwarzschrift dargestellt. Der Vorteil liegt nicht nur darin, daß der Benutzer des Systems selbst nicht Braille kennen muß, sondern auch in der Möglichkeit, die Zeichnung auf einem Schwarzschriftdrucker auszugeben.

## 3 Systembeschreibung

Systemstruktur

## 4 Herstellungskonzept

Sobald am Bildschirm ein zufriedenstellendes Ergebnis vorliegt, wird mit Hilfe des NC-Fräsers die für das Tiefziehen erforderliche dreidimensionale Vorlage hergestellt. Die Fräse erhält die erforderlichen Daten vom PC im HP-GL Code (Hewlett Packard Graphical Language). Von diesem Modell werden mit einer Vakuum-Tiefziehvorrichtung unter Wärmeeinwirkung Abzüge auf PVC-Folien hergestellt.

Als Formate sind DIN A4 und DIN A3 vorgesehen. Tastbare Vorlagen enthalten nur relativ grobe Bildelemente. Um dennoch eine ausreichende Menge an Information vermitteln zu können, muß eine ausreichend große Tastfläche (Relief-Fläche) zur Verfügung stehen.

Als Benutzer des Systems ist vor allem an Lehrer gedacht, die blinde Schüler unterrichten (als Klasse oder im integrierten Unterricht). Aber auch für Autoren von Büchern für blinde Menschen (für Illustrationen) und andere Interessierte ist das System geeignet.

# Adaptable User Interfaces for People with Special Needs

Christian Bühler, Helmut Heck, Rainer Wallbruch

Forschungsinstitut Technologie-Behindertenhilfe
of Evangelische Stiftung Volmarstein
D-58300 Wetter, Germany
hk@FTB-Volmarstein.DE, Fax: +49 2335 9681-19

**Abstract.** The operation of computer-based aids by disabled and elderly people leads to enormous difficulties because of different control philosophies and user interface concepts for various applications. The developed UIMS allows an assistive person to tailor a human computer interface to the user's individual needs and capabilities, which allows the handicapped user to operate different aids for communication, environmental control, manipulation and mobility by the same principle and mechanism of control.

## 1 User Tailorable Computers for People with Special Needs

People with special needs are often dependent on electrical or electronic devices. In our rehabilitation centre we found that the great variety of assistive devices apply different human machine interface concepts. This means a crucial problem not only for the disabled users but even more for the training staff (occupational therapists, teachers etc.). Often much of the functionality of devices is not used because trainers are not able to adapt user interfaces to the users' needs. Most of these devices could be controlled be computer. However, people with disabilities are often not able to use standard computer hardware and software due to various impairments, e.g. physical impairment, mental retardation, perceptual disorders, or combinations of these. Sometimes it is only possible for them to use a single switch as an input device.

Therefore we developed a user interface management system (UIMS) that takes into account the special needs of disabled people.

## 2 The User Interface Management System

**Requirements.** From the point of view of a *disabled person*, the UIMS should generate a very special, individually adapted and uniform *user interface* with an individual input device, an individual presentation of information on the monitor screen, and an individual selection/activation method of choices in menues suitable for the use of several different electronic aids (the computer included) at the same time. To the user a created user interface should appear uniform (with respect to operation) for all applications.

From the point of view of a *training person*, the UIMS should have *one uniform configuration interface* for all the different options of user interfaces and electronic aids. It comprises description tools for

- the choice of input devices and output devices (buttons, switches, pointing devices, microphon touchscreen, colour monitor screen),
- the way of presentation of the pictures/symbols/text on the screen (choice of symbols/pictures, scanned photographs, free-hand drawings; their size and order on the screen; colour of the background and the high-lighting, display of text strings related to the symbols, combination of related symbols, organisation of menus),
- the assignment of actions to symbols (change of menues, speech, operation), and
- the mode of selection of symbols (direct, different ways of scanning, timing restrictions for activation of symbols).

**Method**. At the moment, the configurations are described in a special configuration language. We are working on a menu-based UIMS with the same functionality.

**Implementation**. The UIMS is implemented in the object-oriented programming language C++ and runs on IBM-compatible personal computers.


## 3   User Involvement and Applications

Before we started this project, there was a request for a versatile communication aid, which came directly from the users, teachers of the special school of our rehabilitation centre. Therefore the users were involved in the project from the very beginning. Besides this we worked out the demands for wheelchair control based on questionaires (300 users) and interviews (50 users) [1].
With the help of the UIMS we generated user interfaces for various applications:
- A *symbol-based communication aid for nonspeaking persons* [2] who cannot read and write.
- A *text-based communication aid* for people who can read and optionally write.
- A *wheelchair control system* for people with multiple and severe disabilities, who cannot perform continuous operation of a wheelchair with the help of a joystick.
- An *environmental control system* for those people who have problems to access directly their surroundings like doors, windows, TV, alarm, light etc.


## 4   Perspective

We will intensify the lines of communication and environmental control. So we have started to generate user interfaces for the wheelchair-mounted manipulator MANUS [3]. Furthermore we will allow more feedback information from the controlled devices in the generated user interfaces.


## References
1. Ch. Bühler, M. Schmidt: User involvement in evaluation and assessment of assistive technology. Europ. C. on the Advancement of Rehabilitation Technology (1993)
2. Ch. Bühler, H. Heck: CAi - A versatile communication aid for the speech impaired. 3rd Int. C. on Computers for Handicapped Persons, 88-96 (1992)
3. H.H. Kwee: Rehabilitation robotics: softening the hardware. Intern. Conf. on Rehabilitation Robotics (1990)

# VIP - Arbeitsplatz für blinde
# und sehbehinderte Studierende

Franz P. Seiler, J. Haider, P. Mayer, A. Zagler, W. Zagler

**fortec** - Arbeitsgruppe für Rehabilitationstechnik,
Technische Universität Wien, Gusshausstr. 27/359/B, A-1040 Wien
vip∂fortec.tuwien.ac.at

VIP wurde aus der im Englischen gebräuchlichen Abkürzung für "Visually Impaired Person" entlehnt. Der in diesem Projekt vorgeschlagene VIP-Arbeitsplatz soll im Zentrum jeder Universität eingerichtet werden. Blinde oder sehbehinderte Studierende erhalten persönliche Betreuung und finden dort jene technische und organisatorische Infrastruktur (PCs, Lesegeräte, Blindenschriftanzeigen und -drucker, Sprachausgabe, spezielle Software etc.), um Schriftgut zu lesen, in Blindenschrift zu übertragen, eigene Arbeiten auszuführen und Prüfungen abzulegen.

Durch schulische Integration und den vom Staat geförderten Einsatz technischer Hilfen können blinde und sehbehinderte SchülerInnen Hochschulreife erlangen. Viele beabsichtigen nach der Matura ein für sie geeignetes Studium zu beginnen. Die Statistik zeigt, daß auf diesem Gebiet ein großer Nachholbedarf besteht: Von allen 18jährigen ÖsterreicherInnen nehmen 17% ein Studium in Angriff, von den 18jährigen stark Sehbehinderten nur 6% und von den gleichaltrigen Blinden lediglich 0,7%. (Quelle: Statistische Nachrichten, 43. Jahrgang, 1988, Heft 2)

In Österreich wurde bisher (im Gegensatz zu vielen ausländischen Vorbildern) nur an der Universität Linz ein Modellversuch ("Informatik für Blinde") eingerichtet. Andere Studien blieben der Eigeninitiative Blinder und Sehbehinderter überlassen. Es fehlt insbesondere an den geeigneten technischen Einrichtungen, über die sich blinde oder sehbehinderte Studierende mit dem für das Studium erforderlichen Lernmaterial versorgen können, und dem dafür notwendigen Betreuungspersonal.

Seit April 1993 ist der Muster-VIP-Arbeitsplatz fertig aufgebaut. Es wurden vorwiegend marktübliche Komponenten eingesetzt. Der Schwerpunkt der weiteren Arbeit liegt auf der intelligenten Integration dieser Komponenten zu einem ganzheitlichen, leicht verständlichen und das Studium fördernden System. Dazu muß vor allem eine eigene Bedienungs- und Verwaltungssoftware geschaffen werden, die durch ein hohes Maß an Selbsterklärung und durch sinnvoll eingebaute Hilfe-Funktionen selbst dem Computerlaien die Verwendung des Arbeitsplatzes nach kurzer Zeit ermöglicht.

Ein weiterer, wesentlicher Bereich unserer Projektarbeit ist die Meinungsbildung und Information der Vortragenden der TU Wien hinsichtlich der technischen Möglichkeiten, die behinderten Menschen zur Verfügung stehen. Bereits zu Projektbeginn wurde eine Fragebogen-Aktion hinsichtlich der Studienmöglichkeiten für blinde und sehbehinderte Personen unter den ProfessorInnen der TU Wien durchgeführt.

Das Ziel dieses Projektes ist ein technisches und organisatorisches Konzept, nach dem es österreichischen Universitäten ermöglicht wird, innerhalb der nächsten Jahre Arbeitsplätze nach dem Muster des an der TU Wien aufgebauten VIP-Arbeitsplatzes einzurichten. Die Bibliothek der Universität Wien hat die Arbeitsgruppe für Rehabilitationstechnik vor kurzem mit der Einrichtung eines VIP-Arbeitsplatzes beauftragt.

Die Oesterreichischen Nationalbank hat anläßlich des 175-Jahr-Jubiläums der Technischen Universität Wien dieses Projekt gefördert.

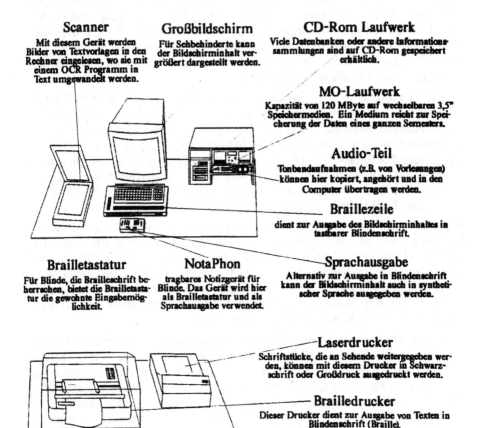

**Scanner**
Mit diesem Gerät werden Bilder von Textvorlagen in den Rechner eingelesen, wo sie mit einem OCR Programm in Text umgewandelt werden.

**Großbildschirm**
Für Sehbehinderte kann der Bildschirminhalt vergrößert dargestellt werden.

**CD-Rom Laufwerk**
Viele Datenbanken oder andere Informationssammlungen sind auf CD-Rom gespeichert erhältlich.

**MO-Laufwerk**
Kapazität von 120 MByte auf wechselbaren 3,5" Speichermedien. Ein Medium reicht zur Speicherung der Daten eines ganzen Semesters.

**Audio-Teil**
Tonbandaufnahmen (z.B. von Vorlesungen) können hier kopiert, angehört und in den Computer übertragen werden.

**Braillezeile**
dient zur Ausgabe des Bildschirminhaltes in tastbarer Blindenschrift.

**Brailletastatur**
Für Blinde, die Brailleschrift beherrschen, bietet die Brailletastatur die gewohnte Eingabemöglichkeit.

**NotaPhon**
tragbares Notizgerät für Blinde. Das Gerät wird hier als Brailletastatur und als Sprachausgabe verwendet.

**Sprachausgabe**
Alternativ zur Ausgabe in Blindenschrift kann der Bildschirminhalt auch in synthetischer Sprache ausgegeben werden.

**Laserdrucker**
Schriftstücke, die an Sehende weitergegeben werden, können mit diesem Drucker in Schwarzschrift oder Großdruck ausgedruckt werden.

**Brailledrucker**
Dieser Drucker dient zur Ausgabe von Texten in Blindenschrift (Braille).

Aufbau des VIP-Arbeitsplatzes

# An Information Exploration and Visualization Approach for Direct Manipulation of Databases

Max M. North and Sarah M. North

Human-Computer Interaction Group
Clark Atlanta University, Atlanta, GA 30314
max@cc.gatech.edu, snorth@cc.gatech.edu

**Abstract.** This research argues that providing a graphical visualization of the databases, queries, and search results will empower users with the complex task of information exploration. To provide and enhance graphical visualization, a new widget called *dynamic slider* (multiple attributes presentation slider) is introduced. The *dynamic slider* enables the user to present multiple value ranges rather than a single or anchored value to minimum or maximum points. The Preliminary results of the pilot studies so far are very encouraging, and users' feedback has been positive.

## 1 Introduction

Generally, information exploration of databases is performed using query languages. Most query languages, such as Structured Query Language (SQL), are based on relational algebra or calculus. While the relational algebra and calculus provide a powerful means to formulate and specify queries, their usage is an extremely tedious and complex task [8] for computer users, especially for *naive* users. In addition, query languages are redundant in the sense that the same query may be expressed in many different ways [5]. In fact, empirical research indicates a wide variation in response times in the implementation of different query languages. This research argues that providing a graphical visualization of the databases, queries, and search results will empower users with the complex task of information exploration [1, 3, 4, 6, 7]. To provide and enhance graphical visualization, a new widget called *dynamic slider* (multiple attributes presentation slider) is introduced [6]. The *dynamic slider* will enable the user to present multiple value ranges rather than a single or anchored value to minimum or maximum points.

## 2 Approach

Several attempts to use direct manipulation for databases have been made. Examples include the user friendly query language called PICASSO [5] and Query-by-Example [8]. Although these approaches are powerful, they do not provide visual presentation of information and actions. The IEVI (Information Exploration and Visualization Interface) provides a more powerful interface by implementing the following guidelines: (i) continuous graphical representation of database, query and information exploration outcome; (ii) visible range of the object by utilizing *dynamic sliders* and other widgets [1]; and (iii) immediate feedback as the user physically manipulates the sliders, selection buttons, etc.

Specifically, the IEVI possesses the following capabilities and characteristics: (i) objects and graphical widgets of interest will be continuously visible to the user [2]; (ii) the outcome of the information exploration will be produced by physical actions [1] such as manipulation of the *dynamic sliders* and other widgets rather than utilizing the complex query syntax; (iii) the provision for incremental, rapid and reversible actions that will be immediately displayed for users; and (iv) a minimal learning curve, so that it will aid naive users as well as expert users in exploration of information. In essence, the IEVI enables users to visualize and explore information similar to human cognitive information processing using minimal cognitive load [3]. In addition, the IEVI enables the user to see in one view objects, actions and results, and assists the user in extracting the meaning and relationship of objects [7].

## 3 Conclusion

Sliders have been used as a metaphor that assists the user in entering either single value or a single range value anchored to minimum or maximum points of a field. The concept of dynamic queries [1] has been extended so that the users can implicitly construct complex queries by utilizing visual and graphical techniques and tools such as *dynamic sliders*. By utilizing *dynamic sliders*, IEVI is able to represent dynamic range(s) rather than a single or anchored value which provides the mechanism for assisting the user in formulating more complex queries.

## Acknowledgement

The Information Exploration and Visualization is an ongoing research project by the Human-Computer Interaction Group that is partially supported by the U.S. Army Center of Excellence in Information Science.

## References

1.  Ahlberg C., Williamson, C. and Shneiderman, B. Dynamic Queries for Information Exploration: An Implementation and Evaluation, *Proceedings of ACM CHI'92 Human Factors in Computing Systems Conference*, May 1992, pp. 619-626.

2.  Beard, D., and Walker, J. Navigational Techniques to Improve the Display of Large Two-dimensional Spaces, *Behaviour & Information Technology*, 1991, Vol. 9, No. 6, pp. 451-466.

3.  Chimera, R. Value Bars: An Information Visualization and Navigation Tool for Multi-attribute Listings, *Proceedings of ACM CHI'92 Human Factors in Computing Systems Conference*, May 1992, pp. 293-294.

4.  Johnson, B. TreeViz: Treemap Visualization of Hierarchically Structured Information, *Proceedings of ACM CHI'92 Human Factors in Computing Systems Conference*, May 1992, pp. 369-370.

5.  Kim, H. Korth, H, and Silberschatz, A. PICASSO: A Graphical Query Language, *Software-Practice and Experience*, 18, 3, March 1988, pp. 169-203.

6.  North, M. Max, and North, M. Sarah, *Sarah:* An Information Exploration and Visualization Interface for Direct Manipulation of Databases, *Proceedings of Graphics Interface '93 Conference*, May 1993.

7.  Sarkar, M., and Brown, M. Graphical Fisheye Views Of graphs, *Proceedings of ACM CHI'92 Human Factors in Computing Systems Conference*, May 1992, pp. 83-91.

8.  Zloof, M. Query-by Example. *Proceedings of National Computer Conference*, AFIPS Press, 1975, PP. 431-437.

# Offices, Balconies, Doors and Corridors : An Experimental Interface Metaphor for Integrating Collaborative Design Styles

Lyn Pemberton

IT Research Institute, University of Brighton
Brighton, BN2 4AT
United Kingdom
lp22@uk.ac.bton.unix

**Abstract:** We describe early research into the use of the metaphor of *office landscape* (Büro-Landschaft) in interfaces for software systems to support co-operative design teams. This work grew out of a study of the problems encountered by a team of engineering designers using a highly distributed work method. A (paper-based) metalanguage based on the office landscape metaphor was developed to ease communication between group members. We suggest that this metalanguage also has the potential to provide a transparent and familiar interface metaphor for software systems to support such work teams. Software for collaborative design would need to be highly flexible and, ideally, user-tailorable: the end users would need to be able to "rearrange the furniture" of their software environment. The office landscape metaphor offers just this facility and has the power to support a rich variety of co-operative and individual work patterns.

## Background

The work described in the proposed poster is early research on the use of the metaphor of *office landscape* in interfaces for software systems to support co-operative design teams. It grew out of a study of the working practices of an automotive components design company which had adopted a highly distributed method of working, with employees working on different stages of the same project at sites in three different countries. Various problems has arisen in the company as a result of failures in collaborative work strategies, with designers prevented from communicating effectively with managers, customers or "downstream" workers such as those involved in manufacturing or marketing, by inflexible communication channels and procedures. We perceived a need for a metalanguage in which to discuss the various styles of working together and apart throughout the design life cycle which were current in the company. This would enable problems to be discussed using a common vocabulary and might lead to suggestions for improved practice. The language we were looking for would enable participants to:

- represent the objects, actors and actions in the domain, via a kind of lexicon of design practice
- represent the current and potential styles of work which would result from linking individual work modes, i.e. it would provide a syntax of collaboration
- analyse existing patterns in order to unearth possible flaws
- specify changes in collaborative work practice

In addition to these basic requirements, we realised it would be an advantage if this "language" were to be as graphically based as possible. There were social reasons for this, but a further motive was the notion that such a language, if sufficiently transparent, rich and flexible, would be an ideal candidate for future use in the user interface to a collaborative design software environment. It is this aspect of the work which is presented in the poster.

## The Office Landscape Approach

The approach we have adopted is based on the recognition that one of the functions of architectural and interior design is to create environments which influence the behaviour of those who use them, in particular the ways in which users communicate with each other. Such patterns of coming together and staying apart are the focus, for instance, of the "Büro-Landschaft" (Office Landscape) movement of the '60's and '70's (Alseleben, 1966), which led to the spread of the open-plan office in Europe. The Office Landscape approach is implemented by first creating a rich model of the communication structures of the existing office and using this model to create groupings of workstations which facilitate frequent communication.

The computer interface can be seen as providing a view into a *virtual office space*, where designers separated in space can nevertheless function as if they were situated in the same location as their collaborators. In addition, the development of automated interface agents now gives designers the opportunity of collaborating with expert advice-giving, information-seeking and critiquing systems in the same computer-based environment as human collaborators. A metaphor based on office buildings is likely to be relevant, realistic and useful and we are in the first stages of designing a set of interface objects and actions, drawn from the domain of office design, which will be capable of expressing in a clear and intuitive way the current and potential patterns of human-human and human-agent interaction.

## Method

We have begun to construct a taxonomy of collaboration styles and techniques in which individual analyses of working practice may be situated. We derive this from an analysis of case studies from a range of design domains - architecture, building, engineering, technical writing, software engineering - in which a number of different methodologies are in use, e.g conventional serial design and manufacturing, concurrent engineering, structural collaborative design, and others which have not been dignified with names. Special note is taken, wherever possible, of the real-life building layouts in which the designers operate and the patterns of communication which operate in the team. The structures uncovered in the analysis of current practice are translated into a vocabulary derived from interior design. We are currently working with a set of over 30 basic objects within the metaphor. To take an example, the Structuralist approach to architectural design outlined in (Peng, 1993) consists in the construction of an initial design sketch or model, the subsequent splitting up of the design team to work on the elaboration of the model according to different specialisms and the final integration of solutions offered by individual designers. In terms of the interior design metaphor, this way of working might suggest a meeting room accessed via doorways to/from individual offices, with the additional facility of a viewing window from office to meeting room (where the common model is stored). The common structure is created and stored in the meeting room, to which an individual designer may return if s/he needs to modify the shared model directly. Alternatively s/he may send a messenger to the meeting room to update the shared model when this is made necessary by some operation on the derivative, non-shared structure. In either case, a messenger must alert other participants of the change to the shared model.

It is easy to envisage further developments of the metaphor: an expert critiquing system might be placed on a balcony running the length of a corridor of individual offices, indicating a shared, active critiquing facility. If this mode of use proved unsatisfactory, the icon representing the expert critic could be dragged onto an icon for a passageway between two rooms, indicating that an evolving design would be checked by the system at the point of hand over between the (human) occupants of the two connected rooms.

The interface metaphor is designed to be not only *descriptive*, i.e. to represent the existing patterns of interaction between team members, but also *proactive*, i.e. to provide a language which enables team members to reflect on their current practice and possibly to make it more effective. It could be used, for instance, by companies implementing the Concurrent Engineering approach. In office landscape language, Concurrent Engineering could be seen as an attempt to go from a long corridor of non-connecting offices, with design representations carried by an uninformed messenger from one office to the next, to something more like a balcony system, where each participant not only inhabits his/her own office, but may also observe the current main worker from the balcony, with messages communicated directly from one to the other.

## References

Alseleben, Kurd. 1966. Neue Technik der Mobiliarornung im Büroraum. Schnelle: Quickborn.
Johansen, R. 1988. Groupware: Computer Support for Business Teams. Free Press: New York.
Peng, Chengzhi. 1993. A Structural Approach in Collaborative Architectural Design. To be presented at AAAI Workshop on AI in Collaborative Design, Washington, D.C., July, 1993.

# POSTER PRESENTATION II

# An Interactive Document Image Description for OCR of Handwritten Forms

David Monger and Graham Leedham

Department of Electronic Systems Engineering
University of Essex, Colchester CO4 3SQ, United Kingdom
email: mongd@essex.ac.uk  C.G.Leedham@essex.ac.uk

**Abstract.** This poster describes an interactive document image specification system currently under investigation which will allow an electronic template to be rapidly developed for any type of handwritten form used in financial services. The template defines the positional layout and content description of a document's constituent fields on a scanned-in image for later automatic processing using appropriate Optical Character Recognition (OCR) algorithms and local syntax constraints for improved recognition performance. The emphasis of this part of the work is on the HCI aspects of producing the electronic template of a new form.

## 1. Introduction

Off-line 'form-filling' handwriting applications usually impose application specific constraints which must be exploited to achieve viable commercial performance. Typically, 'form-filling' OCR applications require the integration of several independent components together with higher level domain-specific knowledge if adequate performance for the complete application is to be achieved. This approach is already being explored in several isolated application areas [1].

## 2. Automatic Form Processing

The advantages of automatic form processing are in the avoidance of data operators being subjected to Repetitive Strain Injury (RSI) and, providing that the OCR is sufficiently accurate, faster throughput of forms. If forms were processed automatically most of the data could be transferred automatically to a company database. This means that a system operator need only scan in the document, call up the relevant image recognition template (and even this may be an automatic process achieved by pattern recognition of the form itself), and allow the system to automatically extract the information using the appropriate OCR algorithm and syntax, with constraints, for each field. After this point, only occasional operator intervention would be required to deal with particular problems associated with badly written forms or information written outside the areas where such information should be entered. Once it has been determined that a document image is admissible as evidence in a court case, then, certainly, financial services companies could seriously consider disposing of many paper documents and files altogether [2].

The typical entries on a form may include fields which only contain numerals and therefore a numeral recognition algorithm needs to be applied, or fields which contain alphabetic characters and thus an alphabetic OCR algorithm is required. Some fields may contain handwritten signatures which may require verification using signature verification techniques whilst others may just require recording and storing as an image. Other fields may contain addresses with a postcode which, for the insurance business say, is very important and other fields may contain free-hand writing, or even sketches, which, using current state-of-the-art technology cannot be accurately recognised, so would have to be stored as images.

The advantage of specifying a local syntax constraint is in improving the overall recognition performance for each field by knowing that there is a limited choice of results at each output and thus only requiring the OCR algorithm to consider the possible alternatives. The application of domain knowledge or syntax has already been successfully applied at the University of Essex to the verification of handwritten addresses [3]. Also, as specified by this application, in addition to domain knowledge, should the fields have any defined inter-relationships then these would have to be stipulated to the OCR machine performing the automatic retrieval of the fields. Any errors subsequently detected by a company's database system, upon receipt of the data input from a form, could be corrected by clerks within the relevant departments.

## 3. Document Image Description System

The prototype of our user-friendly graphical tool runs under the X Windows environment and forms are scanned using a flat-bed scanner and stored as 300 dpi binary images in TIFF format. The tool can accommodate white, single-sided, A4 size documents, and their image is displayed in a main system window, while a panning rectangle can be moved within a smaller overlapping window to select the required area of the image to view. The borders of the various fields that go to make up a document are defined using 'rubber-band' line techniques. The data describing each field is entered through a 'form-filling' command dialogue system. At present, the definition of a field's relationship with others is confined to naming those related fields in the data structure. A magnifying 'inspection' window is also provided to ensure that such field border definitions account for any writing that may have strayed over the pre-defined area on the form. The tool also has the ability to add and remove the electronic templates to and from the form images.

The presentation of this poster will show the derived design of the prototype interactive document description tool and then concentrate on the solution to the HCI aspects of the design.

## References

1. Downton A.C., and Leedham C.G., Pre-processing and pre-sorting of envelope images for automatic sorting using OCR, Pattern Recognition, v.23 No. 3/4, pp. 347-362, 1990
2. Queree, A. (Ed.), Section Five: Legal Issues, DIP in the Financial Services Industry, IBC Publishing, March 1993, pp 59-64.
3. Downton A.C., Tregidgo R.W.S., Leedham C.G., and Hendrawan, Recognition of handwritten British postal addresses, Proc. Second Int. Workshop on Frontiers in Handwriting Recognition, Bonas, France, 23-27 September 1991, pp 132-147. Also published in 'From Pixels to Features III', Elsevier, 1992

# Electronic Meeting Assistance

Johannes Bumiller and Stefanie Räther

DaimlerBenz AG, Research Information Technology
Wilhelm-Runge Str. 11
D-7900 Ulm, Germany
bumiller@dbulm1.uucp, raether@dbulm1.uucp

## 1. Introduction

Organisations coordinate work and exchange information via multiple communication mechanisms ranging from the formal meeting to the transmission of electronic mail messages. Communication forms a necessary part of the organisation infrastructure that maintains the organisation's culture and achievement of objectives. Organisational efforts come to limit and further acceleration of organisational processes is impossible, if organisational structures and working forms are not supported by adequate technical tools. So it is important to look at the design of advanced technologies and how they could support the range of formal and informal corporate communications necessary for coordination.

In this context the main objective of the project "Electronic Meeting Assistance" (EMA) is to improve specifically the effectiveness of meetings.

## 2. Environment

The Electronic Meeting Assistance is a virtually co-located mixed system. That means that all participants of the meeting are present at the same time but not necessary at the same location (for example some people meet in a room and an external, remote expert is included via a local area network).

## 3. Hardware

We expect for the future that people will be using a wide range of small, easy to use NotePad computers as intelligent electronic "paper" devices (something like NoteBooks, NotePads, PenTops, PDAs etc.). This devices will integrate comunication features and there will be standards to which these different machines will adhere: data communication standards such as ISDN or GSM; operating system standards such as (Pen-)Windows or PenPoint.

Within the project EMA, we will use a device which will also be used in the Esprit project TELESTATION. This NotePad computer will be pen-based and integrates the DECT as well as the GSM standard for radio communication.

## 4. Configuration

During the meeting the personal NotePads of the participants are linked together using a radio LAN. In addition an interactive white-board e.g. the Xerox LiveBoard is used for visualisation and manipulation of common data (shown in Figure 1).

## 5. Basic System

The basis is a general platform for the development of groupware tools. This platform provides different administration and management functions for distributed systems and will be used to realize various functionality for the support of cooperative work. The

Firgure 1 : Meeting Szenario

implementation of the groupware platform is based on an object-oriented toolkit.

## 6. Tools

To assist cooperative work, the EMA system supports the exchange of information during meetings. Various information can be exchanged between meeting members, for example contact information, prepared notes and diagrams; electronic presentations could be given or a paper could be edited by the group.
Following tools are in progress:

- A document exchange tool will allow the distribution of text and graphics among the participants. As a special form electronic business cards can be automatically exchanged between the members of the meeting.

- A presentation tool will support the visualisation and distribution of information. The presentation of slides (on the interactive whiteboard) will be controlled via NotePad and distributed via radio communication to the other NotePad machines (instead of a lot of paper copies). So during the presentation each participant will be able to make annotations and remarks on his own electronic copy of the slides.

- A joint editing tool. This tool will allow to make both textual and graphical changes in parallel on common data using the NotePad computers, for example on a document which is written jointly by the meeting-group. The work will include support for local and distributed editing of documents and also methods for synchronisation of the users activities.

To extent the support of cooperative work, we intent to realize further tools, for example a tool to support brainstorming, a decision support tool and tools to help organizing meetings, e.g. to schedule dates, to inform people, to maintain addresses, to send invitations etc.

A first demonstrator of such a meeting assistant system will be realized within the Esprit Project No. 5233 [ TELESTATION].

# Harmonization Criterion for the Man-Machine Interaction

Edward M. Soroko* and  Sergey V. Kirpich**

*Institute of Philosophy Law
**Institute of Engineering Cybernetics
Academy of Sciences, 220012 Minsk, Belarus', CIS
Fax: 7 0172 / 31 84 03
mahaniok % adonis@sovam.com

**Abstract.** The concept of the synthesis of the objective integrity (harmonicity) measure of the systems has been substantiated. This measure is based on the formal criterion for the structural harmony of the systems.
Key words: man-machine-system, interaction, harmonization, measure, invariant.

## 1 Introduction

In using complex systems (e.g., man-machine-environment), the scientists and engineers still more often take into account the system performance criteria, whose use allows more complete account of the emergency effect.

## 2 Criterion

The system performance criterion is based on the integrity (harmonicity) concept, by which here is understood as a rigorous ratio (proportion) of interacting elements or processes in a system.

The integrity (harmonicity) measure of a system to be substantiated below expresses: (a) the presence of many factors and (b) the simultaneity (parallelism) of the actions of such factors that determine the state and the regimes of the system functioning.

A man as an active part in the man-machine interaction is drawn to make integral estimates of an object characterized by a set of the factors (e.g., complexity, hierarchy, reliability, adaptivity, evolution, controllibility, etc.). In this case, the integrity measure of such an object may be presented in the form of a mean-geometrical value of $M_1$ of partial measures $\{ m_i \}$, whose number is equal to the number of the factors s ( $i = 1, 2, ..., S$ )

$$M = \sqrt[s]{m_1 \cdot m_2 \cdot \ldots \cdot m_s}$$

and also to make the analysis it is necessary to use the s-th degree of this mean quantity $M$, i.e., $M_1 = M^s$.

A man as the subject of the activity reflects this object, i.e., the man–machine interaction in the form of the integer image. The amount of the information in a synthetic image of the object perceived by the man may be given (according to Hartley) as $M_2 = \log M^s = s \cdot \log M$.

It is assumed that the perception of the man–machine interaction by the man obeys the stability reguirements; following Lyapunov's theory the small variation of an object is satisfied with the small variation of the image (i,e., the reflection on the object).

This means that the ratio of the elementary increments (delta) of the above measure enables one to include the 3rd measure $M_3 = \dfrac{\delta s \cdot \log M}{\delta M} = \dfrac{s}{M}$.

The obtained measure $M_3$ serves as the control function of the object reflection additivity in the man's activity.

The functional

$$A = M_1 + M_2 + M_3 = M^s + s \cdot \log M + \frac{s}{M}$$

may serve as the generalized quality criterion, i.e., the harmonization criterion for the man–machine interaction. The extremum of the given functional in attained at the critical points, which are the solutions (roots) of the equation of the form

$$M^{s+1} + M = 1, \quad s = 0, 1, 2, 3, \ldots .$$

The roots of then equation are the generators of the invariants of the system organization measure: $0.500 \ldots$ ; $0.618 \ldots$ ; $0.682 \ldots$ ; $0.725 \ldots$ .

Each value of the invariant coresponds to the define system quality, i.e., to the quality of the man–machine interaction.

## 3 Applications

There are many examples that support the validity of the proposed concept. For example, in performing the discrete activity the man-operator forms an optimal strategy of the behaviour (minimum of errors). Objectively, the time ratio of the man's activity is subdivided into subranges, which for different regimes of the activity correspond to the above invariants of the activity organization measures irrespective of the individual specific features and specificity of the activity.

Thus, the concept of the synthesis of the objective integrity (harmonicity) measure of the systems has been substantiated. This measure is based on the formal criterion for the structural harmony of the systems.

# Three-Dimensional Visual Representations for Graphical User Interfaces: the Art of User-Involvement

Peter Thomas and Keith Goss

Department of Computer Science, Brunel University

Uxbridge, Middlesex, UK

Fax: (+44) 895 251686

Email: Peter.Thomas@brunel.ac.uk

**Abstract.** This paper reports on work to develop enhanced visual representations for graphical user interfaces in the form of three-dimensional icons designed as access points to information spaces. The aim is to enhance the interaction between user and interface object by adding 'information depth' and 'information breadth' to interface objects. The paper discusses the approach and describes some issues in the development of 3-dimensional representations.

## 1 Introduction

A commonly-accepted definition of 'icon' is 'a representation used to indicate characteristics of the system's objects by sharing graphic elements' icons exploit our natural abilities to contextualise visual images without *a priori* interpretive rules. Recent work has attempted to challenge the *de rigueur* status of icons in graphical user interfaces and transform the icon from simple static representation to dynamic interface component. Current directions are the use of sound and animation, and the development of picture icons, rotating icons, 'emotional' icons and movie icons.

Further developments are possible by considering icons to be representations of complex information spaces comprising the interface environment and the properties of the objects within it, rather than only as representations of objects themselves. Icons can thus been seen not as expressions of a known idea which exploit conventional appearances but as objects for information visualisation. On this view, issues in icon design are not those of learnability or identifiability, but of expert usability, and icons are not replacements for other forms of representation, but a way of arriving at more natural and efficient representations. Importantly, icons may be designed beyond the traditional 2-D 'illusionary' mode of representation which is a result of the stranglehold exerted by metaphor in graphical interface design: current icons only exploit the degrees of expressiveness provided by the arrangement and interplay of flat pictorial forms on the flat surface of the display. Properties such as visual depth, ambient light, perspective, and size – by dissolving the two-dimensionality of the display – can be systematically manipulated to reveal structure and provide user focus.

The essential issue here is that of interactivity. Interactivity is a matter of degree of engagement, and users will have no sense of engagement as long as 'the interface' is conceived of as standing between the user and task, rather than as a representation within which users act. The notion of 'direct engagement' suggests that we should focus on human-computer interaction as a designed experience and view 'functionality' not as 'what the system can do', but as 'what a user can do with a system'. Here much can be learned from visual art. In particular, we have found the assumptions, aims and techniques of Cubist painting useful in framing understandings of representation, interactivity, and designed experience which can be used in the creation of computer-based representations. Cubism is a genre of modernist art which addressed issues of interaction and representation by challenging the one-point perspective, the dominant system for depicting reality since the Renaissance, which had been elevated to a mathematical process which abstracted and schematised what the viewer saw. Cubism asserted that our knowledge of an object is made up of many possible views of it, and attempted to compress viewers' inspection of a scene or object into a synthesised view. The aim was to involve the viewer, who can then become a participant: this implies that the eye and its object inhabit the same space, bound by a strong 'internal language' of the representation.

## 2 Three-Dimensional Visual Representations

We have been employing these notions to develop icon forms which are not only indices to simple system objects, as are current icons, but indices to objects and associated processes, external and internal information sources. Such icons can provide information not about the immediate identity and function of the object itself, but about properties such as history, usage, and other relevant parameters in relation to its environment. The possibility is that the user can interact with a non-representational icon containing a number of visible facets which display not only what the user can immediately see but what is 'known' (both by the user and by the system) about the object. Such icons use techniques of flattening of form, simplification of representation, and compression into shallow pictorial space to deny 2-D illusionism. They serve to provide both information breadth (the ensembling of diverse information and resources within one representation) and also information depth (objects which provide semantic information about themselves without extensive interrogation of the interface). We are currently developing two types of icon: the first is *static* and *reactive* and serves to add information depth to the object. These icons provide information by displaying that information on different faces of a 3-D graphic object. The second is *dynamic* and *proactive* and allows the user to ensemble and manipulate heterogeneous information and thus serves to add information breath to the object.

The notion of 3-D icons, particularly those which are dynamic and proactive, involve a number of issues which are far from straightforward, and require the extension and of theories and approaches from human-computer interaction as well as providing further empirical support for established theories and approaches. The two particular areas we are developing [1, 2] are computer graphics techniques (topology, rendering and software architectures) and human factors issues (manipulation, control, visual design and the user's 'language of interaction').

## 3 Visual Representations, Art and User-involvement

The use of 'art' in contemporary interface design is mostly 'scientific' – a part of a 'good design'. This fails to recognise that human-computer interaction is fundamentally a process concerned with media and involvement. The approach we have taken attempts to bring such issues into the foreground through a particular interactional technique.

## References

1. Thomas, P. (1992) Cubist Icons. *Proceedings of EC2 Informatique Conference on 'Real and Virtual Worlds'*, Montpellier, 1992.

2. Thomas, P. and Goss, K. (forthcoming) Visual Interaction as Art: Cubist Icons. *Journal of Visual Languages and Computing.*

# Guidelines for Choosing Interaction Objects

François Bodart, Monique Noirhomme-Fraiture, Jean Vanderdonckt

Facultés Universitaires Notre-Dame de la Paix, Institut d'Informatique
Rue Grandgagnage, 21, B-5000 Namur (Belgium)
Tel : + 32- (0)81- 72 49 75 - Fax : + 32- (0)81- 72 49 67 - Telex : 59.222 Fac. Nam.B
E-mail : jvanderdonckt@info.fundp.ac.be

**Abstract.** Every designer faces the problem of choosing appropriate interaction objects when designing a human-computer interface. This should depend on the user capabilities, the data model and the target environment. Because the designer must rely on the experience and because there exists no way to assess that presentation consistency of the user-interfacefe is preserved, research results are presented as explicit selection rules.

## 1 Introduction

Each human-computer interaction consists of three dimensions: the user, the task and the environment. So, when designing the interface, the designer has to pay attention to all those three aspects during the whole process of developing the interface [2,3]. In this process, three steps can be identified [5]: the selection of appropriate abstract interaction objects, the transformation of abstract interaction objects into concrete interaction objects and the placement of the concrete interaction objects to form the final observable interface. J. Larson writes: "Specifying rules for selecting simple interaction objects is an ongoing research problem" ([3], p. 281). This paper is devoted to the first step by presenting an extended set of selection rules.

## 2 Selection Rules

Selection rules fall into two categories: rules for selecting objects to input data and to display data. They cover elementary data, elementary data for a list of data, list of data and group of data. Each data belongs to one of the nine supported data types: hour, date, logical, graphical, integer, numeric, real, alphabetic, and alphanumeric. Different observations led to these rules:

- input and output data should be differentiated to signify to the user the difference in the presentation;
- when the data already has predefined values, it is recommended to present these data to the user so that the desired value can be selected rather than keyed in;
- the higher the user experience is, the less guidance the user needs;
- the higher the user experience is, the higher the screen density can be and the shorter the commands, the labels are.

### 2.1 Parameters

Selection rules uses different parameters depending on the type of the data :

1. every application data is specified as a quadruplet d = (V, dt, nvc, dv) where $V$ is the domain of $d$ (if known); $dt$ belongs to one of the implemented data types; $nvc$ is the number of values to choose; $dv \in V$ is the default value of $d$ (if known). $V$ is partitioned into two sub-sets of principal values and secondary values.

2. six information refine each data when relevant: *precision-* whether precision is low, moderate or high; *orientation-* whether the data should be presented horizontally, vertically, circularly or is undefined; *known values-* whether $V$ is well defined; *ordered list-* whether $V$ is sorted according to a particular order (numerical, logical, temporal, physical, by frequence); *expandable list-* whether the user can add extend $V$ ; *continuous range-* whether the values are contained in a continuous range or interval.

3. one parameter specifies *constrained display space-* whether the selection must consider screen density to avoid too large objects. The more constrained is the screen space, the less large object is selected.

4. a user model is given by a *user experience level* (beginner, novice, intermediate, expert, master) and a *user selection preference* (low or high)- whether the use is more skilled to select one value among a list or to enter it with the keyboard.

## 3 Conclusion

Selection rules can be presented in a decision tree fashion [5] in order to provide the designer the ability to clearly visualize the conditions for using selection rules. The decision tree technique can also be included in a methodology and in an automatic interface generation tool in order to pilot the selection phase. Despite the fact that these rules are studies and presented as completely as possible (217 rules for input data, 28 for display data) [1], they remain experimental: the rules are subject to change in one particular environment and need to be rigorously validated during the development process. The aim of this work was mainly to suggest such a complete set of guidelines for highly-interactive business-oriented applications. A future work will be dedicated to tailor these rules for special users with others parameters such as: motor, ocular and mental abilities for users with disabilities, display time, scrolling time, acoustical feedaback and associated imagery in case of special interaction objects [4] which should be taken into account with users with cerebral palsy.

### Acknowledgments

This work was supported by the "Informatique du Futur" project of "Service de la Politique et de la Programmation Scientifique" under contract N°IT/IF/1. Any opinions, findings, conclusions or recommendations expressed in this paper are those of the authors, and do not necessarily reflect the view of the Belgian Authorities.

### References

1. F. Bodart, J. Vanderdonckt: Expressing Guidelines into an Ergonomical StyleGuide for Highly Interactive Applications. In S. Ashlund et al. (eds.): Adjunct Proc. of InterCHI'93 (Amsterdam, 24-29 April 1993), New York: ACM Press 1993, pp. 35-36
2. J. Coutaz: Interfaces homme-ordinateur. Paris: Bordas, 1990
3. J. A. Larson: Interactive Software - Tools for Building Interactive User Interfaces. Yourdon Press Computing Series. Englewood Cliffs: Prentice Hall, 1992
4. M. Noirhomme-Fraiture, J. Vanderdonckt: Screen Usability Guidelines for Persons with Disabilities, In S. Ashlund et al. (eds.): Adjunct Proc. of InterCHI'93 (Amsterdam, 24-29 April 1993), New York: ACM Press 1993, pp. 25-26
5. J. Vanderdonckt, F. Bodart: Encapsulating Knowledge for Intelligent Automatic Interaction Objects Selection. In: S. Ashlund et al. (eds.): Proc. of InterCHI'93 "Bridges Between Worlds" (Amsterdam, 24-29 April 1993). New York: ACM Press 1993, pp. 424-429

# Eine computergestützte multimediale Dokumentation über den Golfkrieg

Wolfgang Hofkirchner, Peter Purgathofer
Ralf Pichler, Anton Bruno Trapp
Karl Berger, Walter Nierer

Institut für Gestaltungs- und Wirkungsforschung, TU Wien
Möllwaldplatz 5, A-1040 Wien
hofi@iguwnext.tuwien.ac.at, purg@iguwnext.tuwien.ac.at
FAX 00431 504 11 90, Tel. 00431 504 11 86

## 1. Der Ausgangspunkt

ist die Überlegung, daß das Exempel Golfkrieg die These von der zunehmenden Unführbarkeit von Kriegen in Frage gestellt hat. Eine interaktive multimediale Dokumentation am Computer soll die interessierten BenutzerInnen zu einer überlegten und kritischen *Bewertung des Kriegs als Mittel der Politik* befähigen, indem sie dazu angeregt werden, sich mit den Folgen und Auswirkungen des Golfkriegs auseinanderzusetzen, den Verlauf des Krieges selbst, mitzuverfolgen, seine Vorgeschichte kennenzulernen und über die Hintergründe nachzudenken. Die Dokumentation beinhaltet dabei Betrachtungen aus militärischer wie auch aus nicht-militärischer Sicht (Geschichte, Geografie, Wirtschaft, Politik, Völkerrecht, Gesundheitswesen, Ökologie etc.).

Um Informationen optimal anzubieten und andererseits auch ein möglichst großes Zielpublikum anzusprechen, soll die Dokumentation alle gängigen Medien wie *Text, Grafik, Landkarten, Fotografie, Ton* und *Video* in einem multimedialen Hypertextsystem zusammenfassen.

Dieses System wird im Zusammenhang mit einem institutsweiten EDV-gestützten *Informationssystem für Forschung und Lehre* entwickelt, das auf der Grundlage des Hypertextsystems eine alternative Art der Informationsaufbereitung und -suche impliziert (Projekt "Ein computerunterstütztes integriertes Lehr- und Forschungssystem" (Leitung Prof. Fleissner), das vom Fonds zur Förderung der wissenschaftlichen Forschung finanziert wird).

## 2. Die Organisation bzw. Realisierungsschritte

schlossen aufgrund des komplexen Umfelds rund um die Fragestellung Golfkrieg (wie, wo, wann und warum) eine Einteilung des ganzen Problemkreises in etwa ein Dutzend mehr oder weniger voneinander unabhängige *thematische Sachgebiete* (z.B. "Streitkräfte", "Kurdenproblem", "Opfer" etc.) ein, die von je 2 bis 3 StudentInnen bearbeitet werden. Eine weitere Gruppe aus 4 Personen ist für die *programmtechnische*

*Umsetzung bzw. Realisierung* zuständig. Die Dokumentation entsteht auf Apple Macintosh-Rechnern unter HyperCard und ist auf allen Mac-Rechnern lauffähig. Zwei Personen aus dieser Gruppe versuchen, die Dokumentation an die PC-Welt anzupassen (ConvertIt und Toolbook).

Die Erstellung der einzelnen Dokumentationsteile durch die einzelnen Gruppen geschieht weitestgehend computerunterstützt: Für die Dokumentation relevante Aussagen aus dem großen Spektrum der zur Verfügung stehenden Literatur werden in sogenannten "*Zitate-Stacks*" festgehalten - sie erfüllen damit die Aufgabe eines elektronischen Notizblocks. Die für Hypertext notwendigen Links werden in diesem Schritt von den AutorInnen durch die Vergabe relevanter Stichworte für jedes Textstück vorbereitet.

In einem zweiten Schritt werden mit Hilfe dieser Zitate-Stacks (fast) fertige Teile der Gesamtdokumentation erstellt, und zwar mittels eines "*Golfbooks*" (hat Buchcharakter) und einer "*Golfmap*" (Landkarten). In (bzw. zwischen) beiden Teilen können zusätzlich Querverweise auf beliebige Themen vorgenommen werden bzw. Ton- und Videosequenzen angehängt werden.

Golfbook und Golfmap beenden die Arbeit der einzelnen PraktikantInnengruppen. Die fertige Dokumentation entsteht durch die computerunterstützte *Generierung* aus den bestichworteten Teildokumentationen. Dabei sollen Vollständigkeit und Konsistenz in einem weitgehend automatisierten Prüf- und Korrekturvorgang gesichert werden.

## 3. Die fertige Dokumentation

setzt sich aus einer großen Anzahl mehr oder weniger stark vernetzter Informationsstücke zusammen. Um den Zugriff auf diese Datenbasis zu ermöglichen, imitieren die MitarbeiterInnen für verschiedene Informationsarten „natürliche" Zugriffsweisen wie etwa einen Kassettenrecorder für Toninformationen. Mittels solcher Metaphern können die LeserInnen der Dokumentation ihr Wissen aus dem Umgang mit diesen Medien in der Wirklichkeit auf das System umlegen und so mit wenig Lernaufwand und geringer zusätzlicher kognitiver Last durch die Daten „wandern".

Die Darstellungsmetaphern sind

• *ein Buch mit gezeichneten Darstellungen*, das z.B. einen Katalog der zur Anwendung gelangten Waffensysteme oder die entsprechenden UNO-Resolutionen enthält;

• *Fotos*, die in einem eigenen Graustufen-Fenster z.B. die Konterfeis der politischen Führer oder Bilder aus der Schlacht zeigen;

• *Kalender*, die z.B. die Chronologie des Kriegsverlaufes oder der diplomatischen Vorgeschichte in zwei Zugriffsebenen (Überblick und Detail) strukturieren;

• *Landkarten*, die z.B. eine Übersicht über die Verschmutzung der Meere oder die Aufmarschpläne geben;

• „*Kassettenrecorder*" und „*Fernsehapparat*" als metaphorische Darstellung des Zugriffs z.B. auf Bush-Reden oder Filmaufnahmen von den brennenden Ölquellen (Ton- bzw. Videodokumente).

Dem allgegenwärtigen Problem des „lost in Hyperspace" soll also durch starke Strukturierung der Information und der Benutzerschnittstelle begegnet werden.

# The Global Window as a Communication Mediator in Public Administration

Terje Grimstad & Riitta Hellman

Norwegian Computing Center
P.O.Box 114 Blindern, N-0314 Oslo, Norway
e-mail: Terje.Grimstad@nr.no & Riitta.Hellman@nr.no

**Abstract**. New types of CSCW-technologies have potential areas of use in other kind of environments than those recognised by the current research. Global window allows two or more conference participants at different sites to spontaneosly run any application in a cooperative multi-user mode. Several application areas of Global Window in the Norwegian Postal Service have been identified: computer-assisted learning, business contacts with customers, budgeting, case-handling, decicion support and systems development.

## 1 Introduction

For the Norwegian Postal Service, we have recognised several untraditional uses of one particular groupware technology called the Global Window (GW). This is also in line with the development that e.g. Grudin calls for: instead of new CSCW-technologies, new uses of *existing* CSCW-technologies should be invented [1].

Global Window (GW) is a concept which describes a *class* of systems. A GW-system allows two or more conference participants at different workstations and potentially different sites to spontaneously run any application in a cooperative, multi-user mode. Facilities for audio teleconfering and telepointing amongst conference participants are also provided [2].

## 2 The Case-Study (The Norwegian Postal Service)

The Norwegian Postal Service has 32000 employees. It is divided into 12 postal regions with approximately 2500 Post Offices and 2300 rural postman distribution routes.

The survey was based on "walking through" a relatively small samle of potential areas of use in the case-study organisation. The working method in the selected units was first to present GW and give examples of its current applications. After this, a group-discussion on possible uses of GW in the sample unit was conducted. Here, the suggested uses of GW came from the employees of the Postal Service.

## 3 Findings

(1) To a large extent, the case-study organisation educates its own personnel. Both basic and follow-up education is given. Special self-study training programs could be provided for this kind of education. In such a context, the student would need to contact the teacher every now and then. This contact could be made via GW. Another learning context is the daily work at the counter of the Post Office. GW could be used to provide online help for unencountered or unexpected situations for the clerk at the counter.

(2) The Postal Giro Service regards GW a useful tool while discussing business prospects and new products and services with customers. Both to provide a technological image and to be able to use technical expertise which is located elsewhere.

The local Post Offices compete with private distribution companies and newspaper distribution routes. The price of these services is set as a result of negotiations. If these negotiations were performed using GW, the effect would be beneficial both for the Post Office and the customer. The Post Office could provide better service, and the customer could actively participate in tailoring a cost-effective product.

(3) GW is also relevant for the yearly budgeting process. The process is as follows: The yearly budget includes both incomes and expenses. A total financial frame is divided iteratively into sub-frames concerning each unit and each organisational level. The budgeting process is based on a *negotiation principle*, such that after being "broadcast" downwards in the organisational hierarchy, requests for changing the local sub-frames will start being returned upwards in the hierarchy. Negotiations implies a number of both telephone calls and ordinary meetings. Finally, a "definite frame" is established. In the regions' opinion, GW would make both the broadcasting phase and the negotiation phase of the budgeting process much easier by increasing mutual understanding.

(4) The case-study organisation covers the whole nation, including its most rural parts. Basically identical services are guaranteed to all customers independent of the geographic location. In such a setting, it is not possible for all the necessary information nor the required special competence to be present in *every* imaginable situation. Therefore, for case-handling, collaboration with experts via GW becomes interesting.

(5) Decision making involves new business strategies, flexible pricing, the foundation of new joint-stock or subsidiary companies, design of new product profiles and so on. Decision making could benefit from the use of GW: "horisontally", at the level of the postal regions; and "vertically", between the region managers and the coordinative organ in the Directorate of the Norwegian Posts. Also, e.g. the monthly meetings in order to coordinate and follow-up the regions could be combined with the use of GW.

## 4 Discussion

It is often claimed that organisations which have which have flat, group-oriented and informal structure should benefit from CSCW-technologies (e.g. [3]). In our case, we found that the opposite sort of structure, namely the bureaucratic, hierarchical organisation could benefit greatly from the GW CSCW-technology. Groups which "should" be potential users of GW, e.g. the top managers' team, would *not* be able to utilise GW to any great extent. This claim is based on the main characteristic of the team: it is small and its work is based on personal contacts in e.g. problem solving situations.

Another observation concerns the use of GW to support the contact between the case-study organisation itself and its environment (the market).

This means that, in addition to the "original" uses of the CSCW-technologies in the "typical" organisation, uses of fundamentally other kind are emerging (see also [4]).

We assume that should GW be used as a collaborative tool between different organisational levels (e.g. the budgeting process), it would act to facilitate learning about others' working domains. Gaining new knowledge would probably apply in both directions in the organisational hierarchy. Higher levels could learn about the practical problems at the lower levels while these, in turn, could learn about the organisational whole.

## References

1. Grudin, J.: Why CSCW-Applications Fail: Problems in the Design and Evaluation of Organizational Interfaces. Proceedings of the Second Conference on Computer-Supported Cooperative Work, 26–28 September 1988. Portland, Oregon, pp. 85–93.
2. Grimstad, T., Maartmann-Moe, E. and Aas, G.: Real Time Multimedia Conference with Voice and Global Window. Proceedings of The Norwegian Informatics Conference. November 17-18 1992. Tromsø, Norway, pp. 281-291.
3. Goodman, G.O. and Abel, M. J.: Communication and Collaboration: Facilitating Cooperative Work through Communication. Office, Technology and People, Vol. 2, No. 3, 1987, pp. 129-145.
4. Hellman, R.: Emancipation of and by Computer-Supported Cooperative Work. The Scandinavian Journal of Information Systems. Vol 1, 1989, pp. 143–161.

# A supporting system for human creativity: Computer aided divergent thinking process by provision of associative pieces of information

Kazushi Nishimoto, Kenji Mochizuki, Tsutomu Miyasato and Fumio Kishino

ATR Communication Systems Research Laboratories,
2-2 Hikaridai, Seika-cho, Soraku-gun, Kyoto, 619-02, Japan
knishi@atr-sw.atr.co.jp

**Abstract.** We propose a new method of supporting human creativity whereby heterogeneous information is provided to users. By extracting data associatively from databases and selecting data by using a user-model of interests and a user-model of knowledge, this system provides pieces of heterogeneous information to users coarsely within the interests or scope of the users' current thinking. In this paper, how heterogeneous information is provided to users is shown as well as experimental results obtained with a prototype system.

## 1 Introduction

We propose a new method of supporting human creativity whereby heterogeneous information is provided to users. This method can typically be applied to support brainstorming. By combining this method with a conference system with realistic sensations in a virtual reality environment[1], we aim at constructing a creative discussion space. How heterogeneous information is provided to users is shown as well as experimental results obtained with a prototype system.

## 2 Background

Two significant processes are said to exist in human creativity thinking: a divergent thinking process and a convergent thinking process. In the divergent thinking process people extract many ideas or pieces of information associatively, and in the convergent thinking process they unify them and look for some relations between some of them. If new (unknown) relations are found, they form *new ideas*. Or, if any relations are found between some pieces of heterogeneous information, they may constitute an *epoch-making discovery*.

Therefore, providing heterogeneous information as well as information directly related to the interests of a person's current thinking is effective in supporting the human creativity process (especially the divergent thinking process). From a similar view point, Dr. Young has been trying to support human creativity by the provision of metaphors[2]. Our approach, on the other hand, is to provide heterogeneous information by using a *more free-associative method*. However, it goes without saying that providing completely heterogeneous information may not be so effective. It is important to provide information coarsely within the interests (or scope) of a person's current thinking.

## 3 Approach

We have been studying methods to achieve the above-mentioned concept and developing a prototype system for experiments, under the assumption that users converse with the system by using only text data. Below, "article" means text data stored in the database and provided to users, and "query-sentence" means text data users input when conversing with the system. The query-sentence, it should be noted, is a natural sentence, not a so-called list of keywords.

Methods to achieve the concept include :

1. Treating all words included in articles or query-sentences as keywords.

This aims to extract heterogeneous articles by treating not only strongly-concerned words (so-called keywords) but also weakly-concerned words as keywords of articles and query-sentences.

2. Applying Associatron (an associative memory technique)[3] to memorize/recall articles into/from the database.

This allows the system to recall articles associatively and chainly by itself, and to provide divergent articles to users. With the function of the Associatron, even if a query-sentence includes noise words, the system can extract a certain article.

3. Using two user-models.

This aims to limit and to enable the selection of extracted articles.

**User-model of interests.** This user-model represents a user's interests. That is, it is used for putting the extracted data into the scope of the user's interests. This model is constructed as lists of keywords selected by a user.

**User-model of knowledge.** This user-model represents a user's knowledge. Here, "knowledge" has two meanings: (a) Articles already read by the user and (b) Articles, related to the current theme of conversation, with which the user has already recognized some relations. This user-model is constructed as a list of already-provided articles (related to the theme of conversation). It is used for providing new articles or articles already read by the user when the user may not recognize any relations between the articles and the current theme.

## 5 Experiment with prototype system

We experimented with a prototype system (with one user) and examined what kinds of articles were extracted associatively. A result we got from a conversation with this system is given below. The user's interests were represented as a list of keywords (user-model of interests).

Current theme : America.　　　　　User's interests : politics, animals.
query-sentence : "A few months ago, an American election for *President* was held."
article 1 : The new President is Mr. *Clinton*.
article 2 : Mr. Clinton is living in the White House with his wife, daughter and *dog*.
article 3 : In Japan, *Shogun* Tsunayoshi enacted a law to protect dogs.
　　　:

The italic words can be regarded as trigger words to get the next article. In this example, the user inputs a query-sentence and then the system recalls and extracts article 1 probably by using the word "President" mainly. Next, the system recalls article 2 chainly by itself probably using the word "Clinton" mainly. Then, the system recalls the remainder in the same way. In this case, article 3 is not within the current theme but among the interests of the user. It is expected that such heterogeneous articles become triggers for the user's creation.

## 6 Conclusion

This system provides us with articles that are not completely related to the theme and/or in the scope of a user's interests, but coarsely within them. With this system, human creativity, especially the divergent thinking process for human creation, can be accelerated.

## References

[1] Kishino, F., et al., "Virtual Space Teleconferencing System - Real Time Detection and Reproduction of 3-D Human Images", Proceedings of HCI International '93 (1993)
[2] Young, L.F., "The Metaphor Machine: A Database Method for Creativity Support", Decision Support Systems, Vol.3, No.4, pp.309-317 (1987)
[3] Nakano, K., "Associatron", Shoukou-dou (1979)

# An Integrated Courseware Editor Based on OLE Technology*

H.W.J. Borst Pauwels
J. Sousa Pinto
B. Sousa Santos
J. A. Martins

Department of Electronics & Telecommunications
INESC/University of Aveiro, 3800, Portugal
Tel. 351.34.20173, Fax.351.34.381128
hbp@zeus.ci.ua.pt

## 1 Introduction

Currently, several hypermedia systems are available and extensively reviewed by Conklin [1] and Nielsen [2]. An important application field of hypermedia is distance education. The aim of distance education environments is to provide learning resources to a large number of students spread over wide geographical areas. The social significance of these systems is twofold. On one hand, they are helpful to bridge the gap between isolated students and learning centers. On the other hand, they allow teachers to be efficiently 'shared' over several geographically distributed students.

Traditionally, learning material in distance learning environments consist of rather static material like printed text, audiocassettes, videocassettes, television and radio programs. Computer supported courseware based on hypermedia technology opens new perspectives for distance education. Hypermedia learning material can be developed in less time, is more flexible for modifications than traditional learning material and can be distributed relatively fast over computer networks in comparison with the traditional way of sending learning material over ordinary mail.

In this paper we describe the objectives and methods of the design of a hypermedia courseware editor for IBM PCs (or compatibles).

## 2 Objectives

Our first objective was to design a hypermedia courseware editor that is capable of integrating existing applications.

Another objective consisted in obtaining a modeless editor which supports both authoring and reading of hypermedia documents based on one underlying metaphor.

## 3 Methods

We implemented a hypermedia courseware editor using Microsoft ® Windows ™ OLE technology [3]. OLE, Object Linking and Embedding, stands for an extensible protocol (that was jointly developed by a group of Independent Software Vendors (ISVs) including Microsoft, Aldus, Micrografx, and others) that enables an application to use the services of other applications.

The central philosophy behind OLE technology is to change from a traditional "application centered" view of computing, towards a "document centered" view.

This document centered view can be obtained by offering the user the possibility of accessing applications through their associated data instead through applications. Basically, this implies that a user does not have to leave an application in order to create or edit application specific data, but instead more comfortably, simply launch an application by a mouse click on the specific data. It is possible to distinguish two kinds of applications: OLE server applications which can create OLE data and OLE client applications which can receive OLE data .

We developed a hypermedia courseware editor that acts as an OLE client capable of receiving OLE data from several commercial OLE servers. An overhead projector was used as the underlying metaphor. Our editor act as an "electronic" overhead projector on which lessons composed of piles of "electronic" transparencies, can be displayed either in simple sequential order or in more sophisticated so-called "web" structures. More precisely, in our approach, one hypermedia node consists of a background transparency which may, or may not, be covered by one or more overlaying transparencies.

Background transparencies can be filled with OLE objects and afterwards connected by means of anchors, either to other background transparencies or to overlaying transparencies. An anchor is an rectangular area on a background transparency. When an anchor is introduced a new blank background transparency will be automatically displayed or, in case the user requested a connection to an overlaying transparency, a new blank overlaying transparency will be automatically inserted over the background transparency. In both cases, the new blank transparency can be filled with OLE objects. A mouse click on an anchor connected to a background transparency will trigger an event that displays again the associated background transparency. A mouse click on an anchor connected to an overlaying transparency will trigger an event that inserts the associated overlaying transparency over the background transparency or, in case the overlaying transparency is already inserted, removes it.

## 3 Conclusions

We described an integrated courseware editor based on OLE technology. Our courseware editor integrates existing applications like, drawing programs, spreadsheets, sound recorders and text processors into one consistent hypermedia environment. Based on a metaphor of an "electronic" overhead projector both authoring and reading of hypermedia documents are combined in one modeless editor. Our current prototype will be demonstrated at the poster session.

## References

1.      J. Conklin: Hypertext: A survey and introduction. IEEE Computer 20, 9, 17-41 (1987)

2.      J. Nielsen: Hypertext and Hypermedia, Academic Press, (1990)

3.      Object linking and embedding programmer's reference, version 1, Microsoft Press, (1992)

(*) Work done as part of CO-LEARN (D2005) , a project financed by the EEC within the DELTA program.

# Empirical Findings on Using Information Technology in the Creativity Stage of Problem Solving

Otto Petrovic

Institut fuer Betriebswirtschaftslehre der Oeffentlichen Verwaltung
und Verwaltungswirtschaft, Karl-Franzens-University of Graz
Babenbergerstrasse 10, A-8020 Graz, Austria
phone: +43 316 9841 200, fax: +43 316 9841 215

## 1    Obective of the research

For some time now the support of meetings in electronic meeting rooms (EMRs) has been researched. These meeting rooms are equipped with special hard- and software and are meant to benefit the ratio of process profits and losses during the meetings. We distinguish between the effects on efficiency and effectivity, and as far as effectivity is concerned, quantity and quality of results as well as the degree of satisfaction of participants are analysed separately.

## 2    Research method used

**External conditions:** *Kinds of participants, the group, the context and the task:* The participants in the meetings studied were natural groups of students of business administration. The seminar was concluded by project presentations in front of an audience made up of business people who assessed the results according to different criteria. The goal of the meetings carried out in the Graz Electronic Meeting Room was to generate as many contributions as possible to obtain the best possible assessment by business people and thus win the first prize. *Technological variation 1:* electronic meeting room and electronic brainstorming. *Technological variation 2:* traditional moderation. **Variables of research:** *Effectivity:* The quantity of contributions generated is expressed in the total number of contributions made and the number of different contributions. Each contribution was attributed a quality value on a seven-step Likert scale by a team of experts. The attitudes of participants towards the results obtained, towards the process and the technology used were obtained both in the computer supported and the traditionally moderated groups by means of an electronic questionnaire and a seven-step Likert scale. *Efficiency:* As a measure for efficiency we use the average time requirement for a "good" contribution.

## 3    Findings and Conclusions

The significantly higher number of generated contributions in the computer supported groups is primarily due to the higher degree of anonymity. This reduces group pressure as well as social control. Communication via an electronic medium also leads to de-personification of contributions, which reduces orientation towards a group but also towards personal ideas. Electronic brainstorming leads to higher media speed which means that reading electronically transmitted contributions and putting in new ones is faster than writing cards and having them collected by a moderator. This greater number of contributions also results in a greater number of "good" contributions. Anonymity, de-personification and higher media speed do not only lead to the positive result of more contributions but also to the negative effect of lower quality on average. This is indicated by a greater number of humorous and irrelevant remarks. The time requirement per "good" contribution is not significantly different because of the fact that computer supported meetings not only last highly significantly longer than traditionally moderated ones but also generate more "good" contributions. The extended length of computer supported meetings is due to better use of the creative potential of participants which is manifest in the higher degree of participation mentioned at the beginning.

| Statement | computer supported | | | traditionally moderated | | | t-value | DF | 2-tail prob. |
|---|---|---|---|---|---|---|---|---|---|
| | mean value | stand. deviation | N | mean value | stand. deviation | N | | | |
| H1: number of contributions | 103,86 | 21,91 | 7 | 61,33 | 13,34 | 6 | -4,13 | | 0,00 |
| H2: number of different contributions | 96,43 | 21,07 | 7 | 54,67 | 11,59 | 6 | -4,31 | | 0,00 |
| H3: number of "good" contributions | 74,15 | 18,52 | 7 | 51,67 | 12,28 | 6 | -2,53 | | 0,02 |
| H4: quality per contribution** | 4,66 | 2,05 | 675 | 5,75 | 1,36 | 328 | 10,02 | 912 | 0,00 |
| H8: time requirement per "good" contribution*** | 0,54 | 0,18 | 7 | 0,45 | 0,14 | 6 | -0,99 | | 0,34 |
| H9: length of meeting*** | 37,43 | 3,87 | 7 | 22,33 | 6,35 | 6 | -5,27 | | 0,00 |

\* No variance homogeneity can be found (test level 5%), hence separate variance estimate in SPSS/PC+ was used
\*\* Values on a seven-step Likert scale
\*\*\* Values in minutes

**Table 1:** The quality and quantity of results achieved and the efficiency of the meeting

| | computer supported | | | | traditionally moderated | | | | t-value | DF | 2-tail prob. |
|---|---|---|---|---|---|---|---|---|---|---|---|
| | mean value | stand. deviation | Cron-bach's α | N | mean value | stand. deviation | Cron-bach's α | N | | | |
| H 5: Attitudes towards results | 4,28 | 1,19 | 0,77 | 38 | 4,71 | 0,90 | 0,64 | 41 | 1,79 | 77 | 0,08 |
| H 6: Attitudes towards process | 5,75 | 1,29 | 0,87 | 38 | 5,59 | 0,59 | 0,35 | 41 | -0,70 | 51 | 0,49 |
| H 7: Attitudes towards technology | 5,39 | 1,17 | 0,72 | 38 | 5,40 | 1,20 | 0,69 | 41. | 0,03 | 77 | 0,98 |
| 1 ... reject totally | | | | | | | | | | | |
| 7 ... agree totally | | | | | | | | | | | |

**Table 2:** Test of hypotheses concerning attitudes of participants

*For a full paper of this research work see:* Petrovic, O., & Krickl, O. (1993). 'Traditionell-moderiertes vs. computergestütztes Brainstorming: Eine vergleichende Betrachtung,' Wirtschaftsinformatik, Vol. 35 Nr. 2 S. 120-128.

# Computers in Local Administrative Offices (Province of Salzburg) — Aspects of Stress, Strain and Training

Eveline Riedling

Institut für Gestaltungs- und Wirkungsforschung
TU Wien
Möllwaldplatz 5
A-1040 Wien
Austria
eriedling@ps1.iaee.tuwien.ac.at

**Abstract.** This study, recently undertaken in communities in the county of Salzburg which are IOZ (Informatics and Organization Center Salzburg) customers, deals with the new situation which computerized administration brought to the offices: It evaluates the software, the ability of the clerks to handle hard- and software, the training of the personnel, the nature and the frequency of training sessions, the conditions under which people were allowed to attend computer training classes, the ergonomic aspects of the working place, and the subjective feelings of the clerks towards computerization (stress, strain, readiness towards training, and so on).

## 1 Introduction

During recent years, most of the local authorities in the province of Salzburg have computerized their administration. Although some tasks are still performed on mainframe computers at the IOZ in Salzburg City, the main goal of the communities is independence and the ability to accomplish administrative tasks locally, which is also commercially supported by the IOZ. Having delivered the second release of their administration programs, the IOZ programming team launched a comprehensive evaluation of computerized administration.

## 2 Objectives of the study

This study was targeted to identify changes in the working conditions in recently computerized administrative offices. Its main objectives were evaluating the software itself, the handling of the hard- and software by the users, the ergonomic aspects of the working environment, the training situation, and the subjective feelings of the personnel towards computerization. Changes which might be necessary to enhance personnel performance or subjective job satisfaction should be pointed out as specifically as possible.

## 3 Research Method

The research method employed was to interview people with standarized questionnaires which covered all aspects mentioned above. Subsequently, an informal conversation targeted aspects of subjective feelings, stress, strain, and the subjective training situation. The interviews took place at the offices, in case of the clerks in absence of their superiors, in case of the mayors in absence of their personnel. This warranted responses largely unbiased by social or hierarchical pressure. Anonymity was guaranteed.

## 4 Results

The result of the study showed a significant general undervaluation of the difficulties of computerized work. In most of the communities, computerization of the office was started without any or with just a minor knowledge of computers, without any intense training, and mostly with just a few hours of introduction to the IOZ programs – and with the deep conviction to be able to manage all outcoming problems fast, efficiently, and alone. The result of this attitude were severe problems in many aspects: Loss of data, many hours of additional work, learning from mistakes while working, and so on.

These problems existed to a much lesser degree in communities where some kind of computer experts existed, most of them trained at former working places, or dealing with computers at home just as a hobby. Even then, the lack of didactical abilities frequently caused problems. Most severe problems occurred where people were not allowed to go to computer training classes, or where the clerks just ignored the importance of training.

As an additional result, we could find significant differences between the working conditions for men and for women. Most of the female clerks are exclusively trained by male colleagues who themselves just managed to handle the programs somehow, whereas at least some male colleagues attended some computer training. In general, the result of trying to save money instead of investing it in good computer training classes for secretaries were a major increase of stress and fear particularly found with female clerks.

Based on the outcome of this study, the IOZ recently started offering additional computer training. The most efficient form of such training could be personalized training classes which address the specific needs of particular communities and their personnel. These classes should take place at the offices. The questionnaire could be a guide to identify the subjective needs of the clerks.

## References

1.      Bullinger, H.J.(ed.): Human Aspects in Computing, Proceedings of the Fourth International Conference on Human-Computer Interaction, Stuttgart, Elsevier 1991.
2.      Landauer, Th.K: Research Methods in Human-Computer Interaction. In: Helander, M.(ed.): Handbook of Human-Computer Interaction, Elsevier 1991.
3.      Riedling, E.: EDV-Einsatz in Gemeinden am Beispiel des Landes Salzburg, Teil 1, (Gemeinden, die vom IOZ betreut werden), Studie Teil 1. IOZ Salzburg (Amt der Salzburger Landesregierung) 1993.

# Configurable Guides for a Seasonal Database

Peter Purgathofer

Technische Universität Wien
Fachgruppe Informatik
Inst. für Gestaltungs- und Wirkungsforschung
Abteilung Sozialkybernetik
Möllwaldplatz 5/187
A-1040 Wien
EMail purg@iguwnext.tuwien.ac.at

Peter Rüppel

Technische Universität Berlin
Fachbereich Informatik
Inst. für Angewandte Informatik
Forschungsgr. Softwaretechnik
Franklinstr. 28/29
1000 Berlin 10
EMail rueppel@cs.tu-berlin.de

## Introduction

Accessing large databases via command or specification languages is a quite powerful but also trying process; while trained user have access to all possible options, especially rare and untrained user will experience an overwhelming overhead from the demand to use an artificial language. Sometimes even experts tend to use direct manipulation interfaces to databases when they have the choice.

[Salo89, Oren90] suggest the usage of "Guides" as a "natural" metaphor to help users access large databases in a natural setting. Guides represent experts on a certain topic of the database and can be activated whenever their point of view is needed. If combined with other "natural" metaphors like a museum, a book or a building, guides can complement user's access even to a large information space yielding in a most usable system with easy comprehensible structures.

## The Project

We developed a prototype for a tourist information system that is to be used by extremely untrained users e.g. in bookstores or tourist information fairs. It is designed to combine all the (multimedia) material already present for touristic information: print, video, sound, etc.

The basic idea was to combine a simple book metaphor that enables the reader to use the system like a book with some guides that are ready to give information on various topics like sport, transportation or culture. While the book metaphor needs some extensions to include multimedia information (video, sound, animation), the guides were designed to act as cartoons that can be asked by clicking at them.

## Changing Information and Guides

However, this structure does not comprehend the need for seasonal changes of a system that carries touristic information. In winter a person talking about skiing e.g. will tell different things from what she tells in summer. Besides that touristic management is forcing yearly or half-yearly trends like bicycle riding or snow boarding.

While seasonal information can be added by using several predefined databases for one guide, the rapidly changing trend information still is difficult to include. One possible solution to this problem is the introduction of configurable guides.

## Configurable Guides

We improved the design by including guides that can be influenced in their behavior by some system administrators. One e.g. represents a quite stylish, trendy living person. This guide is used to inform about the ever changing in's and out's and of special offers available.

To represent such a character in our prototype, the topics of "interest" and the visual representation of the guide had to be adaptable for the various trend and seasonal information and the task of changing the behavior of such guides had to be easy enough for non-programmers.

This implies that a configurable guide is more a kind of template for a role or character.

## Possible Problems

The main problem on configurable guides is that changes are only allowed following the structure (the stereotypic character) of the guide: Everybody would inspect a professor in art history to give valuable information about art and culture, but would be bewildered when getting information about new trends of winter sports or the prices of train tickets from him.

Because of this it is important to formulate restrictions to define a character's stereotypic kernel. These restrictions can be formulated into guidelines, laid on the process of authoring or act as basic topics of the character template: a trendy person should always be interested in things which are "new".

But besides the problems which arise from the behavioral side of configurable guides, there are also difficult aspects in the visual representation of a stereotypical character: how does a trendy person look like? Is it possible to represent the various trends in one guide or will you need more? How can you formulate certain aspects of the visual representation in a guideline or in the character template?

To answer these questions will be part of our future work.

## Bibliography

[Oren90] Oren, Salomon, Kreitman, Don. "Guides: Characterizing the Interface" in "The Art of Human-Computer Interface Design" by Brenda Laurel, Addison-Wesley, 1990, pp. 367-382

[Salo89] Salomon, Gitta, Oren, Kreitman. "Using Guides to Explore Multimedia Databases" Proc. 22nd Hawaii International Conference on System Sciences, Kailua-Kona, Hawaii, January 3-6, 1989, pp. 3-12

# Offering Different Perspectives in a Learning Environment

Simon H Gill & David K Wright
Department of Design,Brunel University
Egham, Surrey
Simon.Gill @ brunel.ac.uk

**Abstract.** We discuss the design and development of a learning system that offers a number of presentation styles and learning perspectives. The system is concerned with the application of a constructivist model of teaching and the benefits of non-linear and interactive structure. The system can present a number of commonly held beliefs, and challenge the learner to choose, modify, and explain the concepts until the correct scientific model is reached. The learner has the ability to choose, and alter the language level and the style of instruction throughout the learning sequence.

## 1. Introduction

The general student perception of computer aided learning is that the packages are of poor quality, difficult to use, and do little to interest them. Hypermedia systems are able to provide a large number of links and cross-references, so that the user can explore their own interests and branch when they feel it is correct to (1). It is also important to offer material that can be read at differing levels, depending on the readers experience and perspective.

## 2. Hypermedia and Interactive Learning

Our system utilises the Constructivist approach of learning (2,3), which benefits extensively from non-linearity by offering a range of possible routes. The work to date has concentrated on Physics material for the over 16s, although the principles involved and specification can be applied to awide range of subjects (4). The pre-instructional ideas of the students are strongly held and it is not generally sufficient to simply provide the accepted or correct model, and check by asking test questions. It is essential that learners explore their own individual models and concepts, and then to have the model challenged as part of the system. The results have been very encouraging in eliciting these ideas. However the acceptance of the correct scientific view does require a great deal of support In order to help facilitate this learning we propose a learning style approach which is sympathetic to the needs of the learner, and one that can cater more specifically for individuals.

## 3. Language Levels

The style and level of language used in teaching is often a barrier to learning. An early implementation of the system allowed the learner to alter the language level of the system 'on the fly'. The levels catered for were child, teenager and student, and were signified by the faces of Donald Duck, Boris Becker (German text), Marilyn Monroe and Albert Einstein respectively (5). On discussion with the students they seemed amazed and excited by such a feature, but on using the package the students tended not to alter the teacher setting, as this feature is not commonly associated with traditional paper text. New ways of communication have been explored in order to represent the material without education levelism, and sexual bias. Earlier additions also visibly changed the learner to a easier level, but this was in conflict with the comfortable low stress 'user in control'approach we are aiming to achieve. However some kind of prompting is necessary, as from previous tests the student would tend to carry on with the same level regardless of difficulty.

## 4. Learning Styles

The pre-instructional ideas of a learner are important to their perception and interpretation of events and phenomena. Previous experience helps shape conceptual frameworks and will also have bearing on preferred learning styles (6). Kolb amongst others has discussed the importance of learning style and indicates that people fall into four main categories of converger, assimilator, diverger and accommodator. A learner with tendencies towards a particular classification will respond in a different manner to other classes (7). Our system attempts to take into account these differing approaches while accepting that other factors such as motivation level, the type of task and style of instruction are also importance. The student's preferred style may also not be their most effective, and we feel that its is very important to allow the learner to be able to change the style (8). Presently four styles are used:
- Practical, hands on approach with real life experiments.
- Mathematical and conceptual approach.
- Visually strong with emphasis on diagrams and abstract representation.
- Visually strong dealing with facts and real incidents.

This dynamic changing at appropriate parts will hopefully modify and extend the user's learning repertoire. These learning directions concentrate on the representation of data, film clips and experiments that are used in the challenging and application phases of the constructivist method.

## 5. Conclusion

As the classroom and education in general change to meet the demands of the 21st Century and high technology, Computer Aided Learning will become far more important and necessary (9). It is important that the packages are flexible, engaging, and concentrate on offering a more individual approach. Our system allows users to explore their own pre-instructional ideas, using a learning style which they feel more comfortable with. They are also encouraged to try new approaches to equip themselves better and provide richer learning. The poster graphically illustrates the theories behind the system, the differences in learning direction and representation on screen, and illustrate the methods and results of interaction, in terms of feedback and prompting as the learner progresses through the system. The research takes note of important HCI work, and aims to maintain graphical integrity and consistence (10,11), whilst offering flexibility and individuality.

## 6. References

1. McAleese, Ray. Hypertext: State of the Art, Intellect Ltd. 1992
2. Osborne, R & Freyberg, P. Learning science, Heineman, Auckland, 1985
3. Scott, P.A A constructivist view of learning and teaching in science, Leeds, 1987
4. Gill, S.H. Computer aided learning with constructivism and interactive multimedia at Compugraphics 92, Lisbon , Portugal, December 1993.
5. Gill, S.H. Multimedia learning and the theories behind individual discovery in the 10th International Conference on Technology in Education, vol.1, March 1993
6. Ackerman, PL, Sternberg, R.J, Glaser, R.l. Learning and Individual Differences, W.H.Freeman and Company, 1989
7.Kolb, D.A Experiential Learning, Prentice Hall, 1984
8. Harri-Augstein, S & Thomas, L. Learning conversations. Routledge, 1992.
9. Ambron, S & Hooper, K. Interactive Multimedia, Microsoft Press, 1989
10. Apple Computer. Macintosh Human Interface Guidelines, Addison Wesley, 1992
11. Cushman W.H & Rosenberg D.J. Human Factors in Product Design, Elsevier Science, 1991

# Author Index

# Springer-Verlag and the Environment

We at Springer-Verlag firmly believe that an international science publisher has a special obligation to the environment, and our corporate policies consistently reflect this conviction.

We also expect our business partners – paper mills, printers, packaging manufacturers, etc. – to commit themselves to using environmentally friendly materials and production processes.

The paper in this book is made from low- or no-chlorine pulp and is acid free, in conformance with international standards for paper permanency.

# Lecture Notes in Computer Science

For information about Vols. 1–660
please contact your bookseller or Springer-Verlag

Vol. 697: C. Courcoubetis (Ed.), Computer Aided Verification. Proceedings, 1993. IX, 504 pages. 1993.

Vol. 698: A. Voronkov (Ed.), Logic Programming and Automated Reasoning. Proceedings, 1993. XIII, 386 pages. 1993. (Subseries LNAI).

Vol. 699: G. W. Mineau, B. Moulin, J. F. Sowa (Eds.), Conceptual Graphs for Knowledge Representation. Proceedings, 1993. IX, 451 pages. 1993. (Subseries LNAI).

Vol. 700: A. Lingas, R. Karlsson, S. Carlsson (Eds.), Automata, Languages and Programming. Proceedings, 1993. XII, 697 pages. 1993.

Vol. 701: P. Atzeni (Ed.), LOGIDATA+: Deductive Databases with Complex Objects. VIII, 273 pages. 1993.

Vol. 702: E. Börger, G. Jäger, H. Kleine Büning, S. Martini, M. M. Richter (Eds.), Computer Science Logic. Proceedings, 1992. VIII, 439 pages. 1993.

Vol. 703: M. de Berg, Ray Shooting, Depth Orders and Hidden Surface Removal. X, 201 pages. 1993.

Vol. 704: F. N. Paulisch, The Design of an Extendible Graph Editor. XV, 184 pages. 1993.

Vol. 705: H. Grünbacher, R. W. Hartenstein (Eds.), Field-Programmable Gate Arrays. Proceedings, 1992. VIII, 218 pages. 1993.

Vol. 706: H. D. Rombach, V. R. Basili, R. W. Selby (Eds.), Experimental Software Engineering Issues. Proceedings, 1992. XVIII, 261 pages. 1993.

Vol. 707: O. M. Nierstrasz (Ed.), ECOOP '93 – Object-Oriented Programming. Proceedings, 1993. XI, 531 pages. 1993.

Vol. 708: C. Laugier (Ed.), Geometric Reasoning for Perception and Action. Proceedings, 1991. VIII, 281 pages. 1993.

Vol. 709: F. Dehne, J.-R. Sack, N. Santoro, S. Whitesides (Eds.), Algorithms and Data Structures. Proceedings, 1993. XII, 634 pages. 1993.

Vol. 710: Z. Ésik (Ed.), Fundamentals of Computation Theory. Proceedings, 1993. IX, 471 pages. 1993.

Vol. 711: A. M. Borzyszkowski, S. Sokołowski (Eds.), Mathematical Foundations of Computer Science 1993. Proceedings, 1993. XIII, 782 pages. 1993.

Vol. 712: P. V. Rangan (Ed.), Network and Operating System Support for Digital Audio and Video. Proceedings, 1992. X, 416 pages. 1993.

Vol. 713: G. Gottlob, A. Leitsch, D. Mundici (Eds.), Computational Logic and Proof Theory. Proceedings, 1993. XI, 348 pages. 1993.

Vol. 714: M. Bruynooghe, J. Penjam (Eds.), Programming Language Implementation and Logic Programming. Proceedings, 1993. XI, 421 pages. 1993.

Vol. 715: E. Best (Ed.), CONCUR'93. Proceedings, 1993. IX, 541 pages. 1993.

Vol. 716: A. U. Frank, I. Campari (Eds.), Spatial Information Theory. Proceedings, 1993. XI, 478 pages. 1993.

Vol. 717: I. Sommerville, M. Paul (Eds.), Software Engineering – ESEC '93. Proceedings, 1993. XII, 516 pages. 1993.

Vol. 718: J. Seberry, Y. Zheng (Eds.), Advances in Cryptology – AUSCRYPT '92. Proceedings, 1992. XIII, 543 pages. 1993.

Vol. 719: D. Chetverikov, W.G. Kropatsch (Eds.), Computer Analysis of Images and Patterns. Proceedings, 1993. XVI, 857 pages. 1993.

Vol. 720: V.Mařík, J. Lažanský, R.R. Wagner (Eds.), Database and Expert Systems Applications. Proceedings, 1993. XV, 768 pages. 1993.

Vol. 721: J. Fitch (Ed.), Design and Implementation of Symbolic Computation Systems. Proceedings, 1992. VIII, 215 pages. 1993.

Vol. 722: A. Miola (Ed.), Design and Implementation of Symbolic Computation Systems. Proceedings, 1993. XII, 384 pages. 1993.

Vol. 723: N. Aussenac, G. Boy, B. Gaines, M. Linster, J.-G. Ganascia, Y. Kodratoff (Eds.), Knowledge Acquisition for Knowledge-Based Systems. Proceedings, 1993. XIII, 446 pages. 1993. (Subseries LNAI).

Vol. 724: P. Cousot, M. Falaschi, G. Filè, A. Rauzy (Eds.), Static Analysis. Proceedings, 1993. IX, 283 pages. 1993.

Vol. 725: A. Schiper (Ed.), Distributed Algorithms. Proceedings, 1993. VIII, 325 pages. 1993.

Vol. 726: T. Lengauer (Ed.), Algorithms – ESA '93. Proceedings, 1993. IX, 419 pages. 1993

Vol. 727: M. Filgueiras, L. Damas (Eds.), Progress in Artificial Intelligence. Proceedings, 1993. X, 362 pages. 1993. (Subseries LNAI).

Vol. 728: P. Torasso (Ed.), Advances in Artificial Intelligence. Proceedings, 1993. XI, 336 pages. 1993. (Subseries LNAI).

Vol. 729: L. Donatiello, R. Nelson (Eds.), Performance Evaluation of Computer and Communication Systems. Proceedings, 1993. VIII, 675 pages. 1993.

Vol. 730: D. B. Lomet (Ed.), Foundations of Data Organization and Algorithms. Proceedings, 1993. XII, 412 pages. 1993.

Vol. 731: A. Schill (Ed.), DCE – The OSF Distributed Computing Environment. Proceedings, 1993. VIII, 285 pages. 1993.

Vol. 732: A. Bode, M. Dal Cin (Eds.), Parallel Computer Architectures. IX, 311 pages. 1993.

Vol. 733: Th. Grechenig, M. Tscheligi (Eds.), Human Computer Interaction. Proceedings, 1993. XIV, 450 pages. 1993.

Vol. 734: J. Volkert (ed.), Parallel Computation. Proceedings, 1993. VIII, 248 pages. 1993.

Vol. 735: D. Bjørner, M. Broy, I. V. Pottosin (Eds.), Formal Methods in Programming and Their Applications. Proceedings, 1993. IX, 434 pages. 1993.

Vol. 736: R. L. Grossman, A. Nerode, A. P. Ravn, H. Rischel (Eds.), Hybrid Systems. VIII, 474 pages. 1993.

Vol. 737: J. Calmet, J. A. Campbell (Eds.), Artificial Intelligence and Symbolic Mathematical Computing. Proceedings, 1992. VIII, 305 pages. 1993.

Vol. 739: H. Imai, R. L. Rivest, T. Matsumoto (Eds.), Advances in Cryptology – ASIACRYPT '91. X, 499 pages. 1993.